HANDBOOK OF RESEARCH ON CREATIVITY AND INNOVATION

Handbook of Research on Creativity and Innovation

Edited by

Jing Zhou

Mary Gibbs Jones Professor of Management, Jones Graduate School of Business, Rice University, USA

Elizabeth D. Rouse

Associate Professor, Department of Management and Organization, Boston College, USA

EE **Edward Elgar**
PUBLISHING

Cheltenham, UK • Northampton, MA, USA

Published by
Edward Elgar Publishing Limited
The Lypiatts
15 Lansdown Road
Cheltenham
Glos GL50 2JA
UK

Edward Elgar Publishing, Inc.
William Pratt House
9 Dewey Court
Northampton
Massachusetts 01060
USA

Paperback edition 2023

A catalogue record for this book
is available from the British Library

Library of Congress Control Number: 2021945072

This book is available electronically in the **Elgar**online
Business subject collection
http://dx.doi.org/10.4337/9781788977272

MIX
Paper | Supporting
responsible forestry
FSC
www.fsc.org   FSC® C013604

ISBN 978 1 78897 726 5 (cased)
ISBN 978 1 78897 727 2 (eBook)
ISBN 978 1 0353 1550 5 (paperback)

Printed and bound by CPI Group (UK) Ltd, Croydon, CR0 4YY

Contents

Figures

Tables

Contributors

Poornika Ananth, Rotterdam School of Management, the Netherlands.

Matthijs Baas, University of Amsterdam, the Netherlands.

Amy P. Breidenthal, Agnes Scott College, USA.

Ronald S. Burt, Bocconi University, Italy; and University of Chicago, USA.

Carsten K.W. De Dreu, Leiden University and University of Amsterdam, the Netherlands.

Olga Epitropaki, Durham University, UK.

Lucy L. Gilson, University of Connecticut, USA.

Jack A. Goncalo, University of Illinois, Urbana-Champaign, USA.

Andrew Hargadon, University of California, Davis, USA.

Sarah Harvey, University College London, UK.

Inga J. Hoever, Erasmus University Rotterdam, the Netherlands.

Ronit Kark, Bar-Ilan University, Israel; and University of Exeter, UK.

Joshua H. Katz, University of Illinois, Urbana-Champaign, USA.

Daan van Knippenberg, Drexel University, USA.

Verena Krause, University College London, UK.

Yuna S.H. Lee, Columbia University, USA.

Robert C. Litchfield, Washington and Jefferson College, USA.

Aleksandra Luksyte, The University of Western Australia, Australia.

Nora Madjar, University of Connecticut, USA.

Charalampos Mainemelis, Alba Graduate Business School, Greece.

Pier Vittorio Mannucci, London Business School, UK.

Jennifer Mueller, University of San Diego, USA.

Bernard A. Nijstad, University of Groningen, the Netherlands.

Michael G. Pratt, Boston College, USA.

Eric F. Rietzschel, University of Groningen, the Netherlands.

Elizabeth D. Rouse, Boston College, USA.

Diana Rus, University of Groningen, the Netherlands.

Christina E. Shalley, Georgia Institute of Technology, USA.

Kerrie L. Unsworth, University of Leeds, UK.

Lynne C. Vincent, Syracuse University, USA.

Barbara Wisse, University of Groningen, the Netherlands; and Durham University, UK.

Shiyu Yang, University of Illinois, Urbana-Champaign, USA.

Yidan Yin, University of California, San Diego, USA.

Jing Zhou, Rice University, USA.

Introduction: shared foundations and diverse inquiries for advancing creativity and innovation research

Jing Zhou and Elizabeth D. Rouse

The field of creativity and innovation has advanced considerably, accumulating an impressive body of knowledge within a relatively short period of time (Anderson et al., 2014; Hennessey & Amabile, 2010). Though closely related and often used interchangeably outside of academia, scholars typically define creativity as the generation of novel and useful ideas and innovation as the implementation of creative ideas (Amabile, 1988; Woodman et al., 1993). A diverse set of theoretical and methodological perspectives has fueled growth in research exploring creativity, innovation, and their intersection. At this exciting and critical juncture of the development of the creativity–innovation research field, this *Handbook* is designed to take stock of where the field has been and examine current trends in order to chart a promising path forward for future research.

Theoretically, the componential model (Amabile, 1988) and the interactional perspective (Woodman et al., 1993), both of which provided much theoretical guidance in the early years of research on creativity in the workplace, have continued to play a prominent role in guiding empirical studies. More recently, researchers have updated and enriched the componential model (Amabile & Pratt, 2016) and have developed the motivational lens model to integrate theory of person-in-situation creativity research (van Knippenberg & Hirst, 2020). Researchers have also made significant theoretical advancements (see, for example, Nijstad, Rietzschel, Baas, & De Dreu, Chapter 2 in this volume; van Knippenberg & Hoever, Chapter 3 in this volume) that deepen our understanding of the psychological mechanisms underlying the creativity–innovation process (that is, affective, cognitive, and motivational; see Zhou & Shalley, 2011 for a more detailed review). Social network theories (e.g., Burt, 2004), with intellectual roots tracing to sociology, have also been extended to, or formulated specifically for, an understanding of creativity (e.g., Perry-Smith & Shalley, 2003) and the creativity–innovation journey (Perry-Smith & Mannucci, 2017).

Moreover, researchers have started to formulate new typologies, develop new constructs, and identify new research streams. For example, scholars have developed theory around different types of creativity (Unsworth, 2001), co-creation (Rouse, 2020), the bias against creativity (Mueller et al., 2012), creativity and ethics (Keem et al., 2018), and creativity receiving (Zhou et al., 2019). These ideas are related to various aspects and stages of the idea generation and implementation processes and are crucial for understanding not only how various forms of creativity come to be, but also how the process from creativity to innovation unfolds. Although the domains of micro-level creativity and macro-level innovation have often been studied in isolation, researchers have expanded our knowledge base by integrating these research streams and by linking research that centers on creativity and innovation with research on entrepreneurship, an adjacent research field (e.g., see Shalley et al., 2015).

Methodologically, the field has witnessed an increase in the use of qualitative research methods (e.g., Rouse & Pratt, Chapter 15 in this volume). Though quantitative research methods have been used widely and have significantly advanced our understanding of creativity and innovation (e.g., Baas et al., 2008; Byron & Khazanchi, 2012; Liu et al., 2016; Shalley & Breidenthal, Chapter 1 in this volume; Shalley et al., 2004), qualitative methods provide unique tools for theory building and hypothesis generating, which complement quantitative methods. Together, qualitative and quantitative methods allow researchers to understand the complex, dynamic creativity–innovation process and its outcomes.

The *Handbook of Research on Creativity and Innovation* offers a great opportunity to showcase some of the most advanced and interesting work in the creativity and innovation field, to provide a platform for idea exchange and cross-fertilization, and to stimulate future research. Authors invited to contribute to this *Handbook* are leading scholars and prolific researchers who have conducted cutting-edge, interesting, and important work. Each individual chapter presents expert scholarly analysis and serves as a vital reference point for future studies.

We cluster the chapters in the *Handbook of Research on Creativity and Innovation* into three parts. Part I includes chapters that review foundations for conducting rigorous creativity research, elaborate on theoretical models that explain individual creativity and team creativity and innovation, and discuss the relationship between creativity and standardization. Part II presents chapters that analyze the social context for creativity and innovation, a thriving area of inquiry. The chapters cover a wide range of social contexts, revealing how macro social network structures and micro influences (from leaders, co-workers, family, and friends) shape individuals' creativity and innovation, and how engaging in creativity affects individuals' connections with others. Part III contains chapters that reveal a number of new topics that stretch the creativity and innovation field into new frontiers of discovery. Taken as a whole, the book represents the most advanced research in creativity and innovation at this time.

To facilitate readers' locating and using materials presented in this volume, in the paragraphs to follow we highlight the primary focus of each chapter, and comment on its contribution to the creativity and innovation literature. When appropriate, we also make connections among the chapters within each part, and discuss how the three parts relate to one another.

FOUNDATIONS OF CREATIVITY AND INNOVATION RESEARCH

Part I, entitled "Foundations of Creativity and Innovation Research," consists of four chapters. In Chapter 1, Shalley and Breidenthal review and discuss how research in management and organizational studies have defined and measured creativity. The empirical source of their review is quantitative studies conducted in the past five years. On the basis of their review and appraisal of the conceptual definition of creativity including its novelty and usefulness dimensions, Shalley and Breidenthal evaluate type of studies, measurement instruments, and rating sources. They reveal conceptual issues and measurement methods about which the field has reached consensus, where divergence occurs, and where future research opportunities lie. Though their review focuses on defining and measuring creativity at the individual level of analysis, the guiding principles and thought processes on which much of their analysis is based generalizes to the group level of analysis. By highlighting old truths and new trends, Shalley and Breidenthal provide definitional and measurement foundations for conducting rigorous quantitative research.

In Chapter 2, Nijstad, Rietzschel, Baas, and De Dreu describe the dual pathway to creativity model (DPCM), evaluate its empirical support, and discuss future directions for extending and testing the model. They review two long-running research streams aimed at understanding cognitive underpinnings for creative idea generation: that creativity is a result of a random process involving remote association, or it is the outcome of a systematic search process. Whereas the former emphasizes cognitive flexibility, the latter underscores cognitive persistence. Nijstad and co-authors introduce the dual pathway for creativity model, which is an integration of the aforementioned two research traditions. Observing that most studies testing their model have been conducted in the behavioral laboratory, Nijstad and co-authors point out promising ways in which the model may be extended and tested in field studies. They also indicate the feasibility of extending their model from its original focus on the individual level of analysis to the team level.

Moving from a primary focus on individual creativity to a focus on team creativity and innovation, in Chapter 3, van Knippenberg and Hoever build on and extend van Knippenberg's (2017) comprehensive and influential review by examining research published subsequently. This examination leads to the conclusion that the team information elaboration perspective has been the dominant theory used in team creativity/innovation research. There has also been increased integration between this perspective and research into team leadership and team climate. Studies on team leadership have theorized how leaders facilitate team information elaboration, and studies on team climate have highlighted the role that climate plays in encouraging information elaboration among team members. These theoretical advancements anchored around team information elaboration for creativity/innovation open the door for van Knippenberg and Hoever to outline a number of exciting theoretical and empirical directions for researchers to pursue. Their fresh ideas regarding the discussion and debate about the degree to which the notions of team creativity and team innovation are meaningfully distinct are also likely to spark future conceptual and empirical work.

As the field of individual and team creativity/innovation continues to grow and generate scientific and actionable knowledge, the question of whether creativity and innovation are in conflict with standardization becomes more and more salient. In Chapter 4, Litchfield, Lee, and Gilson tackle this question. Reviewing research conducted at individual, team, or organizational level of analysis, they seek to understand the tension between creativity and standardization within each of these levels of analysis, as well as commonalities across different levels of analysis. They find that the relationship between creativity and standardization is more complex than previously assumed: under certain conditions they are adversaries, and under other conditions they are complements. The authors note that despite the importance for organizations to achieve the right balance of creativity and standardization, the literature on this topic is rather small. With an emphasis on individual and team levels of analysis, Litchfield et al. suggest possible research directions.

Taken together, the first set of four chapters (Chapters 1 to 4) present a number of key conceptual, methodological, and theoretical building blocks for research on individual and team creativity/innovation. Reflecting on these chapters, the methodological building blocks center around quantitative research methods. As the development of the creativity and innovation research field accelerates, studies using quantitative research methods will continue to play a significant role in knowledge creation. At the same time, qualitative research methods will also add significant value in advancing our understanding of creativity and innovation. Rouse and Pratt provide a comprehensive treatment of qualitative methods for creativity research in Chapter 15 of this volume. These first chapters also suggest an increased integration of social influences and interactions (for example, leadership and team climate; van Knippenberg & Hoever, Chapter 3 in this volume) with cognitive, affective, and motivational underpinnings of creativity and innovation. Part II of this *Handbook* presents chapters highlighting the role of a wide range of social influences, interactions, and processes.

THE ROLE OF SOCIAL INFLUENCES, INTERACTIONS, AND PROCESSES IN CREATIVITY AND INNOVATION

Contemporary research on creativity and innovation has emphasized the role of the social context in shaping individual and team creativity. Part II of this *Handbook*, entitled "The Role of Social Influences, Interactions, and Processes in Creativity and Innovation," consists of six chapters (Chapters 5 to 10) that address various aspects of the social context. Early creativity research attempted to identify personal attributes that separate creative individuals from those who are not creative (Barron & Harrington, 1981). By contrast, current theory recognizes the role that social influences play in fostering creativity and innovation. For example, social network scholars have revealed the significant impact of social network structures in affecting the quality of ideas generated by individuals embedded in their networks (e.g., Burt, 2004). In the first chapter in this set (Chapter 5), Burt describes the association between social networks and creativity and explains why network structure facilitates or inhibits information flow, creativity, and good ideas. He combines rich conceptual analysis with interesting sociogram illustrations of network structure. Citing evidence from field studies conducted in companies operating in the United States, Europe, and Asia, he underscores the essential role of network brokerage in creativity. In addition to his seminal work on structural holes and good ideas, Burt reviews and appraises extensions and advancements concerning social network structure and creativity. He then points out a number of promising avenues for future research.

When considering social influences, it is necessary to understand the role that leaders play in the process of creativity and innovation. The next two chapters address leadership for achieving creativity and innovation. In Chapter 6, Mainemelis, Epitropaki, and Kark provide an analysis of creative leadership. They maintain that though Selznick (1984 [1957]) coined the term decades ago, creative leadership is more important than ever. They conceptualize three ways in which leaders demonstrate creative leadership, and categorize extant empirical studies on leadership and creativity according to this conceptualization. Mainemelis and co-authors theorize that classifying creative leadership in its three types of manifestations facilitates understanding of why different contexts demand different manifestations of creative leadership. Sensitizing researchers to the context, their analysis provides guidelines for future research concerning creative leadership.

Chapter 7 continues the theme of leadership, albeit with a different focus that complements Chapter 6. Anchoring their analysis at the team level, Rietzschel, Rus, and Wisse focus on leadership behaviors for achieving effectiveness at different stages of team innovation. They emphasize the distinction between leading creativity (idea generation) and leading idea implementation, outline various team design factors (for example, a shared goal) and team interaction processes (for example, managing divergence versus convergence) essential for idea generation and implementation, and analyze leadership behaviors suitable for dealing with team work challenges at different stages of the team innovation journey. Comparing their analysis of what needs to be done in order to develop a full-range understanding of leadership behaviors for team innovation with the existing literature reveals substantial knowledge gaps. Rietzschel and co-authors conclude Chapter 7 by drawing attention to these knowledge gaps and future research opportunities.

As organizations increasingly rely on teams as the organizing unit for completing work tasks, it is beneficial to undertake a deep dive into the processes through which teams achieve creativity and innovation. In Chapter 8, Harvey and Ananth present such a deep dive. They describe an inductive investigation of how constraints influence the team creative processes. Situated in the asset management industry, their investigation builds on the notion of creative synthesis and captures the dynamic processes through which three types of constraints facilitated fund management teams' production of creative ideas. This qualitative investigation sheds light on the underlying reasons for why, paradoxically, the constraints actually exerted a positive impact on the interactions among team members in their collective effort to produce creative ideas. Harvey and Ananth reveal the functional, though counterintuitive, value of constraints in the team creative process, and show the utility of conducting qualitative studies for deepening our understanding of the rich context and dynamic processes of teams' creative work. Their deep dive provides impetus for future research to both extend our understanding of constraints and team creativity and use qualitative research methods in advancing our understanding. Rouse and Pratt provide a more detailed discussion on qualitative methods and creativity research in Chapter 15 of this book.

In addition to social influences from professional networks, leaders, and team members, family may also influence employees' creativity in the workplace. In Chapter 9, Madjar reviews and appraises the research stream concerning creativity-relevant influences from family. Casting family members as potential cognitive and emotional resources, Madjar's review of this literature takes stock of agreed-upon findings, inconsistent results, and topics that have not received sufficient research attention. This systematic review and appraisal demonstrates that social influence from those outside of the organization can exert substantial influence on employee creativity inside the organization; influences from family may promote or hinder employee creativity at work. Madjar concludes the chapter by providing special recommendations for future research concerning both the work–family interface and the influences of family on employee creativity.

Whereas Chapters 5 to 9 deal with effects of social influences and interactions on individual employee and team creativity, Chapter 10 examines effects of creativity on social connections at work. In this chapter, Goncalo, Katz, Vincent, Krause, and Yang point out the need to examine a broader range of consequences of creativity beyond the premise that employee creativity brings business benefits to organizations. Specifically, Goncalo and co-authors identify that engaging in creativity increases social connections. They analyze why engaging in creativity may propel employees to form social connections, and the processes through which this occurs. They also discuss when engaging in creativity combats a sense of loneliness, and when creativity results in rejection, social isolation, and increased loneliness. Overall, the authors suggest that organizations take into consideration the social connections (or lack thereof) that employees make when they engage in creativity. They also discuss a number of interesting directions for future research.

When the creativity research field emerged, much research focused on identifying individuals' traits and attributes in an attempt to understand and predict creativity. Recognizing the significant role that context plays in shaping individual creativity (e.g., Amabile, 1988) has substantially advanced the creativity research field. As our understanding of creativity broadens, encompassing the journey from creativity to innovation, and at multiple levels of analysis, the field has increasingly placed social relationships, interactions, and processes front and center. The six chapters included in Part II represent important research streams that have yielded, and will continue to deliver, productive results in this regard. Similarly, the chapters presented in Part III also hold considerable promise in stimulating future research. Whereas the set of chapters in Part II converge on their emphasis on social relationships and interactions in creativity and innovation, the set of chapters in Part III address diverse and stretching topics.

STRETCHING HOW WE MAKE SENSE OF AND STUDY CREATIVITY AND INNOVATION

Part III, descriptively entitled "Stretching How We Make Sense of and Study Creativity and Innovation," consists of five chapters (Chapters 11 to 15). In Chapter 11, Hargadon introduces a new construct called creative spirals. This construct captures an interesting phenomenon with regard to the generation of a series of creative ideas. Understanding this phenomenon requires researchers to uncover how contexts enable creative spirals to materialize. While the chapters in Part II of this volume focus on the social context for creativity and innovation, Hargadon takes a systems view and brings the sociomaterial context and temporal conditions to the fore. Using a microhistorical lens, he describes creative spirals in context, analyzing how sociomateriality and temporality shape the discovery of solutions to existing problems and the emergence of new questions. Hargadon concludes the chapter by detailing opportunities for future theoretical development, empirical research, and methodological innovation: the use of microhistorical methods to study creative spirals in sociomaterial and temporal contexts.

Whereas Hargadon centers his discussion on the meso level of analysis (for example, how the Edison lab as a collective produced creative spirals), Mannucci in Chapter 12 primarily addresses the creativity trajectory over the course of an individual's career. He reviews and appraises research on not only how creativity trajectories vary, but also why variations transpire. From person, product, and process perspectives, he analyzes factors that result in different trajectories. He also discusses factors that are beneficial to creativity at various career stages. Following the comprehensive and thoughtful review, Mannucci reveals a number of interesting future research directions.

Chapter 13 focuses on the bias against novelty. Though much research effort has been devoted to an understanding of how to increase employees' knowledge, skills, and motivation in order to boost their creativity, less research has been conducted on what happens after creative ideas have been generated and how ideas are received by others. In this chapter, Mueller and Yin highlight the challenge that ideas generators and organizations attempting to benefit from the creativity exhibited by their employees face: there is a profound bias against novelty that can translate into a bias against creativity. Mueller and Yin review this emergent literature and point out the importance of furthering this line of inquiry. They present two approaches to studying the bias against novelty, categorize existing work accordingly, and discuss future research opportunities in the emergent area of studying creativity evaluation.

Continuing a theme around creativity evaluation, Unsworth and Luksyte wonder whether idea evaluators truly evaluate creative ideas along the novelty and usefulness dimensions. In Chapter 14, they ask a provocative and important question: Does it matter who the creator is? They point out that the characteristics of the creator are likely to influence observers' evaluation of the ideas generated by the creator. They theorize the psychological drivers that direct the evaluator's attention toward the idea creator, instead of the idea itself. Among the characteristics of the creator, Unsworth and Luksyte identify two characteristics – age and gender – and analyze how they may influence the observers' evaluation of the idea. Given the statistics regarding workforce composition, understanding how these two characteristics affect observers' creativity evaluation is crucial for both research and management practice. Using these two characteristics to illustrate their theorizing, Unsworth and Luksyte integrate the emergent creativity evaluation literature with several extant research streams, such as the theoretical work unpacking types of creativity (Unsworth, 2001). Their theoretical analysis and integration with earlier work opens the door for quite a few interesting avenues for future research.

Chapters 1 through 14 focus on various theoretical perspectives and diverse research streams in the broad creativity and innovation arena, reviewing a wealth of knowledge created, and identifying ample research opportunities to be pursued. Chapter 15 serves as a conclusion to this volume and a call for action. In this chapter, Rouse and Pratt emphasize the need for radical theory building in research on creativity and innovation, echoing the concern that convergence may stagnate development of the field, and emphasize the value of injecting greater divergence in research questions asked, theoretical perspectives taken, and research methods used. They explain why qualitative methods are helpful in this regard, detail types of qualitative methods, and offer three shifts of focus that may especially benefit from using qualitative methods.

INTENDED READERSHIP

A variety of readers will find the book interesting and useful. PhD students and other aspiring researchers may use the book as a major reference source that helps them to become acquainted with the creativity and innovation research field. If you are a PhD student or an aspiring researcher, here is our suggestion: whether or not you have already chosen creativity and innovation as your area of specialization, you are likely to enjoy studying the book in the order in which we present the chapters. Approaching the material in this sequence will enable you to both acquire knowledge accumulated by the creativity and innovation research field and generate ideas for your own research. More specifically, going through the book in this sequence will facilitate your thinking about how to identify a research question that is interesting and important, generate your own research ideas, develop a theoretical model, and design an empirical study, taking either a quantitative or qualitative approach.

Experienced researchers who already specialize in the creativity and innovation research arena are likely to discover fresh ideas and thought-provoking analysis in these pages. If you are an experienced researcher, you may find it beneficial to jump to the chapters that intrigue you, irrespective of how we have organized the chapters. Researchers whose primary field is not creativity and innovation are likely to find the chapters interesting and useful. Getting a sense of the rapid development of the creativity and innovation field, as evident in the ideas elaborated in the chapters, is likely to stimulate the generation of fresh ideas for your research programs beyond creativity and innovation.

Finally, practicing managers and employees who are interested in understanding creativity and innovation are also likely to find the book useful. If you have already had experience in leading or engaging in idea generation, selection, and implementation, reading the chapters in this volume will help you to reflect, make sense of your own experiences, as well as plan and execute future creativity and innovation more effectively and efficiently. If you do not have much experience in creativity and innovation, thumbing through the pages of this volume will help you to appreciate the complexity and joy of the creativity–innovation journey, and seize future opportunities to engage in creativity and innovation.

REFERENCES

Amabile, T.M. 1988. A model of creativity and innovation in organizations. *Research in Organizational Behavior*, 10: 123–167. Greenwich, CT: JAI Press.

Amabile, T.M., & Pratt, M.G. 2016. The dynamic componential model of creativity and innovation in organizations: Making progress, making meaning. *Research in Organizational Behavior*, 36: 157–183.

Anderson, N., Potocnik, K., & Zhou, J. 2014. Innovation and creativity in organizations: A state-of-the-science review, prospective commentary, and guiding framework. *Journal of Management*, 40, 1297–1333.

Baas, M., De Dreu, C.K.W., & Nijstad, B.A. 2008. A meta-analysis of 25 years of mood creativity research: Hedonic tone, activation, or regulatory focus? *Psychological Bulletin*, 134: 779–806.

Barron, F., & Harrington, D.M. 1981. Creativity, intelligence, and personality. *Annual Review of Psychology*, 32: 439–476.

Burt, R.S. 2004. Structural holes and good ideas. *American Journal of Sociology*, 110: 349–399.

Byron, K., & Khazanchi, S. 2012. Rewards and creative performance: A meta-analytic test of theoretically derived hypotheses. *Psychological Bulletin*, 138: 809–830.

Hennessey, B.A., & Amabile, T.M. 2010. Creativity. *Annual Review of Psychology*, 61: 569–598.

Keem, S., Shalley, C.E., Kim, E. & Jeong, I. 2018. Are creative individuals bad apples? A dual pathway model of unethical behavior. *Journal of Applied Psychology*, 103: 416–431.

Liu, D., Jiang, K., Shalley, C.E., Keem, S., & Zhou, J. 2016. Motivational mechanisms of employee creativity: A meta-analytic examination and theoretical extension of the creativity literature. *Organizational Behavior and Human Decision Processes*, 137: 236–263.

Mueller, J.S., Melwani, S., & Goncalo, J.A. 2012. The bias against creativity: Why people desire but reject creative ideas. *Psychological Science*, 23: 13–17.

Perry-Smith, J., & Mannucci, P.V. 2017. From creativity to innovation: The social network drivers of the four phases of the idea journey. *Academy of Management Review*, 42: 53–79.

Perry-Smith, J., & Shalley, C.E. 2003. The social side of creativity: A static and dynamic social network perspective. *Academy of Management Review*, 28: 89–106.

Rouse, E.D. 2020. Where you end and I begin: Understanding intimate co-creation. *Academy of Management Review*, 45: 181–204.

Selznick, P. 1984 [1957]. *Leadership in administration*. Berkeley, CA: University of California Press.

Shalley, C.E., Hitt, M.A., & Zhou, J. (eds). 2015. *The Oxford handbook of creativity, innovation, and entrepreneurship*. New York: Oxford University Press.

Shalley, C.E., Zhou, J., & Oldham, G.R. 2004. The effects of personal and contextual characteristics on creativity: Where should we go from here? *Journal of Management*, 30: 933–958.

Unsworth, K.L. 2001. Unpacking creativity. *Academy of Management Review*, 26: 289–297.

van Knippenberg, D. 2017. Team innovation. *Annual Review of Organizational Psychology and Organizational Behavior*, 4: 211–233.

van Knippenberg, D., & Hirst, G. 2020. A motivational lens model of person X situation interactions in employee creativity. *Journal of Applied Psychology*, 105: 1129–1144.

Woodman, R.W., Sawyer, J.E., & Griffin, R.W. 1993. Toward a theory of organizational creativity. *Academy of Management Review*, 18: 293–321.

Zhou, J., & Shalley, C.E. 2011. Deepening our understanding of creativity in the workplace: A review of different approaches to creativity research. In S. Zedeck, et al. (eds), *APA handbook of industrial and organizational psychology*, Vol. 1: 275–302. Washington, DC: American Psychological Association.

Zhou, J., Wang, X., Bavato, D., Tasselli, S., & Wu, J. 2019. Understanding the receiving side of creativity: A multidisciplinary review and implications for management research. *Journal of Management*, 45: 2570–2595.

PART I

FOUNDATIONS OF CREATIVITY AND INNOVATION RESEARCH

1. Conducting rigorous research on individual creativity

Christina E. Shalley and Amy P. Breidenthal

Individual creativity, or the generation of novel and useful ideas by individuals at work (Amabile, 1996; Oldham & Cummings, 1996; Shalley, 1991), is often seen as the fundamental building block of organizational innovation (Anderson et al., 2014; Liu et al., 2017). Innovation, in turn, is increasingly cited as paramount for organizations to achieve a sustainable competitive advantage (Amabile, 1996; Lee & Hsieh, 2010; Lengnick-Hall, 1992; Thornhill, 2006). Hence, over the past few decades, research on individual creativity has flourished within the organizational behavior literature (Anderson et al., 2014; Shalley et al., 2004). While this research undoubtedly provides great insights overall, scholars' ability to accurately interpret and aggregate these findings relies heavily on the way creativity is operationalized and measured across studies (Barbot et al., 2019; Batey, 2012; Hinkin, 1998). Therefore, the purpose of this chapter is to review the measurement of individual creativity in organizational studies and highlight some meaningful issues that need to be addressed in order to conduct rigorous research on individual creativity.

In order to conduct this review, we looked broadly at creativity research in the management domain with a particular focus on meta-analyses, reviews, and seminal articles. In addition, we took a closer look at the research published within the last five years by conducting an in-depth review of empirical articles on individual creativity that were published in a sample of top management journals[1] from January 2014 through June 2019. We restricted our scope to empirical investigations of individual-level creativity.[2] As this review will show, in general, creativity scholars have reached consensus around an overall definition of creativity and common measurement approaches for both experimental and field studies. We begin with a brief overview of these points of consensus and look to relevant recent research to highlight the most common approaches for studying creativity. However, this same research has also highlighted several points of discrepancy or areas in which there are debates over the conceptualization of creativity. Such points of active debate include how the elements of novelty and usefulness interact; who should rate one's creativity; whether creativity refers to a person, a process, or a product; and how to differentiate creativity from individual innovation. Through the lens of creativity measurement, we investigate the natural assumptions that the common methods of measurement are making regarding these debates. Finally, we highlight new trends in the creativity literature that seek to measure creativity in novel ways.

COMMON MEASURES OF INDIVIDUAL CREATIVITY

Our focus is on the management literature, and we begin by highlighting the conceptual definition of the construct of creativity as the foundation for construct measurement (Eysenck, 1996; Hinkin, 1998). Creativity is often defined as having two elements: the first relating to the novelty, originality, or uniqueness of an idea or outcome; and the second relating to the idea or outcome's perceived usefulness, appropriateness, or value (Amabile, 1983; Shalley, 1991; Woodman et al., 1993). Overwhelmingly, researchers have coalesced around the definition of creativity as the generation of novel and useful ideas (Barbot et al., 2019; Batey, 2012). Nearly every article published in top management journals over the last five years has used a slight variation of this definition (e.g., González-Gómez & Richter, 2015; Li et al., 2017; Seibert et al., 2017). What is interesting is that some of the older work on creativity defined it as an idea or product that is both original and appropriate (Barron, 1955; Stein, 1974), while Amabile (1983) said that "a product or response will be judged as creative to the extent that (a) it is both novel and appropriate, useful, correct, or valuable to the task at hand, and (b) the task is heuristic rather than algorithmic." Heuristic, as opposed to algorithmic, tasks do not have clear and readily identifiable paths to a solution. Although some people still use this definition, of novel and appropriate, more researchers seem to use novelty and usefulness as the definition. We think it could be said that Amabile (1983) seems to view usefulness and appropriateness as interchangeable terms.

From our review of the creativity studies published in the last five years, the empirical methods used for studying creativity in the management literature are, in the order of frequency, field studies, experiments, and archival studies. Field studies that take place within an organization are predominantly conducted outside the United States (for example, in China: Hirst et al., 2015; Hon et al., 2014; Kwan et al., 2018; in Denmark: Soda et al., 2019; and in Columbia: González-Gómez & Richter, 2015). Across all field studies, creativity is primarily measured through surveys, and employees' creativity is assessed most often by the employees' supervisor. In some cases, creativity assessments are completed by one or more co-workers (e.g., Harris et al., 2014), or the employees are asked to self-rate their own creativity (e.g., Kauppila et al., 2018; Rosen et al., 2014).

There also appears to be a great deal of consensus concerning the top scales used for measuring employee creativity. In our five-year review, the 13-item measure introduced both in Zhou and George (2001) and in George and Zhou (2001)[3] was by far the most frequently utilized; 18 of the 32 studies that used a scale to measure creativity utilized this 13-item scale or a subset of these items. All other scales were reported across only 1–3 studies each. Among these, the scales that were cited more than once were the three- or four-item scales introduced by Oldham and Cummings (1996), Tierney et al. (1999) and Farmer et al. (2003). This finding parallels the finding of a 2011 meta-analysis on creativity and individual innovation (Hammond et al., 2011) which reported that the following creativity scales were the most frequently cited: Tierney et al. (1999), Zhou and George (2001), and Oldham and Cummings

(1996). Anderson et al.'s (2014) review of the creativity and individual innovation literature also cited these three scales as the most commonly used, with Zhou and George (2001) as the most frequently cited.

In the management literature, experimental investigations of individual creativity also share strong commonalities across studies. The majority of these studies ask subjects to complete a complex heuristic task during which they produce one or more ideas, solutions, or products. Then a version of Amabile's (1982) consensual assessment technique (CAT) is used, wherein multiple judges conduct a blind review of the documented ideas, solutions, or products and either rate their overall level of creativity, or they rate the novelty and usefulness of the ideas, solutions, or products separately. In the latter case, the scores are then aggregated in order to compose an individual's creativity score from each rater. For both approaches, if agreement is strong enough between the multiple raters, creativity scores provided by the different raters are aggregated to form the participant's overall creativity score. Less common, but occasionally done in management research, is when participants are asked to engage in a creative thinking task such as a remote association thinking task, a divergent thinking task, or the Dunker candle problem (Duncker, 1945). Participants for the experimental studies that were contained in our five-year review were most often recruited either through panels such as Amazon's Mechanical Turk or Qualtrics (Huang et al., 2015; Jung & Lee, 2015) or by using college students (Brown & Baer, 2015; Perry-Smith, 2014). The experimental studies found in our five-year study were predominantly conducted in the United States.

The tasks given to subjects for creative idea generation vary between studies, but some common themes can be seen across studies such as solving organizational problems or creating new marketing campaigns and products. Shalley (1991) introduced a memo task that has the participants assume the role of a human resources (HR) manager who is tasked to deal with multiple management problems (Perry-Smith, 2014). Madjar et al. (2019) asked participants to develop a creative solution for a newspaper that was faced with a number of strategic challenges. Goncalo et al. (2015) used a task that asked subjects to generate ideas for a new business to fill a vacant space on campus. Madjar and Oldham (2006) presented multiple tasks including creation of a new marketing campaign and generation of new models for a refrigerator (Madjar & Shalley, 2008). Chua (2018) asked subjects to generate a marketing campaign for a new flavored water product.

Archival studies are much less common in management studies of creativity (Hülsheger et al., 2009), however, scholars are increasingly looking for opportunities to utilize objective measures of creativity (Liao et al., 2010). In such cases, archival measures of creativity may include citations (e.g., Arts & Fleming, 2018) or invention disclosures and research reports (Tierney et al., 1999). Additionally, recent archival studies have tested hypotheses using public information in creative fields such as movies and television (Clement et al., 2018; Mannucci & Yong, 2017). In these examples, creativity was assessed by viewership ratings and box office success.

Across all study types, but especially in field studies, scholars vary regarding which variables they measured and controlled for in statistical analyses. The most common controls included demographic and role variables and creativity-related personality variables or self-beliefs. For example, gender, age, education, and organizational tenure are the most commonly utilized control variables across all studies. Interestingly, none of these variables significantly correlated with creativity in the majority of the studies conducted over the last five years (although each does in certain instances). Openness to experience (Costa & McCrae, 1992) and creative self-efficacy (Tierney & Farmer, 2002) were also included in multiple studies as control variables, and were typically, but not always, significantly correlated with creativity.

ONGOING DEBATES ON CONDUCTING RIGOROUS RESEARCH ON INDIVIDUAL CREATIVITY

While the above summary shows that creativity researchers operate with a great deal of consistency across organizational studies, this is not to say that there are no debates among scholars regarding how to conduct rigorous research on individual creativity. Among the top questions to be resolved are the following: (1) How do novelty and usefulness work together to define creativity (Berg, 2014; Miron-Spektor & Beenen, 2015; Sullivan & Ford, 2010)? (2) Who is the best person to assess an individual's creativity (Ng & Feldman, 2012)? (3) Does creativity refer to a person, process, or product (Montag et al., 2012)? and (4) Where is the line differentiating creativity from individual innovation (Anderson et al., 2014)? In order to contribute to these conversations, we next review how creativity has been measured in the recent management literature.

Creativity: How do Novelty and Usefulness Work Together?

As noted above, the common definition of creativity is the generation of novel and useful ideas. While this appears straightforward initially, it is essentially a double-barreled definition and therefore researchers, to date, have interpreted this definition in a few different ways both in theory and in measurement. Theoretically, as noted above, the most common definition of creativity gives equal weight to both elements, essentially suggesting that increases (decreases) in either novelty or usefulness would increase (decrease) one's overall creativity. However, some variations in this conceptualization suggest that novelty is the primary indicator of creativity, while usefulness plays a secondary role (Diedrich et al., 2015). For example, previous work also has considered creativity as "a novel work that is accepted as tenable or useful" (Stein, 1953: 311), or similarly, "new or original ideas ... which are accepted by experts as being of scientific, aesthetic, social, or technological value" (Vernon, 1989: 94). Therefore, we will next summarize how the elements of novelty and usefulness have been measured in recent creativity studies in the management domain to highlight how this theoretical debate is impacting the measurement of creativity, and what measurement has to say for the theoretical debate.

In our review of the recent literature, a few scholars defined creativity as the generation of "novel and potentially useful" ideas (Harris et al., 2014; Soda et al., 2019). Yet, interestingly, these articles do not measure creativity any differently than those that omit the term "potentially," and this applies to both experimental and field studies. In experimental studies, as noted above, the CAT is typically applied in which subjects are asked to generate ideas and raters assess the creativity of these ideas. In such studies, some researchers instruct the judges to rate idea novelty separately from idea usefulness, and then aggregate the two utilizing a product function (for example, product: Brown & Baer, 2015; or square root of the product: Perry-Smith, 2014). Similarly, scholars have asked raters to assess ideas on up to four dimensions assessing both novelty and usefulness and averaging the scores (for example, novelty, originality, usefulness, and feasibility; Zhou et al., 2017). Other researchers, however, asked the raters to assess overall creativity (Madjar et al., 2019) or combined overall creativity, novelty, and usefulness into a composite measure (Koseoglu et al., 2017b). While some report that the definition of "novel and useful" was provided to the rater (Jung & Lee, 2015), others do not specify what, if any, direction was provided to the raters. In these cases, the rater may be utilizing their own lay definition of creativity to assess the creativity of the ideas presented. Notably, in one study, raters were asked to assess the extent to which the presented ideas were novel, unique, unconventional, and creative (Chua, 2018). In this study, usefulness or feasibility was not included in the measure of creativity, yet creativity was defined as "the creation of a new product or idea that satisfies some value functions," thereby putting the element of novelty as dominant over the element of usefulness or value.

In field studies, some common scales similarly assess the creativity of an individual's output. Unlike the CAT, none of the scales we identified assess usefulness or practicality as a unique element. Instead, commonly used scales either merge the elements of novelty and usefulness into individual items (Oldham & Cummings, 1996), or assess creativity, novelty, and originality without highlighting the usefulness element (Shalley et al., 2009). In the most common measure of creativity (Zhou & George, 2001), four items assess novelty alone (that is, is a good source of creative ideas, exhibits creativity on the job when given the opportunity to, comes up with creative solutions to problems, and often has new and innovative ideas), while five items assess one's creativity applied in a useful or practical domain (for example, suggests new ways to achieve goals or objectives, and suggests new ways to increase quality).[4]

Hence, in field studies, the measurement of creativity generally emphasizes novelty over usefulness and assesses one's novelty applied in a useful or appropriate domain. However, in archival studies, where creativity is often measured by evaluating the success of any outcomes (for example, patents, ratings, and box office success), it is possible that the usefulness element of creativity is more heavily weighted, although the measure is not as clearly distinguished between these two elements. Overall, from looking at the measurement of creativity in the management literature, it appears that the interpretation of creativity as novelty that has the potential to be useful, or novelty that is applied in an appropriate way, is more aligned to the way creativity is assessed, especially in the most commonly conducted type of study: that of field studies. This approach is further supported by studies that investigate novelty and usefulness separately, which we discuss below.

Creativity: Who is the Best Person to Assess it?

More elaborate definitions of creativity take into account the inherently subjective nature of the assessment of novelty and usefulness. For example, Ford defines creativity as the "domain-specific, subjective judgment of the novelty and value of an outcome of a particular action" (Ford, 1996: 1115). In other words, creativity is subjective, and when an idea is considered creative in the domain in which it was introduced, it may not be very novel in other domains. Hence, the person subjectively assessing an individual's or idea's creativity may substantively impact the rating of creativity assigned. Furthermore, research is starting to uncover that rater characteristics and environmental characteristics may impact how individuals perceive creativity (Zhou et al., 2019). Hence, special attention should be paid in creativity studies to who is rating creativity.

In experimental studies published in our sample of top management journals over the last five years, the CAT raters were a mix of creativity experts (e.g., Černe et al., 2014), experienced managers (e.g., Jung & Lee, 2015), and independent coders (e.g., Brown & Baer, 2015). Regarding field studies that utilized survey measures for employee creativity ratings, 26 studies asked supervisors to rate employee creativity (e.g., Hirst et al., 2015; Kwan et al., 2018; Parke et al., 2015), compared to only four studies that used self-reports (e.g., Harrison & Wagner, 2016; Rosen et al., 2014), and two that used multiple co-worker reports (Harris et al., 2014; Marinova et al., 2019). In addition, one study that focused on the leader's level of creativity asked a number of their subordinates to rate their leader's creativity, and then using a modified version of CAT aggregated these ratings to form one creativity score for each leader (Koseoglu et al., 2017a). The preponderance of supervisors serving as the most likely rater of employee creativity aligns with recent reviews of the creativity literature (e.g., Anderson et al., 2014), and this trend may help to reduce concerns about common method bias (Podsakoff et al., 2003). However, it is possible that it opens up individual creativity ratings to other types of bias such as liking and any other halo effects (Liao et al., 2010). Hence, some researchers have pursued more objective ratings of creativity. However, objective ratings of creativity are harder to define, as they can span a wide range of measures. For example, creativity measures coined "objective" can include measures ranging from citations (Seibert et al., 2017) to bonuses awarded by top leaderships' review of ideas (Liu et al., 2015), to using an "objective count" of the number of correct answers provided on an associative thinking task (Jung & Lee, 2015). Putting all of this together with burgeoning research regarding the myriad of influences that can affect one's judgments of another's creativity (Kay et al., 2018; Mueller et al., 2018; Randel et al., 2011; Zhou et al., 2019) highlights how utilizing different raters of creativity may substantially impact exactly what one is assessing.

Creativity: Is it a Person, Process, or Product?

An issue that has been repeatedly highlighted in the broader psychology literature is the use of the single term "creativity" to refer to creativity as a person (that is, creativity-related individual differences), a process (that is, cognitive processes used to generate novel and useful ideas), a product (that is, novel and useful outcomes), and "press" (that is, environmental influences, creativity climate) (Barbot et al., 2019; Batey, 2012; Rhodes, 1961). In our review of the recent management literature, a similar issue exists, however, with some variation. For example, the "press" or environmental factors appear to be better distinguished from "individual creativity" within the management literature. Factors such as having a climate for creativity (Amabile et al., 1996) and a creative team environment (González-Gómez & Richter, 2015) are investigated as predictors of individual creativity or seen as boundary conditions. In our review, we did not find any instances of environmental factors being referred to as "creativity." However, in the management literature, the term "creativity" is used in theoretical models to represent creativity as a person, process, and product.

Several constructs at the "person" level have been differentiated from creativity and studied in their own right. For example, creative self-efficacy (Tierney & Farmer, 2002; Zhang & Zhou, 2014), creative identity (Farmer et al., 2003; Vincent & Kouchaki, 2015), and dispositional creativity (Gough, 1979; Keem et al., 2018) have been investigated uniquely from creative processes or outcomes. Yet, there is still some debate at the "person" level when it comes to creativity-related skills. Theoretically, these have been identified as predictors of individual creativity (Amabile, 1996), and at times classified as creativity traits (Eysenck, 1996). Yet in our review of creativity studies in management journals over the last five years we identified multiple studies that assessed individual creativity through creative-thinking tasks, such as divergent thinking tasks and remote association thinking tasks (Huang et al., 2015; Jung & Lee, 2015; Lu et al., 2017). Hence, according to the measurement of creativity, there is still some discrepancy regarding whether creative-thinking tasks represent creative potential or actual creativity. However, overall, creative traits do seem to be well distinguished from the actual generation of novel and useful ideas in organizational research.

In the management literature, the most significant open question is regarding how to distinguish between creativity as a process and creativity as a product. Theoretically, scholars have often articulated the distinction between the two (Amabile, 1983; Woodman et al., 1993). For example, Montag et al. (2012) defined creative behaviors (that is, process) as ranging from behaviors such as problem construction to idea evaluation, and distinguished these from creative outcome effectiveness (that is, product) that they define as the "joint novelty and usefulness (that is, quality) of a product or service or of an outcome as judged by relevant stakeholders"

(Montag et al., 2012: 1369). While theoretically distinct, studies of creativity in the management literature may be theoretically investigating the creative process, the creative product, or a mix of the two. The measures of creativity also may focus on one, the other, or both. Interestingly, in our review, it appears that the two are not always aligned.

Some measures have been generated that clearly assess the creative process. For example, creative process engagement is a construct that was introduced by Zhang and Bartol (2010). This measure is often used in field studies and tends to be self-reported, assessing the frequency with which one engages in problem identification, information searching and encoding, and idea generation behaviors. Meanwhile, other measures more clearly assess the evaluation of the novelty and usefulness of an idea or product that has been produced, presumably from engaging in some type of creative process. Archival studies look at evidence of creative outcomes such as citations (Arts & Fleming, 2018) and an audience's reception to television shows and movies (Clement et al., 2018; Mannucci & Yong, 2017). Some field survey measures such as the three-item measure from Oldham and Cummings (1996) ask one's supervisor to assess one's creative outcomes at work. An example of an item from this scale asks supervisors about their employees: "How original and practical is this person's work? Original and practical work refers to developing ideas, methods, or products that are both totally unique and especially useful to the organization" (Oldham & Cummings, 1996). Additionally, some scholars are moving away from using the general term "creativity" and instead hypothesizing about the specific elements of creativity that they are measuring, such as the number of publications or citations (Seibert et al., 2017), idea quantity and quality (Kier & McMullen, 2018), and creative responses (Perry-Smith, 2014). However, many other measures of creativity are not as clearly aligned to either a process or a product.

The CAT used in experimental studies asks judges who are blind to the experimental manipulations to assess the overall creativity of the ideas or products produced. On one hand, this can be considered an assessment of the creative product, in that expert judges are assessing the novelty and usefulness of one's creative outputs. However, some scholars have argued that this is also an assessment of idea generation, which is one step in the creative process (Montag et al., 2012). Looking at the most commonly used measure in field studies (Zhou & George, 2001), this scale includes behavioral items such as "searches out new technologies, processes, techniques, and/or product ideas" and outcome items such as "often has new and innovative ideas." Similarly, Farmer et al.'s (2003) scale includes both searching behaviors (that is, "seeks new ideas and ways to solve problems") and novel outcomes (that is, "generates ground-breaking ideas related to the field") within their four-item creativity scale.

Drawing on the distinction between studies of the creative process that could lead to creative outcomes is additionally confusing because of the broader meaning and use of the terms "behaviors" and "outcomes." The term "behavior" relates to any observable variable, as opposed to attitudes and cognitions. Therefore, we discuss job performance as being a behavior even though we may be assessing behaviors in one's job or the outcome of one's behaviors such as the quantity or quality of output.

Scholars also use the term "outcome" to refer to any dependent variable in a predictive model. So even in articles that highlight creativity as an outcome (that is, the thing being predicted), the aspect of creativity under investigation may be creative behavior or engaging in the creative process (for example, Rosen et al., 2014). Hence teasing apart the research predicting creative behaviors from creative outcomes can be even more complicated when the terminology used in the hypotheses is the same (that is, creativity) and the measures are not clearly distinguished.

Creativity: How to Distinguish it from Individual Innovation?

A similar area of conceptual overlap, both theoretically and empirically, lies in the distinction between creativity and innovation at the individual level. To creativity scholars, these constructs are considered separately since they represent the beginning and ending phases of implementing a new idea or solution in an organization (Amabile, 1996; Anderson et al., 2014). Creativity is the first step: from problem identification to idea generation or, at times, idea evaluation, selection, and development within an individual or group generating the idea. Innovation at the individual level begins with communicating and championing an idea out in the larger organization and ends at the implementation of the new idea (Anderson et al., 2014). However, this distinction is not universally agreed upon in the management literature. To individual innovation scholars, individual innovation is often conceptualized as the entire process including idea generation (Hammond et al., 2011; Scott & Bruce, 1994; Yuan & Woodman, 2010).

Research on individual innovation often uses Scott and Bruce's (1994) six-item scale that assesses an employee's creative behaviors (for example, information searching, idea generation) and implementation-related behaviors (for example, promoting ideas, securing funds to implement ideas, and planning implementation schedules). Interestingly, there is overlap between this scale and the most commonly used scale to assess individual creativity. Zhou and George (2001) noted that they adapted three items from the Scott and Bruce (1994) scale, two of which are distinctly within the domain of innovation ("promotes and champions ideas to others" and "develops adequate plans and schedules for the implementation of new ideas"). The other shared item, "searches out new technologies, processes, techniques, and/ or product ideas" overlaps with the information searching behaviors characteristic of many creative process models (Zhang & Bartol, 2010). While the idea-championing and implementation focused items are only two of the 13 total items in this creativity scale, this does blur the line between creativity and innovation empirically, even in research that often holds a theoretical distinction between creativity and innovation as the point between idea generation and idea championing. Additionally, archival studies that look at the success of implemented ideas that are considered to be creative are at times measured as creativity (Clement et al., 2018; Mannucci & Yong, 2017; Tierney et al., 1999), and inherently include the implementation phase within the definition of creativity. It is also worth noting that a large number of creativity meta-analyses conducted in the last few decades have included both creativity and innovation in the literature review search terms (Byron & Khazanchi, 2012; Byron et al., 2010; Davis, 2009); meta-analyses of individual innovation include creativity in search terms (Hammond et al., 2011); and recent reviews of creativity incorporate the two into a definition statement (Anderson et al., 2014).

NEW TRENDS IN CREATIVITY MEASUREMENT

Two of the biggest trends in recent research relate directly to the concerns highlighted above: first, the investigation of novelty and usefulness as separate, unique constructs; and second, research on how people judge or perceive ideas to be more or less creative. A related third trend is in exploring cultural differences in the experience of and understanding of creativity. Given our findings about the same scales being used and the unidimensional definition of creativity that exists in research across the globe, finding that different cultures might interpret the phrases "creative" and "novel" uniquely could bring important guidance to the interpretation and aggregation of such studies.

As noted above, ratings of originality or novelty have been shown to have an inverse relationship, at times, with ratings of usefulness or the appropriateness of an idea (Ford & Gioia, 2000; Runco & Charles, 1993). Hence, researchers have recently brought an increased focus to the direct investigation of novelty and usefulness as independent constructs, especially investigating which constructs impact novelty versus which constructs impact usefulness (Berg, 2014; Ford & Gioia, 2000). Many of these studies utilize an experimental research design and CAT rating, rating the usefulness and novelty of the ideas separately, but not aggregating them in the end (Berg, 2014; Miron-Spektor & Beenen, 2015).

Notably, some of these studies have investigated the unique contribution that each aspect of creativity (novelty and usefulness) makes to the overall assessment of creativity. Findings suggest that novelty assessments play a greater role in creativity assessments than usefulness (Diedrich et al., 2015; Runco & Charles, 1993). These studies also find interactive effects, but the interaction results are less consistent across studies. Further research in this vein can provide refined guidance to the issue stated above: confirming how we should incorporate these two elements of the definition of creativity into our measurement of creativity in both field and experimental settings.

Another trend in measuring creativity is in explicitly investigating the way individuals make assessments of creativity (e.g., Mueller et al., 2018; Randel et al., 2011; Zhou et al., 2017). A recent review coins this research as the receiving side of creativity (Zhou et al., 2019). This research highlights that there are characteristics of the context, the creator, the evaluator, and the creative object that impact one's assessment of an object's creativity (Zhou et al., 2019). Given that most measures of creativity involve one or more raters (for example, expert raters, supervisors, co-workers) assessing the novelty and usefulness of an output, much of this research may be conflating influences on objective creativity with influences on one's perceptions of creativity. We echo the call from the researchers for future work to study the "generative and evaluative processes [of creativity] in combination, rather than independently" (Zhou et al., 2019: 2590). The struggle still remains, however, to define a truly "objective" measure of creative idea generation.

Finally, while the idea that different cultures experience and view creativity differently is not old, the creativity literature to date has not incorporated these potential differences into the measurement of creativity (Glaveanu, 2019). As shown in the above review, the research methods and scales used to assess creativity are quite consistent across studies. For example, Zhou and George's (2001) 13-item scale is used in studies in Slovenia (Černe et al., 2014), Columbia (González-Gómez & Richter, 2015), Denmark (Soda et al., 2019), China (Zhang et al., 2014), and the United States (Parke et al., 2015), to name a few. Research conducted on cultural influences on creativity assessments typically investigate the differences between the East (for example, China) and the West (for example, the United States). These studies continually report that while individuals, in general, associate creativity with originality and imagination (Glaveanu, 2019; Niu & Kaufman, 2013), Eastern cultures place a greater emphasis on usefulness and social value, while Western cultures place a greater emphasis on novelty and individual originality (Loewenstein & Mueller, 2016; Morris & Leung, 2010; Niu & Kaufman, 2013; Niu & Sternberg, 2002). Hence, when raters or supervisors are responding to survey questions about an employee's overall creativity, different behaviors and outcomes might drive ratings in each of these contexts. Building on the perspective of the receiving side of creativity mentioned above, these cultural influences on creativity assessments are a critical contextual factor that should be considered in the measurement of creativity and the aggregation and understanding of extant creativity studies.

CONCLUSION

We have reviewed the measurement of individual creativity in organizational studies, and in particular empirical studies that have been published over the last five years in top management journals. Overall, we find that the same unidimensional definition of creativity exists in both experimental and field studies across the world. In addition, the same few scales are used to measure creativity, with one scale (Zhou & George, 2001) predominating in the research. We highlight issues to consider going forward in measuring individual creativity, as well as three recent trends in creativity measurement.

NOTES

1. *Academy of Management Journal, Administrative Science Quarterly, Journal of Applied Psychology, Journal of Management, Management Science, Organization Science,*

Organizational Behavior and Human Decision Processes, Personnel Psychology, and *Strategic Management Journal*.

2. Search included all articles with the term "creativ*" in the abstract. Initial search returned 116 articles. After removing non-quantitative articles and articles on team- or organizational-level creativity, 57 articles remained.
3. This scale will be referred to as Zhou & George (2001) going forward for parsimony as the items are exactly the same in both references.
4. The remaining four items assess other behaviors such as information search, risk-taking, idea-championing and implementation-planning.

REFERENCES

Amabile, T.M. 1982. Social psychology of creativity: A consensual assessment technique. *Journal of Personality and Social Psychology*, 43(5): 997–1013.

Amabile, T.M. 1983. The social psychology of creativity: A componential conceptualization. *Journal of Personality and Social Psychology*, 45(2): 357–376.

Amabile, T.M. 1996. *Creativity in context: Update to "The Social Psychology of Creativity"*, Vol. 18. Boulder, CO: Westview Press.

Amabile, T.M., Conti, R., Coon, H., Lazenby, J., & Herron, M. 1996. Assessing the work environment for creativity. *Academy of Management Journal*, 39(5): 1154–1184.

Anderson, N., Potočnik, K., & Zhou, J. 2014. Innovation and creativity in organizations: A state-of-the-science review, prospective commentary, and guiding framework. *Journal of Management*, 40(5): 1297–1333.

Arts, S., & Fleming, L. 2018. Paradise of novelty – or loss of human capital? Exploring new fields and inventive output. *Organization Science*, 29(6): 1074–1092.

Barbot, B., Hass, R.W., & Reiter-Palmon, R. 2019. Creativity assessment in psychological research: (Re)setting the standards. *Psychology of Aesthetics, Creativity, and the Arts*, 13(2): 233–240.

Barron, F.X. 1955. The disposition toward originality. *Journal of Abnormal Social Psychology*, 51: 478–485.

Batey, M. 2012. The measurement of creativity: From definitional consensus to the introduction of a new heuristic framework. *Creativity Research Journal*, 24(1): 55–65.

Berg, J.M. 2014. The primal mark: How the beginning shapes the end in the development of creative ideas. *Organizational Behavior and Human Decision Processes*, 125(1): 1–17.

Brown, G., & Baer, M. 2015. Protecting the turf: The effect of territorial marking on others' creativity. *Journal of Applied Psychology*, 100(6): 1785–1797.

Byron, K., & Khazanchi, S. 2012. Rewards and creative performance: A meta-analytic test of theoretically derived hypotheses. *Psychological Bulletin*, 138(4): 809–830.

Byron, K., Khazanchi, S., & Nazarian, D. 2010. The relationship between stressors and creativity: A meta-analysis examining competing theoretical models. *Journal of Applied Psychology*, 95(1): 201–212.

Chua, R.Y.J. 2018. Innovating at cultural crossroads: How multicultural social networks promote idea flow and creativity. *Journal of Management*, 44(3): 1119–1146.

Clement, J., Shipilov, A., & Galunic, C. 2018. Brokerage as a public good: The externalities of network hubs for different formal roles in creative organizations. *Administrative Science Quarterly*, 63(2): 251–286.

Costa, P.T.J., & McCrae, R.R. 1992. *Revised NEO Personality Inventory (NEO-PI-R) and NEO Five-Factor Inventory (NEO-FFI) professional manual*. Odessa, FL: Psychological Assessment Resources.

Černe, M., Nerstad, C.G.L., Dysvik, A., & Škerlavaj, M. 2014. What goes around comes around: Knowledge hiding, perceived motivational climate, and creativity. *Academy of Management Journal*, 57(1): 172–192.

Davis, M.A. 2009. Understanding the relationship between mood and creativity: A meta-analysis. *Organizational Behavior and Human Decision Processes*, 108(1): 25–38.

Diedrich, J., Benedek, M., Jauk, E., & Neubauer, A.C. 2015. Are creative ideas novel and useful? *Psychology of Aesthetics, Creativity, and the Arts*, 9(1): 35–40.

Dunker, K. 1945. On problem-solving. *Psychological Monographs*, 58(5, Whole No. 270).

Eysenck, H.J. 1996. The measurement of creativity. In M.A. Boden (ed.), *Dimensions of creativity*: 199–242. Cambridge, MA: MIT Press.

Farmer, S.M., Tierney, P., & Kung-Mcintyre, K. 2003. Employee creativity in Taiwan: An application of role identity theory. *Academy of Management Journal*, 46(5): 618–630.

Ford, C.M. 1996. A theory of individual creative action in multiple social domains. *Academy of Management Review*, 21(4): 1112–1142.

Ford, C.M., & Gioia, D.A. 2000. Factors influencing creativity in the domain of managerial decision making. *Journal of Management*, 26(4): 705–732.

George, J.M., & Zhou, J. 2001. When openness to experience and conscientiousness are related to creative behavior: An interactional approach. *Journal of Applied Psychology*, 86(3): 513–524.

Glaveanu, V.P. 2019. Measuring creativity across cultures: Epistemological and methodological considerations. *Psychology of Aesthetics, Creativity, and the Arts*, 13(2): 227–232.

Goncalo, J.A., Chatman, J.A., Duguid, M.M., & Kennedy, J.A. 2015. Creativity from constraint? How the political correctness norm influences creativity in mixed-sex work groups. *Administrative Science Quarterly*, 60(1): 1–30.

González-Gómez, H.V., & Richter, A.W. 2015. Turning shame into creativity: The importance of exposure to creative team environments. *Organizational Behavior and Human Decision Processes*, 126: 142–161.

Gough, H.G. 1979. A creative personality scale for the adjective check list. *Journal of Personality and Social Psychology*, 37(8): 1398–1405.

Hammond, M.M., Neff, N.L., Farr, J.L., Schwall, A.R., & Zhao, X. 2011. Predictors of individual-level innovation at work: A meta-analysis. *Psychology of Aesthetics, Creativity, and the Arts*, 5(1): 90–105.

Harris, T.B., Li, N., Boswell, W.R., Zhang, X., & Xie, Z. 2014. Getting what's new from newcomers: Empowering leadership, creativity, and adjustment in the socialization context. *Personnel Psychology*, 67(3): 567–604.

Harrison, S., & Wagner, D.T. 2016. Spilling outside the box: The effects of individuals' creative behaviors at work on time spent with their spouses at home. *Academy of Management Journal*, 59(3): 841–859.

Hinkin, T.R. 1998. A brief tutorial on the development of measures for use in survey questionnaires. *Organizational Research Methods*, 1(1): 104–121.

Hirst, G., Van Knippenberg, D., Zhou, J., Quintane, E., & Zhu, C. 2015. Heard it through the grapevine: Indirect networks and employee creativity. *Journal of Applied Psychology*, 100(2): 567–574.

Hon, A.H.Y., Bloom, M., & Crant, J.M. 2014. Overcoming resistance to change and enhancing creative performance. *Journal of Management*, 40(3): 919–941.

Huang, L., Gino, F., & Galinsky, A.D. 2015. The highest form of intelligence: Sarcasm increases creativity for both expressers and recipients. *Organizational Behavior and Human Decision Processes*, 131: 162–177.

Hülsheger, U.R., Anderson, N., & Salgado, J.F. 2009. Team-level predictors of innovation at work: A comprehensive meta-analysis spanning three decades of research. *Journal of Applied Psychology*, 94(5): 1128–1145.

Jung, E.J., & Lee, S. 2015. The combined effects of relationship conflict and the relational self on creativity. *Organizational Behavior and Human Decision Processes*, 130: 44–57.

Kauppila, O.P., Bizzi, L., & Obstfeld, D. 2018. Connecting and creating: Tertius iungens, individual creativity, and strategic decision processes. *Strategic Management Journal*, 39(3): 697–719.

Kay, M.B., Proudfoot, D., & Larrick, R.P. 2018. There's no team in I: How observers perceive individual creativity in a team setting. *Journal of Applied Psychology*, 103(4): 432–442.

Keem, S., Shalley, C.E., Kim, E., & Jeong, I. 2018. Are creative individuals bad apples? A dual pathway model of unethical behavior. *Journal of Applied Psychology*, 103(4): 416–431.

Kier, A.S., & McMullen, J.S. 2018. Entrepreneurial imaginativeness in new venture ideation. *Academy of Management Journal*, 61(6): 2265–2295.

Koseoglu, G., Liu, Y., & Shalley, C.E. 2017a. Working with creative leaders: Exploring the relationship between supervisors' and subordinates' creativity. *Leadership Quarterly*, 28(6): 798–811.

Koseoglu, G., Shalley, C.E., & Herndon, B. 2017b. Task context changes: teams' maladaptive responses to unanticipated change. *Journal of Applied Social Psychology*, 47(4): 195–212.

Kwan, H.K., Zhang, X., Liu, J., & Lee, C. 2018. Workplace ostracism and employee creativity: An integrative approach incorporating pragmatic and engagement roles. *Journal of Applied Psychology*, 103(12): 1358–1366.

Lee, J.S., & Hsieh, C.J. 2010. A research in relating entrepreneurship, marketing capability, innovative capability and sustained competitive advantage. *Journal of Business and Economics Research*, 8(9): 109–120.

Lengnick-Hall, C.A. 1992. Innovation and competitive advantage: What we know and what we need to learn. *Journal of Management*, 18(2): 399–429.

Li, Y., Li, N., Guo, J., Li, J., & Harris, T.B. 2017. A network view of advice-giving and individual creativity in teams: A brokerage-driven, socially perpetuated phenomenon. *Academy of Management Journal*, 61(6): 2210–2229.

Liao, H., Liu, D., & Loi, R. 2010. Looking at both sides of the social exchange coin: A social cognitive perspective on the joint effects of relationship quality and differentiation on creativity. *Academy of Management Journal*, 53(5): 1090–1109.

Liu, D., Gong, Y., Zhou, J., & Huang, J.C. 2017. Human resource systems, employee creativity, and firm innovation: The moderating role of firm ownership. *Academy of Management Journal*, 60(3): 1164–1188.

Liu, D., Wang, S., & Wayne, S.J. 2015. Is being a good learner enough? An examination of the interplay between learning goal orientation and impression management tactics on creativity. *Personnel Psychology*, 68(1): 109–142.

Loewenstein, J., & Mueller, J. 2016. Implicit theories of creative ideas: How culture guides creativity assessments. *Academy of Management Discoveries*, 2(4): 320–348.

Lu, J.G., Hafenbrack, A.C., Eastwick, P.W., Wang, D.J., Maddux, W.W., & Galinsky, A.D. 2017. "Going out" of the box: Close intercultural friendships and romantic relationships spark creativity, workplace innovation, and entrepreneurship. *Journal of Applied Psychology*, 102(7): 1091–1108.

Madjar, N., & Oldham, G.R. 2006. Task rotation and polychronicity: Effects on individuals' creativity. *Human Performance*, 19(2): 117–131.

Madjar, N., & Shalley, C.E. 2008. Multiple tasks' and multiple goals' effect on creativity: Forced incubation or just a distraction? *Journal of Management*, 34(4): 786–805.

Madjar, N., Shalley, C.E., & Herndon, B. 2019. Taking time to incubate: The moderating role of "what you do" and "when you do it" on creative performance. *Journal of Creative Behavior*, 53(3): 377–388.

Mannucci, P.V., & Yong, K. 2017. The differential impact of knowledge depth and knowledge breadth on creativity over individual careers. *Academy of Management Journal*, 61(5): 1741–1763.

Marinova, S.V., Cao, X., & Park, H. 2019. Constructive organizational values climate and organizational citizenship behaviors: A configurational view. *Journal of Management*, 45(5): 2045–2071.

Miron-Spektor, E., & Beenen, G. 2015. Motivating creativity: The effects of sequential and simultaneous learning and performance achievement goals on product novelty and usefulness. *Organizational Behavior and Human Decision Processes*, 127: 53–65.

Montag, T., Maertz, C.P., & Baer, M. 2012. A critical analysis of the workplace creativity criterion space. *Journal of Management*, 38(4): 1362–1386.

Morris, M.W., & Leung, K. 2010. Creativity east and west: Perspectives and parallels. *Management and Organization Review*, 6(3): 313–327.

Mueller, J., Melwani, S., Loewenstein, J., & Deal, J.J. 2018. Reframing the decision-makers' dilemma: Towards a social context model of creative idea recognition. *Academy of Management Journal*, 61(1): 94–110.

Ng, T.W., & Feldman, D.C. 2012. A comparison of self-ratings and non-self-report measures of employee creativity. *Human Relations*, 65(8): 1021–1047.

Niu, W., & Kaufman, J.C. 2013. Creativity of Chinese and American cultures: A synthetic analysis. *Journal of Creative Behavior*, 47(1): 77–87.

Niu, W., & Sternberg, R. 2002. Contemporary studies on the concept of creativity: The East and the West. *Journal of Creative Behavior*, 36(4): 269–288.

Oldham, G.R., & Cummings, A. 1996. Employee creativity: Personal and contextual factors at work. *Academy of Management Journal*, 39(3): 607–634.

Parke, M.R., Seo, M.G., & Sherf, E.N. 2015. Regulating and facilitating: The role of emotional intelligence in maintaining and using positive affect for creativity. *Journal of Applied Psychology*, 100(3): 917–934.

Perry-Smith, J.E. 2014. Social network ties beyond nonredundancy: An experimental investigation of the effect of knowledge content and tie strength on creativity. *Journal of Applied Psychology*, 99(5): 831–846.

Podsakoff, P.M., MacKenzie, S.B., Lee, J.Y., & Podsakoff, N.P. 2003. Common method biases in behavioral research: A critical review of the literature and recommended remedies. *Journal of Applied Psychology*, 88(5): 879–903.

Randel, A.E., Jaussi, K.S., & Wu, A. 2011. When does being creative lead to being rated as creative? The moderating role of perceived probability of successfully bringing ideas to a supervisor's attention. *Creativity Research Journal*, 23(1): 1–8.

Rhodes, M. 1961. An analysis of creativity. *Phi Delta Kappan*, 42(7): 305–310.

Rosen, C.C., Ferris, D.L., Brown, D.J., Chen, Y., & Yan, M. 2014. Perceptions of organizational politics: A need satisfaction paradigm. *Organization Science*, 25(4): 1026–1055.

Runco, M., & Charles, R.E. 1993. Judgments of originality and appropriateness as predictors of creativity. *Personality and Individual Differences*, 15(5): 537–546.

Scott, S.G., & Bruce, R.A. 1994. Determinants of innovative behavior: A path model of individual innovation in the workplace. *Academy of Management Journal*, 37(3): 580–607.

Seibert, S.E., Kacmar, K.M., Kraimer, M.L., Downes, P.E., & Noble, D. 2017. The role of research strategies and professional networks in management scholars' productivity. *Journal of Management*, 43(4): 1103–1130.

Shalley, C.E. 1991. Effects of productivity goals, creativity goals, and personal discretion on individual creativity. *Journal of Applied Psychology*, 76(2): 179–185.

Shalley, C.E., Gilson, L.L., & Blum, T.C. 2009. Interactive effects of growth need strength, work context, and job complexity on self-reported creative performance. *Academy of Management Journal*, 52(3): 489–505.

Shalley, C.E., Zhou, J., & Oldham, G.R. 2004. The effects of personal and contextual characteristics on creativity: Where should we go from here? *Journal of Management*, 30(6): 933–958.

Soda, G., Stea, D., & Pedersen, T. 2019. Network structure, collaborative context, and individual creativity. *Journal of Management*, 45(4): 1739–1765.

Stein, M. I. 1953. Creativity and culture. *Journal of Psychology*, 36(2): 311–322.

Stein, M.I. 1974. *Stimulating creativity (Volume 1): Individual procedures.* New York: Academic Press.

Sullivan, D.M., & Ford, C.M. 2010. The alignment of measures and constructs in organizational research: The case of testing measurement models of creativity. *Journal of Business and Psychology*, 25(3): 505–521.

Thornhill, S. 2006. Knowledge, innovation and firm performance in high- and low-technology regimes. *Journal of Business Venturing*, 21(5): 687–703.

Tierney, P., & Farmer, S.M. 2002. Creative self-efficacy: Its potential antecedents and relationship to creative performance. *Academy of Management Journal*, 45(6): 1137–1148.

Tierney, P., Farmer, S.M., & Graen, G.B. 1999. An examination of leadership and employee creativity: The relevance of traits and relationships. *Personnel Psychology*, 52(3): 591–620.

Vincent, L.C., & Kouchaki, M. 2015. Creative, rare, entitled, and dishonest: How commonality of creativity in one's group decreases an individual's entitlement and dishonesty. *Academy of Management Journal*, 59(4): 1451–1473.

Vernon P.E. 1989. The nature–nurture problem in creativity. In J.A. Glover, R.R. Ronning, and C.R. Reynolds (eds), *Handbook of creativity*: 93–110. Boston, MA: Springer.

Woodman, R.W., Sawyer, J.E., & Griffin, R.W. 1993. Toward a theory of organizational creativity. *Academy of Management Review*, 18(2): 293–321.

Yuan, F., & Woodman, R.W. 2010. Innovative behavior in the workplace: The role of performance and image outcome expectations. *Academy of Management Journal*, 53(2): 323–342.

Zhang, H., Kwan, H.K., Zhang, X., & Wu, L.Z. 2014. High core self-evaluators maintain creativity: A motivational model of abusive supervision. *Journal of Management*, 40(4): 1151–1174.

Zhang, X., & Bartol, K.M. 2010. Linking empowering leadership and employee creativity: The influence of psychological empowerment, intrinsic motivation, and creative process engagement. *Academy of Management Journal*, 53(1): 107–128.

Zhang, X., & Zhou, J. 2014. Empowering leadership, uncertainty avoidance, trust, and employee creativity: Interaction effects and a mediating mechanism. *Organizational Behavior and Human Decision Processes*, 124(2): 150–164.

Zhou, J., & George, J.M. 2001. When job dissatisfaction leads to creativity: Encouraging the expression of voice. *Academy of Management Journal*, 44(4): 682–696.

Zhou, J., Wang, X.M., Bavato, D., Tasselli, S., & Wu, J. 2019. Understanding the receiving side of creativity. *Journal of Management*, 45(6): 2570–2595. https://doi.org/10.1177/0149206319827088.

Zhou, J., Wang, X.M., Song, L.J., & Wu, J. 2017. Is it new? Personal and contextual influences on perceptions of novelty and creativity. *Journal of Applied Psychology*, 102(2): 180–202.

2. The dual pathway to creativity model: implications for workplace creativity

Bernard A. Nijstad, Eric F. Rietzschel, Matthijs Baas, and Carsten K.W. De Dreu

WHERE DO IDEAS COME FROM?

In Ancient Greece, it was custom to turn to the Muses for inspiration. In the opening lines of the *Odyssey*, for example, Homer famously calls upon the Muse to help him tell the story of Odysseus:

> Sing in me, Muse, and through me tell the story
> of that man skilled in ways of contending,
> the wanderer, harried for years on end,
> after he plundered the stronghold
> on the proud height of Troy.
> (Translation by Robert Fitzgerald, 1961)

Although few people may believe that mythical creatures such as muses exist, the image of a muse who quietly whispers words of inspiration into the ears of the artist (or scientist) remains powerful. For example, the American singer-songwriter Judy Collins said, "When inspiration does not come, I go for a walk, go to the movie, talk to a friend, let go … The muse is bound to return again, especially if I turn my back!" (quoted in Packer, 2006: 213). Similarly, the American author Elizabeth Gilbert proposed that perhaps an artist may not be a genius, but may rather have a genius; which she refers to as a "disembodied spirit" who would assist the artist with their work.[1] The image of a muse (or genius) is so strong and persistent partly because it resonates with many accounts of breakthrough ideas. For example, the structure of the benzene molecule allegedly came to August Kekulé when dozing off in front of the fire; Paul McCartney claimed that the song "Yesterday" came to him in a dream; and the mathematical theory of Fuchsian functions apparently came to Henri Poincaré when he was getting on a horse-drawn omnibus (see Ghiselin, 1952). What these accounts have in common is that great ideas seem to appear "out of thin air" at moments in which the creator is not actively thinking about them; indeed, as if a muse whispers into one's ear.

Naturally, the answer to the question "Where do ideas come from?" is not that they come from the muses or appear out of nowhere; instead, ideas are generated in someone's brain (or during a discussion among several "brains"). Yet, it is true that ideas (sometimes) come when least expected and when not actively trying to generate them. For example, research attests to the value of distraction, daydreaming, and defocused attention for creativity (e.g., Baird et al., 2012; Dietrich & Kanso, 2010; Dijksterhuis & Meurs, 2006; Smallwood & Schooler, 2015), and a period of incubation, in which one is not actively thinking of a particular problem, may help one to solve that very problem (Sio & Ormerod, 2009, for a meta-analysis). A somewhat unfortunate consequence of this seems to be that creativity remains unpredictable, and that the only thing one can do is sit back, daydream, and hope that good ideas will somehow come.

Although popular, this account of creativity is incomplete and, therefore, wrong. Although creativity may benefit from defocused attention and incubation, it is also often – and perhaps more often – the result of hard work, concentrated effort, and persistence (Baas et al., 2015; Lucas & Nordgren, 2015). This means, on the one hand, that being creative is cognitively demanding, which may at times be unpleasant (see e.g., Roskes et al., 2012). On the other hand, working hard and concentrating for long periods of time may be a more certain recipe for generating creative ideas than waiting for the muses. Indeed, as the thriller author Helen Hanson (2010) has noted: "Inspiration is the windfall from hard work and focus. Muses are too unreliable to keep on the payroll."

Thus, putting the muses aside, this chapter recognizes that creativity necessarily involves cognitive processes, and that an understanding of these processes will be helpful when trying to stimulate or enhance (one's own or others') creativity. The chapter further builds on the insight that creativity may come about through different (cognitive) processes. We first elaborate on the mental processes that allow people to generate ideas. We then present our dual pathway to creativity model (DPCM; De Dreu et al., 2008; Nijstad et al., 2010), which integrates different views on creativity in a single model. The DPCM proposes that there are two qualitatively different ways to be creative – through cognitive flexibility and through cognitive persistence – and that situational and personal factors drive which (if any) of these two pathways people will use. We next present evidence for this model, which mainly derives from laboratory studies on idea generation, and then go into the implications of the model for workplace creativity. Finally, we discuss directions for future research.

THEORIES OF CREATIVITY

Random Process and Remote Associations

One influential theoretical perspective of creativity – defined as the production of ideas that are both original and useful (Amabile, 1983) – assumes that creativity essentially involves a Darwinian process of random variation and selective retention (e.g., Campbell, 1960; Simonton, 1999). For example, in Simonton's (1999, 2003) model, creators during their life acquire a set of ideas (for example, concepts, techniques, themes) in a certain domain (for example, physics). These ideas are subjected to quasi-random permutations, and by changing or combining existing ideas, new ideas arise. When these ideas are found to be useful, they are retained and passed on to other creators in the field (for example, other physicists); otherwise they are not selected and are often forgotten (see also Csikszentmihalyi, 1999).

These combinatory processes, however, cannot be completely random (hence "quasi-random" in Simonton's model), because of the way the brain works. Most cognitive scientists would agree that knowledge in the brain is stored in an associative network, where certain pieces of knowledge (for example, potential ideas) are connected to other pieces of knowledge (e.g., Collins & Loftus, 1975; also Nijstad & Stroebe, 2006). These connections vary in strength, and pieces of knowledge that are semantically related are presumed to have strong mutual ties. For example, the word "dog" will usually have strong ties with words such as "cat" or "food" because of the semantic relations between these words. As a consequence, combinations that are (randomly) formed will often involve elements that are already related, and these combinations will often not be new or original. Indeed, most associations that are formed through quasi-random processes will be either "old" (ideas that already exist) or "useless" (strange combinations that make no sense); but occasionally something extraordinary happens (by chance) and a truly creative (new and useful) idea is born. Consistent with this account, truly creative breakthroughs are very rare; moreover, creators who are more productive overall (that is, generate more ideas) have a higher chance of generating really good ideas as well as a higher chance of generating poor ideas; as one would expect if the creative process involves some randomness (Simonton, 1997, 2003).

This perspective also suggests that people will be more creative when they are capable of making original or semantically remote (rather than close) associations; that is, for instance, when they associate "dog" also with "leash," "park," or "tail." For example, Mednick's (1962) associative theory of creativity assumes that individuals differ in their association hierarchies. Perhaps because of differences in the functional anatomy of the brain or the availability and transmission of certain neurotransmitters, some people have steep (or narrow) associative hierarchies, in which each element in memory is associated very strongly with only a few other elements. Others will have flatter (or broader) association hierarchies, in which associations are manifold and much weaker. It is assumed that individuals who have a flatter association hierarchy will be more creative, because they are more capable of making remote and original associations. Evidence indeed suggests that those individuals that are recognized as being creative are capable of forming more and more uncommon associations (e.g., Gough, 1976; Mendelsohn, 1976; but see Benedek & Neubauer, 2013, for a critical discussion).

The steepness of an association hierarchy not only varies between individuals, but may also vary within persons from moment to moment. It is possible, for example, that certain temporary psychological states, such as distraction and mind-wandering, but also certain mood states (for example, happiness) or motivational orientations (for example, an approach motivation), enhance creativity because they facilitate making remote connections in memory (see also Baas et al., 2008; Friedman & Förster, 2001; Isen & Daubman, 1984). States of defocused attention and mind-wandering are associated with reduced top-down cognitive control (for example, a lack of concentration or focus), and the same is true for positive mood states (e.g., Dreisbach & Goschke, 2004). Such loose top-down control may increase distractibility and reduce one's ability to focus on a specific task, but may also facilitate creativity: it allows for the intrusion of more remote elements, which leads to higher creativity. These more remote elements may effectively be "blocked out" when in a more focused, concentrated state of mind (see also Carson et al., 2003; Zhang et al., 2020; Zmigrod et al., 2015).

In sum, one important account of creativity assumes that new ideas essentially result from "happy accidents" in the mind. When these "accidents" involve elements that are only remotely associated, the chance is higher that the resulting idea is in fact original (but only occasionally also useful). Remote associations, in turn, are more likely for people who have a flatter association hierarchy, or for people who are in a state of reduced top-down cognitive control (for example, daydreaming, happy). Importantly, whether creative ideas are generated is unpredictable and mostly outside of the control of the creator. Rather, the essential cognitive processes that are involved are relatively passive and unconscious or undeliberate (such as automatic spreading of activation).

Systematic Search

There is, however, a second account of creativity, which emphasizes the importance of systematic search processes. Newell and Simon's (1972) classic work on problem-solving, for example, suggests that problems have an initial state, a goal state, and a set of operators and constraints. Solving a problem (creatively) involves finding a path in "search space" (that is, a domain or set of options that can be searched for solutions; the set of all possible solutions[2]) that would lead from the initial state to the goal state. Finding such a path can be highly systematic and may involve the application of well-known operators (for example, algorithms). However, sometimes problems are "ill-defined," because the initial state, the goal state, and/or the operators are unknown, in which case the problem-solver must apply heuristics to solve the problem. Such an approach may include systematic trial and error, which will initially often be unsuccessful. However, even trial and error may eventually – after persistence – result in creative ideas that actually work.[3]

The idea of systematic search processes resonates with the "creative cognition approach" that was introduced by Finke, Smith, and Ward (e.g., Finke et al., 1992; Smith et al., 1995; Ward, 1994). The basic assumption of this approach is that creativity results from "ordinary" cognitive processes, such as memory retrieval, combination, and categorization, that can be studied using the tools of cognitive science. This approach has found that, as a consequence of the application of these processes, the creative products generated by people – even in response to ill-defined problems – tend to be fairly predictable. For example, when people are asked to generate an alien that lives on a planet that is very different from Earth, most people include typical features of Earth mammals, such as a head, limbs, and bilateral symmetry; and when asked to draw a creature with feathers, many people also include a beak and wings (Ward, 1994; see also Rietzschel et al., 2007a). Furthermore, when confronted with examples of creative solutions before generating their own, people tend to include features of these earlier solutions in their own ideas (e.g., Smith & Blankenship, 1991; Smith et al., 1993). In contrast to the conceptualization of creativity as involving random processes, however, the creative cognition approach assumes that creativity is the result of the application of deliberate effort.

The finding that creative products tend to be fairly predictable has led to the conclusion that people who perform creative tasks tend to retrieve a highly accessible exemplar from memory (for example, a bird) and make minor adjustments to this to generate "creative" ideas. They seem to follow the "path of least resistance" (Ward, 1994): they invest minimal effort in their creative endeavors and then stop. An important implication of this is that people would be more creative if they were motivated to put in more effort. Indeed, this has been observed. For example, when Ward (1994) asked his participants to think a bit more about the features of the imagined planet, people drew more original aliens. Furthermore, the notion that most people end idea generation prematurely has inspired creative techniques such as brainstorming, in which the explicit goal is to generate many ideas: assuming that earlier ideas that are "within easy reach" will be relatively unoriginal, and that one therefore needs to generate many ideas to become creative (Osborn, 1953; Perkins, 1981; Stein, 1975; see also Nijstad et al., 2010). In fact, when people receive extra time to generate ideas after the initial time window to respond has ended, the ideas generated in extra time are more creative than those generated initially (Lucas & Nordgren, 2015).

This second general approach to creativity, in sum, proposes that creativity results from normal, predictable, and deliberate cognitive processes. These processes initially do not lead to highly creative products, because initial ideas or associations tend not to be very original. Furthermore, many people have the tendency to follow the path of least resistance, stop prematurely, and will therefore not be creative. However, given time and/or effort, people are capable of producing more creative (original) output, even when working in a systematic way. These deliberate, effortful, and controlled cognitive processes make creativity more predictable (as compared to the randomness in the Darwinian approach), and more under control of the creator. Rather than to sit and let one's mind wander, creativity is predicted to occur after thinking long and hard about an issue.

THE DUAL PATHWAY TO CREATIVITY MODEL

The dual pathway to creativity model (DPCM) integrates these two seemingly contradictory approaches to creativity. The model proposes that there are two qualitatively different ways in which creative outcomes can be achieved, namely either through flexibility (the ease of switching to a different approach or considering a different perspective) or through persistence (the degree of sustained and focused task-directed cognitive effort). These two pathways differ mainly in terms of cognitive control. The flexibility pathway involves relatively low (top-down) cognitive control, and relies on (more or less) spontaneous activation of material in memory (for example, through spreading activation; Collins & Loftus, 1975) and on the formation of spontaneous associations. The persistence pathway is more systematic and requires more cognitive control (that is, focused effort) and more information processing capacity. As a consequence, being creative through persistence is more cognitively depleting, and involves working memory to a greater extent than being creative through flexibility (Roskes et al., 2012).

Because the persistence pathway is associated with less distractibility and higher cognitive control, responses that are produced through persistence are more predictable than those produced through flexibility. Because focused attention (that is, persistence) will generally lead to more predictable responses, it will – in the short term – be associated with lower levels of creativity (and especially with low originality). With sustained effort, however, this may change. Even though the initial responses may be unoriginal, over time the unoriginal responses get depleted and more original responses will follow. In other words, being creative through the persistence pathway indeed, quite literally, requires persistence (see also Lucas & Nordgren, 2015; Ward, 1994).

This difference in cognitive control between the two pathways suggests a trade-off, which in cognitive psychology is referred to as the flexibility–stability trade-off (e.g., Boot et al., 2017; Dreisbach & Goschke, 2004; Zhang et al., 2020). It also suggests that flexibility and persistence are incompatible, and that people use either one or the other. Although this is likely the case in the short term (in which one of the two processes naturally dominates), in the longer term, even in a matter of minutes, people are able to switch between flexible and focused processing (e.g., Finke, 1996; Leber et al., 2008). Therefore, over time, flexibility does not exclude persistence or vice versa. In fact, for many truly creative outcomes, both high flexibility and high persistence may be needed. Indeed, some work suggests that real-life creative achievements involve a combination of distractibility and flexible processing on the one hand, with high mental abilities, including the ability to focus on a task, on the other (Carson et al., 2003).

Importantly, the DPCM further assumes that certain predictors, including individual difference variables and situational variables, impact creativity because of their effects on flexibility, persistence, or both. A general hypothesis is that situations that are benign (that is, are appraised as non-threatening to the organism) and traits and states that are associated with an approach motivation – the motivation to move towards positive and desirable events and possibilities (Elliot & Thrash, 2002: 804) – increase flexible processing. Benign situations and an approach motivation allow individuals to explore their environment open-mindedly, with a willingness to look for opportunities to reach some desired end-state. In contrast, situations that are perceived as problematic (that is, as potentially threatening to the organism), and states that associate with an avoidance motivation – the motivation to move away from negative and undesirable events and possibilities (Elliot & Thrash, 2002: 804) – may undermine flexibility, but may also stimulate creativity through persistence (Nijstad et al., 2010). Problematic situations and an avoidance motivation trigger careful processing to avert any potential threats, which leads to more narrow attention, increased cognitive control, and reduced flexibility (see e.g., Derryberry & Reed, 1998; Koch et al., 2008). However, these states may only lead to creativity when narrow and focused attention is sustained over longer periods of time.

EXPERIMENTAL EVIDENCE FOR THE DPCM

Evidence for the DPCM derives mainly from experimental work in which participants' levels of creativity as well as their flexibility and persistence were assessed. A first type of evidence comes from studies that show that creativity can in fact be achieved through both flexible and systematic (persistent) processing. In ideation tasks such as brainstorming (generating as many ideas as possible on some topic), generated ideas cover a small or large number of semantic categories. Surveying many categories during idea generation is seen as a sign of cognitive flexibility, because it signifies the ability to use different approaches and perspectives (e.g., Guilford, 1950; Torrance, 1966). It has been found that flexibility, as measured by the number of categories used, is related to idea originality, because surveying more categories means that also the less popular and more original categories are used (see Nijstad et al., 2010, for a meta-analysis). However, it has also been found that systematically exploring one or a few semantic categories in depth can lead to higher levels of creativity as well, even in the absence of flexibility. For example, Rietzschel et al. (2007b) asked participants to generate ideas to improve their own health. Before idea generation, some participants were asked to reflect briefly on certain health-related topics, such as sports (in one condition) or healthy food (in another condition). Those participants who had reflected on sports (healthy food) generated more sports (food) ideas, and those sports (food) ideas were also more original than ideas generated by other participants (see Nijstad et al., 2010; Rietzschel et al., 2014, for additional evidence). Thus, creativity can result from flexible processing, but also from systematically exploring a limited number of idea categories in depth.

Secondly, research has shown that different traits and psychological states affect creativity through different pathways. For example, De Dreu et al. (2008) examined the effects of mood states on creativity. Mood states were either manipulated or measured, and relations with creative processes and outcomes were assessed. Across four studies, De Dreu et al. (2008) found that active, positive moods (for example, happiness) increased creativity through flexibility (for example, using more categories in idea generation), and that active, negative moods (for example, anger, anxiety) could increase it through persistence (for example, generating more ideas per category, or spending more time). Passive mood states, either positive or negative (for example, sadness, calmness), did not relate to creativity. This finding was subsequently also confirmed in a meta-analysis (Baas et al., 2008) and survey studies in organizational settings (Madrid et al., 2014; To et al., 2012).

Other research has shown that the strength of people's cognitive needs may affect their use of the two different pathways. In a series of studies, Rietzschel et al. (2007a) looked at the relation between personal need for structure (PNS) – a strong desire for predictability and aversion to ambiguity – and creativity. Although one might expect a high PNS to predict low levels of creativity, results showed that people with a high PNS performed quite creatively as long as they also had a low personal fear of invalidity (a fear of making a wrong choice or decision). Moreover, they did so by using the persistence pathway, thinking more deeply within a limited set of semantic categories (rather than thinking flexibly across multiple categories).

Other evidence shows that approach-related motivation associates positively with creativity through flexibility (see Baas et al., 2011; De Dreu et al., 2011; Roskes et al., 2012). For example, De Dreu et al. (2011) related individual differences in approach motivation, as measured by Carver and White's (1994) Behavioral Activation Scale (BAS), to creativity (see also Shao et al., 2018). They found that behavioral activation was only positively related to creativity when the situation afforded or sustained flexible processing, but not when this was impossible or difficult. For example, creativity in an ideation task was positively associated with behavioral activation when the topic of the ideation task was broad and allowed for the use of many different semantic categories ("How can teaching at your university be improved?"), but not when the topic was narrowly defined and did not allow as strongly for flexible processing ("How can classroom teaching at your university be improved?").

On the other hand, avoidance-related motivation has been associated with increased creativity as well, but only under specific conditions (Baas et al., 2011; Roskes et al., 2012). Firstly, Roskes et al. (2012) argued that avoidance motivation would focus attention, and could therefore lead to creativity through persistence. However, because persistence is cognitively depleting, they also proposed that participants would be reluctant to engage in this fatiguing type of processing. They therefore predicted that avoidance motivation would increase persistence and creativity only when participants were sufficiently motivated to expend effort. In a series of experiments, Roskes et al. (2012) found that avoidance motivation could in fact stimulate creativity through persistence, but only if creativity was functional in reaching a person's avoidance goals (and not when it was not). Secondly, evidence indicates that the persistence pathway does not depend only on sufficient motivation to expand effort, but also on processing capacity. For example, De Dreu et al. (2012) found that working memory capacity, as a measure of processing capacity, was positively related to creativity, and that this effect was mediated by cognitive persistence rather than flexibility. Thus, avoidance motivation may increase creativity through persistence, but only if motivation and processing capacity are sufficiently high.

In sum, there is experimental evidence showing that creativity (for example, original ideas) can be achieved by thinking broadly and flexibly (for example, using many idea categories) or by thinking in a focused way (for example, exploring categories and approaches in depth). Furthermore, some psychological states (for example, active positive moods) and traits (for example, behavioral activation) relate to creativity through flexibility, and other states (for example, active negative moods) and traits (for example, PNS) through persistence. Certain facets of the model, however, have not yet been systematically investigated. For example, how do people switch between flexible and persistent processing? To what degree are flexible and persistent processing involved in producing really important work and groundbreaking discoveries? And, a topic to which we turn now, how can these insights be used to understand creativity at work?

IMPLICATIONS FOR WORKPLACE CREATIVITY

Although these results offer good support for the DPCM, most of the evidence was gathered in controlled laboratory environments. This leaves open the question whether and how the DPCM may be applied in less controlled settings, such as the workplace. We believe that there are two ways in which these results are relevant to workplace creativity. Firstly, the results suggest that different and seemingly incompatible predictors (for example, approach and avoidance motivation; positive and negative moods) may both lead to creativity, but through different pathways. Secondly, they suggest that to allow, sustain, and reinforce creativity at work, the circumstances have to match (or fit with) the cognitive pathway used by a particular person. We will discuss these two possibilities in turn.

Different Predictors for Different Pathways: Freedom versus Pressure and Constraints

Research on employee creativity has long been dominated by Amabile's foundational work (e.g., Amabile, 1983, 1988; Amabile et al., 1996; Hennessey & Amabile, 2010). One central principle in this work is the intrinsic motivation principle, which states that doing something out of intrinsic interest will generally lead to higher creativity than doing it to obtain some external reward (for example, money or praise). Indeed, meta-analyses show a strong correlation between intrinsic work motivation and creativity (De Jesus et al., 2013; Liu et al., 2016). The work by Amabile further suggests that intrinsic motivation and creativity will flourish when conditions are positive and supporting. Thus, Amabile et al. (1996) proposed that a work environment that is characterized by encouragement and support for creativity, by autonomy and freedom, and by sufficient resources, will generally benefit creativity. Many of these ideas have been confirmed. For example, one meta-analysis (Hunter et al., 2007) suggests that work-related aspects such as positive supervisor relations, management support, autonomy, and resources are all positively related to employee creativity. Furthermore, meta-analytic evidence indicates that the effects of autonomy and supportive leadership on employee creativity are at least partly mediated by intrinsic motivation (Liu et al., 2016).

Applying the DPCM, we propose that intrinsic motivation and the factors that contribute to it (for example, support, autonomy) generally signal that the (work) situation is benign (that is, non-threatening). This will allow for a broader and more explorative mindset, will reduce top-down cognitive control, and will stimulate creativity through flexibility. In other words, variables such as manager and co-worker support, autonomy, and intrinsic motivation signal that the environment is safe, and that risk-taking and exploration are possible in order to identify opportunities for gains. This leads to reduced top-down cognitive control, a broader attentional focus, and increased creativity through the flexibility pathway.

Amabile et al. (1996) have also suggested that other external factors, such as workload pressure, controlling leadership or feedback styles, and certain organizational impediments (for example, rigid management structures), will reduce intrinsic motivation and constrain creativity. However, empirical results are less straightforward when it comes to these negative factors. For example, meta-analysis has shown that the effect of stressors (for example, workload pressure) on creativity is not uniformly negative (Byron et al., 2010), and some studies indicate that stressors can actually have positive effects on creativity (Binnewies & Wörnlein, 2011; Sacremento et al., 2013; also see De Dreu & Van Dijk, 2018). A recent review also suggests that constraints may sometimes be a blessing in disguise, and can aid rather than hinder creative performance (Acar et al., 2019). For example, a lack of resources may create a necessity to be creative (see also Zhou & George, 2001), and formalization and routinization may free up resources to be used for creative endeavors (Gilson et al., 2005; Ohly et al., 2006). Finally, research indicates that extrinsic factors, such as rewards for creativity, and extrinsic demands or expectations to be creative, are in fact positively (rather than negatively) related to employee creativity. For example, meta-analysis has shown that people who are rewarded for their creative performance actually are more creative than those who are not (Byron & Khazanchi, 2012). Similarly, leaders who expect their employees to be creative (e.g., Tierney & Farmer, 2004), and jobs that require people to be creative (e.g., Unsworth & Clegg, 2010), stimulate higher creativity in employees than those that do not. It thus appears that extrinsic motivators often do not undermine creativity, as originally proposed in the intrinsic motivation principle, but can in fact stimulate it.

These effects do not fit well with the intrinsic motivation principle, but can potentially be (better) understood through the lens of the DPCM (see also Gutnick et al., 2012). The DPCM suggests that conditions that are more demanding or potentially threatening may stimulate effort to more thoroughly think about this problematic situation, and may lead to higher creativity through the persistence pathway. Thus, workload and time pressure may be a strong activator and trigger creativity that would not be needed when more (time) resources would be available. Similarly, extrinsic cues such as rewards and creative expectations may also trigger cognitive effort, and such focused effort may, through persistence, lead to creative outcomes (see also Eisenberger & Rhoades, 2001; Harkins, 2006). Moreover, providing employees with task structure may reduce the options available to them, but may also increase the motivation to invest cognitive effort by making the task less overwhelming and cognitively demanding (see also Tierney & Farmer, 2002).

There is, however, an important caveat, which is that in the workplace people often do not have to be creative, but can in fact choose to focus their cognitive energy on something else (e.g., Ford, 1996). That is, even though autonomy or supervisor support may trigger more flexible mental processes, these processes are not necessarily used to produce creative output. Similarly, stressors and constraints may trigger focused effort, but these efforts are not necessarily used to be creative (see also Roskes et al., 2012). It therefore stands to reason that factors such as autonomy and support are more strongly related to creativity in situations in which engaging in creativity is presumed to be worthwhile. This may be the case either because an individual enjoys creative activities (for example, has a creative personality or high openness to experience) or because extrinsic conditions suggest that being creative brings benefits (for example, leader creative expectations). Similarly, it is likely the case that stressors (for example, tight deadlines) or constraints (lack of budget) will only translate to creative behaviors when employees wish to express their creativity or perceive that creativity is valued or needed. Consistent with this, Orth and Volmer (2017) found that job autonomy was more strongly linked to innovative behavior among employees with high levels of creative self-efficacy, and Aleksíc et al. (2016) found that the presence of clear outcome goals at work were most likely to translate into employee creativity when employees had a high preference for creativity.

Thus, applying the DPCM may help to understand why seemingly conflicting conditions (for example, intrinsic and extrinsic motivation; autonomy and constraints) can both stimulate creativity. Furthermore, this approach suggests some new and testable hypotheses about workplace creativity. For example, workplace variables such as autonomy and support will trigger flexible processing, but will be more strongly associated with employee creativity when employees have either an internal drive (for example, creative personality or a strong need for creative self-expression) or an external drive (for example, external demands or rewards) to be creative. Similarly, stressors (for example, tight deadlines) and constraints (for example, low budget) may stimulate persistence, but will only lead to creativity when at the same time there are internal or external reasons to be creative.

Creativity from Fit

A second way in which the DPCM can yield new insights for workplace creativity is because it suggests that to allow, sustain, and reinforce creativity, the circumstances have to match (or fit with) the cognitive pathway used by a particular employee. Partly, this is a matter of person–environment fit (PE-Fit). That is, an employee may be naturally inclined towards either flexible or persistent processing (see Baas et al., 2013), and will be more creative when the (job) circumstances match this processing style. However, because flexible and persistent processing can also be triggered by situational factors, it may also mean that different situational factors need to be aligned rather than misaligned to stimulate creativity. We will discuss both possibilities.

Previous research suggests that certain personality characteristics associate with a tendency towards cognitive flexibility. For example, certain traits, such as extraversion, openness to experience, and positive affectivity, are associated with approach motivation (Elliot & Thrash, 2002), and an approach motivation relates to creativity through cognitive flexibility (De Dreu et al., 2011; Shao et al., 2018). Such traits are consequently more likely to stimulate creativity in situations in which flexible processing is possible and can be sustained. This is also what the evidence seems to suggest. For example, George and Zhou (2001) found that openness to experience was more strongly related to creativity in jobs that allowed for more heuristic, loose processing, because the job could be done in multiple ways (rather than one single way). This resonates with findings from De Dreu et al. (2011), who found that dispositional approach motivation related to creativity only in situations where flexible processing was possible. We suggest that this will be the case in situations in which there are no or few clear rules and regulations (see also Roskes, 2015), in which relatively many options and opportunities present themselves, and in which much and diverse stimulation is available (for example, when working in a more diverse team).

In contrast, neuroticism, anxiety, and negative affectivity are generally associated with avoidance motivation (Elliot & Thrash, 2002). In turn, avoidance motivation is associated with a narrower focus of attention, which may limit cognitive flexibility but can trigger creativity through persistence. Similarly, conscientiousness is a personality trait that is related to achievement motivation and hard work, and conscientiousness may stimulate creativity through persistence. However, we propose that these traits will stimulate creativity only when creative performance is seen as valuable or necessary (Roskes et al., 2012), and when sufficient processing capacity is available (De Dreu et al., 2012). For example, research suggests that avoidance-motivated people do not perform well when they are distracted by time pressure (Roskes et al., 2013). Furthermore, cognitive persistence is likely sustained better in situations in which options and opportunities are limited, and potentially when there are important constraints (Roskes, 2015). For example, experimental evidence suggests that creativity may be more easily achieved through persistence in tasks that are relatively narrowly defined (Rietzschel et al., 2014), and field research shows that conscientiousness may relate positively to creativity when employees are closely monitored, perhaps because this reduces the available behavioral options (George & Zhou, 2001).

Similarly, situational cues, such as signals of opportunities, demands, and threats, may trigger a certain processing style and this may more readily lead to creativity when other situational factors sustain and reinforce this type of processing. For example, certain leadership styles, such as transformational leadership, create a focus on opportunities and gains, and may trigger flexible processing (e.g., Kark & Van Dijk, 2007). Creativity would benefit from this type of leadership, especially in situations in which flexible processing is possible and sustained (for example, in which there are few rules and constraints). Other situational variables, such as threats, may restrict attentional scope and lead to inflexible and rigid thinking (e.g., Staw et al., 1981). However, given persistence, creativity may still be achieved, but mainly when creativity is perceived to be important to address the threat, and when options and opportunities are limited rather than broad (see also De Dreu & Nijstad, 2008).

In sum, certain individual differences and external factors may trigger a specific processing style (that is, flexibility or persistence), and this processing style is likely more successful under some rather than other conditions. In earlier research, often certain person–situation interactions have been found (see Zhou & Hoever, 2014), and the DPCM may help to more clearly understand these interactions and predict the type of interactions that may be found.

FUTURE DIRECTIONS

So far, the DPCM has mainly been tested in laboratory research. However, as we have highlighted in this chapter, the model has implications for workplace creativity. It suggests: (1) that different and seemingly incompatible workplace predictors may lead to creativity, but through different cognitive processes; and (2) that the circumstances that enable and sustain one type of processing (for example, flexibility) may be different from those that enable and sustain another type of processing (for example, persistence). Some previous work seems consistent with these ideas, but direct tests are missing, and this presents a clear opportunity for future research. In the remainder of this section we will highlight some further opportunities: we integrate the DPCM with constraint theory, look at dynamic processes, and extend the DPCM to groups and teams.

The Role of Constraints

In the previous section, we proposed that constraints (for example, time pressure) may sometimes facilitate creativity, because of the need for (immediate) action, but that constraints may also distract people from their task. We also proposed that other constraints (for example, rules and procedures) may sometimes benefit creativity because they channel cognitive effort towards creative outcomes. However, the precise role of constraints in relation to the DPCM is not completely clear, and this may benefit from an integration with theories of constraints (Acar et al., 2019; Rietzschel, 2018; Roskes, 2015). In particular, this literature suggests two conclusions: that there are different types of constraints, and that the effects of constraints may differ depending on the type of constraint and additional variables.

Firstly, the emerging literature on constraints suggests that there are different types of constraints. Thus Acar et al. (2019) distinguished between input constraints (for example, lack of resources), process constraints (for example, rules, formalization), and output constraints (for example, output standards, outcome requirements). Taking a cognitive perspective, Roskes (2015) made a distinction between limiting constraints, which refer to constraints that consume or limit cognitive resources (for example, time pressure, dual task demands, and noise), and channeling constraints, which lead people to focus their cognitive resources (for example, procedures, task structure, or restricted goals).

Secondly, effects of constraints will not be uniformly positive or negative, but will depend on the type and amount of constraint and other variables. Thus, Acar et al. (2019) proposed that constraints may affect creativity because they influence motivation, cognitive processes, or social processes, and that effects will often be curvilinear: facing a moderate amount or degree of constraints may counteract complacency, necessitate creative action, and channel behavior towards desired outcomes, but having too many or too strict constraints will limit people's behavioral repertoires or undermine their motivation. Rietzschel (2018) argued that a lack of constraints may actually cause people to rely on the path of least resistance (and hence perform less creatively), as unconstrained tasks can be cognitively overwhelming and stimulate the use of heuristics. Limiting the possibilities in a creative task (for example, narrowing the topic, giving fewer choices, providing specific procedures to follow) can therefore stimulate creativity (also see Finke et al., 1992). Finally, Roskes (2015) proposed that effects of constraints on creativity depend on motivational orientation (approach versus avoidance). For example, she assumed that avoidance motivation would lead to a narrow cognitive focus, and to systematic and resource-demanding cognitive processes. Consequently, limiting constraints would easily lead to cognitive overload and reduce creativity, but channeling constraints could focus attention and facilitate creative achievements under avoidance motivation.

Integrating these ideas with DPCM suggests that different types of constraints may play a different role. For example, certain input and output constraints potentially impact creativity by influencing the cognitive pathway that is activated. Thus, some constraints, such as time pressure or output constraints, may be seen as external demands placed upon people. These demands may trigger cognitive effort and lead to creativity through the persistence pathway when creativity is perceived to be necessary to meet demands. Other constraints, such as process constraints, in contrast, may not necessarily trigger a specific type of processing, but may be more compatible with one cognitive pathway (persistence) than with another (flexibility; cf. Roskes, 2015), and consequently have positive or negative effects depending on the type of processing. Alternatively, process constraints may make a creative task more palatable for people with certain traits (such as a high PNS), who are a priori more likely to use a particular pathway. Developing these ideas further and testing them in future research could be fruitful.

Dynamic Processes

As mentioned earlier, flexibility and persistence do not exclude each other over time. There is, however, no research on how people use flexible and persistent processing over time, and on what the consequences are for creative performance. Previous work suggests that, in relatively mundane laboratory tasks, flexibility and persistence can both lead to equal levels of creativity, and that they may therefore be substitutes (e.g., De Dreu et al., 2008; Roskes et al., 2012). However, it is possible that when it comes to less mundane creative achievements, this is not the case. In particular, it may be that both flexible and persistent processing are required to generate breakthrough ideas or make important creative contributions to some domain. In addition, it may be the case that these processes normally follow each other in a specific sequence, or series of iterations. For example, more flexible processing can be useful to identify new perspectives or approaches to some issue, after which more focused effort and persistence is required to explore these new directions in greater depth (cf. Amabile, 1996). These processes can be iterated several times to lead to a finished creative product.

This raises the question, however, of which kinds of meta-skills are required to engage in this kind of pathway-switching. Similar to constructs such as ambidexterity (e.g., Rosing et al., 2011; Caniëls et al., 2017), high and sustained levels of workplace creativity require more than the ability to be both flexible and persistent: people need to know when the different pathways are most likely to be effective. This also has developmental implications in that people may need to learn how (and when) to use (or not use) their non-preferred pathway. Depending on the lay theory that employees or managers hold (random process versus systematic search), it may be difficult to accept the effectiveness of another pathway to creativity (or to accept the limitations of one's preferred pathway), let alone to make use of it (cf. Baas et al., 2015).

Creativity of Teams

A final direction for future research would be to extend the DPCM to dyads and teams. Rouse (2020) has recently proposed that creative collaborations (in dyads) can be characterized by a free flow of ideas, trust, psychological safety, and positive affect. In turn, these processes stimulate a feeling of "we-ness" that allows participants to constructively address certain tensions that are inherent to creative work, such as those between originality and usefulness, between learning and performance, between being passionate and disciplined, and between flexibility and persistence (see Miron-Spektor & Erez, 2017). These processes may enable participants to combine, over time, flexibility and persistence. As proposed above, this mixing of flexibility and persistence may be pivotal to achieving true creative breakthroughs.

Similarly, when it comes to creativity in teams, team composition will also be important (e.g., Paulus & Nijstad, 2019; Nijstad, 2015). In relation to the DPCM, it would be interesting to examine how team composition in terms of members' tendency towards flexible or persistent processing would affect creativity of the team. Some evidence indicates that groups which are composed of diverse members in terms of cognitive styles (for example, preferred ways of information processing) may have a benefit when it comes to team creativity (Miron-Spektor et al., 2011). Thus, a hypothesis could be that a mix of people with a preference for or tendency towards either flexible or persistent processing would be better for team creativity than having a team that is more homogeneous in terms of preferred processing style. In essence, it could be that those with more flexible processing styles can identify promising directions, and those with a more persistent processing style can explore these in greater depth. However, given the difficulty in reaping the benefits of diversity in teams (e.g., Van Knippenberg & Schippers, 2007), this is only speculative.

CONCLUSION

Creative ideas are necessarily born in someone's brain, and the DPCM therefore puts cognitive processes at center stage. Evidence suggests that: (1) two qualitatively different processes (flexibility and persistence) can lead to creative output; and (2) that these processes are influenced and/or facilitated by a host of different person- and situation-related variables. The DPCM thus offers a promising way to look at creativity in context, such as the work context, and suggests unique new predictions. Examining these implications may further creativity research and practice, and may provide a theoretical foundation for future work.

ACKNOWLEDGEMENT

Writing this chapter was facilitated by grant 453-15-002 of the Netherlands Organization for Scientific Research (NWO) awarded to Bernard Nijstad.

NOTES

1. See, for example, her Ted talk at https://www.ted.com/talks/elizabeth_gilbert_your _elusive_creative_genius.
2. For example, in chess the search space would consist of all possible moves at a given point in time.
3. For example, this is how Edison developed the light bulb (see e.g., https://www.livescience .com/43424-who-invented-the-light-bulb.html) and how restaurant chef and inventor of molecular cuisine Ferran Adrià has created many of his famous dishes (see e.g., https:// www.fastcompany.com/3027589/cataloging-creativity-ferran-adria-showcases-7-years -of-culinary-art-science).

REFERENCES

Acar, O.A., Tarakci, M., & van Knippenberg, D.L. 2019. Creativity and innovation under constraints: A cross-disciplinary integrative review. *Journal of Management*, 45: 96–121.

Aleksić, D., Černe, M., Dysvik, A., & Škerlavaj, M. 2016. I want to be creative, but … Preference for creativity, perceived clear outcome goals, work enjoyment, and creative performance. *European Journal of Work and Organizational Psychology*, 25: 363–383.

Amabile, T.M. 1983. The social psychology of creativity: A componential conceptualization. *Journal of Personality and Social Psychology*, 45: 357–376.

Amabile, T.M. 1988. A model of creativity and innovation in organizations. *Research in Organizational Behavior*, 10: 123–167.

Amabile, T.M. 1996. *Creativity in context*. Boulder, CO: Westview.

Amabile, T.M., Conti, R., Coon, H., Lazenby, J., & Herron, M. 1996. Assessing the work environment for creativity. *Academy of Management Journal*, 39: 1154–1184.

Baas, M., De Dreu, C.K.W., & Nijstad, B.A. 2008. A meta-analysis of 25 years of research on mood and creativity: Hedonic tone, activation, or regulatory focus? *Psychological Bulletin*, 134: 739–756.

Baas, M., De Dreu, C.K.W., & Nijstad, B.A. 2011. When prevention promotes creativity: The role of mood, regulatory focus, and regulatory closure. *Journal of Personality and Social Psychology*, 100: 794–809.

Baas, M., Koch, S., Nijstad, B.A., & De Dreu, C.K.W. 2015. Conceiving creativity: The nature and consequences of laypeople's beliefs about the realization of creativity. *Psychology of Aesthetics, Creativity, and the Arts*, 9: 340–354.

Baas, M., Roskes, M., Sligte, D., Nijstad, B.A., & De Dreu, C.K.W. 2013. Personality and creativity: The dual pathway to creativity model and a research agenda. *Social and Personality Psychology Compass*, 7: 732–748.

Baird, B., Smallwood, J., Mrazek, M.D., Kam, J.W., Franklin, M.S., & Schooler, J.W. 2012. Inspired by distraction: Mind wandering facilitates creative incubation. *Psychological Science*, 23: 1117–1122.

Benedek, M., & Neubauer, A.C. 2013. Revisiting Mednick's model on creativity-related differences in associative hierarchies: Evidence for a common path to uncommon thought. *Journal of Creative Behavior*, 47: 273–289.

Binnewies, C., & Wörnlein, S.C. 2011. What makes a creative day? A diary study on the interplay between affect, job stressors, and job control. *Journal of Organizational Behavior*, 32: 589–607.

Boot, N., Baas, M., Van Gaal, S., Cools, R., & De Dreu, C.K.W. 2017. Dopaminergic modulation of creativity. *Neuroscience and Biobehavioral Reviews*, 78: 13–23.

Byron, K., & Khazanchi, S. 2012. Rewards and creative performance: A meta-analytic test of theoretically derived predictions. *Psychological Bulletin*, 138: 809–830.

Byron, K., Khazanchi, S., & Nazarian, D. 2010. The relationship between stressors and creativity: A meta-analysis examining competing theoretical models. *Journal of Applied Psychology*, 95: 201–212.

Campbell, D.T. 1960. Blind variation and selective retention in creative thought as in other knowledge processes. *Psychological Review*, 67: 380–400.

Caniëls, M. C., Neghina, C., & Schaetsaert, N. 2017. Ambidexterity of employees: The role of empowerment and knowledge sharing. *Journal of Knowledge Management*, 21: 1098–1119.

Carson, S.H., Peterson, J.B., & Higgins, D.M. 2003. Decreased latent inhibition is associated with increased creative achievement in high-functioning individuals. *Journal of Personality and Social Psychology*, 85: 499–506.

Carver, C.S., & White, T.L. 1994. Behavioral inhibition, behavioral activation, and affective responses to impending reward and punishment: The BIS/BAS scales. *Journal of Personality and Social Psychology*, 67: 319–333.

Collins, A.M., & Loftus, E.F. 1975. A spreading-activation theory of semantic processing. *Psychological Review*, 82: 407–428.

Csikszentmihalyi, M. 1999. Implications of a systems perspective for the study of creativity. In R.J. Sternberg (ed.), *Handbook of creativity*: 313–335. New York: Cambridge University Press.

De Dreu, C.K.W., Baas, M., & Nijstad, B.A. 2008. Hedonic tone and activation in the mood–creativity link: Towards a Dual Pathway to Creativity model. *Journal of Personality and Social Psychology*, 94: 739–756.

De Dreu, C.K.W., & Nijstad, B.A. 2008. Mental set and creative thought in social conflict: Cognitive load versus motivated focus. *Journal of Personality and Social Psychology*, 95: 648–661.

De Dreu, C.K.W., Nijstad, B.A., & Baas, M. 2011. Behavioral activation links to creativity because of increased cognitive flexibility. *Social Psychological and Personality Science*, 2: 72–80.

De Dreu, C.K.W., Nijstad, B.A., Baas, M., Roskes, M., & Wolsink, I. 2012. Working memory benefits creative insight, musical improvisation and original ideation through maintained task-focused attention. *Personality and Social Psychology Bulletin*, 38: 656–669.

De Dreu, C.K.W., & Van Dijk, M.A. 2018. Climatic shocks associate with innovation in science and technology. *PLoS ONE*, 13: e0190122.

De Jesus, S.N., Rus, C.L., Lens, W., & Imaginario, S. 2013. Intrinsic motivation and creativity related to product: A meta-analysis of the studies published between 1990–2010. *Creativity Research Journal*, 25: 80–84.

Derryberry, D., & Reed, M.A. 1998. Anxiety and attentional focusing: Trait, state, and hemispheric influences. *Personality and Individual Differences*, 25: 745–761.

Dietrich, A., & Kanso, R. 2010. A review of EEG, ERP, and neuroimaging studies of creativity and insight. *Psychological Bulletin*, 136: 822–848.

Dijksterhuis, A., & Meurs, T. 2006. Where creativity resides: The generative power of unconscious thought. *Consciousness and Cognition*, 15: 135–146.

Dreisbach, G., & Goschke, T. 2004. How positive affect modulates cognitive control: Reduced perseveration at the cost of increased distractibility. *Journal of Experimental Psychology: Learning, Memory, and Cognition*, 30: 343–353.

Eisenberger, R., & Rhoades, L. 2001. Incremental effects of reward on creativity. *Journal of Personality and Social Psychology*, 81: 728–741.

Elliot, A.J., & Thrash, T.M. 2002. Approach–avoidance motivation in personality: Approach and avoidance temperaments and goals. *Journal of Personality and Social Psychology*, 82: 804–818.

Finke, R.A. 1996. Imagery, creativity, and emergent structure. *Consciousness and Cognition*, 5: 381–393.

Finke, R.A., Ward, T.B., & Smith S.M. 1992. *Creative cognition: Theory, research and applications*. Cambridge, MA: MIT Press.

Fitzgerald, R. 1961. *The Odyssey of Homer*. Minneapolis, MI: The Franklin Library.

Ford, C.M. 1996. A theory of individual creative action in multiple social domains. *Academy of Management Review*, 21: 1112–1142.

Friedman, R.S., & Förster, J. 2001. The effects of promotion and prevention cues on creativity. *Journal of Personality and Social Psychology*, 81: 1001–1013.

George, J.M., & Zhou, J. 2001. When openness to experience and conscientiousness are related to creative behavior: An interactional approach. *Journal of Applied Psychology*, 86: 513–524.

Ghiselin, B. 1952. *The creative process*. Toronto: Penguin Group.

Gilson, L.L., Mathieu, J.E., Shalley, C.E., & Ruddy, T.M. 2005. Creativity and standardization: Complementary or conflicting drivers of team effectiveness? *Academy of Management Journal*, 48: 521–531.

Gough, H.G. 1976. Studying creativity by means of word association tests. *Journal of Applied Psychology*, 61: 348–353.

Guilford, J.P. 1950. Creativity. *American Psychologist*, 9: 444–454.

Gutnick, D., Walter, F., Nijstad, B.A., & De Dreu, C.K.W. 2012. Creative performance under pressure: An integrative framework. *Organizational Psychology Review*, 2: 189–207.

Hanson, H. 2010. For writers. https://www.helenhanson.com/.

Harkins, S.G. 2006. Mere effort as the mediator of the evaluation–performance relationship. *Journal of Personality and Social Psychology*, 91: 436–455.

Hennessey, B.A., & Amabile, T.M. 2010. Creativity. *Annual Review of Psychology*, 61: 569–598.

Hunter, S.T., Bedell, K.E., & Mumford, M.D. 2007. Climate for creativity: A quantitative review. *Creativity Research Journal*, 19: 69–90.

Isen, A.M., and Daubman, K.A. 1984. The influence of affect on categorization. *Journal of Personality and Social Psychology*, 47: 1206–1217.

Kark, R., & Van Dijk, D. 2007. Motivation to lead, motivation to follow: The role of the self-regulatory focus in leadership processes. *Academy of Management Review*, 32: 500–528.

Koch, S., Holland, R.W., & Van Knippenberg, A. 2008. Regulating cognitive control through approach–avoidance motor actions. *Cognition*, 109: 133–142.

Leber, A.B., Turk-Browne, N.B., & Chun, M.M. 2008. Neural predictors of moment-to-moment fluctuations in cognitive flexibility. *Proceedings of the National Academy of Sciences*, 105: 13592–13597.

Liu, D., Jiang, K., Shalley, C.E., Keem, S., & Zhou, J. 2016. Motivational mechanisms of employee creativity: A meta-analytic examination and theoretical extension of the creativity literature. *Organizational Behavior and Human Decision Processes*, 137: 236–263.

Lucas, B.J., & Nordgren, L.F. 2015. People underestimate the value of persistence for creative performance. *Journal of Personality and Social Psychology*, 109: 232–243.

Madrid, H.P., Patterson, M.G., Birdi, K.S., Leiva, P.I., & Kausel, E.E. 2014. The role of weekly high-activated positive mood, context, and personality in innovative work behavior: A multilevel and interactional model. *Journal of Organizational Behavior*, 35: 234–256.

Mednick, S.A. 1962. The associative basis of the creative process. *Psychological Review*, 69: 220–232.

Mendelsohn, G.A. 1976. Associative and attentional processes in creative performance. *Journal of Personality*, 44: 341–369.

Miron-Spektor, E., & Erez, M. 2017. Looking at creativity through a paradox lens: Deeper understanding and new insights. In M. Lewis, W. Smith, P. Jarzabkowski, & A. Langley (eds), *Handbook of organizational paradox: Approaches to plurality, tensions and contradictions*: 434–451. Oxford: Oxford University Press.

Miron-Spektor, E., Erez, M., & Naveh, E. 2011. The effects of conformist and attentive-to-detail members on team innovation: Reconciling the innovation paradox. *Academy of Management Journal*, 54: 740–760.

Newell, A., & Simon, H.A. 1972. *Human problem solving*. Englewood Cliffs, NJ: Prentice Hall.

Nijstad, B.A. (2015). Creativity in groups. In J. Dovidio & J. Sherman (eds), *Handbook of social psychology: Group processes and intergroup relations*: 35–65. Washington, DC: American Psychological Association.

Nijstad, B.A., De Dreu., C.K.W., Rietzschel, E.F., & Baas, M. 2010. Towards a dual-pathway to creativity model: Creative ideation as a function of flexibility and persistence. *European Review of Social Psychology*, 21: 34–77.

Nijstad, B.A., & Stroebe, W. 2006. How the group affects the mind: A cognitive model of idea generation in groups. *Personality and Social Psychology Review*, 10: 186–213.

Ohly, S., Sonnentag, S., & Pluntke, F. 2006. Routinization, work characteristics and their relationships with creative and proactive behaviors. *Journal of Organizational Behavior*, 27: 257–279.

Orth, M., & Volmer, J. 2017. Daily within-person effects of job autonomy and work engagement on innovative behaviour: The cross-level moderating role of creative self-efficacy. *European Journal of Work and Organizational Psychology*, 26: 601–612.

Osborn, A. (1953). *Applied imagination: Principles and procedures of creative problem solving*. New York: Charles Scribner's Sons.

Packer, A.J. 2006. *Wise highs: How to thrill, chill, and get away from it all without alcohol or other drugs*. Minneapolis, MI: Free Spirit Publishing.

Paulus, P.B., & Nijstad, B.A. 2019. *The Oxford handbook of group creativity and innovation*. New York: Oxford University Press.

Perkins, D.N. 1981. *The mind's best work*. Cambridge, MA: Harvard University Press.

Rietzschel, E.F. 2018. Freedom, structure, and creativity. In R. Reiter-Palmon, V.L. Kennel, & J.C. Kaufman (eds), *Individual creativity in the workplace* (pp. 203–222). Cambridge, MA: Academic Press.

Rietzschel, E.F., De Dreu, C.K., & Nijstad, B.A. 2007a. Personal need for structure and creative performance: The moderating influence of fear of invalidity. *Personality and Social Psychology Bulletin*, 33: 855–866.

Rietzschel, E.F., Nijstad, B.A., & Stroebe, W. 2007b. The effects of knowledge activation on the quantity and quality of ideas. *Journal of Experimental Social Psychology*, 43: 933–946.

Rietzschel, E.F., Nijstad, B.A., & Stroebe, W. 2014. Effects of problem scope and creativity instructions on idea generation and selection. *Creativity Research Journal*, 26: 185–191.

Rosing, K., Frese, M. and Bausch, A. 2011. Explaining the heterogeneity of the leadership–innovation relationship: Ambidextrous leadership. *Leadership Quarterly*, 22: 956–974.

Roskes, M. 2015. Constraints that help or hinder creative performance: A motivational approach. *Creativity and Innovation Management*, 24: 197–206.

Roskes, M., De Dreu, C.K.W., & Nijstad, B.A. 2012. Necessity is the mother of invention: Avoidance motivation stimulates creativity through cognitive effort. *Journal of Personality and Social Psychology*, 103: 242–256.

Roskes, M., Elliot, A.J., Nijstad, B.A., & De Dreu, C.K.W. 2013. Time pressure undermines performance more under avoidance than approach motivation. *Personality and Social Psychology Bulletin*, 39: 803–813.

Rouse, E.D. 2020. Where you end and I begin: Understanding intimate co-creation. *Academy of Management Review*, 45: 181–204.

Sacramento, C.A., Fay, D., & West, M.A. 2013. Workplace duties or opportunities? Challenge stressors, regulatory focus, and creativity. *Organizational Behavior and Human Decision Processes*, 121: 141–157.

Shao, Y., Nijstad, B.A., & Täuber, S. 2018. Linking self-construal to creativity: The role of approach motivation and cognitive flexibility. *Frontiers in Psychology*, 9: 1929. doi: 10.3389/fpsyg.2018.01929.

Simonton, D.K. 1997. Creative productivity: A predictive and explanatory model of career trajectories and landmarks. *Psychological Review*, 104(1): 66–89.

Simonton, D.K. 1999. *Origins of genius: Darwinian perspectives on creativity*. New York: Oxford University Press.

Simonton, D.K. 2003. Scientific creativity as constrained stochastic behavior: The integration of product, person, and process perspectives. *Psychological Bulletin*, 129: 475–494.

Sio, U.N., & Ormerod, T.C. 2009. Does incubation enhance problem solving? A meta-analytic review. *Psychological Bulletin*, 135: 94–120.

Smallwood, J., & Schooler, J.W. 2015. The science of mind wandering: Empirically navigating the stream of consciousness. *Annual Review of Psychology*, 66: 487–518.

Smith, S.M., & Blankenship, S.E. 1991. Incubation and the persistence of fixation in problem solving. *American Journal of Psychology*, 104: 61–87.

Smith, S.M., Ward, T.B., & Finke, R.A. (eds). 1995. *The creative cognition approach*. Cambridge, MA: MIT Press.

Smith, S.M., Ward, T.B., & Schumacher, J.S. 1993. Constraining effects of examples in a creative generations task. *Memory and Cognition*, 21: 837–845.

Staw, B.M., Sandelands, L.E., & Dutton, J.E. 1981. Threat-rigidity effects in organizational behavior: A multilevel analysis. *Administrative Science Quarterly*, 26: 501–524.

Stein, M.I. (1975). *Stimulating creativity*. Cambridge, MA: Academic Press.

Tierney, P., & Farmer, S.M. 2002. Creative self-efficacy: Its potential antecedents and relationship to creative performance. *Academy of Management Journal*, 45: 1137–1148.

Tierney, P., & Farmer, S.M. 2004. The Pygmalion process and employee creativity. *Journal of Management*, 30: 413–432.

To, M.L., Fisher, C.D., Ashkanasy, N.M., & Rowe, P.A. 2012. Within-person relationships between mood and creativity. *Journal of Applied Psychology*, 97: 599–612.

Torrance, E.P. 1966. *Torrance tests of creative thinking*. Princeton, NJ: Personnel Press.

Unsworth, K.L., & Clegg, C.W. 2010. Why do employees undertake creative action? *Journal of Occupational and Organizational Psychology*, 83: 77–99.

Van Knippenberg, D., & Schippers, M.C. 2007. Work group diversity. *Annual Review of Psychology*, 58: 515–541.

Ward, T.B. 1994. Structured imagination: The role of category structure in exemplar generation. *Cognitive Psychology*, 27: 1–40.

Zhang, W., Sjoerds, Z., & Hommel, B. 2020. Metacontrol of human creativity: The neurocognitive mechanisms of convergent and divergent thinking. *NeuroImage*, 210: 116572.

Zhou, J., & George, J.M. 2001. When job dissatisfaction leads to creativity: Encouraging the expression of voice. *Academy of Management Journal*, 44: 682–696.

Zhou, J., & Hoever, I.J. 2014. Research on workplace creativity: A review and redirection. *Annual Review of Work and Organizational Psychology*, 1: 333–359. https://doi.org/10.1146/annurev-orgpsych-031413-091226.

Zmigrod, S., Zmigrod, L., & Hommel, B. 2015. Zooming into creativity: Individual differences in attentional global-local biases are linked to creative thinking. *Frontiers in Psychology*, 6: 1647. doi: 10.3389/fpsyg.2015.01647.

3. Team creativity and innovation
Daan van Knippenberg and Inga J. Hoever

Creativity and innovation are core to work in organizations in meeting day-to-day work challenges as well as in developing the organization and its products, services, and processes to adapt to changing circumstances. As part of the trend towards team-based organization of work (Mathieu et al., 2017), teams are a key source of creativity and innovation (Wuchty et al., 2007). This makes the study of team creativity and innovation an increasingly important research domain. In this chapter we take stock of the state of the science in this domain both to capture what we know and to identify important directions for future research. To avoid redoing and rehashing earlier reviews more than is needed, we anchor our review on a recent review of the team creativity and innovation literature by van Knippenberg (2017a) that is arguably the most recent high-profile review of this literature. We first concisely summarize the key conclusions of that review, and then position our review of the literature since then (2016–19) to capture ongoing research streams and newer developments.

In research in creativity and innovation, there is widespread agreement on the definition of creativity as the generation of novel and useful outcomes: products, processes, solutions to problems, and so on (Amabile, 1996; Zhou & Hoever, 2014). Innovation researchers sometimes differentiate innovation from creativity by suggesting that creativity is limited to idea generation and that it is the actual implementation of these ideas that constitutes innovation. We find that in reviewing the literature, this is not a very helpful distinction. Most studies of creativity in organizations can be understood to concern implemented ideas, and research in innovation also shows that attempts at differentiating idea generation and implementation in measurement often fail because of very high intercorrelations between the two (e.g., Eisenbeiss et al., 2008), suggesting that in these studies idea generation is typically recognized because of idea implementation. Thus, we follow earlier reviews of the team creativity and innovation literature by treating creativity and innovation as interchangeable, and review both studies using the label "team creativity" and using the label "team innovation" (Hülsheger et al., 2009; van Dijk et al., 2012; van Knippenberg, 2017a). That said, given the above-mentioned tradition in the literature to define them as separate, we revisit the question of whether their combination is warranted for specific subsections of the review and in our discussion of the findings.

The exception to this general rule of interchangeability is a stream of research on idea generation that, inspired by the notion of brainstorming, is explicitly limited to idea generation and involves neither idea development nor implementation. This research is atypical for creativity and innovation in organizations, where brainstorming is at best only a step in the creativity process, and moreover a step that in all likelihood is more typically not taken. Therefore, we follow van Knippenberg (2017a) as well as earlier reviews by Hülsheger et al. (2009) and van Dijk et al. (2012), and exclude these studies from review.

The aim of our review was not to be exhaustive but to be representative of the most important developments in the field. In reviewing research in team creativity and innovation for the period 2016–19, we therefore limited ourselves to published research in management and organizational behavior. Because we anchor on the van Knippenberg (2017a) review, we first briefly discuss the key takeaways from that review to set the stage for our review of the literature.

A 2017 STATE OF THE SCIENCE

The van Knippenberg (2017a) review identified two dominant themes in research in team creativity and innovation. The first, and arguably primary, theme is the focus on team information elaboration as the core process driving team creativity and innovation. Within the reviewed research, there are a number of interrelated processes that we group together under the label of elaboration (defined as the exchange, discussion, and integration of task-relevant information; van Knippenberg et al., 2004). These processes that capture elaboration or highly overlapping team processes are information exchange, information sharing, knowledge sharing, information integration, and knowledge integration. Although concept labels including exchange or sharing may suggest the emphasis is purely on the first element of information elaboration, it is good to realize that operationally these measure often also reference the discussion and integration of information, and moreover that information sharing can be considered an extremely proximal process antecedent of discussion and integration. There thus is a strong communality underlying all these different but overlapping labels and measures: that they capture the processes that entail an integration of information and perspectives that is crucial to the emergence of new ideas and insights.

Strongly implied in this notion of information elaboration as driving team creativity and innovation is that these outcomes benefit from diversity in information and perspectives; it is the integration of different insights from different members that allows teams to be creative, and presumably more creative than any of their members could be by themselves. It is hence an integral part of this information elaboration perspective that concepts which reflect teams' access to diverse information and perspectives represent "input" that can drive team creativity and innovation (that is, through information elaboration). This is evident in research on team diversity in composition as well as in research on the team's social network (in which ties represent conduits of and access to information). The focus on team diversity also allows team creativity and innovation research to draw on the broader team diversity literature and its strong emphasis on moderation in the relationship between team diversity and team information elaboration (and thus also the outcomes of information elaboration such as creativity and innovation; van Dijk et al., 2012; van Knippenberg et al., 2004).

By means of illustration, consider a study in which these elements were brought together. Hoever et al. (2012) studied the relationship between diversity of perspectives and team creativity. They proposed that diversity of perspectives would result in information elaboration to the extent that team members engaged in perspective taking: efforts to understand other members' perspective on the task at hand. As predicted, they found that diversity of perspectives and perspective taking interacted to predict team creativity. They also found that this effect was mediated by information elaboration.

The second major perspective identified in the van Knippenberg (2017a) review is the team climate perspective (Hülsheger et al., 2009; West & Farr, 1990). Team climate is understood to reflect a shared perception by team members of what the team values in terms of objectives and interaction patterns (Schneider & Reichers, 1983). Team climate is important because it may guide members to focus on certain objectives and behave in certain ways (as well as discourage pursuits seen as less appropriate and desirable). Team climate aspects that would encourage a focus on creativity and innovation, or encourage certain attitudes and actions that drive team processes conducive to innovation (for example, psychological safety to share one's perspective even when it deviates more from what others in the team think; Edmondson, 1999), would thus be a positive influence on team creativity and innovation.

Influential work by West and Farr (1990) followed this logic and sparked a stream of research on team climate for innovation comprising four major climate factors that contribute to it. These comprise support for innovation (through for example, time, resources, and cooperation); participative safety (similar to the more commonly used concept of psychological safety); clear, shared, and meaningful objectives; and a task orientation defined by a climate for excellence (Anderson & West, 1998). Teams with a stronger climate for innovation are more innovative, as for instance illustrated by Bain et al. (2001), who found that climate for innovation was positively related to team innovation, and more strongly so in research teams than in development teams. The relationship between the four elements of team climate for innovation and team creativity and innovation was also meta-analytically established by Hülsheger et al. (2009). Related to this focus on climate for innovation is research emphasizing the importance of a cooperative climate (e.g., Tjosvold et al., 2004), which arguably overlaps in part with notions of participative safety and shared objectives.

The team climate perspective is probably best seen as complementary to the team information elaboration perspectives, in that team climate would capture some of the conditions under which teams engage in information elaboration to integrate diverse perspectives (van Knippenberg, 2017a). A good illustration to this effect is found in a study by Fay et al. (2006), who showed that team diversity and team climate interacted to predict innovation, such that team diversity was more positively related to innovation with a better climate for innovation.

In addition to identifying these two main themes, or streams of research, van Knippenberg (2017a) highlighted two research angles that stood out as being under-represented. The first was research on team leadership. The growing emphasis on the team-based organization of work has invited increasing attention to team leadership (Burke et al., 2006; van Knippenberg, 2017b). From that perspective, the number of studies of leadership and team creativity and innovation was surprisingly small. This holds even more when we exclude findings concerning transformational leadership, as we do in this review (see van Knippenberg, 2017a for related arguments). Transformational leadership is one of the leadership aspects studied in research in team creativity and innovation, but its conceptual and empirical invalidity has been established beyond dispute (van Knippenberg & Sitkin, 2013). In short, the issue is that transformational leadership is defined in terms of its effectiveness and thus confounded with the outcomes it is expected to predict, that the concept lacks theory to explain its proposed multidimensional nature, and that its measurement fails to replicate its multidimensional nature and distinctiveness from its perceived effects and non-transformational leadership. As a result, any evidence concerning transformational leadership must be considered invalid (van Knippenberg & Sitkin, 2013).

The second issue that van Knippenberg (2017a) pointed to is the study of team composition in terms of the creativity of individual team members. The emphasis in research in creativity and innovation is firmly on how creativity and innovation are driven by team process, but complementary to this perspective is the notion that team creativity and innovation also benefit from the creativity that individual members bring to the team (e.g., West & Anderson, 1996). A fundamental question for research in team creativity and innovation is thus how team composition in member creativity impacts team process and team creativity and innovation. This issue too was addressed only by what is perhaps a surprisingly modest number of studies.

A 2020 STATE OF THE SCIENCE

The state of the science as captured by the van Knippenberg (2017a) review was the starting point for our own review and literature search. As noted, our search focused on the 2016–19 period, considered only published work, and excluded pure idea generation research and findings concerning transformational leadership. In addition, we made a very mild quality selection to exclude some studies that we believed fell below the bar in terms of data quality and conceptual development (inclusion of which would not change any of the conclusions from the review). To identify relevant studies to include, we conducted a Web of Science search (with the terms "group creativity," "team creativity," "group innovation," and "team innovation" published since 2016) and screened the results in two steps. In a first step, we read titles and abstracts to select papers that focused on team creativity or innovation as an outcome (excluding papers relying purely on brainstorming measures), relied on non-clinical adult samples, were written in English, and provided empirical results for our review published in a journal article (rather than, for example, conference proceedings).

The 102 resultant papers from the first step were evaluated more thoroughly in a second step to ascertain that they indeed reported empirical data on a relationship between one or more antecedents and team creativity and innovation (which turned out not to be the case for all studies). In addition, we made lenient judgment calls on the quality of the reported research and excluded a few studies that in terms of quality of evidence and conceptual development seemed to be neither representative of the literature at large nor adding value-added insights (all of these concerned publications in what would typically not be considered esteemed journals). This resulted in a final selection of 46 studies.

We reviewed these papers from the perspective of whether and how they fit into the main streams of research identified in the van Knippenberg (2017a) review, or whether they signified newer developments. As the following review shows, the studies reviewed by and large could be understood as either further developments of the information elaboration perspectives, or new angles on the climate perspective that are consistent with the 2017 state of the science, or reflect growing attention to the influence of team leadership. Because there is more overlap between studies from these different perspectives than in the 2017 review, studies are often reviewed addressing more than one theme.

The Information Elaboration Perspective

The strongest theme within research from an information elaboration perspective was a focus on team diversity as a factor driving creativity and innovation mediated by an indicator of, or proxy for, team information elaboration. Consistent with the state of the science in team diversity research, there was also a strong emphasis on moderation of the relationship between diversity and information elaboration (cf. van Knippenberg & Mell, 2016). Following common practice in team diversity research, we group these studies as concerning job-related diversity attributes, demographic diversity, or so-called deep-level diversity, referring to more psychological attributes (e.g., van Dijk et al., 2012).

Firstly, we consider studies of job-related diversity. Zhang (2016) found that functional diversity was more strongly related to creativity with higher team longevity, mediated by knowledge sharing and group cohesion. Cheung et al. (2016) found that functional diversity was negatively related to team innovation with low affective trust (but see van Knippenberg, 2018) and unrelated with higher trust, mediated by knowledge sharing. Luan et al. (2016) found that educational diversity interacted with team knowledge integration capability (a precondition for information elaboration; van Knippenberg et al., 2004) such that teams were more creative with moderate diversity and higher integration capability (that is, a curvilinear relationship consistent with the notion that high levels of diverse information can create processing overload; van Knippenberg et al., 2004). Park et al. (2018) found that knowledge diversity is more positively related to creativity the lower a team's tenure-based status inequality. Li, Q., et al. (2018) show that expertise diversity is good for innovation, mediated by perspective taking, and moderated by paradoxical leadership. Qu and Liu (2017) found that informational diversity faultlines are good for creativity when teams have a prosocial motivation (that is, are focused on cooperation), mediated by external knowledge acquisition and internal knowledge integration. Hoever, Zhou, and van

Knippenberg (2018), experimentally show that informational diversity and feedback valence interact such that diversity promotes creativity through information elaboration with negative feedback, and homogeneity is better for creativity with positive feedback, mediated by generative processing. Finally, Moser et al. (2019) report that information sharing and helping (cf. cooperation) interacted with occupational diversity such that teams were more innovative with greater diversity at higher levels of information sharing and helping. Beyond diversity specifically, they also found that information sharing and helping were more strongly related to innovation in larger teams.

Next, we review studies of demographic diversity. Lisak et al. (2016) found that cultural diversity was more positively related to innovation with higher leader global identity, because such identity resulted in more shared innovation goals and thus in more inclusive communication (that is, presumably setting the stage for information elaboration). Li et al. (2017) observed that cultural diversity predicted creativity mediated by information sharing contingent on climate for inclusion. Bodla et al. (2018) observed that inclusive climate moderated the relationship between demographic diversity and creativity, mediated by knowledge sharing, such that demographic diversity is not a negative influence within a more inclusive climate. Lu et al. (2018) find that cultural diversity is negatively related to information elaboration and thus to creativity, attenuated by benevolent paternalistic leadership.

Finally, there were studies of deep-level diversity. Tang and Naumann (2016) observed that team value diversity was more positively related to team creativity when member positive mood was higher, and that this interaction was mediated by knowledge sharing. Toader and Kessler (2018) showed experimentally that diversity in mental models caused greater information elaboration with higher learning goal orientation and thus resulted in greater creativity. Bodla et al. (2018) also studied deep-level diversity, finding that deep-level diversity is a positive influence with more inclusive team climates, mediated by knowledge sharing. Aggarwal and Woolley (2019) find that cognitive diversity works as signal to locate information in the team and thus stimulates creativity.

What these studies show in combination is highly consistent with the information elaboration perspective (van Knippenberg, 2017a) and team diversity theory (van Knippenberg et al., 2004). The studies offer further evidence that indicators of information elaboration are proximal drivers of team creativity and innovation. They also show, consistent with team diversity theory, that diversity can be a positive driver of such information elaboration, provided that moderating conditions are met, but that diversity can also disrupt information elaboration when such moderating conditions are not met (that is, presumably because diversity can also invite interpersonal tensions and communication challenges when team members are not motivated and able to integrate diverse perspectives; van Knippenberg et al., 2004). In this respect, it is also noteworthy that these conclusions hold regardless of whether the focus is on job-related diversity, demographic diversity, or deep-level diversity. This is consistent with the notion that all diversity attributes may introduce valuable diversity of perspectives as well as invite tensions that disrupt team process (van Knippenberg et al., 2004). What these findings also illustrate is that it is inconsequential whether the outcome of interest was defined as creativity or innovation; very similar theory was associated with very similar conclusions regardless of the label used.

In addition to the strong focus on diversity, a number of other studies also fit the information elaboration perspective. The strongest theme here – overlapping with some of the diversity studies discussed in the previous – is leadership. More specifically, within the information elaboration perspective, leadership seems to be understood from the perspective that information elaboration benefits from substantial autonomy to be self-leading. Accordingly, the main focus is on the related concepts of shared leadership, empowering leadership, leader coaching, and leader humility.

Sun et al. (2016) found that shared leadership predicts creativity mediated by constructive controversy (arguably a proxy for information elaboration) when members are higher in learning goal orientation. Gu et al. (2018) report that shared leadership is positively related to creativity mediated by knowledge sharing with higher task interdependence (where task interdependence moderated both the first step and the second step in this process). Li and Zhang (2016) observed that empowering leadership predicted creativity mediated by team learning (an expression of information integration; van Knippenberg & Mell, 2020). Li, R., et al. (2018) found that empowering leadership leads to creativity mediated by a feedback seeking climate (an expression of information search), but only with low status conflict. Schaubroeck et al. (2016) found that leader coaching was positively related to innovation mediated by team learning, but only when there is interpersonal contentious communication. Liu et al. (2017) found that leader humility was positively related to creativity mediated by voice climate (that is, encouraging the sharing of ideas for change), moderated by interdependence such that the leader humility and interdependence substitute for each other. Goncalves and Brandão (2017) reported that leader humility predicted psychological safety and psychological capital and thus creativity. Hu et al. (2018) showed that leader humility was good for creativity mediated by information sharing and psychological safety, and moderated by team power distance (such that power distance reduced these positive influences).

Taking a different perspective on leadership and information elaboration, Madrid et al. (2016) showed that leader affective presence (a trait capturing how contagious leader affect is) predicted innovation through information sharing such that positive affect was a positive influence and negative affect was a negative influence. What all these leadership studies share is the notion that leadership can impact team creativity and innovation by stimulating information elaboration.

In addition, there are a number of other studies within the information elaboration perspective. Some of these mainly show that an indicator of information elaboration predicts creativity and innovation. Fan et al. (2016) showed that team transactive memory system (the team's knowledge and use of their diversity of expertise) predicted innovation. In a study of research and development (R&D) teams, Kowlaser and Barnard (2016) showed that relationships external to the team but internal to the R&D unit contributed most to team innovation. Dong et al. (2017) showed that knowledge sharing is positively related to creativity. Reiter-Palmon et al. (2018)

found that reflexivity (that is, a driver of team learning) was positively related to innovation.

Other studies focused on an eclectic set of precursors to information elaboration. Ma et al. (2017) found that ability-focused human resources (HR) practices affected creativity mediated by team efficacy, whereas motivation-focused HR practices affected creativity mediated by knowledge sharing. Chen et al. (2018) report that technological turbulence stimulates innovation through new knowledge acquisition and reduced dependence on team experts, and more so with greater autonomy. Jiang and Chen (2018) showed that cooperative norms predicted knowledge sharing and thus innovation, moderated by external knowledge acquisition. Finally, Liang et al. (2019) found that promotive voice stimulated knowledge utilization and reflexivity and thus creativity, whereas prohibitive voice stimulated reflexivity and had diminishing returns on creativity.

Again, we may note that a first conclusion is that in combination these studies underscore the importance of information elaboration for team creativity and innovation. Directly following from this, some of these studies also show that factors which influence information elaboration, in doing so, have an indirect influence on creativity and innovation.

The Team Climate Perspective

Where the 2017 review was characterized by a strong presence of the West and Farr (1990) team climate for innovation perspective and a stream of research on cooperation climate (e.g., Tjosvold et al., 2004), the explicit (measurement) reliance on these perspectives seems to have mostly disappeared. There is still a range of studies that can be understood as consistent with these perspectives on team climate, however. Note that several of these were reviewed in the previous section as part of the information elaboration perspective.

The positive influence of shared innovation goals in Lisak et al. (2016) is consistent with the climate for innovation perspective; so is the positive role of climate for inclusion (cf. psychological safety) in Li et al. (2017) and in Bodla et al. (2018) and the focus on psychological safety in Erdogan et al. (2018). Also speaking to psychological safety, Lee et al. (2018) show that status conflict reduces psychological safety at the expense of creativity, but less so with a greater proportion of women. Consistent with the climate for innovation perspective, Lyubovnikova et al. (2018) show that shared objectives are positively related to innovation.

In a related vein, findings for prosocial motivation by Qu and Liu (2017) and for helping reported by Moser et al. (2019) are consistent with the proposed positive influence of cooperation climate, as are Jiang and Chen's (2018) findings for cooperative norms. Consistent with this perspective are also findings by Bastian et al. (2018) that adversity enhances support (cf. cooperation) which in turn enhances creativity.

Possibly also fitting in here are findings by Salazar et al. (2017) that dual identity (that is, identification with the team as well as with the own demographic subgroup) is positively related to creativity. Identification could be interpreted as a proxy for shared objectives or for cooperation climate, which would make these findings consistent with the team climate perspective more broadly. When identification is understood as a precursor to cooperation or shared objectives, Lee, E.-S., et al.'s (2019) findings are particularly interesting. They found that group identification interacted with promotion focus and prevention focus, such that with a higher identification promotion focus was a more positive influence on creativity, but prevention focus a more negative influence. This is consistent with the notion that identification invites (cooperative) efforts for shared objectives, but that whether this is good or bad for creativity and innovation depends on what these shared objectives are perceived to be (Hekman et al., 2016).

These climate findings are well aligned with earlier climate findings, as captured in the 2017 state of the science (van Knippenberg, 2017a). At the same time, much more than in the 2017 state of the science, they also fall within the information elaboration perspective (see the previous section). A positive development thus has been an increased integration of these perspectives. The conclusion to emerge here is that team climate indicators which are understood to be a positive influence on creativity and innovation exert this positive influence because they either stimulate information elaboration directly or moderate the relationship between precursors to elaboration and elaboration (interestingly, and perhaps not coincidentally, a conclusion advanced by van Knippenberg, 2017a, in the integrative model he proposed as a framework to guide future research).

We do not want to overstate conclusions based on a low number of studies. That said, we do see another indication of the growing integration of the information elaboration perspective and the team climate perspective in the work on feedback seeking climate (Li, R., et al., 2018) and voice climate (Liu et al., 2017). Arguably, these are team climate angles that can be understood as fitting under the umbrella of "team information elaboration climate" in that they both concern climates encouraging introducing new information into the team. As van Ginkel and van Knippenberg (2008) and van Knippenberg et al. (2013) have outlined, it is not a given that teams understand the value of information elaboration. As a result, team cognition (that is, members' understanding of their team and teamwork; Salas & Fiore, 2004) emphasizing information elaboration can be an important influence on team information elaboration. Team cognition and team climate are different constructs, but they are obviously overlapping in team members' perception of what is desirable and effective in teamwork. Accordingly, it may be valuable to incorporate these notions of team cognition or team climate for elaboration more in research on team creativity and innovation.

Team Leadership

Where the 2017 state of the science seemed surprisingly low in its attention to leadership, leadership has emerged as a major theme in research in team creativity and innovation. Moreover, where the few leadership studies reviewed by van Knippenberg (2017a) were separate from the main information elaboration perspective, many leadership studies are now an integral part of this perspective (see our review above). We have already observed that an important angle here is not just that leadership may influence team creativity and innovation by stimulating information elaboration, but also that an important element in this leadership process is team empowerment and self-leadership (cf. Chen et al., 2018, on autonomy).

This is evident in the studies of shared leadership (Gu et al., 2018; Sun et al., 2016), empowering leadership (Li & Zhang, 2016; Li, R., et al., 2018), leader coaching (Schaubroeck et al., 2016), and leader humility (Goncalves & Brandão, 2017; Hu et al., 2018; Liu et al., 2017) reviewed in the previous paragraphs. Without such a clear focus on information elaboration, this is complemented by research by Oedzes et al. (2019) showing that with lower empowering leadership, informal hierarchies in the team are more detrimental to creativity; and by Li, G., et al. (2018) who showed that participative leadership is good for creativity, and directive leadership is bad for creativity. (Li, G., et al. also found that leader regulatory mode predicted leadership, such that leader locomotion mode predicted directive leadership and leader assessment mode predicted participative leadership.) Also speaking to the importance of empowered teamwork, Rousseau and Aubé (2018) reported that abusive supervision reduced innovation mediated by proactive behavior, and more so with greater member interdependence.

Other leadership studies offer a more eclectic set of findings. We have already discussed the Madrid et al. (2016) findings for leader affective presence, Lisak et al. (2016) on leader global identity, Li, Q., et al. (2018) on paradoxical leadership, and the Lu et al. (2018) findings for paternalistic leadership. Yang et al. (2017) found that servant leadership was positively related to creativity mediated by team efficacy, and more so with lower power distance. Cai et al. (2019) also focused on the mediating role of team (creative) efficacy (Shin & Zhou, 2007), showing that it mediated the relationship between entrepreneurial leadership and team creativity. Mo et al. (2019) found that ethical leadership had an inverted U-shaped relationship with creativity, moderated such that the relationship was stronger with weaker diversity faultlines (that is, here diversity is treated as disruptive rather than as an informational resource). Li et al. (2016) found that leader–member exchange (LMX) differentiation (that is, the variance in quality of leader–member relationships) had an inverted U-shaped relationship with creativity that was stronger the lower the mean LMX level in the team.

Thus, as before, not all studies of leadership and team creativity and innovation are easily tied into the main perspectives in research in team creativity and innovation. One question this sparks is whether these studies may signal a potential new perspective in addition to the increasingly integrated information elaboration and climate perspectives. As we discuss below when we reflect on the state of the science as captured in our review as a whole, it would make sense to start with the consideration of whether the more eclectic studies, that are not clearly part of the information elaboration or climate perspective report findings, can be integrated into the more elaborate and more broadly supported perspectives. We believe it is for future research to conceptually and empirically either make the case for their integration into the information elaboration perspective, or to explicitly position itself conceptually and empirically as complementary or alternative to this perspective. That said, for the majority of studies, a strong theme is to connect leadership to information elaboration, and moreover to do so primarily through leadership perspectives that emphasize empowered, self-leading teamwork.

Creativity Versus Innovation

As discussed in the introduction to this review, there is a stronger case to treat creativity and innovation as interchangeable than as distinct outcomes. Our review so far supports this conclusion in that it does not reveal a pattern of different theory and findings for creativity as compared with innovation. Even so, we recognize that there are contexts such as new product development in which the implementation decision lies outside of the team, and creative ideas are more likely to be denied than approved for implementation. In such contexts, the distinction between the creativity of a proposed product and its implementation is very real and relevant, because in such contexts there are often forces in play that render organizations more hesitant to adopt more radically creative products (e.g., Alexander & van Knippenberg, 2014). That is, in such contexts it is far from a given that the more creative idea is more likely to be implemented.

Our discussion and decision to treat creativity and innovation as interchangeable was not to deny this reality. Rather it was to recognize that in the practice of team creativity and innovation research it makes more sense to treat the two as interchangeable. As van Knippenberg (2017a) also noted, adopting the distinction between creativity and innovation as idea generation (and development) versus idea implementation (and further development) would suggest research to speak to the creativity–innovation relationship, and to study the conditions that affect the extent to which more creative ideas are more likely to be implemented, or to study factors that differentially impact creativity and innovation.

Van Knippenberg (2017a) only included one study to that effect (Somech & Drach-Zahavy, 2013). The 2020 state of the science is no different: we found only one study that speaks to the team creativity–team innovation distinction. Huang et al. (2017) found that higher mean member traditionalism (a cultural value) was bad for idea generation, but good for idea implementation. They also found that greater diversity in member traditionalism was good for idea generation, but bad for idea implementation.

There are two ways to look at the state of the science in the study of team creativity versus team innovation. The first is to conclude that in research practice, it remains a distinction that is not very useful. In the studies reviewed here and linking back to earlier reviews, some studies refer to the outcome as team creativity whereas others refer to team innovation, but they essentially reference the same thing and use the same theory to predict the outcome. The second way to look at the state of the science in this respect is to recognize that there are contexts in which the distinction between developing a creative idea and deciding to implement (and further develop) it are distinct outcomes worth studying in relationship to each other. This perspective makes it stand out as an important omission in research in team creativity and innovation that research seems to hardly concern such contexts in which the distinction between idea generation and idea implementation is worth studying.

Combining these two perspectives, we would suggest that it may be good to at least make our language less ambiguous, and to recognize that in research practice as well as in organizational practice creativity is typically understood in a way that it includes the implementation of the creative outcome that is generated. From this perspective, it then makes sense to refer to idea generation, and not to creativity, when one is interested in the distinction between idea generation and idea implementation.

Creativity Composition

Following the themes highlighted in the van Knippenberg (2017a) review, a final issue to address is the study of the relationship between team composition in terms of member creativity, and team creativity and innovation, for which the main issue was the question of whether mean member creativity or highest member creativity is a better predictor of team creativity. At first blush, it may seem self-evident that teams are more creative when their members are more creative, but on closer inspection there are two different takes on this notion that both receive inconsistent empirical support (van Knippenberg, 2017a). The first take is that teams are more creative when the mean (or sum) of individual member creativity is higher; the second take is that teams are more creative when the most creative member is more creative.

The extent to which the one or the other accounts for the relationship between member creativity and team creativity was an issue that received only very modest research attention in the 2017 state of the science, and this state of affairs has not changed. Our search resulted in the inclusion of only one study on this count, and it speaks indirectly rather than directly to the member creativity–team creativity relationship. Lee, H.-W., et al. (2019) showed that creativity-focused human resource management (HRM) practices (for example, staffing and training focused on creative skills) was positively related to team creativity, presumably because the practices result in teams with more creative members.

IN CONCLUSION: MOVING FORWARD

A positive development in research in team creativity and innovation is that there is increasing integration between research perspectives. In van Knippenberg's (2017a) review of the state of the science, the information elaboration and team climate perspectives emerged as by and large separate perspectives, and there was only limited research on team leadership that was separate from these two prominent perspectives. Our review shows that research on team climate and team leadership since then has anchored strongly on team information elaboration (that is, including information or knowledge exchange, sharing, or integration) as the core process driving team creativity and innovation. Increasingly, then, the study of team creativity and innovation has become the study of: (1) factors representing informational resources (diversity, social network ties); (2) factors stimulating the use of these informational resources as either moderating or direct influence (mostly team leadership and team climate); and (3) the information elaboration process that drives team creativity and innovation. As important next steps in developing this perspective further, we highlight two issues for research to address moving forward.

Firstly, there is a smaller and more eclectic set of studies that does not clearly anchor on information elaboration as the driver of team creativity and innovation, and that either does not include mediating evidence or focuses on another mediator (for example, team creative efficacy). The dominant focus on team information elaboration should not be taken to mean that information elaboration is the only relevant mediating process (Hoever et al., 2018). For the further development of the field, it would be valuable, however, to position future studies more clearly vis-à-vis the information elaboration perspective. If one focuses on other processes than information elaboration, how should these processes be understood in relationship to information elaboration? Are they alternative mediating paths, and if so, do they occur in parallel with information elaboration, or does one or the other occur contingent on moderating influences? Are they mediating influences explaining moderation? For instance, when the influence of servant leadership is mediated by team efficacy (Yang et al., 2017), is this because team efficacy is positively related to information elaboration, or because team efficacy moderates the relationship between team informational resources and team information elaboration (cf. van Knippenberg et al., 2004)? Are they mediating influences representing informational resources? For instance, we would understand the mediation evidence concerning feedback-seeking climate (Li, R., et al., 2018) and voice climate (Liu et al., 2017) as concerning influences on team informational resources (that is, feedback, voice) that can invite information elaboration. The point here is not that everything should be linked back to information elaboration. Rather, the point is that the theory and evidence that information elaboration is a core driver of team creativity and innovation is so strong and consistent that further development of the field benefits from positioning alternative perspectives in relationship to the information elaboration perspective. Importantly, this would ideally be done not only in conceptual analysis, but also empirically: given the state of the science, it would be a relatively weak case to focus on other mediators than information elaboration without empirically positioning these mediators vis-à-vis information elaboration.

The second issue we highlight is the proliferation in ways to capture informational resources, climate, and leadership. Our review identifies a range of leadership influences and it would seem implausible that there is so little overlap between these influences that the conclusion is that team leadership should engage in all these actions to stimulate team creativity and innovation. For instance, shared leadership, empowering leadership, coaching leadership, and leader humility all would seem to have in common that they reflect a context in which teams can be self-leading to at least some degree. Leader humility may be a precursor to leader coaching and empowering leadership more than a direct influence, and leader coaching and empowering leadership may help to develop shared leadership. Moving forward, it would thus be helpful to identify how different leadership constructs overlap or relate to each other in influencing team creativity and innovation, to identify more proximal and more distal influences, and to reduce redundancies in the knowledge base.

Similar observations hold for team climate. For instance, are climate for inclusion and psychological safety different enough to treat them as separate influences? Are prosocial motivation and cooperative norms different enough to treat them as separate antecedents? Does prosocial motivation or a cooperative norm result in psychological safety or a climate for inclusion? Here too, it would be valuable to identify how different constructs overlap or relate to each other in influencing team creativity and innovation, to identify more proximal and more distal influences, and to reduce redundancies in the knowledge base.

By and large, similar observations hold for concepts reflecting team informational resources. How separate are team diversity and team social network links? There is a case that more diverse teams may, as a result of their diversity, have more diverse external networks (Ancona & Caldwell, 1992). This does not mean that external networks can be "reduced" to team diversity, but it does mean that there is value-added in recognizing their linkages in conceptual and empirical analysis. In a related vein, one may also ask how much functional and educational diversity overlap, or to what extent the influence of cultural diversity is explained by value diversity. Again, this is not to reduce one to an instantiation of the other; but to move the field towards integration it is helpful to have a sense of the overlap between these different ways of thinking about team informational resources.

We end on an optimistic note here. The 2020 state of the science compared with the 2017 state of the science reflects clear steps towards integration. These steps towards integration also make clearer than perhaps was the case in 2017 what important next steps to achieve further integration would be. More than ever before, then, the state of the science in research in creativity and innovation is a call to arms for integrative efforts.

REFERENCES

Aggarwal, I., & Woolley, A.W. 2019. Team creativity, cognition, and cognitive style diversity. *Management Science*, 65: 1586–1599.

Alexander, L., & van Knippenberg, D. 2014. Teams in pursuit of radical innovation: A goal orientation perspective. *Academy of Management Review*, 39: 423–438.

Amabile, T.M. 1996. *Creativity in context: Update to the social psychology of creativity*. Boulder, CO: Westview.

Ancona, D.G., & Caldwell, D.F. 1992. Bridging the boundary: External activity and performance in organizational teams. *Administrative Science Quarterly*, 37: 634–665.

Anderson, N., & West, M.A. 1998. Measuring climate for group innovation: Development and validation of the team climate inventory. *Journal of Organizational Behavior*, 19: 235–258.

Bain, P.G., Mann, L., & Pirola-Merlo, A. 2001. The innovation imperative: The relationship between team climate, innovation, and performance. *Small Group Research*, 32: 55–73.

Bastian, B., Jetten, J., Thai, H.A., & Steffens, N.K. 2018. Shared adversity increases team creativity through fostering supportive interaction. *Frontiers in Psychology*, 9: 1–10.

Bodla, A.A., Tang, N., Wan, J., & Tian, L. 2018. Diversity and creativity in cross-national teams: The role of team knowledge sharing and inclusive climate. *Journal of Management and Organization*, 24: 711–729.

Burke, C.S., Stagl, K.C., Klein, C., Goodwin, G.F., Salas, E., & Halpin, S.M. 2006. What type of leadership behaviors are functional in teams? A meta-analysis. *Leadership Quarterly*, 17: 288–307.

Cai, W., Lysova, E.I., Khapova, S.N., & Bossink, B.A.G. 2019. Does entrepreneurial leadership foster creativity among employees and teams? The mediating role of creative efficacy beliefs. *Journal of Business and Psychology*, 34: 203–217.

Chen, T., Li, F., Chen, X.-P., & Ou, Z. 2018. Innovate or die: How should knowledge-worker teams respond to technological turbulence? *Organizational Behavior and Human Decision Processes*, 149: 1–16.

Cheung, S.Y., Gong, Y., Wang, M., Zhou, L., & Shi, J. 2016. When and how does functional diversity influence team innovation? The mediating role of knowledge sharing and the moderating role of affect-based trust in a team. *Human Relations*, 69: 1507–1531.

Dong, Y., Bartol, K.M., Zhang, Z.-X., & Li, C. 2017. Enhancing employee creativity via individual skill development and team knowledge sharing: Influences of dual-focused transformational leadership. *Journal of Organizational Behavior*, 38: 439–458.

Edmondson, A. (1999). Psychological safety and learning behavior in work teams. *Administrative Science Quarterly*, 44: 350–383.

Eisenbeiss, S.A., van Knippenberg, D., & Boerner, S. 2008. Transformational leadership and team innovation: Integrating transformational leadership and team climate models. *Journal of Applied Psychology*, 93: 1438–1446.

Fan, H.-L., Chang, P.-F., Albanese, D., Wu, J.-J., Yu, M.-J., & Chuang, H.-J. 2016. Multilevel influences of transactive memory systems on individual innovative behavior and team innovation. *Thinking Skills and Creativity*, 19: 49–59.

Fay, D., Borrill, C., Amir, Z., Haward, R., & West, M.A. 2006. Getting the most out of multidisciplinary teams: A multi-sample study of team innovation in health care. *Journal of Occupational and Organizational Psychology*, 79: 553–567.

Goncalves, L., & Brandão, F. 2017. The relation between leader's humility and team creativity: The mediating effect of psychological safety and psychological capital. *International Journal of Organizational Analysis*, 25: 687–702.

Gu, J., Chen, Z., Huang, Q., Liu, H., & Huang, S. 2018. A multilevel analysis of the relationship between shared leadership and creativity in inter-organizational teams. *Journal of Creative Behavior*, 52: 109–126.

Hekman, D.R., van Knippenberg, D., & Pratt, M.G. 2016. Channeling identification: How perceived regulatory focus moderates the influence of organizational and professional identification on professional employees' diagnosis and treatment behaviors. *Human Relations*, 69: 753–780.

Hoever, I.J., van Knippenberg, D., van Ginkel, W.P., & Barkema, H.G. 2012. Fostering team creativity: Perspective taking as key to unlocking diversity's potential. *Journal of Applied Psychology*, 97: 982–996.

Hoever, I.J., Zhou, J., & van Knippenberg, D. 2018. Different strokes for different teams: The contingent effects of positive and negative feedback on the creativity of informationally homogeneous and diverse teams. *Academy of Management Journal*, 61: 2159–2181.

Hu, J., Erdogan, B., Jiang, K., Bauer, T.N., & Liu, S. 2018. Leader humility and team creativity: The role of team information sharing, psychological safety, and power distance. *Journal of Applied Psychology*, 103: 313–323.

Huang, L., Gibson, C.B., Kirkman, B.L., & Shapiro, D.L. 2017. When is traditionalism an asset and when is it a liability for team innovation? A two-study empirical examination. *Journal of International Business Studies*, 48: 693–715.

Hülsheger, U.R., Anderson, N., & Salgado, J.F. 2009. Team-level predictors of innovation at work: A comprehensive meat-analysis spanning three decades of research. *Journal of Applied Psychology*, 94: 1128–1145.

Jiang, Y., & Chen, C.C. 2018. Integrating knowledge activities for team innovation: Effects of transformational leadership. *Journal of Management*, 44: 1819–1847.

Kowlaser, K., & Barnard, H. 2016. Tie breadth, tie strength and the location of ties: The value of ties inside an emerging mnc to team innovation. *International Journal of Innovation Management*, 20: 1–31.

Lee, E.-S., Park, T.-Y., & Paik, Y. 2019. Does shared group identification lead to group creativity? Group regulatory focus as a moderator. *Journal of Applied Social Psychology*, 49: 117–129.

Lee, H.W., Choi, J.N., & Kim, S. 2018. Does gender diversity help teams constructively manage status conflict? An evolutionary perspective of status conflict, psychological safety, and team creativity. *Organizational Behavior and Human Decision Processes*, 144: 187–199.

Lee, H.-W., Pak, J., Kim, S., & Lee, L.-Z. 2019. Effects of human resource management systems on employee proactivity and group innovation. *Journal of Management*, 45: 819–846.

Li, C.-R., Lin, C.-J., Tien, Y.-H., & Chen, C.-R. 2017. A multilevel model of team cultural diversity and creativity: The role of climate for inclusion. *Journal of Creative Behavior*, 51: 163–179.

Li, G., Liu, H., & Luo, Y. 2018. Directive versus participative leadership: Dispositional antecedents and team consequences. *Journal of Occupational and Organizational Psychology*, 91: 645–664.

Li, M., & Zhang, P. 2016. Stimulating learning by empowering leadership: Can we achieve cross-level creativity simultaneously? *Leadership and Organization Development Journal*, 37: 1168–1186.

Li, Q., She, Z., & Yang, B. 2018. Promoting innovative performance in multidisciplinary teams: The roles of paradoxical leadership and team perspective taking. *Frontiers in Psychology*, 9: 1–10.

Li, R., Wang, H., & Huang, M. 2018. From empowerment to multilevel creativity: The role of employee self-perceived status and feedback-seeking climate. *Journal of Leadership and Organizational Studies*, 25: 430–442.

Li, Y., Fu, F., Sun, J.-M., & Yang, B. 2016. Leader–member exchange differentiation and team creativity: An investigation of nonlinearity. *Human Relations*, 69: 1221–1238.

Liang, J., Shu, R., & Farh, C.I.C. 2019. Differential implications of team member promotive and prohibitive voice on innovation performance in research and development project teams: A dialectic perspective. *Journal of Organizational Behavior*, 40: 91–104.

Lisak, A., Erez, M., Sui, Y., & Lee, C. 2016. The positive role of global leaders in enhancing multicultural team innovation. *Journal of International Business Studies*, 47: 655–673.

Liu, W., Mao, J., & Chen, X. 2017. Leader humility and team innovation: Investigating the substituting role of task interdependence and the mediating role of team voice climate. *Frontiers in Psychology*, 8: 1–12.

Lu, L., Li, F., Leung, K., Savani, K., & Morris, M.W. 2018. When can culturally diverse teams be more creative? The role of leaders' benevolent paternalism. *Journal of Organizational Behavior*, 39: 402–415.

Luan, K., Ling, C.-D., & Xie, X.-Y. 2016. The nonlinear effects of educational diversity on team creativity. *Asia Pacific Journal of Human Resources*, 54: 465–480.

Lyubovnikova, J., West, H.R., Dawson, J.F., & West, M.A. 2018. Examining the indirect effects of perceived organizational support for teamwork training on acute health care team productivity and innovation: The role of shared objectives. *Group and Organization Management*, 43: 382–413.

Ma, Z., Long, L., Zhang, Y., Zhang, J., & Lam, C.K. 2017. Why do high performance human resource practices matter for creativity? The mediating role of collective efficacy and knowledge sharing. *Asia Pacific Journal of Management*, 34: 565–586.

Madrid, H. P., Totterdell, P., Niven, K., & Barros, E. 2016. Leader affective presence and innovation in teams. *Journal of Applied Psychology*, 101, 673–686.

Mathieu, J.E., Hollenbeck, J.R., van Knippenberg, D., & Ilgen, D.R. 2017. A century of work groups in the *Journal of Applied Psychology*. *Journal of Applied Psychology*, 102: 452–467.

Mo, S., Ling, C.-D., & Xie, X.-Y. 2019. The curvilinear relationship between ethical leadership and team creativity: The moderating role of team faultlines. *Journal of Business Ethics*, 154: 229–242.

Moser, K.S., Dawson, J.F., & West, M.A. 2019. Antecedents of team innovation in health care teams. *Creativity and Innovation Management*, 28: 72–81.

Oedzes, J.J., Rink, F.A., Walter, F., & van der Vegt, G.S. 2019. Informal hierarchy and team creativity: The moderating role of empowering leadership. *Applied Psychology: An International Review*, 68: 3–25.

Park, W.W., Lew, J.Y., & Lee, E.K. 2018. Team knowledge diversity and team creativity: The moderating role of status inequality. *Social Behavior and Personality*, 46: 1611–1622.

Qu, X., & Liu, X. (2017). Informational faultlines, integrative capability, and team creativity. *Group and Organization Management*, 42: 767–791.

Reiter-Palmon, R., Kennel, V., Allen, J., & Jones, K.J. 2018. Good catch! Using interdisciplinary teams and team reflexivity to improve patient safety. *Group and Organization Management*, 43: 414–439.

Rousseau, V., & Aubé, C. 2018. When leaders stifle innovation in work teams: The role of abusive supervision. *Journal of Business Ethics*, 151: 651–664.

Salas, E., & Fiore, S.M. 2004. *Team cognition: Understanding the factors that drive process and performance*. Washington, DC: APA.

Salazar, M.R., Feitosa, J., & Salas, E. 2017. Diversity and team creativity: Exploring underlying mechanisms. *Group Dynamics*, 21: 187–206.

Schaubroeck, J., Carmeli, A., Bhatia, S., & Paz, E. 2016. Enabling team learning when members are prone to contentious communication: The role of team leader coaching. *Human Relations*, 69: 1709–1727.

Schneider, B., & Reichers, A.E. 1983. On the etiology of climates. *Personnel Psychology*, 36: 19–39.

Shin, S.J., & Zhou, J. 2007. When is educational specialization heterogeneity related to creativity in research and development teams? Transformational leadership as a moderator. *Journal of Applied Psychology*, 92: 1709–1721.

Somech, A., & Drach-Zahavy, A. 2013. Translating team creativity to innovation implementation: The role of team composition and climate for innovation. *Journal of Management*, 39: 684–708.

Sun, X., Jie, Y., Wang, Y., Xue, G., & Liu, Y. 2016. Shared leadership improves team novelty: The mechanism and its boundary condition. *Frontiers in Psychology*, 6: 1–12.

Tang, C., & Naumann, S.E. 2016. Team diversity, mood, and team creativity: The role of team knowledge sharing in Chinese R&D teams. *Journal of Management and Organization*, 22: 420–434.

Tjosvold, D., Tang, M.M.L., & West M. 2004. Reflexivity for team innovation in China: The contribution of goal interdependence. *Group and Organization Management*, 29: 540–559.

Toader, A.F., & Kessler, T. 2018. Team mental models, team goal orientations, and information elaboration, predicting team creative performance. *Creativity Research Journal*, 30: 380–390.

van Dijk, H., van Engen, M.L., & van Knippenberg, D. 2012. Defying conventional wisdom: A meta-analytical examination of the differences between demographic and job-related diversity relationships with performance. *Organizational Behavior and Human Decision Processes*, 119: 38–53.

van Ginkel, W.P., & van Knippenberg, D. 2008. Group information elaboration and group decision making: The role of shared task representations. *Organizational Behavior and Human Decision Processes*, 105: 82–97.

van Knippenberg, D. 2017a. Team innovation. *Annual Review of Organizational Psychology and Organizational Behavior*, 4: 211–233.

van Knippenberg, D. 2017b. Team leadership. In E. Salas, R. Rico, & J. Passmore (eds), *The Wiley Blackwell handbook of the psychology of team working and collaborative processes*: 345–368. Chichester: Wiley.

van Knippenberg, D. 2018. Affect-based trust: A reconsideration and implications for a new research agenda. In R. Searle, A.-M. Nienaber, & S.B. Sitkin (eds), *The Routledge companion to trust*: 3–13. New York: Routledge.

van Knippenberg, D., De Dreu, C.K.W., & Homan, A.C. 2004. Work group diversity and group performance: An integrative model and research agenda. *Journal of Applied Psychology*, 89: 1008–1022.

van Knippenberg, D., & Mell, J.N. 2016. Past, present, and potential future of team diversity research: From compositional diversity to emergent diversity. *Organizational Behavior and Human Decision Processes*, 136: 135–145.

van Knippenberg, D., & Mell, J.N. 2020. Team diversity and learning in organizations. In L. Argote & J. Levine (eds), *Handbook of Group and Organizational Learning*: 475–490. New York: Oxford University Press.

van Knippenberg, D., & Sitkin, S.B. 2013. A critical assessment of charismatic-transformational leadership research: Back to the drawing board? *Academy of Management Annals*, 7: 1–60.

van Knippenberg, D., van Ginkel, W.P., & Homan, A.C. 2013. Diversity mindsets and the performance of diverse teams. *Organizational Behavior and Human Decision Processes*, 121: 183–193.

West, M.A., & Anderson, N.R. 1996. Innovation in top management teams. *Journal of Applied Psychology*, 81: 680–693.

West, M.A., & Farr, J.L. 1990. *Innovation and creativity at work: Psychological and organizational strategies*. Chichester: Wiley.

Wuchty, S., Jones, B.F., & Uzzi, B. 2007. The increasing dominance of teams in production of knowledge. *Science*, 316: 1036–1039.

Yang, J., Liu, H., & Gu, J. 2017. A multi-level study of servant leadership on creativity: The roles of self-efficacy and power distance. *Leadership and Organization Development Journal*, 38: 610–629.

Zhang, Y. 2016. Functional diversity and group creativity: The role of group longevity. *Journal of Applied Behavioral Science*, 52: 97–123.

Zhou, J., & Hoever, I.J. 2014. Research on workplace creativity: A review and redirection. *Annual Review of Organizational Psychology and Organizational Behavior*, 1: 333–359.

4. Creativity and standardization: tension, complementarity, and paradox

Robert C. Litchfield, Yuna S.H. Lee, and Lucy L. Gilson

Individuals, teams, and organizations need creativity to thrive in a changing world (Anderson et al., 2014), yet performance also requires "routine-based, history-dependent, target-oriented" (Levitt & March, 1988: 336) action that can make creativity unattractive (e.g., Christensen, 1997; Ford, 1996; March, 1991). A significant literature dating back to Taylor's original ideas of "scientific management" contends that routine actions become more effective as they are specified in more detail with an eye toward improving their efficiency at meeting organizational goals. Accordingly, habits and routines are often systematically examined, documented, questioned, changed (if necessary), and then formalized in order to increase efficiency and deliver consistent quality. In the modern era, Benner and Tushman (2003: 240) note that this translates into "mapping processes, improving processes, and adhering to systems of improved processes." Collectively, these practices, which can be executed at any level of analysis from the individual to the organization, constitute standardization.

A stated purpose of standardization is to reduce unwanted variation at work. Concurrent with the need for standardization is the need for individuals, teams, and organizations to engage in creative processes and generate creative outcomes that encompass novel and useful ideas, products, and solutions. To this end, creativity has been described as essential for innovation, individual and team performance, along with organizational flexibility, survival, and competitiveness (Anderson et al., 2014; Gilson, 2007b). By its very nature, however, creativity implies that variance is not only required, but also highly sought after. Although it is easy to suggest that such variance might be tolerable in certain jobs where creativity is obviously wanted (for example, research and development, artists, marketing, and so on), researchers have argued that some level of creativity is needed even in jobs that are described as mainly comprised of routine work (Shalley & Gilson, 2017; Shalley et al., 2000). In more routine jobs, the notion of variance becomes problematic, as it may be associated with error more than with creativity. While it may be attractive to imagine a world in which only the positive variation associated with creativity occurs, research firmly concludes that creativity is a messy business that encompasses both desirable and undesirable variation (Campbell, 1960; Simonton, 2003; Staw, 1990, 1995) and can even have a dark side (Gilson, 2007a; Gino & Ariely, 2012).

Scholars have puzzled extensively over the question of how to make room for both creativity and standardization. For instance, following Benner and Tushman's

(2003) seminal work defining "ambidextrous" organizations as "composed of multiple tightly-coupled subunits that are themselves loosely coupled with each other" (Benner & Tushman, 2003: 247), perhaps the dominant theoretical perspective is to resolve tension between creativity and standardization at a higher level of analysis. Through this theoretical lens, organizational leadership or senior teams seek to integrate standardization and creativity performed by separate, lower-level subunits (Benner & Tushman, 2003). A second, alternative approach is to attempt to resolve tensions at the level of analysis where they occur. This may be best achieved though activities such as promoting multifaceted skill sets in individual managers (Mom et al., 2009), assigning simultaneous goals to individuals (Miron-Spektor & Beenen, 2015), or by separating activities across time (Ford & Sullivan, 2004).

Although these approaches seem to offer a wealth of potential for understanding competing goals, intervention strategies, and other aspects of individual and group work, most research has focused on ambidexterity as a firm-level phenomenon concerned with balancing exploration (that is, the pursuit of new knowledge) and exploitation (that is, the use and improvement of existing knowledge; Turner et al., 2013). While creativity can be central in both exploration and exploitation (often referred to as radical and incremental creativity; Gilson & Madjar, 2011; Litchfield, 2008; Mumford & Gustafson, 1988), standardization is primarily a phenomenon of exploitation. Thus, creativity and standardization are perhaps best considered jointly within processes labeled "exploitation" in ambidexterity and innovation research. When the focus is on innovation (as opposed to standardization), research has most often concentrated on the contrast between routine and creative work. In management research, this has often resulted in an assumed backdrop of routine against which creativity is studied, with some research considering the degree of routinization embedded in work as a variable (e.g., Ohly et al., 2006). In other research, routinization is treated as a form of constraint on creativity (Roskes, 2015). Thus, research that truly attempts to study standardization and creativity as co-equals seems to be rare (for an exception, see Gilson et al., 2005).

In this chapter, we review research relevant to creativity and standardization and suggest future directions for scholars to consider as they investigate the intersection of these two complex, yet essential, aspects of organizational life. The fact that creativity and standardization exist simultaneously, can be contradictory to one another, are often highly interrelated, and may persist over time, leads naturally to considering them in terms of paradox (Lewis, 2000; Smith & Lewis, 2011; Smith & Tushman, 2005). Interestingly, however, only some of the research we review uses this theoretical lens. Yet even when creativity and standardization turn out to have complementary aspects, tension and paradox seem to characterize many of the conceptualizations. For instance, while there is some consistency within the extant literature with regard to creativity appearing mostly as an outcome, the paradox becomes clear when standardization is entered into the equation, as the two constructs are sometimes described in opposition to one another (for example, exploration versus exploitation, March, 1991; energy restoring creativity versus energy depleting standardization, Cain et al., 2017; "lean" versus creative, Pakdil & Leonard, 2017). That said, research also suggests ways that creativity and standardization may be mutually reinforcing (Chae & Choi, 2019; Gilson et al., 2005; Roskes, 2015). To unravel this tension, complementarity, and paradox, we organize our chapter by levels of analysis. In doing so, we consider the level of analysis of creativity and the level of analysis where tension is addressed, as well as several instances where the research crosses levels (for example, individual–team, individual–work environment, individual–organization, society–organization). We focus our efforts on the individual and team levels because this is where most creativity research concentrates. Although we also briefly address higher levels of analysis, we specifically do not attempt to review the large literature on organization-level ambidexterity.

INDIVIDUAL CREATIVITY

Although creativity is considered at all levels of analysis within the broader management literature (e.g., Woodman et al., 1993), it is most commonly conceptualized at the individual level (e.g., Amabile, 1996). Standardization, in contrast, is often considered as a higher-level phenomenon that imposes constraints downward onto the individual through organizational structures (for example, bureaucracy; Hirst et al., 2011). In this section, we delve more deeply into research focused at the individual level of analysis.

One relatively pure approach to standardization at the individual level is to consider standardization as overlearning, or automaticity with regard to routine work. In a study pioneering this approach, Ohly et al. (2006) used a self-report survey design to gather data from 278 individuals employed in a German technology firm. They found that routinization, described through agreement to prompts about the extent to which common work behaviors were "something ... I do automatically" (ibid.: 266), was positively associated with self-reports of creativity (the amount of novel and useful ideas employees had at work) and innovation (the degree that novel and useful ideas are implemented) on the job. Despite this promising result, it would be more than a decade before Chae and Choi (2019) revisited this finding and began unpacking the underlying mechanisms in more detail. Specifically, in their study of engineers and technicians working in South Korean manufacturing firms, Chae and Choi introduced the construct of free cognitive resources into the creativity–standardization equation. Free cognitive resources are a form of mental slack, or the feeling employees get when they are free from stress, anxiety, and overload associated with a complex and demanding mental workload. Here, Chae and Choi found that routinization (measured in the same way as Ohly et al., 2006) and creativity (assessed through supervisor ratings) may be related through the mechanism of free cognitive resources. That is, routinization and creativity may not be in conflict with one another, and routinization may in fact facilitate creativity, when routinization leads individuals to experience more free cognitive resources with which to consider creative actions. Chae and Choi found that the positive effect of routinization on creativity through free cognitive resources was moderated by learning goal orientation and leaders' support for creativity such that each of these additional variables led to a strengthening of the mediation effect.

A second way to consider the interplay between creativity and standardization in individuals is through the goals they pursue. The classic study here remains that of Shalley (1991), who showed in laboratory research that productivity and creativity goals can coexist without penalizing output or creativity. However, this type of research offers, at best, weak evidence regarding standardization because it considers only the output and not the way in which the output is pursued (that is, through some sort of process formalization).

A variation on a motivated approach at the individual level is to examine how individuals use their time to pursue creativity when they are confronted with varying levels of standardization. For example, in a study of "bootlegging" in research and development (R&D) contexts (that is, working on ideas that may benefit the company, but have no formal support), Criscuolo et al. (2014) found that when standardization increased in the organization, individuals who engaged in more bootlegging suffered reduced innovation performance. The notion of tension is at the core of this study, in that the key research questions it seeks to address relate to the balance between accountability and autonomy that R&D workers need to have in order to explore new ideas, and whether underground R&D efforts help individuals to develop innovations based on the exploration of uncharted territory and delayed assessment of embryonic ideas. With the accountability requirements imposed by organizations to ensure employees are meeting company strategies, objectives, and priorities, how do employees use their time to engage in creative projects? Interestingly, in the technology-intensive multinational studied, R&D employees were not given slack time to work on creative "pet projects," and management relied on formal, audited work plans to ensure accountability. However, the authors find that R&D professionals engage in bootlegging activities to gain "strategic autonomy through nonprogrammed, underground R&D efforts" (Criscuolo et al., 2014: 1300). Bootlegging activities resulted in both proactive and deviant creativity, and its impact on innovative performance varied based on alignment with organizational objectives, meaning that bootlegging out of frustration with the organization often resulted in a negative impact due to a misalignment of objectives. Furthermore, "an individual's bootlegging efforts tended to be successful only in high performance work settings and in the presence of fellow bootleggers" (ibid.: 1301). These findings suggest that the deviant side of creativity in a standardized work environment necessitates a social norming component in order to deliver positive outcomes.

At the individual level of analysis, these examples suggest that the tensions that emanate from contradictory yet interwoven demands may be managed at the conscious and/or unconscious levels. In the Chae and Choi example, complementarity is achieved through the freeing up of cognitive resources, a relatively unconscious resolution of the tension. In the Criscuolo study, frustration leads employees to become more flexible as a means to "escape" from accountability, suggesting a more consciously motivated approach. However, it should be noted that in both instances several other outside variables also come into play, such as learning goal orientation, leader support, and the presence of others who are also "bootlegging."

Although we avoid reviewing higher-level ambidexterity research here, Mom et al. (2009) considered drivers of ambidexterity in individual managers; which may have implications for understanding dual prioritization of creativity and standardization for individuals. It should be noted that this study does not cleanly target either creativity or standardization: items related to exploration were more concerned with ambiguity and learning than with creativity per se; items related to exploitation were partially concerned with standardization and partially with time horizons and customer choice. However, we mention this study because it suggests that decision-making authority (a form of autonomy for managers), participation in cross-functional interfaces, and connectedness across hierarchical levels are all possible mechanisms for building ambidexterity in individuals. Given that autonomy, broad networks, and good relationships with leaders are all known drivers of creativity, these ideas may warrant follow-up in studies more explicitly devoted to understanding creativity and standardization.

Returning to themes of automaticity, autonomy, and cognitive resources, Elsbach and Hargadon (2006) theorized benefits of designing a degree of "mindless work," which they defined as low in cognitive difficulty and performance pressure, into the jobs of busy professionals tasked heavily with producing creativity. Similar to the other studies reviewed above, Elsbach and Hargadon suggested that such work would build cognitive capacity, psychological safety, and positive affect that could then be poured back into additional creativity.

TEAM LEVEL OF ANALYSIS

The relationship between team-level standardization and creativity was first examined by Gilson and colleagues in a 2005 study of service technicians employed in a large multinational organization that was consistently recognized for the quality of its products and services through a number of prestigious international awards. In this setting, standardization was seen as critical to maintaining quality standards. Concurrently, the organization empowered its employee teams to work independently and engage in creative processes where necessary to meet performance, financial, and customer satisfaction metrics. Results from this study found that when considered independently of one another, creativity was positively associated with objective performance, whereas standardization was the driver of customer satisfaction. However, when examined in concert with one another, high levels of creativity and standardization resulted in the highest levels of customer satisfaction. In contrast, the highest levels of objective performance were achieved when teams engaged in high levels of creativity and low levels of standardization. Conversely, the lowest levels of objective performance were associated with low levels of creativity and low standardization. The tension here appears to be at the level of the team, and how to engage in both critical processes, but at the appropriate time.

At the team level another way of framing this question is how the standardization of team processes might affect team-level creativity. Here, Goncalo et al. (2015) considered how standardizing a group's interaction processes around a norm to be "politically correct" might affect creativity in same-sex versus mixed-sex work groups. Across two studies of undergraduate students, they found that a supposedly restrictive norm toward "politically correct" conversation increased creativity in mixed-sex groups. This research is particularly notable for showing how process standardization can improve team performance on a task that is explicitly creative (that is, idea generation).

More in line with the traditional supposition that standardization and creativity may be in opposition with one another, a small qualitative study of a healthcare team surveyed quarterly over an 18-month period found that the standardization of what had been meaningful work led workers to feel emotionally depleted, whereas exercising creativity on the job helped them to feel emotionally rewarded (Cain et al., 2017). Specifically, the majority of team members (62 percent) identified standardization of meaningful work as energy depleting; while at the same time the majority of team members (54 percent) identified working in teams, connecting with patients, practicing autonomy and creativity, as energy restoring; and lastly, emotional exhaustion was potentially decreased by increasing the energy restoring aspects of work.

It is interesting to note here that the examples of the standardization of meaningful work that led to energy draining and emotional exhaustion included excessive required documentation, trying to break the work down into manageable steps, and the fact that while convenient, technology was making it harder for team members to disengage from work while at home. All of these examples can easily be explained through a quality assurance lens, the need to reduce variance in the caring of adults with serious illnesses, and the formalization of processes for increased efficiency. And yet, they are at odds with the organizational values of autonomy and creativity and the more emotionally rewarding work examples that included flexibility, freedom to problem-solve creatively, and being treated as an autonomous professional (cf. Cain et al., 2017).

Individual-Level Creativity and Organizational Culture: Team Climate

Two studies by Hirst and colleagues consider how standardization in teams might affect creativity in individuals. In the first, Hirst et al. (2011) considered how two forms of standardization associated with bureaucracy – centralization of decision-making and formalization of procedures – might affect individual creativity within the Taiwan Customs Bureau. They found that standardization generally suppressed creative tendencies spurred by employees' goal orientations, with the caveat that greater formalization ameliorated negative effects of avoidance orientation on creativity.

In a second cross-level study, of engineering teams from Australia, Taiwan, and China, Hirst et al. (2018) explored how team climate affected the dual demands of performance and creativity. In this research, performance was measured as completing job-specified duties, meeting formal requirements, responsibilities, and never neglecting aspects of the job that one is obligated to perform; whereas creativity comprised the frequency with which individuals came up with creative solutions. This delineation suggests that performance is conceptualized as efficient, in-role, and related to one's job description; whereas creativity, while necessary for organizational success, is a job enhancement (ibid.: 28) where individuals employ new and useful approaches to solving complex problems and challenges. Exploitation was measured in terms of energy invested in standardization-related practices (for example, consistent and efficient methods, refining existing methods). Results suggest that exploration climates help creativity, and exploitation climates help performance. However, when team exploration and exploitation climate are examined in conjunction with the individual's creative self-efficacy, the results are more complex. Specifically, when individual creative self-efficacy is low, team climates that encourage either exploration or exploitation can deliver performance and creative benefits. However, when individuals' creative self-efficacy is high:

> up to a moderate level increasing team encouragement of exploitation and exploration is associated with clear performance and creative returns. When team encouragement for exploitation and exploration increase beyond this point, the returns on such encouragement diminish and individuals with high levels of self-efficacy show less additional performance and creative returns. (ibid.: 17)

Perhaps most interesting of all for our purposes here, exploration and exploitation climates were fairly strongly correlated (r = 0.63 at the individual level, r = 0.55 at the team level), suggesting that teams may develop climates encouraging both.

In an examination of personal characteristics and organizational culture, Miron et al. (2004) found that individuals can attend to both creativity and detail, and that an innovative culture does not necessarily compete with one that is focused on quality and efficiency. More specifically, engineers and technicians in R&D roles were asked to assess their creativity, attention to detail, and conformity to group rules, and these characteristics were examined in concert with the cultural dimension of innovation, attention to detail, and outcome orientation on individual performance. At the individual and organizational levels there can exist a balance between creativity and attention to detail, and being creative did not impede efficiency, but it did not contribute to it either. However, for individuals to attain high levels of innovation, creative people need a culture that is supportive of innovation.

Team-Level Creativity and Unit-Level Standardization

Naveh and Erez (2004) examined team-level innovation-related behaviors and team-level standardization behaviors in the form of attention to detail in the context of quality improvement initiatives in four production plants. They found that both concepts, which they conceptualized as values, but measured through reports of behavioral tendencies, complemented each other and that each contributed uniquely to improving productivity and lowering the costs of non-quality. In addition, they found that while implementing the specific standardization of ISO 9002 improved productivity, it lowered team-level creativity and innovation. Because innovative behaviors positively affected productivity, the authors concluded that "ISO 9002 would have had a stronger effect on productivity if it had not impaired innovation" (ibid.: 1583).

ORGANIZATIONAL LEVEL OF ANALYSIS (AND BEYOND)

As we noted at the outset, most research at the organization level of analysis that considers both creativity and standardization addresses it through the ambidexterity paradigm. Nevertheless, there are a few instances of such higher-level discussions of creativity and standardization that draw on other approaches. In a qualitative study, Obstfeld (2012) considers organizational routines and creative projects as two different types of "action trajectories" that organizations pursue to accomplish work. Obstfeld (2012) considers the language of "creative projects" and project management as ways to describe actions that depart from routines and that may or may not ultimately change them. However, Obstfeld specifically explicates creativity and routine as projects in organizations that differ in the amount of repetition involved, pointing toward a view of organizations as portfolios of varying mixes of these types of actions.

This focus on routines also features in the work of Sonenshein (2016). Drawing on theories suggesting that routinization can produce both stability and change (Feldman & Pentland, 2003), Sonenshein investigated how creativity and standardization might coexist within a retail organization that conceptualized itself as a "boutique" (seeming to imply creativity) while growing as a "chain" (seeming to imply standardization). In his qualitative study, Sonenshein develops the concept of "familiar novelty," claiming that it allows employees to simultaneously use their agency to be creative while remaining true to whatever level of guidelines managers require. In so doing, he gives empirical life to the idea that creativity is tied to traditions that must be upheld. Yet Sonenshein's work also questions the validity of pursuing too much standardization. For instance, Sonenshein's extensive description of the merchandising process makes it clear that this process is heavily decentralized in the sense that store-level employees have substantial latitude about what items are to be displayed and how, constrained only by loose guidelines and the need to coordinate with others on the store-level team to attain a coherent look that still communicates the brand. Sonenshein notes that this is not typical, and that other retail chains commonly detail exactly how each display should look and what items it should contain.

Finally, one theoretical work that we reviewed considered factors in the larger society. Here, Pakdil and Leonard (2017) proposed that cultural dimensions rather than organizational factors might play a key role in understanding the tension between creativity and standardization. Grounding their theoretical work in the prevalence of lean processes that have become a well-accepted means of employee-driven quality improvement, automation, specialization, and waste elimination, they posed the question: Does societal culture impact the implementation and sustainment of lean processes as a means of improving overall operational performance? Using Hofstede's 1991 dimensions of individualism and collectivism, uncertainty avoidance, power distance, long versus short-term orientation, and masculinity versus femininity they developed a number of propositions linking cultural dimensions to lean processes. In general, their analysis suggests that creativity and standardization are facilitated by different factors in the broader culture. However, they proposed that the cultural dimensions of collectivism and long-term orientation would facilitate both.

DISCUSSION

The tension between the needs for creativity and standardization appears to manifest at all levels of analysis. However, in contrast to ideas ranging from the individual (Ford, 1996) to organizational level (Benner & Tushman, 2003) suggesting that creativity and standardization are likely adversaries, extant research paints a somewhat more complex picture. Indeed, studies at the individual (Ohly et al., 2006; Chae & Choi, 2019) and team (Gilson et al., 2005; Goncalo et al., 2015) levels, as well as some aspects of cross-level research (Hirst et al., 2018; Naveh & Erez, 2004), have suggested that creativity and standardization exhibit complementarity under the right conditions. Yet our review also suggests that the number of studies that have focused simultaneously on standardization and creativity is quite small. On one hand, this lack of literature is surprising given the ubiquity of these twin pressures of organizational life and the proliferation of the paradox literature in recent years. On the other hand, the siloing of research on standardization versus creativity suggests that this state of play is perhaps a predictable, if regrettable, casualty of the fact that few researchers likely see it as their calling to examine how organizations might improve standardization and creativity in tandem and with equal fervor.

"Wanted" Variance versus Standardization

A central concept in both creativity and standardization is variation. Accordingly, we propose that examining the contestable terrain of "wanted" variance is foundational to an improved understanding of the intersection between standardization and creativity. Yet this terrain might equally be represented in terms of "wanted" standardization. For instance, standardization in healthcare might at times suggest a preference to serve only patients who best meet the parameters of standardization, despite creativity of clinicians (especially regarding thoughtful diagnosis) traditionally being heralded as the mark of superior performance (Devi, 2015). In the case of Shouldice Hospital, this has resulted in highly trained specialized physicians with high performance quality and a very high level of customer satisfaction for patients requiring routine hernia surgery (Heskett, 2003 [1983]). However, for patients whose surgery is not routine, or for those who suffer from additional medical complications, this practice could obviously have undesirable consequences, and more so if broadly applied (Shalley & Gilson, 2017). Indeed, standardization was shown to have its limits in a study of 877 patients with breast cancer in Germany, which found that deviation from practice guidelines of breast cancer, a condition in which patients may have distinct clinical, psychological, and social characteristics, resulted in increased five-year survival (Jacke et al., 2015).

Sonenshein's (2016) study of the balance between standardization and creativity in a retail chain also speaks to this question of desirable variation. Although this study is at the level of the chain, his merchandising example raises interesting questions about how the level of analysis for standardization and creativity might vary. The stores he studied exhibit more variation because lower-level employees are empowered to be creative. That is, looser standardization at the store level enabled creativity in merchandising at the store level. However, one might also argue that iron-fisted centralization of merchandising decisions could be a legitimate choice in an organization enacting the vision of a directive creative leader (cf., Mainemelis et al., 2015). Thus, while Sonenshein illustrates a duality of creativity and standardization, his qualitative study suggests many questions about how organizations might choose to balance these pursuits. An example from healthcare that underscores Sonenshein's finding is the case of the cancer field, where medical experts suggest that the multidisciplinary team (where patients and their care team members creatively discuss treatment approaches, including deviations from guidelines) may be a productive solution for the integration of macro/system-level standardization and the need for micro/patient-level variation at the individual level (Ansmann & Pfaff, 2018).

Dual pressures for creativity and standardization are commonly manifest in the reliance on digital technologies that have enabled individuals, teams, and organizations to accelerate the pace of all forms of working. Of course, it is also true that the drivers of standardization are what were, at one time, considered to be creative endeavors in and of themselves. For example, if we examine the history of technological disruptions and consider the innovations that have taken place from the introduction of the telephone to the proliferation of Wi-Fi, we quickly note that technology has changed the way people and teams approach both task and teamwork (Cascio & Montealegre, 2016). Mainframe computers were introduced into the general work environment[1] in the 1950s and 1960s, for the first time allowing employees to share work documents by centralizing the computing resources in data processing centers. These computers were an example of radical creativity or exploration that enabled a complete break from the status quo, while at the same time increasing both the standardization of work output and productivity. Linking this to the work of Chae and Choi (2019) it is easy to extrapolate that these computers freed up employee cognitive resources, allowing them to engage in creative endeavors without the need to "bootleg" their time. In fact, this has always been the argument of technological optimists. However, one can also imagine that at the same time employees, similar to the findings of Cain et al. (2017), may have resented the need to use and interact with computers rather than having the autonomy to decide how to solve their own work problems creatively.

Future Research

As for future research, our chapter clearly points to a need for more – much more – research that jointly considers creativity and standardization. In considering how to conduct studies in this area, researchers might proceed in many ways. Here, we highlight three issues that we think merit particular attention: (1) the role of each variable in the context to be studied; (2) the perspective to be adopted; and (3) the level of analysis for complementarity.

Our first suggestion is to consider the status of creativity and standardization in the focal context. One possibility is to examine creativity in standardized environments and standardization in creative environments. This type of research might particularly make use of qualitative techniques to examine, in detail, nuances with regard to how people think about creativity in a highly standardized environment (or standardization in a creative environment). Yet we also recommend research studying contexts where creativity and standardization can both be treated as variables for quantitative investigation. The fact that creativity and standardization can sometimes be complementary and at other times at odds with one another suggests the possibility for interactions between them (Gilson et al., 2005), but also potentially implicates a host of moderators that might determine their effects when applied in the same context.

Future research might also carefully consider the perspective to be adopted in understanding creativity and standardization. In creativity research, for instance, theorists have posed the question "Creative for whom?" as a means of acknowledging that creativity from one perspective might be seen as disruptive and unwanted variance from another vantage point (George, 2007). In a similar fashion, one might question who benefits from standardization relative to creativity. Such debates are already ongoing in fields such as medicine (Ansmann & Pfaff, 2018; Devi, 2015), but might be relevant to many other fields. A better understanding of the relative costs and benefits of creativity and standardization might even help managers to consider what balance to strike in making tradeoffs within creative processes between, say, idea generation and reuse. For instance, increased standardization in knowledge management might improve the reuse of ideas in ways that would benefit organizational efficiency in executing creative processes from the perspective of managers (Litchfield & Gilson, 2013); reduced standardization of knowledge management might improve perceptions of value generation in the eyes of customers by offering them at least the appearance of bespoke solutions (Sutton & Hargadon, 1996). Either path might be profitable, depending on the circumstances and capabilities of the organization, and research might illuminate factors that should affect managers' choices.

Finally, if creativity and standardization are to be complementary, we need more information on how inevitable tensions are resolved. Ambidexterity research suggests higher levels of analysis as natural points of resolution (Benner & Tushman, 2003), but the research we have reviewed here suggests the possibility for complementarity within the levels of analysis where they occur. Yet, little research has been designed explicitly to probe for such complementarity. Future studies might contribute by unpacking more of the dynamics of individuals and teams that lead them to integrate (or fail to integrate) standardization with creativity.

In conclusion, there is much unstudied terrain with regard to creativity and standardization. We hope that this short chapter inspires researchers to look beyond framing creativity and standardization exclusively as competitors, and to work to improve our knowledge of these important phenomena.

NOTE

1.   Computers had been used in scientific research and the military prior to this. For example, in 1941, the British used Bombe, an electro-mechanical means of decrypting Nazi ENIGMA-based military communications during World War II. Similarly, ENIAC (Electronic Numerical Integrator and Computer) was used to calculate artillery firing tables for the United States Army's Ballistic Research Laboratory. In science, the Williams–Kilburn tube was developed and tested in 1947 at the University of Manchester and is reported to be the first high-speed electronic memory.

REFERENCES

Amabile, T.M. 1996. *Creativity in context: Update to the social psychology of creativity.* Boulder, CO: Westview Press.

Anderson, N., Potocnik, K., & Zhou, J. 2014. Innovation and creativity in organizations: A state of science review, prospective commentary, and guiding framework. *Journal of Management*, 40: 1297–1333.

Ansmann, L., & Pfaff, H. 2018. Providers and patients caught between standardization and individualization: Individualized standardization as a solution. *International Journal of Health Policy and Management*, 7: 349–352.

Benner, M.J., & Tushman, M.L. 2003. Exploitation, exploration, and process management: The productivity dilemma revisited. *Academy of Management Review*, 28: 238–256.

Cain, C.L., Taborda-Whitt, C., Frazer, M., Schellinger, S., White, K.M., et al. 2017. A mixed methods study of emotional exhaustion: Energizing and depleting work within an innovative healthcare team. *Journal of Interprofessional Care*, 31: 714–724.

Campbell, D.T. 1960. Blind variation and selective retention in creative thought as in other knowledge processes. *Psychological Review*, 67: 380–400.

Cascio, W.F., & Montealegre, R. 2016. How technology is changing work and organizations. *Annual Review of Organizational Psychology and Organizational Behavior*, 3: 349–375.

Chae, H., & Choi, J.N. 2019. Routinization, free cognitive choices, and creativity: The role of individual and contextual contingencies. *Human Relations*, 72: 420–443.

Christensen, C. 1997. *The innovator's dilemma.* Cambridge, MA: Harvard Business School Press.

Criscuolo. P., Salter, A., & Ter Wal, A.L.J. 2014. Going underground: Bootlegging and individual innovative performance. *Organization Science*, 25: 1287–1305.

Devi, G. 2015. Creativity in medicine. *Neurology*, 84: e53–e54.

Elsbach, K.D., & Hargadon, A.B. 2006. Enhancing creativity through "mindless" work: A framework of workday design. *Organization Science*, 17: 470–483.

Feldman, M.S., & Pentland, B.T. 2003. Reconceptualizing organizational routines as a source of flexibility and change. *Administrative Science Quarterly*, 48: 94–121.

Ford, C.M. 1996. A theory of individual creative action in multiple social domains. *Academy of Management Review*, 21: 1112–1142.

Ford, C., & Sullivan, D.M. 2004. A time for everything: How the timing of novel contributions influences project team outcomes. *Journal of Organizational Behavior*, 25: 279–292.

George, J.M. 2007. Creativity in organizations. *Academy of Management Annals*, 1: 439–477.

Gilson, L.L. 2007. *Exploring the dark side of creativity: Conflicts and complementarities*. Paper presented at the Society for Industrial and Organizational Psychology Leading Edge Consortium, Kansas City, MO.

Gilson, L.L. 2007. Why be creative: A review of the practical outcomes associated with creativity at the individual, group, and organizational levels. In C. Shalley & J. Zhou (eds), *Handbook of Organizational Creativity*: 303–322. Mahwah, NJ: Lawrence Erlbaum Associates.

Gilson, L.L., & Madjar, N. 2011. Radical and incremental creativity: Antecedents and processes. *Psychology of Aesthetics, Creativity, and the Arts*, 5: 21–28.

Gilson, L.L., Mathieu, J.E., Shalley, C.E., & Ruddy, T.M. 2005. Creativity and standardization: Complementary or conflicting drivers of team effectiveness. *Academy of Management Journal*, 48: 521–531.

Gino, F., & Ariely. D. 2012. The dark side of creativity: Original thinkers can be more dishonest. *Journal of Personality and Social Psychology*, 102: 445–459.

Goncalo, J.A., Chatman, J.A., Duguid, M.M., & Kennedy, J.A. 2015. Creativity from constraint? How the political correctness norm influences creativity in mixed-sex work groups. *Administrative Science Quarterly*, 60: 1–30.

Heskett, J.L. 2003 [1983]. *Shouldice Hospital Limited*. Harvard Business School Case, 683-068. Revised, 2003. Cambridge, MA: Harvard Business School.

Hirst, G., van Knippenberg, D., Chen, C., & Sacramento, C.A. 2011. How does bureaucracy impact individual creativity? A cross-level investigation of team contextual influences on goal orientation-creativity relationships. *Academy of Management Journal*, 54: 624–641.

Hirst, G., van Knippenberg, D., Zhou, Q., Zhu, C.J., & Tsai, P.C. 2018. Exploitation and exploration climates' influence on performance and creativity: Diminishing returns as function of self-efficacy. *Journal of Management*, 44: 870–891.

Hofstede, G. 1991. *Cultures and organizations: Software of the mind*. London: McGraw-Hill.

Jacke, C.O, Albert, U.S., & Kalder, M. 2015, The adherence paradox: guideline deviations contribute to the increased 5-year survival of breast cancer patients. *BMC Cancer*, 15: 734.

Levitt, B., & March, J.G. 1988. Organizational learning. *Annual Review of Sociology*, 14: 319–338.

Lewis, M. 2000. Exploring paradox: Toward a more comprehensive guide. **Academy of Management Review**, 25: 760–776.

Litchfield, R.C. 2008. Brainstorming reconsidered: A goal-based view. *Academy of Management Review*, 33: 649–668.

Litchfield, R.C., & Gilson, L.L. 2013. Curating collections of ideas: Museum as metaphor in the management of creativity. *Industrial Marketing Management*, 42: 106–112.

Mainemelis, C., Kark, R., & Epitropaki, O. 2015. Creative leadership: A multi-context conceptualization. *Academy of Management Annals*, 9: 393–482.

March, J.G. 1991. Exploration and exploitation in organizational learning. *Organization Science*, 2: 71–87.

Miron, E., Erez, M., & Naveh, E. 2004. Do personal characteristics and cultural values that promote innovation, quality, and efficiency compete or complement each other? *Journal of Organizational Behavior*, 25: 175–199.

Miron-Spektor, E., & Beenen, G. 2015. Motivating creativity: The effects of sequential and simultaneous learning and performance achievement goals on product novelty and usefulness. *Organizational Behavior and Human Decision Processes*, 127: 53–65.

Mom, T.J.M., van den Bosch, F.A.J., & Volberda, H.W. 2009. Understanding variation in managers' ambidexterity: Investigating direct and interaction effects of formal structural and personal coordination mechanisms. *Organization Science* 20: 812–828.

Mumford, M.D., & Gustafson, S.B. 1988. Creativity syndrome: Integration, application, and innovation. **Psychological Bulletin**, 103: 27–43.

Naveh, E., & Erez, M. 2004. Innovation and attention to detail in the quality improvement paradigm. *Management Science*, 50: 1576–1586.

Obstfeld, D. 2012. Creative projects: A less routine approach toward getting new things done. *Organization Science*, 23: 1571–1592.

Ohly, S., Sonnentag, S., & Pluntke, F. 2006. Routinization, work characteristics and their relationships with creative and proactive behaviors. *Journal of Organizational Behavior*, 27: 257–279.

Pakdil, F., & Leonard, K.M. 2017. Implementing and sustaining lean processes: the dilemma of societal culture effects. *International Journal of Production Research*, 55: 700–717.

Roskes, M. 2015. Constraints that help or hinder creative performance: A motivational approach. *Creativity and Innovation Management*, 24: 197–206.

Shalley, C.E. 1991. Effects of productivity goals, creativity goals and persona discretion on individual creativity. *Journal of Applied Psychology*, 76: 179–185.

Shalley, C.E., & Gilson, L.L. 2017. Creativity and the management of technology: Balancing creativity and standardization. *Production and Operation Management (POM) Journal*, 26: 605–616.

Shalley, C.E., Gilson, L.L., & Blum, T.C. 2000. Matching creativity requirements and the work environment: Effects on Satisfaction and Intentions to leave. *Academy of Management Journal*, 43: 215–223.

Simonton, D.K. 2003. Scientific creativity as constrained stochastic behavior: The integration of product, person, and process perspectives. *Psychological Bulletin*, 129: 475–494.

Smith, W.K., & Lewis, M.W. 2011. Toward a theory of paradox: A dynamic equilibrium model of organizing. *Academy of Management Review*, 36: 381–403.

Smith, W.K., & Tushman, M.L. 2005. Managing strategic contradictions. A top management model for managing innovation streams. *Organization Science*, 16: 522–536.

Sonenshein, S. 2016. Routines and creativity: From dualism to duality. *Organization Science*, 27: 739–758.

Staw, B.M. 1990. An evolutionary approach to creativity and innovation. In M.A. West & J.L. Farr (eds), *Innovation and creativity at work*: 287–308. Hoboken, NJ: Wiley.

Staw, B.M. 1995. Why no one really wants creativity. In C.M. Ford & D. Gioia (eds), *Creative action in organizations*: 161–166. Thousand Oaks, CA: SAGE Publications.

Sutton, R.I., & Hargadon, A. 1996. Brainstorming groups in context: Effectiveness in a product design firm. *Administrative Science Quarterly*, 41: 685–718.

Turner, N., Maylor, H., & Swart, J. 2013. Ambidexterity in managing business projects – An intellectual capital perspective. *International Journal of Managing Projects in Business*, 6: 379–389.

Woodman, R.W., Sawyer, J.E., & Griffin, R.W. 1993. Toward a theory of organizational creativity. *Academy of Management Review*, 18: 293–321.

PART II

THE ROLE OF SOCIAL INFLUENCES, INTERACTIONS, AND PROCESSES IN CREATIVITY AND INNOVATION

5. Social network and creativity

Ronald S. Burt

In theory, social networks are not essential to creativity. People are creative when they produce novel and useful ideas or works. Creativity is a judgment about the produced idea or work. The fact that people are not equally creative encourages stories about the people associated with creative acts being more intuitive, smarter, or otherwise blessed with a predisposition to creativity. Hero stories of creative individuals and teams abound in the popular press. However, whatever a person's predisposition to creativity, the social network around them can be responsible for creativity displayed. Not essential in theory, social networks in practice can be a deciding factor in who emerges among us as creative individuals. How that is so is the subject of this chapter. I first sketch the connection between information and network structure, which is the foundation for a network–creativity association. I then discuss illustrative evidence of network associations with good ideas, creative work, and delivered performance, which together illustrate my central point that creativity is an act of network brokerage. I close by discussing network implications for two areas of new research on creativity: the overlapping effects of micro versus macro network structure, and the idea of illegitimate creativity.

FOUNDATION: SOCIAL NETWORK AND INFORMATION

Foundation for the network–creativity association is provided by two facts established during the 1950s "golden age" of social psychology (especially, Festinger et al., 1950; Asch, 1951; Leavitt, 1951; Katz and Lazarsfeld, 1955) that allow the structure of social networks to proxy for the distribution of information: (1) people cluster into groups as a result of interaction opportunities defined by the places where people meet; and (2) communication is more frequent and influential within than between groups, such that people in the same group display similar behavior and beliefs.[1]

Sticky Information

Within their group, people tire of repeating arguments and stories explaining why they believe and behave the way they do. They invent phrasing, opinions, symbols, and behaviors that contribute to defining what it means to be a member of the group. Beneath familiar arguments and experiences are new, emerging arguments and experiences awaiting a label; the emerging items more understood than said within the group. What was once explicit knowledge interpretable by anyone becomes tacit knowledge meaningful primarily to insiders. With more time, information in the group becomes "sticky": nuanced, interconnected, implicit meanings difficult to understand in other groups (Von Hippel, 1994). For reasons of division of labor, in which groups specialize in separate bits of work, or variation due to the independent evolution of separate social groups (Salganik et al., 2006), holes tear open in the flow of information between groups. These holes in the social structure of communication, or more simply "structural holes," are missing relations indicating where information is likely to differ on each side of the hole and not flow easily across the hole. In short, the bridge and cluster structure of social networks is a proxy for the distribution of information in a population, indicating where information is relatively homogeneous (within group) and where information is likely heterogeneous (between groups).

For example, Figure 5.1 is a sociogram of the social network among senior leaders in a large European Union (EU) healthcare organization. Each symbol is a person. Lines between symbols indicate relationships between people. People are close together in the sociogram to the extent that they have a strong connection with each other and with the same colleagues (spring embedding algorithm; Borgatti, 2002). Note the clusters. To the east in the sociogram, company leaders in the United States (US) are strongly connected with one another, with little connection overseas. To the northeast in the sociogram, company leaders in Asia are strongly connected to one another with little connection outside Asia. To the southeast in the sociogram, an important group in the company's research and development (R&D) operations floats cut off from the rest of company leadership. Business practice varies between the clusters. People in the R&D cluster are guided by state-of-the-art scientific practice. They explain and describe their activities in terms of science. People in the US cluster are adapted to American legal code, business practice, and local institutions. Similarly, people in the Asian, European, front office, and back office clusters are efficient with their local language, within the social and professional institutions associated with each cluster.

Network Brokers: Breadth, Timing, and Arbitrage

The connections between groups in Figure 5.1 are "bridge" relations. A bridge in graph theory is a link that connects two people not otherwise connected, but it is customary to discuss as bridges any connection between groups unlikely to otherwise coordinate with each other. The people labeled "Bill" and "Bob" in Figure 5.1 are "network brokers" (along with several others identified by the letter "B" in the figure), and their network behavior is "brokerage." Characterized by their location in social structure, network brokers correspond to Merton's (1868 [1949]) and Gouldner's (1957) "cosmopolitans," and Katz and Lazarsfeld's (1955) "opinion leaders" (see Burt, 1999, 2005: 84–86, on network brokers versus opinion leaders), and more distantly, Schumpeter's and Hayek's touchstone images of what it means for a person to be an entrepreneur (see Burt, 2005: Ch. 5, for details).

Network brokers such as Bill and Bob have three information advantages over people who do not have bridge connections: breadth, timing, and arbitrage. With respect to breadth, Bill and Bob's bridge relations across groups give them access

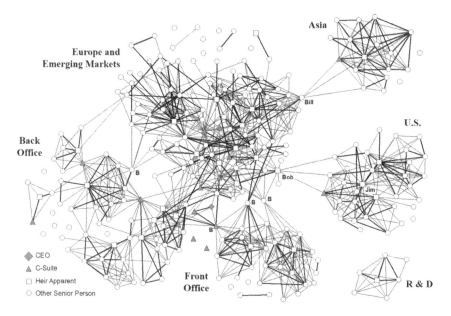

Note: Lines indicate frequent and substantive work discussion; bold lines especially close relations.
Source: Burt (2019a), reprinted with permission.

Figure 5.1   Social network at the top of a leading EU company

to more diverse information. Bob, looking at European operations, can see where certain practices in America could be an improvement. Bill, looking at European operations, can see where certain practices in Asia could be an improvement. With respect to timing, Bill and Bob are positioned at crossroads in the flow of information between groups, so they are early to learn about activities in other groups and are often the person introducing to one group information from another. There is no one other than Bob and Bill positioned to look at European operations through an American or Asian lens. Bill and Bob are more likely to know when it would be rewarding to bring together separate groups, which gives them a disproportionate say in whose interests are served when the contacts come together, which brings in arbitrage. Network brokers have an advantage in translating opinion and behavior familiar from one group into the dialect of a target group. Bob and Bill can express their proposals from overseas in terms familiar to their European colleagues.

The information advantages of network brokers are less about getting novel information than they are about applying novel interpretations to existing information, and combining previously disparate bits of information into novel interpretations. For one thing, technology continues to expand our exposure to information, such that getting information is not as difficult as making sense of information. Secondly, the benefit of access to structural holes does not come from indirect access: it comes from direct access to disconnected people (Burt, 2010). It is one thing to hear about diverse knowledge and practice that defines an opportunity; it is quite another to recognize and develop the opportunity (Soda et al., 2018). Diverse information is readily available from professionals, social media, or by word of mouth. It is easy to look up a business concept in Wikipedia and cite a reputable article on the concept; it is quite another to know the concept well enough to transform it into concepts familiar to a target audience. Experience in coordinating people with different understandings develops in one a talent for converting and synthesizing information between groups. People behaving as network brokers develop skill with analogy, metaphor, and simile. They develop tolerance for ambiguity, for conflict between contrasting colleague understandings, for seeing when the time is ripe to propose new combination of knowledge or practice. The social capital of brokering structural holes is a kind of forcing function for human capital (Burt, 2010). Relative to a person who has spent all their time in a single business function, a person connected to multiple business functions is more likely to see a novel solution that integrates or synthesizes knowledge and practice across functions. The same holds for recombinant information across industries, countries, products, or channels.

In sum: the structural holes in a network are potentially valuable contexts for action; brokerage is the act of coordinating across a hole via bridges between people on opposite sides of the hole; and network brokers are the people who build the bridges, and become more able brokers as they gain experience with diversity in their immediate social environment. Brokers operate somewhere between the force of corporate authority and the dexterity of markets, building bridges between disconnected parts of markets and organizations where it is valuable to do so, translating what is known here into what can be understood to be valuable over there. Network brokers are the social mechanism that clears a sticky-information market.

CREATIVITY IS AN ACT OF NETWORK BROKERAGE

To their European colleagues, Bill and Bob in Figure 5.1 are likely to appear creative. The European colleagues are not familiar with Asian or American operations, so good ideas articulately proposed by Bill or Bob (from their contacts overseas) look like creative innovations to their European colleagues. For example, suppose that Bob and Jim in Figure 5.1 have the same idea for an entrepreneurial spin-off from the organization. Jim knows how to express the idea in terms of American operations. The more nuanced the idea, the more embedded in American operations, and the more different the American versus European operations (as indicated by the structural hole in Figure 5.1 between the two), then the less successful Jim will be in explaining the value of the idea to potential investors at the European headquarters. Jim can explain only in terms of American operations. In contrast, Bob is embedded in European operations and familiar with American operations, so he is better positioned to explain the value of the idea to potential investors in familiar terms.

Put yourself in the position of a manager working with a high-priced management consultant, Ana. You lead a team addressing a general problem in your company operations. A viable solution has not developed within the team, so you hire Ana. After becoming familiar with your company and the problem, Ana suggests solution XYZ and offers a list of cautions and enthusiasms specific to your company. XYZ sounds like a good way to manage the problem. You and your team are dazzled: "Ana is a genius. What a creative person." No, Ana just gets out more than you do. Ana learned about solution XYZ in the course of working with a previous client. People in the prior client organization had initiated and worked out the bugs in XYZ, so they knew what it did well and where it required monitoring. For the prior client, XYZ became a taken-for-granted commodity element in its operations. Ana is a network broker. Like a mother bird who eats worms out of the ground and regurgitates them in a form digestible for her chicks, Ana took the XYZ solution from the prior client, shrouded it in the language of your company, and sold it to you as an idea tailored for your company. And her seemingly facile effort is worth the several hundred thousand you will pay Ana. She saved you the time and effort and risk involved in your team detecting and evaluating alternative solutions. You are at a conference some months later, and a friend in another company mentions that he is working on the problem for which you adopted XYZ. You suggest that he might consider doing X and Y and Z. "Terrific idea. That's really creative."

In short, creativity is an act of network brokerage. Ideas and works are not inherently creative. An idea deemed creative by this audience can be no more than a familiar commodity to that audience. Value is decided by the audience. Network brokers move complex information from a place where it is a commodity to places where it will be valuable. Experienced, intelligent people have an advantage in brokerage as they do in most intellectual tasks, but the essential variation is in the audience. Every time a network broker moves information to a place where it is valued, it is an act of creativity: Ana to you, you to your friend in the other company. Creativity lives in relationships, not people. Hence the network proverb: "The easiest way to feel creative is to find people more ignorant than yourself" (*New York Times*, 2004, May 22: A17). The proverb sounds cynical, hypocritical, but it is at once true, inclusive, and practical. It is how people of variable gifts can create value by reusing proven knowledge in new combinations and applications.

Note that the network role in creativity is one of facilitation (or inhibition), not necessity. Consider the following quote in which an executive explains the creativity and success of a prominent biotech entrepreneur:

> His value as a scientist is that he is reading and thinking very widely. He is totally unafraid of any new technology in any area of human creativity. And he reads voluminously. He has wonderful contacts with people in many different areas, and he sees the bridges between otherwise disparate fields.[2]

The first three sentences are about the entrepreneur as an individual. He reads and thinks widely about any new technology in any area of human creativity. That activity benefits from intelligence, education, and access to a good library and/or the internet, but it does not depend on the entrepreneur's social network. People in closed networks can read widely just as easily as people in open networks.

But they do not. Confirmation bias sharpens our eyes to detect things consistent with what we already know or suspect, and we typically work under time pressure such that we do not get around to investigating novel things that catch our interest. Enter the network. It is referenced in the last sentence in the above quotation: the entrepreneur has contacts in many different areas. He sees bridges between otherwise disparate fields. In other words, the entrepreneur's network alerts him to structural holes where brokerage could be valuable. People who socialize with people of diverse belief and behavior are at higher risk of seeing new combinations; in the words of the above quoted executive, network brokers are at higher risk of seeing "bridges between otherwise disparate fields." You are more likely to bump into things you did not know that you did not know, pressuring you to rethink what you thought you knew. When you rethink what you know, the pieces come together in a slightly different way. Taking on unusual work assignments can lead to such a rethinking (Kleinbaum, 2012). The extreme case is immigration, which asks for adaptation to a whole new social and cultural environment. Not surprisingly, immigrants are disproportionately the source of good ideas that develop into intellectual property (Maddux and Galinsky, 2009; Godart et al., 2015; Weiner, 2016). The inescapable diversity of surrounding oneself with friends who hold contradictory beliefs and practices makes a person accustomed to resolving inconsistency between friends, increasing one's skill in playing with alternative ways of thinking, and enhancing skill with recombinant knowledge. At the other extreme, by protecting a person from diverse belief and behavior, a closed network of homogeneous friends is prophylactic against such skill. Friends in a closed circle share stories reinforcing their stereotyped image of us, and their social support attributing failure to forces other than ourselves can obscure the wisdom that failure could provide. Closed networks are the habitat of idiot savants (see Adams, 2019, for an entertaining application to American society).[3]

The core network prediction about creativity is that network brokers, like Bob in Figure 5.1 with his connections to multiple groups, are more likely to be discussed as creative, relative to managers embedded in closed networks, like Jim (Burt, 2000: 362–367; Burt, 2004). The prediction has empirical support. Network brokers score high on creativity when creativity is measured by a supervisor's summary opinion of a subordinate's work (Perry-Smith, 2006; Jang, 2017; Carnabuci and Quintane, 2018), by executive opinion of a manager's ideas for improving the organization (Burt, 2004; Burt, 2005: Ch. 2), or by external critical opinion of the final product (Fleming and Marx, 2006; Fleming et al., 2007; deVaan et al., 2015; Soda et al., forthcoming). Other factors held constant, network brokers come up with more creative ideas, produce more creative work, and deliver higher performance.

Good Ideas

Let me illustrate. Figure 5.2A displays the network–creativity association with respect to good ideas. Taken from early work on the network origin of good ideas (Burt, 2004), the graph summarizes data on 455 supply chain managers in a large American electronics company. Each manager was asked to write online his or her best idea for improving the value of the company's supply chain. The company's two executive vice presidents rated each idea from 1 to 5 for its value to the company. Their average evaluation defines a manager's location on the vertical axis in Figure 5.2A.

Managers are distinguished by their networks on the horizontal axis in Figure 5.2A, from network brokers at the left (like Bob in Figure 5.1, note the network illustration below the horizontal axis to the left) to managers embedded in closed networks to the right (like Jim in Figure 5.1). Networks were measured by asking each manager to name the colleagues with whom they had the most frequent and substantial work contact, then asking them to describe relations with and between the named colleagues (similar to the network data displayed in Figure 5.1). Managers are distinguished on the horizontal axis by network constraint, an index measuring the extent to which a manager's network time and energy are consumed by one group. Multiplied by 100 so I can talk in terms of points of constraint, a constraint score of 100 indicates that a person's contacts are all strongly connected with one another (no access to structural holes). Constraint decreases toward zero with the extent to which a person has many contacts (network size or degree), increases with the extent to which the person's network is closed by strong direct connections between contacts (network density), and increases with the extent to which the person's network is closed by an individual through whom contacts are strongly connected indirectly (network hierarchy or centralization). Related popular measures of brokerage opportunities in a person's network are the number of nonredundant clusters in the network (effective size), or a count of the structural holes to which the person has monopoly access (Freeman's, 1977 betweenness; see Burt et al., 2013: 531–534, for a comparative discussion).

The data in Figure 5.2A cluster along a nonlinear negative association between good ideas and network constraint. The more closed a manager's network, the lower the rating executives gave the manager's idea. The Figure 5.2A association is robust to controls for a manager's job rank, experience, education, job function, and company division (Burt, 2004: 381).

Note the importance of having poor ideas in the analysis. To the extent that everyday people think about creativity, they want to be more creative rather than less. It is therefore natural to focus on obviously creative ideas, and to emulate the qualities of people who propose creative ideas. Interested in networks, I could focus on ideas at the top of the executive rating scale, and ask what kinds of networks surround the people who proposed those ideas. The data in Figure 5.2A show that the networks associated with good ideas are large, open networks rich in structural holes. The problem with that research strategy is that I would not know how often the same

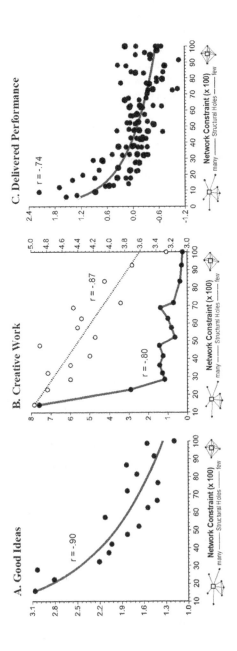

Notes: Plotted data are average scores on X and Y within five-point intervals of network constraint (horizontal) in each study population. Correlations are computed from the plotted data for the displayed association. Vertical axis in graph A is executive rating of the value of 455 manager best ideas for improving company operations (adapted from Burt, 2004: 382).

Two vertical axes in graph B are based on expert evaluations of the episode-specific creativity of 200 writers, directors, and producers in the *Dr Who* television series (adapted from Soda et al., forthcoming: Fig. 6). Axis to the right in graph B is the highest level of creativity a person reached in any episode (dashed line through hollow dots). Axis to the left is the cumulative number of "highly creative" episodes on which a person worked over their career with the series (solid line through solid dots).

Vertical axis in graph C is z-score performance relative to peers for 3179 managers in ten European or US firms, where performance is measured with in study populations by annual evaluations, compensation, or early promotion (see text; graph adapted from Burt, 2019b: 38).

Figure 5.2   *Network–creativity associations*

kind of network is associated with poor ideas. In a population of investment bankers, almost everyone has a large, open network, but only a subset of the bankers are credited with coming up with the good ideas that guide the bank. Generalizing from people known to have proposed good ideas is an example of a problem discussed as a halo effect in business (Rosenzweig, 2007) or, more generally, sample selection bias (Morgan and Winship, 2007). The power of the data in Figure 5.2A is that across managers with diverse kinds of networks, and variably poor to good ideas, executive rating of ideas systematically increases with the extent to which a manager's network is rich in structural holes.

How much do a manager's experience and intelligence matter? Initially I expected less experienced, less intelligent managers to be the people in closed networks, which I expected from network theory to be the source of pedestrian ideas and work. I was wrong about the ability of people in closed networks. It is not that they are unable; the problem is that they are extremely specialized (cf. Merluzzi and Phillips, 2016, on overspecialized MBA students hoping to be hired by investment banks). The supply chain managers in Figure 5.2A are useful on this point. I do not have intelligence scores for the managers, but I know their education, job rank, and years of experience. None of these human capital factors matter for the executive opinion of a manager's idea (Burt, 2004: 381). The 455 managers are similarly middle-aged, with a similar education, and had been in the industry for many years. The strong correlate of positive executive opinion is having relations to disconnected parts of the company, as illustrated in Figure 5.2A. The more closed the network around a manager, the more likely the manager has an idea that the executives see as trivial, or has an idea that the executives dismiss out of hand, or does not offer an idea (Burt, 2004: 381).

Looking through the 455 idea texts, I had a sense that the texts from managers in closed networks included more specialized language specific to their work site, such as program and technical terms. Within a closed network, people know similar things, so shared understanding of familiar things can be assumed. That assumption, valid for local conversations, does not apply to conversations with outsiders, especially senior executives at corporate headquarters. I did not measure the extent to which managers use language specific to their work site, but I can measure the extent to which they use language likely to be familiar to the executive judges. I ran the 455 idea texts through the language software LIWC (Pennebaker et al., 2003), which reports the percentage of words found in the LIWC dictionary. The average idea text from the managers has 79.32 words in the LIWC dictionary, and 33.67 words not in the dictionary. Technical and local terms are not in the dictionary. The first row of Table 5.1 shows that more words in the idea texts from network brokers are in the LIWC dictionary. With respect to dismissing ideas, an executive judge explained (Burt, 2004: 379): "for ideas that were either too local in nature, incomprehensible, vague or too whiny, I didn't rate them." The second row of the table shows that the managers embedded in closed networks are more likely to have their ideas dismissed as not worth rating.

Table 5.1   *Network brokers use more familiar language*

	Network brokers: relatively open networks	Average networks	Clique managers: relatively closed networks	Probability no difference
Familiar text	56.32	46.67	34.34	P < 0.001
Idea dismissed	14.38%	36.94%	43.42%	P < 0.001

Note: Columns distinguish the bottom, middle, and top third of managers on network constraint in the Figure 5.2A population (horizontal axis in the figure). "Familiar text" is the number of words in a manager's text that are familiar in the sense that they are found in the LIWC language software dictionary. Probability test is based on a -9.49 z-score from a Poisson regression of word count over the three network categories (-1, 0, and 1), controlling for number of words in the manager's idea text. "Idea dismissed" is the percentage of managers whose idea is dismissed by the executives as not worth rating. Probability test is based on a 5.14 chi-square with 2 degrees of freedom, controlling for number of words in the manager's idea text.

Creative Work

Of course, creating a valuable product is a process, not an event. Good ideas morph as they wind their way from inception to delivery, through colleague opinions and technical issues. What begins as a good idea finishes as one of many possible implementations, the original idea subject to reframing or reimagining each step along the way (see Lingo and O'Mahony, 2010; Rahman and Barley, 2017, for illustrative detail; Latour, 2008: 5 for the succinct phrasing that design "is never a process that begins from scratch: to design is always to redesign"). Network advantage at the beginning and end of the creative process is likely advantage at critical decision points during the process (Stuart and Sorenson, 2007; Sorenson and Stuart, 2008; Anderson et al., 2014; Perry-Smith and Mannucci, 2017; although good ideas seem to be used to impress friends more often than improve operations, Burt, 2004: 389–394).

Figure 5.2B displays an illustrative network–creativity association with respect to work product. Taken from a recent network study of creative work (Soda et al., forthcoming), the graph summarizes data on all 200 producers, directors, and writers who worked on episodes of the British television series *Dr Who*. The negative associations in Figure 5.2B replicate results from other studies in which industry experts see less creativity in the work of people in closed networks, typically closed team networks (Fleming and Marx, 2006; Fleming et al., 2007; deVaan et al., 2015).

Two measures of creativity are reported in Figure 5.2B: a contributor's most creative work, and the number of episodes in which they contributed high-quality work. The hollow dots summarize expert opinion on a 1–5 scale of the creativity of a person's most creative contribution in their role as a producer, director, or writer (right-hand vertical axis). Given the episodes on which a person worked, each evaluated for the person's creativity, what is the highest score the person ever received? The dashed line through the hollow dots in Figure 5.2B shows that network brokers reach a high level of creativity in their best work. The more closed the network, the less creative a contributor's best work (-0.87 correlation).

The tendency for network brokers to reach higher levels of creativity in their best work cumulates across episodes. Network brokers end up contributing to multiple episodes rated as highly creative. The solid dots in Figure 5.2B describe the number of episodes on which a person worked that experts judged as highly creative for the contributor's role as a producer, director, or writer (left-hand vertical axis). Notice how the highly creative work is concentrated to the left in Figure 5.2B. Network brokers not only reach a higher level of creativity in their best work (dashed line in the graph), but they also more frequently reach high levels of creativity (solid line in the graph; -0.80 correlation with log network constraint).

The above paragraph reads as though contributors worked as individuals. In fact, they worked in teams. For Figure 5.3B, an individual's network of colleagues is constructed from the individual's history of teams. Figure 5.3 illustrates team histories generating low versus high network constraint scores. Consider a director indicated by individual A in Figure 5.3. In the first row of Figure 5.3, director A is in a team with three colleagues, typically a producer and two writers. He worked with the same three people on his previous episode of *Dr Who*, and worked with the same three people on the episode before that. When the team history is aggregated, director A has a network of three colleagues, all maximally connected with each other, where the connection between persons A and B is the number of episodes on which they both worked. Network constraint is a high 92.6 points, which would put director A close to the extreme right in Figure 5.2B. By working with the same colleagues again and again, director A in the first row of Figure 5.3 is expected from a 92.6 constraint score in Figure 5.2B to have a personal best of low creativity, and never to have worked on an episode that the experts judge as highly creative.

In the second row of Figure 5.3, director A comes to the current team with a more varied history. He worked with B and C on the previous episode, and with B on a prior episode. D was brought in, recommended by C from C's prior work with D. In the second row, director A has an aggregate network of five variably connected colleagues. Network constraint is 59.9 points; about average. With director A's history, and a 59.9 constraint score, Figure 5.2B shows that he would be unlikely to produce an episode deemed highly creative (bold line in Figure 5.2B), but would be likely to reach a level of creativity in his best work that is higher than the level reached by the people in the first row of Figure 5.3 (dashed line in Figure 5.2B).

Finally, in the third row of Figure 5.3, director A comes to the current team with the most diverse history (of the three histories in Figure 5.3). The current team involves contributors who rarely work with one another. Director A has eight weakly connected colleagues. Network constraint is a below-average 33.1 points. Working with colleagues from diverse histories, director A in the third row of Figure 5.3 is expected from a 33.1 constraint score in Figure 5.2B to have worked on at least one episode the experts judge highly creative (solid line in Figure 5.2B), and to have a personal best creativity rating in the high 4s (dashed line).

In sum, Figure 5.2B illustrates cross-sectional evidence of the expected network association with creative work, in this case team work. The evidence is cross-sectional in that aggregate networks are correlated with measures of maximum and cumula-

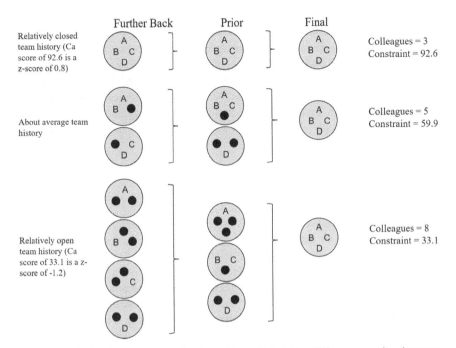

Note: Persons B, C, and D are members in A's final team. Each dot is a different person in prior teams. "Colleagues" is the number of people with whom A has worked. "Constraint" is 100 x A's network constraint score (horizontal axis in Figure 5.2B).

Figure 5.3   Person A in three team histories

tive creativity across a history of projects. Soda et al. (forthcoming) show that the network–creativity association is robust to controls for episode content, contributor experience, contributor role (producer, director, writer), and they extend the analysis to study the association over time.

Delivered Performance

Creativity is only one of the performance metrics associated with network brokers. The networks associated with creativity are also associated with work evaluations more positive than peers, compensation higher than peers, more likely recognition as a leader, and promotion faster than peers. The robust nature of the success-brokerage association is illustrated in Figure 5.2C with data on a few thousand managers and executives in the United States and Europe. With each of the ten management populations combined in Figure 5.2C, a manager's performance relative to peers (vertical axis) is measured by a studentized residual from an equation in which raw performance is adjusted for correlates in the population (for example, job rank, job function, location, age, education, gender, and so on). A score of zero indicates a manager whose success is what would be expected in their study population for someone with their characteristics. Positive numbers indicate managers ahead of expected. Negative numbers indicate managers below expected. For the horizontal axis, a network around each manager is computed from survey, email, or 360 data (details in the source publication, Burt, 2019b). As predicted by network theory, a manager's relative success decreases as their network becomes more closed (and the -0.74 correlation in Figure 5.2C is similar across managers within the United States [-0.75] and Europe [-0.73], as well as 1000 Chinese managers not presented here [-0.78]; Burt, forthcoming: Fig. 2).

IMPLICATIONS FOR FUTURE RESEARCH

Given a network association with creativity (Figures 5.2A and 5.2B) similar to the network association with performance in general (Figure 5.2C), substantial knowledge about the network–performance association can be used to generate ideas for creativity research. Replication is an obvious implication. Given the initial studies, how robust is the evidence? Replication is our protection against overgeneralizing results from unusual study populations, and management research is prone to idiosyncratic results given our reliance on access to managers in a particular division or company (for example, Figure 5.2A), or participants in a particular activity (for example, Figure 5.2B). A result is not a fact until it is reported in a substantial probability sample from a heterogeneous population, or in multiple, diverse study populations (for example, Figure 5.2C). In that spirit, what does the network–creativity association look like in diverse study populations and in domains other than business? It should be found in science, politics, nonprofits, as well as the arts and humanities (for popular press, search the internet for "everything is a remix"). Looking over time, how does inevitable network decay and renovation affect the association (Zaheer and Soda, 2009; Burt and Merluzzi, 2016; Quintane and Carnabuci, 2016)? How does the network effect mix with personality (Mehra et al., 2001; Zhou et al., 2009; Baer, 2010; Burt, 2012) and culture (Morris and Leung, 2010)? How does the association vary with broker tactics (Soda et al., 2018)? I discuss these questions and others elsewhere with respect to research on network brokerage (Burt, forthcoming). Here, I sketch two implications of the network–creativity association for creativity research in particular.

Micro versus Macro Network Structure

I have focused on the network around a person (known as a personal network, or an ego-network, Perry et al., 2018), but the network around any one individual is embedded in a broader network across the population from which the individual is drawn. For example, Bob is a network broker in Figure 5.1 between his organization's European and American operations. I display at the top of Figure 5.4 Bob's personal network pulled out of the broader management network. Bob has the same

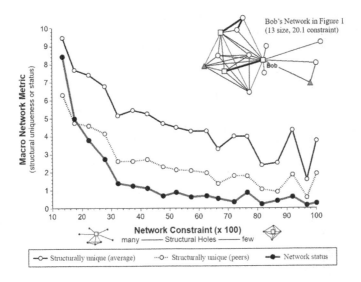

Bob's Network in Figure 1
(13 size, 20.1 constraint)

Notes: Plotted data are average scores within five-point intervals of network constraint for people in the Figure 5.2A management population. Status is an eigenvector expressed in multiples of average (solid dots). Structural uniqueness is Euclidean distance from networks of other managers in the population, on average (solid line through hollow dots) and relative to five most similar managers (dashed line through hollow dots).

Figure 5.4   Micro network structure is correlated with macro

network in Figure 5.1 and Figure 5.4, and the abundance of structural holes in Bob's network indicated by his low network constraint score of 20.1 implies that Bob is one of the more creative managers in the population.

When viewed in the broader context of Figure 5.1, however, Bob's network has additional qualities. For example, it has a level of status in the management network (Podolny, 1993). Bob has a personal connection with the head of the company's European operations (triangle symbol) and Bob is the only European who has a personal connection with the chief executive officer (CEO) of American operations (triangle). The senior people with whom Bob is connected not only hold high-ranking jobs, but they are also especially well-connected occupants of high-ranking jobs. Connections with well-connected people mean that Bob has high status in the management network. If Bob turns out to be one of the company's more creative executives, how much of his creativity comes from his access and confidence associated with occupying a high-status position (van den Born et al., 2018), rather than from the breadth, timing, and arbitrage advantage of his access to structural holes in his network?

Bob is also structurally unique. His network is unlike anyone else's. He is similar to several people in terms of being a network broker. Bill is another network broker, as are the several people marked with a "B" in Figure 5.1. But Bob is the only network broker connecting European and American operations. How much of Bob's creativity comes from him occupying a unique position in the management network (he sees things differently because he has a unique perspective on things), rather than from the breadth, timing, and arbitrage advantage of his access to the structural holes in his network?

These alternatives, two among many, raise a micro–macro question. With respect to the above paragraphs, are the network–creativity associations in Figures 5.2A and 5.2B in some part associations with network status, or with having a structurally unique position in the broader management network?

The question will not be easy to answer because micro and macro network variables are often highly correlated. Figure 5.4 illustrates the point. The horizontal axis for the graph in Figure 5.4 is the same as in Figure 5.2A, defined by the level of constraint in the personal network around each of the 455 supply chain managers: brokers to the left, and clique managers in closed networks to the right. The vertical axis in Figure 5.4 describes manager status and structural uniqueness (Burt, 2004: 364, displays the broader network). Status is the usual eigenvector measure, here normalized by the average score, so a status score of 1.0 indicates a manager of average status, a status score of 2.0 indicates a manager of status twice the average, and so on. The solid line through solid dots in Figure 5.4 shows that network brokers have high status on average, while managers in closed networks tend to have low status on the periphery of the management network. Lines through the hollow dots in Figure 5.4 show that network brokers also tend to occupy structurally unique positions in the management network. The solid line through hollow dots in Figure 5.4 describes average distances to other managers (network brokers are more distant on average), and the dashed line through hollow dots describes average distances to a manager's five closest people (lower than the overall average, but network brokers are still more distant from their closest colleagues than are managers in closed networks).[4]

To sort out the alternative network stories, Table 5.2 displays correlations among good ideas, constraint, status, and structural uniqueness. Each network variable has a statistically significant association with good ideas when used separately to predict good ideas. Good ideas are less likely in more closed networks (-7.55 t-test with constraint), more likely from a manager high in network status (6.85 t-test), and more likely from managers who occupy more unique positions in the management network (4.27 t-test). Network constraint is the primary predictor when all three network variables predict together, but correlations among the network variables are so high that the balance could shift to another network variable with minor change in the network correlations with good ideas, as could be expected in another study population, or even a later replication in the same study population. The point is that creativity is likely to be associated with both micro and macro network structure. Sorting out the most active network mechanism requires replication studies, and more detail on creative acts.

Table 5.2   *Micro and macro network–creativity associations*

	Regressions (t-tests)			Correlations		
	Each predictor separately	All three predictors	Good idea	Network constraint	Network status	Structurally unique
Network constraint	-7.55	4.9	0.3	1.0		
Network status	6.85	2.51	0.30	-0.63	1.00	
Structurally unique position	4.27	0.15	0.19	-0.46	0.51	1.00

Note: The three network variables are log scores to capture the nonlinear association with good ideas (Figure 5.2A). First column is the vertical axis in Figure 5.2A regressed across each network variable separately. Second column is all three network variables in same regression. Network status is eigenvector of network (solid line through solid dots in Figure 5.4). Structurally unique position is average Euclidean distance from manager to all other supply-chain managers (solid line through hollow dots in Figure 5.4).

Illegitimate Creativity

Studies of performance and network brokerage reveal contingency on social standing. People with low social standing in a population often enjoy little or no advantage from network brokerage in the population (Burt, 1997, 1998, forthcoming; Rider, 2009; Burt and Merluzzi, 2014). Divide the people in a study population into two categories: insiders (people with social standing sufficient to operate as a network broker) versus outsiders (people with social standing insufficient in the study population to operate as a network broker). Most management populations I have studied contain no outsiders. Everyone is eligible to operate as a network broker. Where outsiders exist, however, their presence and treatment is starkly apparent.

The graphs in Figure 5.5 are the same as Figure 5.2C – relative performance is predicted by level of network constraint – except that insiders are distinguished from outsiders in Figure 5.5. Perhaps the most familiar indicator of social standing in management studies is job rank. Figure 5.5A contains the same people displayed in Figure 5.2C but here managers in senior job ranks (solid line through solid dots) are distinguished from managers in job ranks at the bottom of the ranks deemed eligible as a source of good ideas (dashed line through hollow dots). People in the lower job ranks, who seem to be outsiders to senior management, show no compensation benefit from network brokerage.[5]

Figure 5.5B is six months after a merger. Before the merger, both companies had strong, contradictory cultures, and a history of using one another as an icon of what we do not want to be. After the merger, senior managers from the acquired company carried the stigma of their legacy. They were outsiders. Senior people in the acquiring company ostentatiously displayed distain for behavioral stereotypes attributed to the acquired company, and did not wish to be seen following advice from legacy managers. The solid line through solid dots in Figure 5.5B shows substantial returns to brokerage for managers in the acquiring firm. The dashed line through hollow dots shows negligible compensation returns for managers from the acquired company

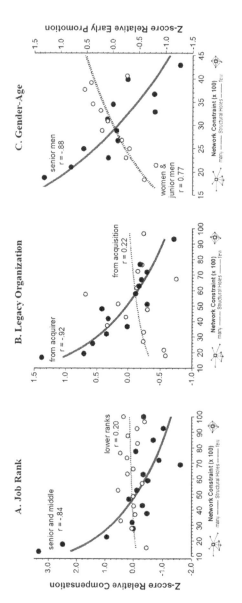

Note: Plotted data are average scores within five-point intervals of network constraint within each study population (electronics company for job rank, computer company for M&A post-integration, and another computer company for gender and age; see notes 5, 6, 7). Hollow dots are data on people deemed illegitimate to be network brokers in their organizations at the time. Correlations are computed from the plotted data using log network constraint.

Figure 5.5   Detecting network brokers deemed illegitimate (and note the absence of any hollow dots in the upper-left in Figure 5.5B; able leaders from the legacy company, outsiders in the post-merger company, left for jobs elsewhere).[6]

In Figure 5.5C, senior men enjoy substantial returns to brokerage, but women and junior men are punished if they try to behave like a network broker. Their promotions are delayed. The women and junior men are outsiders to senior management. The benefits of networks rich in structural holes were the domain of senior men (in the study population at the time when the Figure 5.5C data were gathered).[7]

The illustrative results in Figure 5.5 show the network–performance association contingent on audience acceptance of a person as a network broker. To the extent that creativity is an act of network brokerage, the same contingency can be expected in creativity. Overlooked creative acts by outsiders can be termed "illegitimate creativity." Expect in Figure 5.5A that important creative ideas are attributed to people in senior job ranks rather than junior ranks. In Figure 5.5B, they are attributed to leaders in the acquiring firm, and especially not to people from the legacy acquired firm. In Figure 5.5C, important creative ideas are attributed to senior men, and especially not, or to youngsters with insufficient experience. People are more likely to recognize creative acts from people "like us," insiders, rather than people they view as "not one of us." I dare say we have each of us at one time or another ignored outsider creativity as arrogant, uninformed, inarticulate, or even crazy. The people of low social standing in each of the Figure 5.5 graphs can offer creative ideas, but the noise will go unnoticed until it comes from an appropriate insider. Having your creative ideas overlooked in favor of insiders offering the same ideas is a disincentive to offer additional creative ideas, and living as an outsider among insiders can be expected to erode confidence and sense of worth (Burt, 2010: 216–218), which can have its own a negative effect on displayed creativity (Isen et al., 1987; Amabile et al., 2005). In short, people not accepted as network brokers are unlikely to be creative. As it turns out, consistent with the prediction, good ideas in Figure 5.2A are less likely to come from managers in lower job ranks, among whom Figure 5.5A shows that compensation is not associated with network brokers (mean executive ratings are 1.63 for ideas from managers in the lower two ranks, 2.42 for managers in more senior ranks, 6.08 t-test, $P < 0.001$). The importance to network brokers of social standing in a target audience raises interesting and tractable empirical questions for research into creativity as an act of network brokerage.

SUMMARY

In this chapter I have sketched the connection between information and network structure, which is the foundation for a network–creativity association. I then discussed illustrative evidence of network associations with good ideas, creative work, and delivered performance; which together illustrate my central point that creativity is an act of network brokerage. I closed the chapter by discussing network implications for future research on creativity, focusing on two new areas: the overlapping effects of micro versus macro network structure (Is it your network or your position in their network?), and the idea of illegitimate creativity (Will the audience accept you as a creative?).

ACKNOWLEDGEMENT

I am grateful to the University of Chicago Booth School of Business for financial support during the work reported here.

NOTES

1. Portions of this section are adapted from broader introductions to the network theory for other audiences: Burt (2010) for management, Burt et al. (2013) for psychology, Burt and Soda (2017) for strategy, Burt (2019a) for entrepreneurship, and Burt (2020) for sociology.
2. The quote is from a video, privately shared by Yves Doz, of his 1998 interview with Russell Howard at Affymax, talking about the Affymax founder Alejandro Zaffaroni.
3. There are, of course, exceptions in which cohesion enhances exchanges among diverse people in a group, thereby providing the benefits of network brokerage (Leavitt, 1996; Farrell, 2001; Aral and Van McAlstyne, 2011; Brothers, 2018; see Burt, 1992: 44–45, on structural autonomy; and cf. Soda et al., 2019), but these are heroic exceptions to be celebrated. Closed networks are more often composed of homogeneous belief and behavior.
4. Each manager has a profile of 454 relations with each other manager. Euclidean distance between the profiles for two managers measures the extent to which the two managers are connected differently in the management population: $d_{ij}^{2} = \sum_k \left(z_{ik} - z_{jk} \right)^2$, $i \neq k \neq j$ where z_{jk} is the strength of connection between managers j and k, and d_{ij} is the squared Euclidean distance between managers i and j. Sort the 454 distances between manager i and each other manager, from closest colleague to colleague furthest away. The hollow dots in Figure 5.4 describe average distance to other managers, and average distance to a manager's five closest colleagues.
5. Predict an individual's annual compensation by the following (plus intercept and residual terms): $\alpha S + \beta \left(log\ C \right) + \lambda S \left(log\ C \right) + \sum_k b_k X_k$, where: S is a binary variable distinguishing people with high social standing in Figure 5.5, C is network constraint on the horizontal axes in Figures 5.2 and 5.5, and various success factors X_k in the population are held constant. The beta coefficient in the model measures the cost of network constraint to people with low social standing (dashed lines in Figure 5.5), and lamda (λ) is the expected negative adjustment for people with high social standing (difference between the slopes of the dashed and solid lines in each graph). Figure 5.5A describes compensation to supply chain managers in a large electronics company, holding constant job function, age, education, division, and geographic location (Burt, 2004: 371). Of the five job ranks distinguished in the analysis, the bottom two are distinguished here as low social standing. Repeating the prediction in the original analysis but now with level and slope adjustments for S, the success–brokerage association is negligible for managers in the bottom two ranks (0.50 t-test for beta, P ~ 0.61) and substantial for managers in the higher ranks (-4.88 t-test for lambda, P < 0.001).

6. Continuing the previous note, Figure 5.5B describes compensation to managers in the merged organization holding constant job rank, age, function, and geography. Removing compensation differences associated with the control variables, the success–brokerage association is negligible for people acquired from the legacy firm (1.02 t-test for beta, $P \sim 0.31$) and significant for people who worked in the acquiring firm (-3.81 t-test for lambda, $P < 0.001$).

7. Continuing the previous two notes, Figure 5.5C describes age at promotion to senior rank in a computer company holding constant manager job rank, function, location, education, and seniority (Burt, 1992: 126–131). Analysis revealed that women in all ranks, and men in the most junior of the senior ranks, suffered promotion delay when they had a network rich in structural holes. Repeating the prediction in the original analysis, but now with level and slope adjustments for S (a dummy variable distinguishing senior men), the success–brokerage association shows delayed promotions to women and junior men who are network brokers (2.32 t-test for beta, $P \sim 0.02$) while promotions to senior men are delayed when they are not a network broker (-5.27 t-test for lambda, $P < 0.001$). Casual readers of Figure 5.5C in the source article often infer that women and junior men in all organizations are denied the benefits of network brokerage. The inference is incorrect. Disadvantage is specific to a study population at the time it is observed (on age discrimination, see Burt, 2018). Figure 5.5C is a rare exception, not the rule.

REFERENCES

Adams, S. 2019. *Loserthink: How untrained brains are ruining America*. New York: Portfolio.

Amabile, T.M., Barsade, S.G., Mueller, J.S., & Staw, B.W. 2005. Affect and creativity at work. *Administrative Science Quarterly*, 50: 367–403.

Anderson, N., Potocnik, K., & Zhou, J. 2014. Innovation and creativity in organizations: a state-of-the-science review, prospective commentary, and guiding framework. *Journal of Management*, 40: 1297–1333.

Aral, S., & Van Alstyne, M. 2011. The diversity–bandwidth trade-off. *American Journal of Sociology*, 117: 90–171.

Asch, S.E. 1951. Effects of group pressure upon the modification and distortion of judgments. In H. Guetzkow (ed.), *Groups, leadership and men*: 177–190. Pittsburgh, PA: Carnegie Press.

Baer, M. 2010. The strength-of-weak-ties perspective on creativity: A comprehensive examination and extension. *Journal of Applied Psychology*, 95: 592–601.

Borgatti, S.P. 2002. *NetDraw*. Boston, MA: Analytic Technologies.

Brothers, T. 2018. *Help! The Beatles, Duke Ellington, and the magic of collaboration*. New York: Norton.

Burt, R.S. 1992. *Structural holes: The social structure of competition*. Cambridge, MA: Harvard University Press.

Burt, R.S. 1997. The contingent value of social capital. *Administrative Science Quarterly*, 42: 339–365.

Burt, R.S. 1998. The gender of social capital. *Rationality and Society*, 10: 5–46.

Burt, R.S. 1999. The social capital of opinion leaders. *Annals of the American Academy of Political and Social Science*, 566: 37–54.

Burt, R.S. 2000. The network structure of social capital. *Research in Organizational Behavior*, 22: 345–423.

Burt, R.S. 2004. Structural holes and good ideas. *American Journal of Sociology*, 110: 349–399.

Burt, R.S. 2005. *Brokerage and closure*. New York: Oxford University Press.

Burt, R.S. 2010. *Neighbor networks*. New York: Oxford University Press.
Burt, R.S. 2012. Network-related personality and the agency question: multirole evidence from a virtual world. *American Journal of Sociology*, 118: 543–591.
Burt, R.S. 2018. Life course and network advantage in organizations: peak and transitional ages. In D.F. Alwin, D.H. Felmlee, & D.A. Kreager (eds), *Social networks and the life course*: 67–87. Basel: Springer.
Burt, R.S. 2019a. Network disadvantaged entrepreneurs: density, hierarchy, and success in China and the West. *Entrepreneurship Theory and Practice*, 43: 19–50.
Burt, R.S. 2019b. The networks and success of female entrepreneurs in China. *Social Networks*, 58: 37–49.
Burt, R.S. Forthcoming. Structural holes capstone, cautions, and enthusiasms. In M.L. Small, B.L. Perry, B. Pescosolido, & E. Smith (eds), *Personal networks: Classic readings and new directions*. New York: Cambridge University Press.
Burt, R.S., Kilduff, M., & Tasselli, S. 2013. Social network analysis: foundations and frontiers on network advantage. *Annual Review of Psychology*, 64: 537–547.
Burt, R.S., & Merluzzi, J. 2014. Embedded brokerage: hubs versus locals. In D.J. Brass, G. Labianca, A. Mehra, D.S. Halgin, & S.P. Borgatti (eds), *Contemporary perspectives on organizational social networks*: 161–177. Bingley: Emerald.
Burt, R.S., & Merluzzi, J. 2016. Network oscillation. *Academy of Management Discoveries*, 2: 368–391.
Burt, R.S., & Soda, G. 2017. Social origins of great strategies. *Strategy Science*, 2: 226–233.
Carnabuci, G., & Quintane, E. 2018. Does bridging structural holes increase innovative performance? Evidence from a field experiment. Paper presented at 8th Intra-Organizational Networks Conference, University of Kentucky, Lexington.
deVaan, M., Vedres, B., & Stark, D. 2015. Game changer: The topology of creativity. *American Journal of Sociology*, 120: 1144–1194.
Farrell, M.P. 2001. *Collaborative circles: Friendship dynamics and creative work*. Chicago, IL: University of Chicago Press.
Festinger, L., Schachter, S., & Back, K.W. 1950. *Social pressures in informal groups: A study of human factors in housing*. Stanford, CA: Stanford University Press.
Fleming, L., & Marx, M. 2006. Managing creativity in small worlds. *California Management Review*, 48: 6–27.
Fleming, L., Mingo, S., & Chen, D. 2007. Collaborative brokerage, generative creativity, and creative success. *Administrative Science Quarterly*, 52: 443–475.
Freeman, L.C. 1977. A set of measures of centrality based on betweenness. *Sociometry*, 40: 35–41.
Godart, F.C., Maddux, W.W., Shipilov, A.V., & Galinsky, A.D. 2015. Fashion with a foreign flair: professional experiences abroad facilitate the creative innovations of organizations. *Academy of Management Journal*, 58: 195–220.
Gouldner, A.W. 1957. Cosmopolitans and locals: toward an analysis of latent social roles. *Administrative Science Quarterly*, 2: 281–306.
Isen, A.M., Daubman, K.A., & Nowicki, G.P. 1987. Positive affect facilitates creative problem solving. *Journal of Personality and Social Psychology*, 52: 1122–1131.
Jang, S. 2017. Cultural brokerage and creative performance in multicultural teams. *Organization Science*, 29: 993–1009.
Katz, E., & Lazarsfeld, P.W. 1955. *Personal influence: The part played by people in the flow of mass communications*. New York: Free Press.
Kleinbaum, A.M. 2012. Organizational misfits and the origins of brokerage in intrafirm networks. *Administrative Science Quarterly*, 57: 407–452.
Latour, B. 2008. *A cautious Prometheus? A few steps toward a philosophy of design (with special attention to Peter Sloterdijk)*. Keynote lecture for the Networks of Design meeting

of the Design History Society, Falmouth, UK. http://www.bruno-latour.fr/sites/default/files/112-DESIGN-CORNWALL-GB.pdf.

Leavitt, H.J. 1951. Some effects of certain patterns of communications on group performance. *Journal of Abnormal and Social Psychology*, 46: 38–50.

Leavitt, H.J. 1996. The old days, hot groups, and managers' lib. *Administrative Science Quarterly*, 41: 288–300.

Lingo, E.L., & O'Mahony, S. 2010. Nexus work: Brokerage on creative projects. *Administrative Science Quarterly*, 55: 47–81.

Maddux, W.W., & Galinsky, A.D. 2009. Cultural borders and mental barriers: The relationship between living abroad and creativity. *Journal of Personality and Social Psychology*, 96: 1047–1061.

Mehra, A., Kilduff, M., & Brass, D.J. 2001. The social networks of high and low self-monitors: Implications for workplace performance. *Administrative Science Quarterly*, 46: 121–146.

Merluzzi, J., & Phillips, D.J. 2016. The specialist discount: negative returns for MBAs with focused profiles in investment banking. *Administrative Science Quarterly*, 61: 87–124.

Merton, R.K. 1968 [1949]. Patterns of influence: local and cosmopolitan influentials. In R.K. Merton (ed.), *Social theory and social structure*, 3rd edn: 441–474. New York: Free Press.

Morgan, S.L., & Winship, C. 2007. *Counterfactuals and causal inference: Methods and principles for social research*. New York: Cambridge University Press.

Morris, M.W., & Leung, K. 2010. Creativity East and West: Perspectives and parallels. *Management and Organization Review*, 6: 313–327.

Pennebaker, J.W., Mehl, M.R., & Niederhoffer, K.G. 2003. Psychological aspects of natural language use: Our words, our selves. *Annual Review of Psychology*, 54: 547–577.

Perry, B.L., Pescosolido, B.A., & Borgatti, S.P. 2018. *Egocentric network analysis: Foundations, methods, and models*. New York: Cambridge University Press.

Perry-Smith, J.E. 2006. Social yet creative: the role of social relationships in facilitating individual creativity. *Academy of Management Journal*, 49: 85–101.

Perry-Smith, J.E., & Mannucci, P.V. 2017. From creativity to innovation: The social network drivers of the four phases of the idea journey. *Academy of Management Review*, 42: 53–79.

Podolny, J.M. 1993. A status-based model of market competition. *American Journal of Sociology*, 98: 829–872.

Quintane, E., & Carnabuci, G. 2016. How do brokers broker? *Tertius gaudens, tertius iungens*, and the temporality of structural holes. *Organization Science*, 27: 1343–1360.

Rahman, H.A., & Barley, S.R. 2017. Situated redesign in creative occupations – An ethnography of architects. *Academy of Management Discoveries*, 3: 404–424.

Rider, C.I. 2009. Constraints on the control benefits of brokerage: a study of placement agents in US venture capital fundraising. *Administrative Science Quarterly*, 54: 575–601.

Rosenzweig, P. 2007. *The halo effect*. New York: Free Press.

Salganik, M.J., Dodds, P.S., & Watts, D.J. 2006. Experimental study of inequality and unpredictability in an artificial culture market. *Science*, 311(5762): 854–856.

Soda, G., Mannucci, P.V., & Burt, R.S. forthcoming. *Networks, creativity, and time: Staying creative through time and space*. Paper presented at the annual meetings of the Academy of Management, Chicago.

Soda, G., Tortoriello, M., & Iorio, A. 2018. Harvesting value from brokerage: individual strategic orientation, structural holes, and performance. *Academy of Management Journal*, 61: 896–918.

Soda, G., Stea, D., & Pedersen, T. 2019. Network structure, collaborative context, and individual creativity. *Journal of Management*, 45: 1739–1765.

Sorenson, O., & Stuart, T.E. 2008. Bringing the context back in: settings and the search for syndicate partners in venture capital investment networks. *Administrative Science Quarterly*, 53: 266–294.

Stuart, T.E., & Sorenson, O. 2007. Strategic networks and entrepreneurial ventures. *Strategic Entrepreneurship Journal*, 1: 211–227.

van den Born, F., Mehra, A., & Kilduff, M. 2018. *The network structure of leadership and team creativity: evidence from New York City Jazz Bands (Circa. 2007–2010)*. Paper presented at the Network Evolution Conference, INSEAD, Fontainebleau.

Von Hippel, E. 1994. Sticky information and the locus of problem solving: implications for innovation. *Management Science*, 40: 429–439.

Weiner, E. 2016. *The geography of genius*. New York: Simon & Schuster.

Zaheer, A., & Soda, G. 2009. Network evolution: the origins of structural holes. *Administrative Science Quarterly*, 54: 1–31.

Zhou, J., Shin, S.J., Brass, D.J., Choi, J., & Zhang, Z.X. 2009. Social networks, personal values, and creativity: Evidence for curvilinear and interaction effects. *Journal of Applied Psychology*, 94: 1544–1552.

6. Creative leadership across contexts

Charalampos Mainemelis, Olga Epitropaki, and Ronit Kark

INTRODUCTION

In the 1950s, Selznick (1984 [1957]) introduced the term "creative leadership" in order to differentiate the more creative manifestations of leadership from both technical administration and decision-making by artificial intelligence systems. He argued that creative leadership entails the art of building institutions that embody new and enduring values, and the creation of the conditions that will make possible in the future what is excluded in the present. Half a century later, Mumford et al. (2002) concluded that creative leadership differs from other forms of leadership in three ways: it induces rather than preserves structure; it cannot rely on influence tactics linked to power, conformity pressure, and organizational commitment; and it has to manage the inherent and often paradoxical conflict between creativity and organization.

More recently, Mainemelis et al. (2018) observed that by 2020 creative leadership has become more important than ever before, for at least four reasons. Firstly, leaders increasingly rely on creativity in order to develop adaptive organizations in the era of digital transformation. Secondly, as creativity and innovation are now business imperatives for many types of organizations, a critical element of many leadership jobs is the ability to foster the creativity of employees, teams, and larger collectives. Thirdly, the exponential growth of the creative economy has created a vast sector of economic activity where the notion of leadership is often virtually indistinguishable from the notion of creative leadership. Last but not least, as artificial intelligence threatens to render many traditional forms of management obsolete, creative leadership has become increasingly important (as Selznick foresaw in the 1950s) as the source of some key human leadership qualities that intelligent machines do not possess (at least not yet); for example, the ability to solve creatively highly complex social problems.

In the last two decades, organizational science has witnessed a rapid and significant increase in the number of studies on creative leadership (Dinh et al., 2014; Mumford et al., 2017). For several years, the resulting body of scientific knowledge had remained dispersed and fragmented across several strands of organizational research. Recently, Mainemelis et al. (2015) integrated the extant literature into a multi-context framework, which offers to creativity and innovation research a valuable metatheoretical tool for revealing underlying patterns of contextual variability in the manifestations of creative leadership.

THE MULTI-CONTEXT FRAMEWORK OF CREATIVE LEADERSHIP

In their metatheoretical analysis of over 200 articles on creative leadership culled from over 60 academic journals, Mainemelis et al. (2015) found that, since Selznick's (1984 [1957]) original formulation of creative leadership, the concept has evolved into three different conceptualizations, which are evident in the different ways that different research strands define creative leadership, as briefly summarized in Table 6.1.

The first conceptualization focuses on the leader's role in fostering the creativity of employees in the work context. This conceptualization has a social-psychological foundation and was originally developed within a strand of organizational research that examines contextual influences on employee creativity. Later, it expanded into a strand of leadership research that examines the influences of various leadership styles on employee creativity. To date, these two research strands have been the most prolific contributors to creative leadership research. Given that three influential theories in the field – Amabile's (1988) componential theory, Woodman et al.'s (1993) interactionist model, and Ford's (1996) theory of creative action – argued that leadership influences employee creativity, subsequent studies sought to understand how leaders foster and hinder employee creativity (e.g., Amabile et al., 1996; George & Zhou, 2001; Liao et al., 2010; Oldham & Cummings, 1996; Tierney et al., 1999). Empirical research in these two research strands usually examines creativity not in the creative industries but in other industry environments where creativity is a relatively less fundamental aspect of organizational activity (Mainemelis, 2018; Vessey et al., 2014). Creative leadership in these research strands refers to facilitating employee creativity.

The second conceptualization focuses on the creative leader as the primary source of creative thinking and behavior, as a master-creator who directs the implementation of their creative vision by other collaborators. This conceptualization of creative leadership is associated with a research strand of neo-institutional studies of haute cuisine chefs (e.g., Bouty & Gomez, 2010; Svejenova et al., 2007); a second stream of studies on orchestra conductors (e.g. Hunt et al., 2004; Marotto et al., 2007); and a third set of studies on top-down corporate innovation (e.g., Eisenmann & Bower, 2000; Vaccaro et al., 2012). Creative leadership in these research strands refers to materializing a leader's creative vision through other people's work.

The third conceptualization focuses on leaders who integrate their own creative ideas with the diverse creative ideas of other collaborators who tend to be professionally unsimilar. This conceptualization is evident in research on creativity in temporary organizations and in contexts of collaborative leadership, including a stream of studies on creative leadership in filmmaking (e.g., Perretti & Negro, 2007), theatrical (e.g., Dunham & Freeman, 2000), and television (e.g., Murphy & Ensher, 2008) settings; a stream of social network studies on creative leadership in the form of brokerage in music production (e.g., Lingo & O'Mahony, 2010) and industrial design (e.g., Obstfeld, 2012) settings; and research on dual (e.g. Hunter et al., 2012; Sicca,

Table 6.1   *Definitions of creative leadership in the creativity literature*

Creative leadership as facilitating	Creative leadership as directing	Creative leadership as integrating
"Leadership as evident as the exercise of influence to increase the likelihood of idea generation by followers and the subsequent development of those ideas into useful products" (Mumford et al., 2002: 706) "Leaders, at least as the occupants of a role where they direct creative people, will not be the ones generating new ideas. Instead, the leader is more likely to evaluate follower ideas" (Mumford et al., 2003: 414) "Creative leadership means leading people through a common process or method of finding and defining problems, solving them, and implementing the new solutions" (Basadur, 2004: 111) "We take as an exemplar of creative leadership the behaviours associated with the role of the team facilitator in the implementation of creative problem-solving systems such as the Parnes–Osborn brainstorming" (Rickards & Moger, 2000: 276) "The role leaders play in the facilitation of creative production in their subordinates" (Reiter-Palmon & Illies, 2004: 56) "The capacity to foster employee creativity" (Tierney, 2008: 95)	"Creativity is important for leadership because it is the component whereby one generates the ideas that others will follow" (Sternberg, 2003: 391) "Some of the most admired companies ... appear to be those whose leader had the creative idea. Under these conditions, a strong corporate culture emphasizing uniformity, loyalty, and adherence to company expectations would be advantageous ... This is not the same as promoting creativity from within the organization. Cohesion, convergent thought, and loyalty help to implement an idea but tend not to enhance the production of a creative idea" (Nemeth, 1997: 66) "There is only the conductor-CEO, with occasional technical and question clarification from the concertmaster and principal players in carrying out the conductor's vision and technical desires ... In the idea generation stage, we expect the conductor to present interpretive vision and direction to the orchestral musicians ... the musicians respond to this vision and ... they must solve creatively the individual technical issues in the music individually while remaining flexible and motivated enough to change artistic direction at the request of a conductor" (Hunt et al., 2004: 148–149)	"Brokers in a collaborative context must not just have a good idea themselves, they must be able to elicit and synthesize the ideas of others" (Lingo & O'Mahony, 2010: 64) "The collaborative nature of creativity is even more apparent in filmmaking ... The typical feature film is the product of the separate contributions of directors, screenwriters, actors, cinematographers, film editors, composers, art directors, costume designers, and a host of specialists in makeup, special effects, and sound. What makes these cinematic collaborations especially intriguing is that the individual contributions are not completely submerged or blended in the final product ... Truly creative directors leave their personal stamp on virtually every movie they make" (Simonton, 2004: 163–170) "Members of orchestras, for instance, are bound by the conductor's decisions. Each member of a string quartet, however, can theoretically have one-fourth of the input in musical and business decisions ... At the same time, the first violinist has most of the musical opportunities and responsibilities in traditional compositions" (Murnighan & Conlon, 1991: 169) "a rather unique solution to this paradox is simply not to have a single leader, but rather share the responsibility between individuals who possess the requisite skills and expertise" (Hunter et al., 2011: 56)

Source: Adapted from Mainemelis et al. (2015: 403–405).

1997) and shared (e.g., Davis & Eisenhardt, 2011; Hargadon & Bechky, 2006) forms of leadership. Creative leadership in these research strands refers to the synthesis of the creative work of the leader with the heterogeneous creative contributions of other professionals.

Across all research strands, creative leadership refers to leading others toward the attainment of a creative outcome. However, different research strands tend to give different meaning to what it actually means to lead others toward the attainment of a creative outcome. These differences are not artifacts of diverse methodological choices, but they reflect actual differences in how creative leadership is enacted across contexts. Creative leadership, hence, entails three alternative manifestations: facilitating employee creativity; directing the materialization of a leader's creative vision; and integrating heterogeneous creative contributions. These manifestations are not leadership styles, leadership processes, or industry contexts, but rather, they are three distinct contexts of creative collaboration that are shaped by the "dynamic confluence of cultural, industry, organizational, professional, personal, and task characteristics" (Mainemelis et al., 2015: 452).

Creativity in organizations requires both creative contributions (for example, generating and developing new ideas), and supportive contributions (for example, psychological, social, and material support) (Amabile, 1988; Madjar et al., 2002; Oldham & Cummings, 1996). The three manifestations of creative leadership differ in terms of the ratios between the creative and supportive contributions made by the leader and those made by the followers, as shown in Figure 6.1. In the facilitating context, employees act as "primary creators," but their actual creative contributions are influenced by the level of leader supportive contributions. In the directing context, the leader acts as the primary creator, but their actual creative contributions are influenced by the level of follower supportive contributions. In the integrating context the ratios of leader–follower creative and supportive contributions are more balanced, and the creative outcomes are more sensitive to the degree of leader–follower creative synergy.

CREATIVE LEADERSHIP IN FACILITATING CONTEXTS

Research conducted in facilitating contexts views employees as primary idea generators, and leaders as a crucial contextual factor that fosters or hinders employee creativity. Mumford et al. (2002, 2003) argued that creative leaders are involved throughout the creative process, from idea generation to idea structuring and idea promotion, and that leader creative cognition is primarily evaluative in nature. Mainemelis et al. (2015) found that among the three manifestations of creative leadership, facilitative creative leadership is more widespread across various industry and organizational contexts.

Competency Perspectives

Past research has found that effective creative leaders possess technical expertise (e.g., Amabile et al., 2004; Mumford et al., 2014), creative thinking skills (e.g., Mumford et al., 2002, 2003), creative process management skills (e.g., Basadur, 2004; Reiter-Palmon & Illies, 2004), awareness of temporal complexity (e.g.,

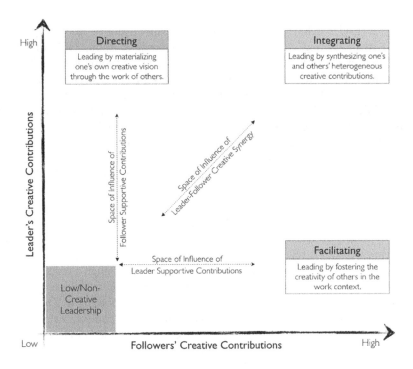

Source: Reproduced with permission from Mainemelis et al. (2015: 401).

Figure 6.1   The multi-context framework of creative leadership

Halbesleben et al., 2003), and emotional intelligence (e.g., Zhou & George, 2003). Three recent conceptual contributions have proposed that facilitative creative leaders should also possess emotional complexity (Rothman & Melwani, 2017), the ability to flexibly switch between regulatory foci (Kark & Van Dijk, 2019), and the ability to effectively channel complex interactions among four dimensions of diversity in teams into higher degrees of team creativity (Kakarika, 2018). In another recent conceptual contribution, Mumford et al. (2018) proposed that leaders must have five sets of skills (creative thinking skills, forecasting, causal analysis skills, constraint analysis skill, and wisdom) in order to effectively execute three dimensions of creative leadership functions: leading the work, leading the people, and leading the firm.

Behavioral Perspectives

Research on leader behaviors has stressed the positive role of leader support in employee creativity (e.g., Amabile et al., 2004; George & Zhou, 2007; Lin et al., 2016; Madjar et al., 2002; Oldham & Cummings, 1996). Specific leader behaviors that have been found to impact employee creativity include assigned goals (e.g., Litchfield et al., 2011; Shalley, 1991, 1995; Sutton & Hargadon, 1996), monitoring (e.g., Amabile et al., 2004; Choi et al., 2009; George & Zhou, 2001; Zhou, 2003), expected evaluation (e.g., Shalley & Perry-Smith, 2001; Shalley, 1995; Yuan & Zhou, 2008), feedback (e.g., George & Zhou, 2001; Mumford et al., 2014; Zhou, 1998, 2003, 2008), playfulness (e.g., Andriopoulos & Gotsi, 2005; Mainemelis & Ronson, 2006; Statler et al., 2009, 2011), empowerment (e.g., Sun et al., 2012; Zhang & Bartol, 2010), authentic leader behaviors (e.g., Rego et al., 2012, 2014), ethical leader behaviors (e.g., Gu et al., 2015; Tu & Lu, 2013), and leader's social network ties (e.g., Elkins & Keller, 2003; Venkataramani et al., 2014).

Recently, Zhang et al. (2018) found that access to resources and organization-based self-esteem mediate the relationship between empowering leadership and employee creativity. Another interesting finding in that study is that although a moderate level of empowering leadership may facilitate employee creativity, excessive empowerment from the leader may not bring additional benefits. According to Zhang et al. (2018), this is because too much leader empowerment may generate risks, such as a lack of managerial control, not enough guidance from the leader, or increased work burden and ambiguity for employees. In another recent study of research and development teams, Zhang and Kwan (2018) found that the positive relationship between empowering leadership and team creativity is mediated by team creative efficacy and team learning behavior, and that these relationships are moderated by team task complexity.

A set of recent studies has examined the role of leader humility in team creativity. Hu et al. (2018) found that leader humility indirectly contributes to team creativity through promoting team members' information exchange, but not through psychological safety climate. Hu et al. (2018) also found that in teams with low power distance, leader humility was positively related to team information seeking but had no significant relation to team psychological safety; while in high power distance teams, leader humility was not related to team information sharing, but was negatively related to team psychological safety. In another study, Wang et al. (2020) found that leader humility promotes team creativity through team creative efficacy, and leader conscientiousness moderates this indirect effect. Other recent studies have examined the role of leaders' listening behavior (Castro et al., 2018), leaders' role in building a culture that encourages employees' "speaking up" (Cunha et al., 2019), and the role that formal visionary leadership plays in the relationship between an employee's proactive personality and their creativity via informal leadership status (Pan et al., 2018).

Relational Perspectives

Past research has found that the leader–follower relation plays an important role in employee creativity (e.g., Atwater & Carmeli, 2009; Clegg et al., 2002; Liao et al., 2010; Olsson et al., 2012; Volmer et al., 2012). A meta-analysis by Hammond et al. (2011) reported a moderate relationship ($r = 0.29$) between leader–member exchange (LMX) and innovative performance. Responding to the scholarly call for greater relational focus in LMX research (e.g., Mainemelis et al., 2015: 420), Stephens and Carmeli (2017) recently proposed a conceptual model of the complex relationships among relational leadership, thriving, meaningfulness in and at work, and individual involvement in creative work.

Transformational Perspectives

The relationship between transformational leadership and employee creativity has gained support from empirical studies (e.g., Eisenbeiss et al., 2008; Kark & Van Dijk, 2007; Ling et al., 2008; Shin & Zhou, 2003). Two meta-analyses by Hammond et al. (2011) and Wang et al. (2011) found positive moderate relationships between transformational leadership and creative performance ($r = 0.13$ and $r = 0.21$, respectively). To date, research has identified many mechanisms through which transformational leadership impacts employee creativity, such as followers' creative self-efficacy (Gong et al., 2009); followers' work engagement, experienced meaningfulness of work, and experienced responsibility for work outcomes (Aryee et al., 2012); educational specialization heterogeneity in the team's composition (Shin & Zhou, 2007); followers' self-regulatory focus as enhancing or hindering creativity (promotion versus prevention; Kark et al., 2018); and team empowerment climate (Si & Wei, 2012). Another meta-analysis by Rosing et al. (2011) showed that transformational leadership may be more effective at the initial opening-up stages of the creative process, whereas transactional leadership may be more effective in the subsequent stages of idea implementation. Furthermore, earlier studies showed that transactional leadership enhances prevention focus motivation, which in turn contributes to the reduction of creativity; and that it is easier for transformational leaders to reduce prevention, which in turn hinders creativity, than it is to enhance creativity. Thus, leaders may be more likely to hold back creativity than to encourage it, at the individual level as well as at the team level (e.g., Kark et al., 2018; Van Dijk et al., 2020).

Van Knippenberg and Sitkin (2013) and Antonakis and House (2014) identified important definitional, conceptual, and methodological limitations of transformational leadership theory and research. An additional point of concern is that empirical evidence for the role of transformational leadership in fostering team creativity and innovation has been scarce and mixed (Anderson et al., 2014). In an attempt to address some of these limitations, Dong et al. (2017) recently analyzed the multi-level influences of dual-focused transformational leadership on employee creativity. They found that individual-focused transformational leadership had an indirect effect on individual creativity via individual skill development; whereas team knowledge sharing partially mediated the relationship between team-focused transformational leadership and team creativity. They suggested that leader behaviors such as providing customized coaching and setting high expectations may not necessarily lead directly to employee creativity. Rather, the leader can provide opportunities for individual team members to develop the task-related knowledge and capabilities needed for creativity, which then prepare and enable them to step up to the creativity work requirements and to more effectively produce creative outcomes.

In three recent literature reviews of research in facilitating creative leadership contexts, Mumford et al. (2017), Shalley and Lemoine (2018), and Thayer et al. (2018) concluded that leaders and leader behaviors may be the most important contextual influences on the success of creative efforts in organizations. In a recent meta-analysis of 266 studies, Lee et al. (2020) found that 13 leadership variables (transformational, transactional, ethical, humble, leader–member exchange, benevolent, authoritarian, entrepreneurial, authentic, servant, empowering, supportive, and destructive), had significant associations with creativity or/and innovation. Lee et al. (2020) suggested that it is possible that any of these 13 leadership variables can help to leverage followers' creativity and innovation; or alternatively, that many of these 13 variables are redundant and their assessment assesses overall attitudes regarding leaders rather than actual behaviors.

Shalley and Lemoine (2018) noted that, given that the field has long assumed creativity to be infrequent or even rare, it seems contradictory to conclude that virtually anything a leader does fosters employee creativity. They offer three possible explanations for this paradox: firstly, creativity may not be as rare as the field has thought, especially in contexts where most cases of employee creativity represent incremental forms of creativity; secondly, there may be a methodological halo-like effect, where evaluations of leaders' behaviors inadvertently tap creative characteristics or processes themselves; and thirdly, the outcomes of leadership and the antecedents of creativity may be very similar. Shalley and Lemoine (2018) noted that all three views have some merit, and they urged future research to focus more sharply on whether, when, and under which conditions a specific leader behavior might impact followers' creativity.

CREATIVE LEADERSHIP IN DIRECTING CONTEXTS

Research conducted in directing contexts tends to view leaders as primary creators who materialize their creative vision through other people's work. Mainemelis et al. (2015: 426) clarified that "If the generation of a creative idea is the hallmark of individual creative thinking, the hallmark of Directive creative leadership is the materialization of a creative idea through inspiring, eliciting, and integrating others' high-quality supportive contributions." While facilitative contexts pose *ex ante* upon leaders the normative expectation to foster the creativity of followers, directive contexts pose *ex ante* upon leaders the normative expectation to generate and effectively communicate a compelling creative vision to the followers. Mainemelis et al. (2015)

found that directive creative leadership is less common than facilitative creative leadership, and that it appears in some specific contexts, such as haute cuisine, symphony orchestras, and episodic top-down corporate innovation.

Past research has suggested that directive creative leaders must possess intelligence, creativity, and wisdom (e.g., Faulkner, 1973a; Mumford et al., 2000; Selznick, 1984 [1957]; Sternberg, 2003). In a recent study, Qin et al. (2019) found that leader creative mindset is associated with state-based moral disengagement, which leads in turn to abusive supervision. Considering that directive creative leaders are normatively expected to act as primary master-creators, wisdom is a particularly important quality that protects them from manifesting negative creativity and abusive supervision. Recently, Sternberg (2018) noted that, because creativity has dark sides, leaders often fail because they lack ethics rather than creativity or intelligence. Sternberg's (2018) proposed a conceptual model which posits that leadership that is both good and effective is a function of creativity in generating ideas, analytical intelligence in evaluating the quality of these ideas, practical intelligence in implementing the ideas, and wisdom to ensure that the decisions and their implementation help to achieve a common good for the greater community.

To date, research on directive creative leadership has focused on the importance of articulating a compelling creative vision for the followers (e.g., Bouty & Gomez, 2010; Conger, 1995; Eisenmann & Bower, 2000; Selznick, 1984 [1957]); the role of followers' evaluation of the competence and inspirational ability of the leader (e.g., Bennis, 2003; Faulkner, 1973b; Hunt et al., 2004); the intimate and challenging relationship between the personal and professional identities of the directive creative leader, who often represents publicly the creative identity of the organization (e.g., Gomez & Bouty, 2011; Messeni Petruzzelli & Savino, 2014; Svejenova et al., 2007, 2014); and the role of the leader's social, symbolic, and technical capital (e.g., Gomez & Bouty, 2011; Jones, 2010, 2011; Marotto et al., 2007). Research has also investigated the dynamics of creative freedom (e.g., Svejenova et al., 2007, 2010), apprenticeship (e.g, Bouty & Gomez, 2010; Stierand, 2015), and creative entrapment of the followers of directive creative leaders (e.g., Faulkner, 1973b).

While research in facilitating contexts tends to focus on how the average person engages creatively with a task in a work context that may not depend primarily on creativity, Bouty et al. (2018) recently proposed a theoretical foundation that is more sensitively attuned to the practices of highly creative leaders in work contexts requiring substantial degrees of creativity. They suggested that haute cuisine chefs direct their team through enabling (configuring the creative space to set the conditions of creative work), orientating (managing creative work to keep it abounded and focused), and complying (assessing ideas to select those that fit). Bouty et al. (2018) posit that the practices of enabling, orientating, and complying are interrelated in nonlinear, non-stable, and often "fuzzy" ways.

In another recent contribution, Svejenova (2018) observed that in the context of artistic innovation the emphasis is less on leading others and more on leading time. Analyzing the creativity of Joan Miro, Svejenova distinguishes between time patterning, the temporal infrastructure of the artist's creative practice that entails different tensions, and temporality work, which involves cultivating serendipity and surprise, extending events' duration, stepping into new temporalities, and considering potentiality. Svejenova (2018) argues that time patterning provides a scaffolding for steady creative work and experimentation; whereas temporal work ensures the materialization of a creative world of novel signs, symbols, and forms. Svejenova's work opens new ways for studying the interplay among directive creative leadership, novelty, and different dimensions of temporality.

CREATIVE LEADERSHIP IN INTEGRATING CONTEXTS

Research in integrating contexts tends to examine forms of creative production that synthesize heterogeneous creative inputs by a number of diverse creative professionals. Creative leaders in such contexts are expected to act as primary creators who generate and materialize their creative vision, but also to elicit and integrate the heterogeneous creative contributions of other professionals into a final creative product. In integrating contexts the creative inputs of different contributors are not always blended, but they may often be discerned in the final creative product (Simonton, 2004). Mainemelis et al. (2015) found that the integrating context appears in the literature in three variants: the film or theatrical director who works intensively with a team for a short period of time; the creative broker who synthesizes creative inputs whose production is usually dispersed in time and space; and work contexts wherein the generation and integration of creative inputs is not achieved by a single leader but by more complex forms of collective leadership.

Research on integrative contexts has focused on how professional role structures influence creative leadership (e.g., Baker & Faulkner, 1991; Bechky, 2006), how creative leaders protect their creative freedom (e.g., Alvarez et al., 2005; Mainemelis et al., 2016), the role that leaders play in the attraction and selection of the members of temporary teams (e.g., Delmestri et al., 2005; Lampel & Shamsie, 2003; Perretti & Negro, 2007), and the role that creative vision (e.g., Dunham & Freeman, 2000; Mainemelis & Epitropaki, 2013; Murphy & Ensher, 2008) and the ability to inspire creative performances (e.g., Faulkner & Anderson, 1987; Murphy & Ensher, 2008) play in crafting a final creative product. Integrative creative leadership research has also examined the role of charismatic leadership (e.g., Dunham & Freeman, 2000; Epitropaki & Mainemelis, 2016), and the importance of the leader's social, symbolic, and technical capital (e.g., Delmestri et al., 2005; Ferriani et al., 2005; Lingo & O'Mahony, 2010; Obstfeld, 2012).

Integrative creative leadership research has welcomed five new contributions that develop it conceptually. Building on the concept of creative synthesis (Harvey, 2014), Harvey et al. (2018) discussed how creative leaders shape and help to materialize a creative vision by drawing out and then enabling integration of group members' diverse inputs. Harvey et al's (2018) process model of leading for creative synthesis consists of three phases: marshalling resources, helping groups to engage in the process facilitators through leader behaviors, and facilitating feedback from the external environment. Harvey et al. (2018) explicate how integrative creative leaders use constraints, boundaries, and other variability reduction practices to help the group generate and integrate ideas. Overall, Harvey et al.'s model places a strong emphasis on collective leadership and on what individual leaders can do to enable collective leadership and creative synthesis.

While Harvey et al. (2018) focused on less dispersed and more temporally stable organizational groups, Lingo (2018) has examined shorter creative projects undertaken by temporary and dispersed networks of heterogeneous professionals. In such contexts, leaders are expected to generate new ideas, elicit new ideas from others, and synthesize new ideas into a cohesive whole, while facing ambiguity over quality, ambiguous occupational jurisdictions, and ambiguity regarding process. Lingo (2018) argued that integrative creative leaders navigate these tensions by engaging in creative brokerage in order to manage the three types of ambiguity, elicit creative contributions, and maintain the commitment of those involved. Building upon the study of Nashville country music producers by Lingo and O'Mahony (2010), Lingo's (2018) process model of integrative creative leadership focuses on four primary phases of the collective creative process: resource gathering, defining project boundaries, creative production, and final synthesis.

Litchfield and Gilson (2018) suggested that creative leaders can achieve higher-level synthesis also by rearranging others' past individual creative products into novel creative collections. Elaborating upon their earlier work on curatorial creativity (e.g., Litchfield & Gilson, 2013; Gilson & Litchfield, 2017), Litchfield and Gilson (2018) analyzed the comparative advantages of curatorial creative leadership over the idea championing and the portfolio management perspectives.

Two other recent contributions focus on the commonalities and differences of various expressions of integrative creative leadership. Observing that scientific breakthroughs to treat complex and intractable diseases depend on a collaborative approach to medical research and practice, Salazar et al. (2019) argued that leaders with integrative capabilities will have greater success in helping disciplinary diverse teams to overcome the obstacles of cross-boundary collaboration. Salazar et al. (2019) proposed a theoretical model that links common integrative leadership capabilities and team emergent states to individual and organizational creative performance outcomes.

In contrast, in their analysis of six acclaimed film directors, Flocco et al. (2018) focus on sources of variability among integrative creative leaders. Filmmaking is an integrative context of creative leadership par excellence, where the film director has to elicit, orient, and integrate the highly heterogeneous inputs of multiple non-similar professionals into a coherent whole, the final cut. However, while the final cut is a collective effort, the act of integrating heterogeneous inputs could be done solely by the director in an autocratic manner, or it could be shared with others in a more democratic manner. Flocco et al. identified seven factors that can help to explain why different directors occupy different locations on the autocratic–democratic continuum: the director's personality; the temporality of involvement of others in crafting the creative vision; director's degree of secrecy; directors' tendency to work with the same crew and cast across different movies; consolidation of roles by the director; the film's technological sophistication; and the production template of the filmmaking process. Flocco et al.'s (2018) work brings a rare and valuable integration of contextual and styles approaches to the study of integrative creative leadership.

Integrative creative leadership has also studied contexts where creative leadership is shared, be it in collective (e.g., Hargadon & Bechky, 2006; Harvey, 2014; Harvey & Kou, 2013), rotating (e.g., Davis and Eisenhardt, 2011), improvisational (e.g., Barrett, 1998; Vera & Crossan, 2004), or dual form (e.g., Hunter et al., 2012; Sicca, 1997; Reid & Karambayya, 2009). In a recent study of the social practices that underpinned the making of a new television production by the Australian Broadcasting Corporation and several partnering organizations and freelance artists, Dovey et al. (2017) identified three leadership practices – wise partnering, collective visioning, and stakeholder empowerment – which fostered dialogue, collective critical reflexivity, and "soft power" relational practices that allowed creative license to the diverse professionals and units employed in the production. A related and critical question in collective leadership contexts is how creative leaders emerged in the first place. Recently, Lee and Farh (2019) found that creative leadership emergence in such contexts is shaped by the type of contributions members express (constructive versus supportive), when those contributions are expressed (idea generation versus idea enactment phase), and the extent to which fellow teammates express constructive or supportive contributions themselves.

Other recent studies have stressed that collective leadership is not synonymous with eliminating the role of the focal leader. Friedrich et al. (2016) tested a set of hypotheses about how individual differences among leaders, the team's network, and problem situation characteristics influence three collective leadership behaviors: communication, network development, and leader–team exchange. Moreover, observing that creative leaders have to manage a broad range of activities that are often at odds with one another, Hunter et al. (2017, 2018) argued that the resulting role conflict hampers creative production by causing strain, stress, and uncertainty on the leaders and the followers. Hunter et al. (2017, 2019) suggested that the tensions and paradoxes of creativity can be tackled through dual leadership, whereby two individuals share the leadership workload and through coordinated efforts engage subordinates toward the accomplishment of the often disparate goals characterizing the generation and implementation of novel ideas. Hunter et al. (2017, 2019) also discuss in detail the challenges, limitations, and opportunities associated with dual forms of creative leadership.

WORKING WITH THE MULTI-CONTEXT FRAMEWORK

Over the years, several scholars have noted that a persistent weakness of research on creativity and leadership is its low contextual sensitivity (Blair & Hunt, 1986; Johns, 2006; Liden & Antonakis, 2009; Thomson et al., 2007), especially with regard to the organizational context (Heath & Sitkin, 2001; Rousseau & Fried, 2001).

The multi-context framework addresses this long-standing criticism in the field by unifying three distinct conceptualizations of creative leadership that reflect essential contextual differences.

The tripartite multi-context model can be used as a metatheoretical tool for revealing significant patterns of contextual variability in creative leadership research. For example, Mainemelis (2018) recently posed the question: What exactly is "organizational" about the facilitating, directing, and integrating contexts of creative leadership? He proposed that the emergence of the three contexts is shaped by different configurations of six dimensions of organizational conditions: strategic role of creativity; functional role of creativity; key learning mode; structure; size; key location in the social structure; and perceived importance of the role of creativity in leadership. Mainemelis (2018) proposed that different configurations of these six organizational conditions place upon leaders and followers different *ex ante* normative expectations about making creative and supportive contributions to the collaborative creative process, and that these *ex ante* normative expectations ultimate influence the emergence of facilitative, directive, or integrative creative leadership.

In another recent conceptual elaboration of the multi-context framework, Epitropaki et al. (2018) observed that in the socio-cognitive domain of leadership perceptions and schemas, leadership and creativity remain not only separate but also contradictory notions. They suggested that connectionist models in the implicit leadership theories (ILTs) literature highlight the context-sensitive, dynamic, and flexible nature of schemas and thus allow for both stability and flexibility of implicit leadership and implicit creativity theories. Epitropaki et al. (2018) proposed that creativity will be automatically activated as a salient trait of leadership in organizational contexts where creativity is a desired quality, innovation is a key strategic objective, positive emotions prevail, and organizational members see themselves as creators. They suggested that this is more likely in directive and integrative creative leadership contexts, where the leader has a strong creator identity, makes visible creative contributions, and creativity and innovation are key strategic objectives of the work contexts. In contrast, they argued that a convergence between creativity and leadership is less likely to occur in facilitative contexts of creative leadership where there is limited requirement for creative contributions on behalf of the leader.

Mainemelis et al. (2015) observed that collaborative contexts can be thought of as falling on a continuum from weakly to strongly structured in terms of how the opportunities for making creative contributions are distributed among the members of the collaborative context. In "strong" contexts, the distribution of opportunities for creative contributions commences long before leaders and followers start collaborating. This happens in part because of the pre-existing organizational conditions (Mainemelis, 2018) and schemas (Epitropaki et al., 2018) discussed earlier. In contrast, in "weak" contexts, leaders (and at times followers) have relatively higher degrees of freedom to determine whether creative leadership will be manifested in the form of facilitating, directing, or integrating. Steele et al.'s (2017) recent recommendation that it is vital for leaders to understand well the motivational and personality profiles of followers, as well as the specific types, behaviors, and outcomes of creativity being sought, is particularly important for prospective leaders in "weak" contexts.

In a recent ethnographic study with chorographers, Abecassis-Moedas and Gilson (2017) examined the drivers of leader behavior, and they found that choreographers had substantial freedom to shape the collaborative context in either a directive or an integrative manner. An interesting observation in their study is that no choreographer acted as a facilitative leader, which implies that contextual pressures play a role even in relatively "weak" contexts. As Abecassis-Moedas and Gilson (2017) note, directive and integrative creative leadership tend to be prevalent across several segments of the arts. Similarly, in another recent interview study with designer Johannes Torpe, Stierand et al. (2020) observed that directive and integrative forms of creative leadership may be more prevalent in segments of the industrial and product design industry where it is desirable to allow consumers, users, and peers to discern the creative identity of the individual designer in the final creative product.

There are also contexts that are so weakly structured in terms of *ex ante* normative expectations that the ensuing collaboration may not include clear or stable patterns of creative leadership. For instance, Svejenova and Christiansen (2018) analyzed an architectural project that aimed to catalyze social change through the design and construction of a new housing model. Unlike the directive forms of creative leadership previously observed among cases of famous creative architects (e.g., Bennis, 2003; Jones, 2010, 2011), the large-scale and highly atypical nature of the project studied by Svejenova and Christiansen (2018) appeared to encompass at different times different expressions of creative leadership.

Mainemelis et al. (2015) noted that changing contextual conditions may trigger a switch between creative contexts. Cunha et al.'s (2017) recent study of the evolution of the independent music label 4AD provides intriguing insights about how the growth and expansion of a new firm exerted considerable pressures upon the identity of its founder, who found it increasingly difficult after a point in time to function as a directive creative leader. Cunha et al. (2017) hence raise a larger question about an underexplored area of creative leadership: namely, the temporal stability of the facilitating, directing, and integrating manifestations.

As shown in Figure 6.1, besides the three manifestations of creative leadership discussed above, the multi-context framework also identifies a fourth possibility: low-/ noncreative leadership. This raises the equally important question of what leads to the emergence of any form of creative leadership in the first place (Gilson & Davis, 2019). Randel and Jaussi (2019) recently proposed a model that articulates the contextual factors (enablers and redundancies) and personal factors (leader's motivation to lead for creativity) that interact to increase the likelihood of creative leadership as opposed to low-/noncreative leadership. Randel and Jaussi's (2019) model also articulates some contextual conditions that may differentially affect the subsequent emergence of facilitative, directive, or integrative creative leadership.

Additional insights on what triggers creative leadership can be gained by adopting an events-based perspective (Morgeson et al., 2015). Disruptive events of high novelty and criticality (such as a pandemic) can be conducive to the emergence of creative leadership forms. For example, Chen et al. (2018) have found disruptive event characteristics (that is, event novelty and criticality) and employee learning orientation to jointly influence employees' creativity via employees' improvisational responses. In the presence of disruptive events, the creativity of learning-goal-oriented employees increased. Thus, facilitative creative leadership may emerge in these conditions to facilitate the creative contributions of followers.

Disruptive events and major crises many times fuel organization innovation in terms of business models, strategies, products, and services (e.g., Archibugi et al., 2013). They may therefore trigger emergence of directive creative leadership (mainly in the form of top-down innovation). Novel and critical events also pose complex problems and grand challenges that require collective creative solutions (e.g., Gilla, 2003; Harvey, 2014). Integrating creative leadership can help to tackle such complex problems by harnessing the creative contributions of both leaders and followers. Thus, a closer look at disruptive events (for example, novelty, criticality), as well as the event space, can perhaps offer us a more nuanced understanding of creative leadership triggers.

In conclusion, the multi-context framework allows creativity and innovation researchers to identify similarities and differences in how creative leadership is manifested and studied across contexts. For example, creativity leadership appears to play a crucial role in the accomplishment of creative outcomes by individuals, teams, and organizations across all three contexts. On the other hand, research on directive contexts tends to set the magnitude and time frame of creativity, as well as the responsibility of the creative leader, much higher than the other two contexts (Mainemelis et al., 2018). Moreover, while research on facilitative contexts tends to rely on variance-based approaches, research on integrative contexts utilizes more process-based methodologies. Kark et al. (2020) recently identified several differences among the methodologies employed by different research strands that study creativity in different contexts. They concluded that the choice of different methodologies is often related to the contextual particularities of each of the three manifestations of creative leadership. Attending to and learning from such patterned conceptual and methodological differences can help the field to improve its cross-pollination of scientific knowledge and insight across various research strands, and ultimately to develop more nuanced and more contextual sensitive theories of creative leadership.

REFERENCES

Abecassis-Moedas, C., & Gilson, L.L. 2017. Drivers and levels of creative leadership: an examination of choreographers as directive and integrative leaders. *Innovation: Organization and Management*, 20: 122–138.
Alvarez, J.L., Mazza, C., Pedersen, J.S., & Svejenova, S. 2005. Shielding idiosyncracy from isomorphic pressures: Towards optimal distinctiveness in European filmmaking. *Organization*, 12: 863–888.

Amabile, T.M. 1988. A model of creativity and innovation in organizations. *Research in Organizational Behavior*, 10: 123–167.

Amabile, T.M., Conti, R., Coon, H., Lazenby, J., & Herron, M. 1996. Assessing the work environment for creativity. *Academy of Management Journal*, 39: 1154–1184.

Amabile, T.M., Schatzel, E.A., Moneta, G.B., & Kramer, S.J. 2004. Leader behaviors and the work environment for creativity: Perceived leader support. *Leadership Quarterly*, 15: 5–32.

Anderson, N., Potočnik, K., & Zhou, J. 2014. Innovation and creativity in organizations: A state-of-the-science review, prospective commentary, and guiding framework. *Journal of Management*, 40: 1297–1333.

Andriopoulos, C., & Gotsi, M. 2005. The virtues of "blue-sky" projects: How lunar design taps into the power of imagination. *Creativity and Innovation Management*, 14: 316–324.

Antonakis, J., & House, R.J. 2014. Instrumental leadership: Measurement and extension of transformational–transactional leadership theory. *Leadership Quarterly*, 25: 746–771.

Archibugi, D., Filippetti, A., & Frenz, M. 2013. Economic crisis and innovation: Is destruction prevailing over accumulation? *Research Policy*, 42: 303–314.

Aryee, S., Walumbwa, F.O., Zhou, Q., & Hartnell, C.A. 2012. Transformational leadership, innovative behavior, and task performance: Test of mediation and moderation processes. *Human Performance*, 25: 1–25.

Atwater, L., & Carmeli, A. 2009. Leader–member exchange, feelings of energy, and involvement in creative work. *Leadership Quarterly*, 20: 264–275.

Baker, W.E., & Faulkner, R.R. 1991. Role as resource in the Hollywood film industry. *American Journal of Sociology*, 97: 279–309.

Barrett, F.J. 1998. Creativity and improvisation in jazz and organizations: Implications for organizational learning. *Organization Science*, 9: 605–622.

Basadur, M. 2004. Leading others to think innovatively together: Creative leadership. *Leadership Quarterly*, 15: 103–121.

Bechky, B.A. 2006. Gaffers, gofers, and grips: Role-based coordination in temporary organizations. *Organization Science*, 17: 3–21.

Bennis, W. 2003. Frank Gehry: Artist, leader, and "neotenic." *Journal of Management Inquiry*, 12: 81–87.

Blair, J.D., & Hunt, J.G. 1986. Getting inside the head of the management researcher one more time: Context-free and context-specific orientations in research. *Journal of Management*, 12: 147–166.

Bouty, I., & Gomez, M.-L. 2010. Dishing up individual and collective dimensions in organizational knowing. *Management Learning*, 41: 545–559.

Bouty, I., Gomez, M-L., & Stierand, M. 2018. The creative leadership practices of haute cuisine chefs. In C. Mainemelis, O. Epitropaki, and R. Kark (eds), *Creative leadership: Contexts and prospects*: 156–170. New York: Routledge.

Castro, D.R., Anseel, F., Kluger, A.N., Lloyd, K.J., & Turjeman-Levi, Y. 2018. Mere listening effect on creativity and the mediating role of psychological safety. *Psychology of Aesthetics, Creativity, and the Arts*, 12: 489–502.

Chen, Y., Tang, G., Liu, D., & Hogan, T.M. 2018. *When and how disruptive events fuel creativity*. Paper presented at Academy of Management, Chicago, IL.

Choi, J.N., Anderson, T.A., & Veillette, A. 2009. Contextual inhibitors of employee creativity in organizations: The insulating role of creative ability. *Group and Organization Management*, 34, 330–357.

Clegg, C., Unsworth, K., Epitropaki, O., & Parker, G. 2002. Implicating trust in the innovation process. *Journal of Occupational and Organizational Psychology*, 75: 409–422.

Conger, J.A. 1995. Boogie down wonderland: Creativity and visionary leadership. In C.M. Ford & D.A. Gioia (eds), *Creative action in organizations*: 53–59. Thousand Oaks, CA: SAGE.

Cunha, M.P.E., Giustiniano, L., & Rego, A. 2017. "Heaven or Las Vegas": Competing institutional logics and individual experience. *European Management Review*, 16: 781–798.

Cunha, M.P.E., Simpson, A.V., Clegg, S.R., & Rego, A. 2019. Speak! Paradoxical effects of a managerial culture of "speaking up." *British Journal of Management*, 30: 829–846.

Davis, J.P., & Eisenhardt, K.M. 2011. Rotating leadership and collaborative innovation: Recombination processes in symbiotic relationships. *Administrative Science Quarterly*, 56: 159–201.

Delmestri, G., Montanari, F., & Usai, A. 2005. Reputation and strength of ties in predicting commercial success and artistic merit of independents in the Italian feature film industry. *Journal of Management Studies*, 42: 975–1002.

Dinh, J.E., Lord, R.G., Gardner, W.L., Meuser, J.D., Liden, R.C., & Hu, J. 2014. Leadership theory and research in the new millennium: Current theoretical trends and changing perspectives. *Leadership Quarterly*, 25: 36–62.

Dong, Y., Bartol, K.M., Zhang, Z-X., & Li, C. 2017. Enhancing employee creativity via individual skill development and team knowledge sharing: Influences of dual-focused transformational leadership. *Journal of Organizational Behavior*, 38: 439–458.

Dovey, K., Burdon, R., & Simpson, R. 2017. Creative leadership as a collective achievement: An Australian case. *Management Learning*, 48: 23–28.

Dunham, L., & Freeman, R.E. 2000. There is business like show business: Leadership lessons from the theatre. *Organizational Dynamics*, 29: 108–122.

Eisenbeiss, S.A., van Knippenberg, D., & Boerner, S. 2008. Transformational leadership and team innovation: Integrating team climate principles. *Journal of Applied Psychology*, 93: 1438–1446.

Eisenmann, T.R., & Bower, J.L. 2000. The entrepreneurial M-form: Strategic integration in global media firms. *Organization Science*, 11: 348–355.

Elkins, T., & Keller, R.T. 2003. Leadership in research and development organizations: A literature review and conceptual framework. *Leadership Quarterly*, 14: 587–606.

Epitropaki, O., & Mainemelis, C. 2016. The "genre bender": The creative leadership of Kathryn Bigelow. In C. Peus, S. Braun, & B. Schyns (eds), *Leadership lessons from compelling contexts*: 275–300. Bigley: Emerald Group Publishing.

Epitropaki, O., Mueller, J.S., & Lord, R.G. 2018. Unpacking the socio-cognitive foundations of creative leadership: Bridging implicit leadership and implicit creativity theories. In C. Mainemelis, O. Epitropaki, and R. Kark (eds), *Creative leadership: Contexts and prospects*: 40–55. New York: Routledge.

Faulkner, R.R. 1973a. Orchestra interaction: Some features of communication and authority in an artistic organization. *Sociological Quarterly*, 14: 147–157.

Faulkner, R.R. 1973b. Career concerns and mobility motivations of orchestra musicians. *Sociological Quarterly*, 14: 334–349.

Faulkner, R.R., & Anderson, A.B. 1987. Short-term projects and emergent careers: Evidence from Hollywood. *American Journal of Sociology*, 92: 879–909.

Ferriani, S., Corrado, R., & Boschetti, C. 2005. Organizational learning under organizational impermanence: Collaborative ties in film project firms. *Journal of Management and Governance*, 9: 257–285.

Flocco, N., Canterino, F., Cirella, S., Coget, J.-F., & Shani, A.B.R. 2018. Exploring integrative creative leadership in the filmmaking industry. In C. Mainemelis, O. Epitropaki, & R. Kark (eds), *Creative leadership: Contexts and prospects*: 244–258. New York: Routledge.

Ford, C.M. 1996. A theory of individual creative action in multiple social domains. *Academy of Management Review*, 21: 1112–1142.

Friedrich, T.L., Griffith, J.A., & Mumford, M.D. 2016. Collective leadership behaviors: Evaluating the leader, team network, and problem situation characteristics that influence their use. *Leadership Quarterly*, 27: 312–333.

George, J.M., & Zhou, J. 2001. When openness to experience and conscientiousness are related to creative behavior: An interactionist approach. *Journal of Applied Psychology*, 86: 513–524.

George, J.M., & Zhou, J. 2007. Dual tuning in a supportive context: Joint contributions of positive mood, negative mood, and supervisory behaviors to employee creativity. *Academy of Management Journal*, 50: 605–622.

Gilla, F. 2003. Collective creativity: A complex solution for the complex problem of the state of our planet. *Creativity Research Journal*, 15(1): 83–90.

Gilson, L.L., & Davis, W.D. 2019. Managing in an age of complexity and uncertainty. *Group and Organization Management*, 44: 243–246.

Gilson, L.L., & Litchfield, R.C. 2017. Idea collections: A link between creativity and innovation. *Innovation: Organization and Management*, 19: 80–85.

Gomez, M.-L., & Bouty, I. 2011. The emergence of an influential practice: Food for thought. *Organization Studies*, 32: 921–940.

Gong, Y., Huang, J., & Farh, J. 2009. Employee learning orientation, transformational leadership, and employee creativity: The mediating role of employee creative self-efficacy. *Academy of Management Journal*, 52: 765–778.

Gu, Q., Li-Ping Tang, T., & Jiang, W. 2015. Does moral leadership enhance employee creativity? Employee identification with leader and leader–member exchange (LMX) in the Chinese context. *Journal of Business Ethics*, 126: 513–529.

Halbesleben, J.R.B., Novicevic, M.M., Harvey, M.G., & Buckley, M.R. (2003). The influence of temporal complexity in the leadership of creativity and innovation: A competency-based model. *Leadership Quarterly*, 14: 433–454.

Hammond, M.M., Neff, N.I., Farr, J.L., Schwall, A.R., & Zhao, X. 2011. Predictors of individual-level innovation at work: A meta-analysis. *Psychology of Aesthetics, Creativity and the Arts*, 5: 90–105.

Hargadon, A.B., & Bechky, B.A. 2006. When collections of creatives become creative collectives: A field study of problem solving at work. *Organization Science*, 17: 484–500.

Harvey, S. 2014. Creative synthesis: Exploring the process of extraordinary group creativity. *Academy of Management Review*, 39: 324–343.

Harvey, S., & Kou, C.Y. 2013. Collective engagement in creative tasks: The role of evaluation in the creative process in groups. *Administrative Science Quarterly*, 58: 346–386.

Harvey, S., Kou, C-Y., & Xie, W. 2018. Leading for creative synthesis: A process-based model for creative leadership. In C. Mainemelis, O. Epitropaki, and R. Kark (eds), *Creative leadership: Contexts and prospects*: 191–207. New York: Routledge.

Heath, C., & Sitkin, S.B. 2001. Big-B versus Big-O: What is organizational about organizational behavior? *Journal of Organizational Behavior*, 22: 43–58.

Hu, J., Erdogan, B., Jiang, K., Bauer, T.N., & Liu, S. 2018. Leader humility and team creativity: The role of team information sharing, psychological safety, and power distance. *Journal of Applied Psychology*, 103: 313–323.

Hunt, J.G., Stelluto, G.E., & Hooijberg, R. 2004. Toward new-wave organizing creativity: Beyond romance and analogy in the relationship between orchestra-conducting leadership and musician creativity. *Leadership Quarterly*, 15: 145–162.

Hunter, S., Allen, J., Heinen, R., & Cushenbery, L. 2018. Proposing a multiple pathway approach to leading innovation: Single and dual leader approaches. In R. Reiter-Palmon, V.L. Kennel, & J.C. Kaufman (eds), *Individual creativity in the workplace*: 269–292. London: Academic Press.

Hunter, S.T., Cushenbery, L., Fairchild, J., & Boatman, J. 2012. Partnerships in leading for innovation: A dyadic model of collective leadership. *Industrial and Organizational Psychology: Perspectives on Science and Practice*, 5: 424–428.

Hunter, S., Cushenbery, L., & Jayne, B. 2017. Why dual leaders will drive innovation: Resolving the exploration and exploitation dilemma with a conservation of resources solution. *Journal of Organizational Behavior*, 38: 1183–1195.

Hunter, S.T., Thoroughgood, C.N., Myer, A.T., & Ligon, G.S. (2011). Paradoxes of leading innovative behaviors: Summary, solutions, and future directions. *Psychology of Aesthetics, Creativity, and the Arts*, 5: 54–66.

Johns, G. 2006. The essential impact of context on organizational behavior. *Academy of Management Review*, 31: 386–408.

Jones, C. 2010. Finding a place in history: Symbolic and social networks in creative careers and collective memory. *Journal of Organizational Behavior*, 31: 726–748.

Jones, C. 2011. Frank Lloyd Wright's artistic reputation: The role of networks and creativity. In C. Matthieu (ed.), *Careers in creative industries*: 151–162. New York: Routledge, Taylor & Francis.

Kakarika, M. 2018. Fostering the creativity of work teams: Creative leadership in the midst of diversity. In C. Mainemelis, O. Epitropaki, & R. Kark (eds), *Creative leadership: Contexts and prospects*: 122–136. New York: Routledge.

Kark, R., Epitropaki, O., & Mainemelis, C. 2020. It's all about context: Research methods of the multi-context framework of creative leadership. In V. Dörfler & M. Stierand (eds), *Handbook of research methods on creativity*: 46–66. Cheltenham, UK and Northhampton, MA, USA: Edward Elgar Publishing.

Kark, R., & Van Dijk, D. 2007. Motivation to lead, motivation to follow: The role of the self-regulatory focus in leadership processes. *Academy of Management Review*, 32: 500–528.

Kark, R., & Van Dijk, D. 2019. Keep your head in the clouds and your feet on the ground: A multifocal review of leadership–followership self-regulatory focus. *Academy of Management Annals*, 13: 509–546.

Kark, R., Van Dijk, D., & Vashdi, D. 2018. Motivated or de-motivated to be creative: The role of self-regulatory focus in transformational and transactional leadership processes. *Applied Psychology: An International Review*, 67: 186–224.

Lampel, J., & Shamsie, J. 2003. Capabilities in motion: New organizational forms and the reshaping of the Hollywood movie industry. *Journal of Management Studies*, 40: 2189–2210.

Lee, S.M., & Farh, C.I.C. 2019. Dynamic leadership emergence: Differential impact of members' and peers' contributions in the idea generation and idea enactment phases of innovation project teams. *Journal of Applied Psychology*, 104: 411–432.

Lee, A., Legood, A., Hughes, D., Tian, A.W., Newman, A., & Knight, C. 2020. Leadership, creativity and innovation: a meta-analytic review. *European Journal of Work and Organizational Psychology*, 29: 1–35.

Liao, H., Liu, D., & Loi, R. 2010. Looking at both sides of the social exchange coin: A social cognitive perspective on the joint effects of relationship quality and differentiation on creativity. *Academy of Management Journal*, 53: 1090–1109.

Liden, R.C., & Antonakis, J. 2009. Considering context in psychological leadership research. *Human Relations*, 62: 1587–1605.

Lin, B., Mainemelis, C., & Kark, R. 2016. Leaders' responses to creative deviance: Differential effects on subsequent creative deviance and creative performance. *Leadership Quarterly*, 4: 537–556.

Ling, Y., Simsek, Z., Lubatkin, M.H., & Veiga, J.F. 2008. Transformational leadership's role in promoting corporate entrepreneurship: Examining the CEO–TMT interface. *Academy of Management Journal*, 51: 557–576.

Lingo, E.L. 2018. Brokerage and creative leadership: Process, practice, and possibilities. In C. Mainemelis, O. Epitropaki, & R. Kark (eds), *Creative leadership: Contexts and prospects*: 208–227. New York: Routledge.

Lingo, E.L., & O'Mahony, S. 2010. Nexus work: Brokerage on creative projects. *Administrative Science Quarterly*, 55: 47–81.

Litchfield, R.C., Fan, J., & Brown, V.R. 2011. Directing idea generation using brainstorming with specific novelty goals. *Motivation and Emotion*, 35: 135–143.

Litchfield, R.C., & Gilson, L.L. 2013. Curating collections of ideas: Museum as metaphor in the management of creativity. *Industrial Marketing Management*, 42: 106–112.

Litchfield, R.C., & Gilson, L.L. 2018. A curatorial metaphor for creative leadership. In C. Mainemelis, O. Epitropaki, and R. Kark (eds), *Creative leadership: Contexts and prospects*: 228–243. New York: Routledge.

Madjar, N., Oldham, G.R., & Pratt, M.G. 2002. There's no place like home? The contributions of work and nonwork creativity support to employees' creative performance. *Academy of Management Journal*, 45: 757–767.

Mainemelis, C. 2018. On the relationship between creative leadership and contextual variability. In C. Mainemelis, O. Epitropaki, & R. Kark (eds) *Creative leadership: Contexts and prospects*: 23–38. New York: Routledge.

Mainemelis, C., & Epitropaki, O. 2013. Extreme leadership as creative leadership: Reflections on Francis Ford Coppola in The Godfather. In C. Giannantonio & A. Hurley-Hanson (eds), *Extreme Leadership: Leaders, Teams, and Situations Outside the Norm*: 187–200. Northampton, MA: Edward Elgar Publishing.

Mainemelis, C., Epitropaki, O., & Kark, R. 2018. Introduction: Connecting creative leadership's strands of research. In C. Mainemelis, O. Epitropaki, & R. Kark (eds), *Creative leadership: Contexts and prospects*: 3–22. New York: Routledge.

Mainemelis, C., Kark, R., & Epitropaki, O. 2015. Creative leadership: A multi-context conceptualization. *Academy of Management Annals*, 9: 393–482.

Mainemelis, C., Nolas, S.-M., & Tsirogianni, S. 2016. Surviving a boundaryless creative career: The case of Oscar-nominated film directors, 1967–2014. *Journal of Management Inquiry*, 25: 262–285.

Mainemelis, C., & Ronson, S. 2006. Ideas are born in fields of play: Towards a theory of play and creativity in organizational settings. *Research in Organizational Behavior*, 27: 81–131.

Marotto, M., Roos, J., & Victor, B. 2007. Collective virtuosity in organizations: A study of peak performance in an orchestra. *Journal of Management Studies*, 44: 388–413.

Messeni Petruzzelli, A., & Savino, T. 2014. Search, recombination, and innovation: Lessons from haute cuisine. *Long Range Planning*, 47: 224–238.

Morgeson, F.P., Mitchell, T.R., & Liu, D. 2015. Event system theory: An event-oriented approach to the organizational sciences. *Academy of Management Review*, 40: 515–537.

Mumford, M.D., Connelly, S., & Gaddis, B. 2003. How creative leaders think: Experimental findings and cases. *Leadership Quarterly*, 14: 411–432.

Mumford, M.D., Durban, C., Gujar, Y., Buck, J., & Todd, M. 2018. Leading creative efforts: Common functions and common skills. In C. Mainemelis, O. Epitropaki, & R. Kark (eds), *Creative leadership: Contexts and prospects*: 59–78. New York: Routledge.

Mumford, M.D., Hemlin, S., & Mulhearn, T.J. 2017. Leading for creativity: Functions, models, and domains. In M.D. Mumford and S. Hemlin (eds), *Handbook of research on leadership and creativity*: 1–14. Cheltenham, UK and Northampton, MA, USA: Edward Elgar Publishing.

Mumford, M.D., Gibson, C., Giorgini, V., & Mecca, J. 2014. Leading for creativity: People, products, and systems. In D. Day (ed.), *The Oxford handbook of leadership and organizations*: 754–779. New York: Oxford University Press.

Mumford, M.D., Marks, M.A., Connelly, M.S., Zaccaro, S.J., & Reiter-Palmon, R. 2000. Development of leadership skills: Experience and timing. *Leadership Quarterly*, 11: 87–114.

Mumford, M.D., Scott, G.M., Gaddis, B., & Strange, J.M. 2002. Leading creative people: Orchestrating expertise and relationships. *Leadership Quarterly*, 13: 705–750.

Murnighan, J.K., & Conlon, D.E. (1991). The dynamics of intense work groups: A study of British string quartets. *Administrative Science Quarterly*, 36: 165–186.

Murphy, S.E., & Ensher, E.A. 2008. A qualitative analysis of charismatic leadership in creative teams: The case of television directors. *Leadership Quarterly*, 19: 335–352.

Nemeth, C.J. 1997. Managing innovation: When less is more. *California Management Review*, 40: 59–74.

Obstfeld, D. 2012. Creative projects: A less routine approach toward getting new things done. *Organization Science*, 23: 1571–1592.

Oldham, G.R., & Cummings, A. 1996. Employee creativity: Personal and contextual factors at work. *Academy of Management Journal*, 39: 607–634.

Olsson, L., Hemlin, S., & Poussette, A. 2012. A multi-level analysis of leader-member exchange and creative performance in research groups. *Leadership Quarterly*, 23: 604–619.

Pan, J., Liu, S., Ma, B., & Qu, Z. 2018. How does proactive personality promote creativity? A multilevel examination of the interplay between formal and informal leadership. *Journal of Occupational and Organizational Psychology*, 91: 852–874.

Perretti, F., & Negro, G. 2007. Mixing genres and matching people: A study in innovation and team composition in Hollywood. *Journal of Organizational Behavior*, 28: 563–586.

Qin, X., Dust, S.B., DiRenzo, M.S., & Wang, S. 2019. Negative creativity in leader-follower relations: a daily investigation of leaders' creative mindset, moral disengagement, and abusive supervision. *Journal of Business and Psychology*, https://doi.org/10.1007/s10869 -019-09646-7.

Randel, A.E., & Jaussi, K.S. 2019. Giving rise to creative leadership: Contextual enablers and redundancies. *Group and Organization Management*, 44: 288–319.

Rego, A., Sousa, P., Marques, C., & Pina e Cunha, M. 2012. Authentic leadership promoting employees' psychological capital and creativity. *Journal of Business Research*, 65: 429–437.

Rego, A., Sousa, P., Marques, C., & Pina e Cunha, M. 2014. Hope and positive affect mediating the authentic leadership and creativity relationship. *Journal of Business Research*, 67: 200–210.

Reid, W., & Karambayya, R. 2009. Impact of dual executive leadership dynamics in creative organizations. *Human Relations*, 62: 1073–1112.

Reiter-Palmon, R., & Illies, J.J. 2004. Leadership and creativity: Understanding leadership from a creative problem-solving perspective. *Leadership Quarterly*, 15: 55–77.

Rickards, T., & Moger, S. (2000). Creative leadership processes in project team development: An alternative to Tuckman's stage model. *British Journal of Management*, 11: 273–283.

Rosing, K., Frese, M., & Bausch, A. 2011. Explaining the heterogeneity of the leadership–innovation relationship: Ambidextrous leadership. *Leadership Quarterly*, 22: 956–974.

Rothman, N.B., & Melwani, S. 2017. Feeling mixed, ambivalent, and in flux: The social functions of emotional complexity for leaders. *Academy of Management Review*, 43: 259–282.

Rousseau, D.M., & Fried, Y. 2001. Location, location, location: Contextualizing organizational research. *Journal of Organizational Behavior*, 22: 1–13.

Salazar, M.R., Widmer, K, Doiron, K., & Lant, T.K. 2019. Leader integrative capabilities: A catalyst for effective interdisciplinary teams. In K.L. Hall, A.L. Vogel, & R.T. Coyle (eds), *Strategies for team science success*: 313–328. Cham: Springer Nature.

Selznick, P. 1984 [1957]. *Leadership in administration*. Berkeley, CA: University of California Press.

Shalley, C.E. 1991. Effects of productivity goals, creativity goals, and personal discretion on individual creativity. *Journal of Applied Psychology*, 76: 179.

Shalley, C.E. 1995. Effects of coaction, expected evaluation, and goal setting on creativity and productivity. *Academy of Management Journal*, 38: 483–503.

Shalley, C.E., & Lemoine, G.J. 2018. Leader behaviors and employee creativity: Taking stock of the current state of research. In C. Mainemelis, O. Epitropaki, & R. Kark (eds), *Creative leadership: Contexts and prospects*: 79–94. New York: Routledge.

Shalley, C.E., & Perry-Smith, J.E. 2001. Effects of social-psychological factors on creative performance: The role of informational and controlling expected evaluation and modeling experience. *Organizational Behavior and Human Decision Processes*, 84: 1–22.

Shin, S.J., & Zhou, J. 2003. Transformational leadership, conservation and creativity: Evidence from Korea. *Academy of Management Journal*, 46: 703–714.

Shin, S.J., & Zhou, J. 2007. When is educational specialization heterogeneity related to creativity in research and development teams? Transformational leadership as a moderator. *Journal of Applied Psychology*, 92: 1709–1721.

Si, S., & Wei, F. 2012. Transformational leadership and transactional leaderships, empowerment climate, and innovation performance: A multilevel analysis in the Chinese context. *European Journal of Work and Organizational Psychology*, 21: 299–320.

Sicca, L.M. 1997. Management of opera houses: The Italian experience of the "Enti Autonomi." *International Journal of Cultural Policy*, 4: 201–224.

Simonton, D.K. 2004. Film awards as indicators of cinematic creativity and achievement: A quantitative comparison of the Oscars and six alternatives. *Creativity Research Journal*, 16: 163–172.

Statler, M., Heracleous, L., & Jacobs, C.D. 2011. Serious play as a practice paradox. *Journal of Applied Behavioral Science*, 47: 236–256.

Statler, M., Roos, J., & Victor, B. 2009. Ain't misbehavin': Taking play seriously in organizations. *Journal of Change Management*, 9: 87–107.

Steele, L.M., McIntosh, T., & Higgs, C. 2017. Intrinsic motivation and creativity: Opening up a black box. In M.D. Mumford and S. Hemlin (eds), *Handbook of research on leadership and creativity*: 100–130. Cheltenham, UK and Northampton, MA, USA: Edward Elgar Publishing.

Stephens, J.P., & Carmeli, A. 2017. Relational leadership and creativity: The effects of respectful engagement and caring on meaningfulness and creative work involvement. In M.D. Mumford and S. Hemlin (eds), *Handbook of research on leadership and creativity*: 273–296. Cheltenham, UK and Northampton, MA, USA: Edward Elgar Publishing.

Sternberg, R.J. 2003. WICS: A model of leadership in organizations. *Academy of Management Learning and Education*, 2: 386–401.

Sternberg, R.J. 2018. Creativity is not enough: The WICS model of leadership. In C. Mainemelis, O. Epitropaki, & R. Kark (eds), *Creative leadership: Contexts and prospects:* 139–155. New York: Routledge.

Stierand, M. 2015. Developing creativity in practice: Explorations with world renowned chefs. *Management Learning*, 46: 598–617.

Stierand, M., Heelein, J., & Mainemelis, C. 2020. A designer on designing: A conversation with Johannes Torpe. *Journal of Management Inquiry*, 29: 350–359.

Sun, L., Zhang, Z., & Chen, Z. X. 2012. Empowerment and creativity: A cross-level investigation. *Leadership Quarterly*, 23: 55–65.

Sutton, R.I., & Hargadon, A. 1996. Brainstorming groups in context: Effectiveness in a product design firm. *Administrative Science Quarterly*, 41: 685–718.

Svejenova, S. 2018. "It must give birth to a world": Temporality and creative leadership for artistic innovation. In C. Mainemelis, O. Epitropaki, & R. Kark (eds), *Creative leadership: Contexts and prospects*: 171–188. New York: Routledge.

Svejenova, S., & Christiansen, L. 2018. Creative leadership for social impact. In C. Joines and M. Maoret (eds), *Frontiers of creative industries: Exploring structural and categorical dynamics*, Research in the Sociology of Organizations, Vol. 55: 47–72. Bingley, UK: Emerald Group Publishing.

Svejenova, S., Mazza, C., & Planellas, M. 2007. Cooking up change in haute cuisine: Ferran Adria as an institutional entrepreneur. *Journal of Organizational Behavior*, 28, 539–561.

Svejenova, S., Planellas, M., & Vives, L. 2010. An individual business model in the making: A chef's quest for creative freedom. *Long Range Planning*, 43: 408–430.

Thayer, A.L., Petruzzelli, A., & McClurg, C.E. 2018. Addressing the paradox of the team innovation process: A review and practical considerations. *American Psychologist*, 73: 363–375.

Thomson, P., Jones, M., & Warhurst, C. 2007. From conception to consumption: Creativity and the missing managerial link. *Journal of Organizational Behavior*, 28: 625–640.

Tierney, P.M. 2008. Leadership and employee creativity. In C.E. Shalley & J. Zhou (eds), *Handbook of organizational creativity*: 95–123. New York: Lawrence Erlbaum.

Tierney, P., Farmer, S.M., & Graen, G.B. 1999. An examination of leadership and employee creativity: The relevance of traits and relationships. *Personnel Psychology*, 52: 591–620.

Tu, Y.D., & Lu, X. X., 2013. How ethical leadership influence employees' innovative work behavior: A perspective of intrinsic motivation. *Journal of Business Ethics*, 116: 441–455.

Vaccaro, I.G., Jansen, J.J.P., Van Den Bosch, F.A.J., & Volberda, H.W. 2012. Management of innovation and leadership: The moderating role of organizational size. *Journal of Management Studies*, 49: 28–51.

Van Dijk, D., Kark, K. Russel, J. & Matte, F. 2020. Collective aspiration: Collective regulatory focus as a mediator between leadership behavior and team creativity. *Journal of Business and Psychology*. https://doi.org/10.1007/s10869-020-09692-6.

Van Knippenberg, D., & Sitkin, S.B. 2013. A critical assessment of charismatic-transformational leadership research: Back to the drawing board? *Academy of Management Annals*, 7: 1–60.

Venkataramani, V., Richter, A., & Clarke, R. 2014. Creative benefits from well-connected leaders? Leader social network ties as facilitators of employee radical creativity. *Journal of Applied Psychology*, 99: 966–975.

Vera, D., & Crossan, M. 2004. Theatrical improvisation: Lessons for organizations. *Organization Studies*, 25: 727–751.

Vessey, W.B., Barrett, J.D., Mumford, M.D., Johnson, G., & Litwiller, B. 2014. Leadership of highly creative people in highly creative fields: A historiometric study of scientific leaders. *Leadership Quarterly*, 25: 672–691.

Volmer, J., Spurk, D., & Niessen, C. 2012. Leader–member exchange (LMX), job autonomy, and creative work involvement. *Leadership Quarterly*, 23: 456–465.

Wang, G., Oh, I.S., Courtright, S.H., Colbert, A.E. 2011. Transformational leadership and performance across criteria and levels: A meta-analytic review of 25 years of research. *Group and Organization Management*, 36: 223–270.

Wang, X., Li, H., & Yin, H. 2020. Antecedents and consequences of creativity in teams: When and how leader humility promotes performance via team creativity. *Journal of Creative Behavior*, 54: 843–856.

Woodman, R.W., Sawyer, J.E., & Griffin, R.W. 1993. Toward a theory of organizational creativity. *Academy of Management Review*, 18: 293–321.

Yuan, F., & Zhou, J. 2008. Differential effects of expected external evaluation on different parts of the creative idea production process and on final product creativity. *Creativity Research Journal*, 20: 391–403.

Zhang, S., Ke, X., Wang, X-H. F., & Liu, J. 2018. Empowering leadership and employee creativity: A dual-mechanism perspective. *Journal of Occupational and Organizational Psychology*, 91: 896–917.

Zhang, X., & Bartol, K.M. 2010. Linking empowering leadership and employee creativity: The influence of psychological empowerment, intrinsic motivation, and creative process engagement. *Academy of Management Journal*, 53, 107–128.

Zhang, X., & Kwan, H.K. 2018. Empowering leadership and team creativity: The roles of team learning behavior, team creative efficacy, and team task complexity. In C. Mainemelis, O. Epitropaki, & R. Kark (eds), *Creative leadership: Contexts and prospects*: 95–121. New York: Routledge.

Zhou, J. 1998. Feedback valence, feedback style, task autonomy, and achievement orientation: Interactive effects on creative performance. *Journal of Applied Psychology*, 83: 261–276.

Zhou, J. 2003. When the presence of creative coworkers is related to creativity: Role of supervisor close monitoring, developmental feedback, and creative personality. *Journal of Applied Psychology*, 88: 413–422.

Zhou, J. 2008. Promoting creativity through feedback. In C.E. Shalley & J. Zhou (eds), *Handbook of organizational creativity*: 125–145. New York: Lawrence Erlbaum Associates.

Zhou, J., & George, J.M. 2003. Awakening employee creativity: The role of leader emotional intelligence. *Leadership Quarterly*, 14: 545–568.

7. Leading groups and teams towards successful innovation

Eric F. Rietzschel, Diana Rus, and Barbara Wisse

Innovation, or the intentional introduction of new and useful applications, products, or procedures (West & Farr, 1990), is receiving more and more attention from researchers and practitioners. Some are interested in innovation because of its economic potential, others consider innovation the hallmark of human civilization, or expect that innovation can facilitate a transition towards a safe, fair, and sustainable society. Whatever the reasons, many agree that innovation is important and that we need a better understanding of the way it can be facilitated.

Despite the persistent myth of the "lone genius," innovation is rarely a purely individual effort. Even if an idea is generated by a single individual, the subsequent development and implementation of the idea usually require concerted effort on the part of a group or collective of individuals working interdependently on the same task or project; in other words, a team. As collections of interdependent individuals, teams require the resources and context to help them coordinate their efforts and perform effectively in a setting where multiple interests, both within and outside of the team, have to be balanced. One crucial factor shaping these processes (and ultimately team innovation) is leadership. Leaders, and team leaders in particular, have the potential to shape a team's goals, activities, coordination and communication, to influence its norms and climate, to deal with interests within and outside the team, and to provide the team with crucial resources to attain its innovative ends. For example, leaders can explicitly instruct their teams to look for innovative solutions and motivate them to go beyond well-known routines and to take risks; they can encourage team members to share their wildest ideas and to refrain from premature criticism. Additionally, leaders can bring team members into contact with crucial stakeholders who may provide the team with political leverage or critical information, or they can provide the team with time or money to pursue creative ideas, for example by deciding that some other projects can be temporarily set aside.

However, the literature on this topic is relatively fragmented and scattered, with little integration or cohesion (see also Hughes et al., 2018). In this chapter, we review the research on leadership and team innovation. We first explain some of the general issues related to team innovation and leadership. Next, we address the link between leadership and team innovation by focusing on three potential roles that leadership can play: (1) as a predictor of team innovation; (2) as a moderator of the effect of other (for example, individual, team-level, or contextual) variables; and (3) as a transition catalyst in moving from creativity to implementation. Finally, we reflect on the reviewed literature, address methodological and theoretical trends and gaps, and point out some potentially valuable avenues for future research.

TERMINOLOGY AND DEFINITIONS

This chapter focuses on the effects of leadership on innovation at the team level (as opposed to, for instance, the effects of leadership on individual followers' innovative behaviors), and as such focuses on team-level processes (as opposed to, for instance, individual-level processes). Nevertheless, teams are multi-level entities, composed of individuals working together, that are often nested in larger collectives (departments, organizations, and so on). As such, any effect that leaders may have on individual members' innovative performance may at some point also affect the team's performance, just as the performance of teams may, in the end, affect the performance of the organization as a whole (Woodman et al., 1993). That said, our main focus in this chapter is on the team level.

A team can be defined as a group of interacting and interdependent individuals with a shared goal, working on an organizationally relevant task within an organizational setting (Kozlowski & Ilgen, 2006). In contrast, the term "group" is often used to refer to ad hoc groups put together for the purpose of a lab study, or to distinguish a level of description or analysis from, say, the individual level (as in: group brainstorming versus individual brainstorming). Thus, every team is a group, but not every group is a team.

Simply stated, team innovation is innovation as performed by teams. Thus, team innovation refers to how teams engage in the intentional introduction and application of novel ideas, processes, products, or procedures in an organizational context (see West & Farr, 1990). Although this process is usually messy and iterative, researchers often distinguish between different stages or components, moving from initial conception of a task, problem, or project to a divergent stage of idea generation and development, on to a more convergent and evaluative stage of idea selection, followed by actual implementation of one or more ideas (e.g., Amabile, 1996; Perry-Smith & Mannucci, 2017; Zhou et al., 2019).

Despite differences in the models or sequences used by researchers, one aspect shared by most stage models is particularly important for this chapter: the differentiation between creativity and idea implementation (e.g., West, 2002; Rietzschel et al., 2019). In theory, these activities should be closely tied together, given that ideas can be implemented only if they are first generated. However, in practice they diverge and may not even always be correlated (see Rietzschel et al., 2019; Rietzschel & Ritter, 2018, for overviews). In this chapter, we use the term "innovation" to refer to the entire process of generating and implementing ideas (and everything in between). We use the term "creativity" to refer to the act of generating ideas or creative insights, and refer to other specific aspects of the innovation process using terms such as "idea development," "idea promotion," or "idea implementation."

Leadership has been defined as "the process of influencing others to understand and agree about what needs to be done and how to do it, and the process of facilitating individual and collective efforts to accomplish shared objectives" (see Yukl, 2013: 7). In this chapter, we focus on team leadership specifically. Team leaders are (formally or informally) responsible for defining team goals and tasks, coordinating activities, providing resources, and motivating the team to accomplish its goals. In other words, a leader's tasks are enormously broad and varied; this, in turn, means that leader behaviors can have a multitude of effects on team creativity and innovation. As we will discuss later on, we adopt a functional perspective on leadership, distinguishing between two main categories of leader behaviors: task-focused (aimed at optimizing task accomplishment) and person-focused (aimed at optimizing team interaction and/or development) behaviors. This distinction will serve as a high-level organizing framework for our review. Naturally, not all leader behaviors fall cleanly into one category or the other; nevertheless, this categorization will help us to make sense of the highly diverse research base. Furthermore, our focus on leader behaviors and leadership styles means that some aspects of leadership remain outside the scope of our review; such as, for example, shared leadership, which is more about the way leadership roles are distributed or configured within teams than about how these roles are enacted, and which has also been linked to team creativity and innovation (Hoch, 2013; Kakar, 2017; Wu & Cormican, 2016).

THE CHALLENGES OF TEAM INNOVATION

Working on innovative projects in a group or team (as opposed to individually) poses specific challenges, several of which are particularly relevant in the context of leadership. Several useful frameworks of team performance exist, such as the four-factor framework of team effectiveness (distinguishing between cognitive, motivational, affective, and coordination processes) proposed by Zaccaro et al. (2001), and the input–process–output (IPO) framework (e.g., Hülsheger et al., 2009). Whichever framework one uses, several clusters of variables seem especially important (or problematic) when it comes to creativity and innovation in teams (Hülsheger et al., 2009; Paulus & Nijstad, 2019); we will briefly discuss these below.

Information Exchange and Diversity

Teams hold innovative potential because they can draw on a wider variety of expertise and perspectives than individuals. Realizing this potential requires that this knowledge is exchanged and processed within the team. This means that the team needs to constructively deal with diversity (Van Knippenberg et al., 2004), and that team members must be motivated to both share and process information for the benefit of the team (De Dreu et al., 2011). This also requires coordination, to ensure that members actually get the opportunity to contribute their ideas or opinions (for example, avoiding "production blocking" during idea generation; Diehl & Stroebe, 1987; Nijstad & Stroebe, 2006).

Cohesion, Psychological Safety, and Dissent

Because creativity is inherently risky (for example, because it is not always known whether an idea will work or will be received favorably), team members may hold back their most creative ideas or their divergent opinions. Thus, team members need to experience sufficient psychological safety and support to actually bring their ideas to the table (e.g., Anderson & West, 1996, 1998). However, meta-analytical results (Hülsheger et al., 2009) suggest that excessively high levels of psychological safety or cohesion may be problematic if the group gets too focused on maintaining harmony and consensus. A certain amount of (task) conflict and dissent can force team members to consider multiple perspectives and challenge some assumptions (Nemeth & O'Connor, 2019). Thus, a team needs to be safe enough for members to share whatever ideas they have, even if these lead to disagreement.

Goals, Vision, and Support

Teams need to share a clear goal to work towards, including the goal to be creative and innovative. Effective teamwork requires alignment of team members' efforts, and if creativity and innovation are desired, these need to be part of the team's goal. Popular stereotypes notwithstanding (e.g., Baas et al., 2015; Ritter & Rietzschel, 2017), creativity does not happen by accident, but is a matter of goal-directed behavior (e.g., Litchfield, 2008). This also means that innovation needs to be supported and encouraged, and that being innovative should itself be among the team's goals (Anderson & West, 1998).

Managing Divergence and Convergence

Because innovation is a multi-stage process, teams will need to be able to effectively switch between divergence (exploring options and generating ideas) and convergence (decision-making). This means that different goals will have to be salient at different moments, and that the nature of the group task and the degree of interdependence are continually changing. For example, whereas group idea generation often is an additive group task (that is, the group's performance is the sum of individual members' performance), idea development and – especially – implementation may be more conjunctive group tasks (that is, all group members must make an adequate contribution for the group to succeed; Steiner, 1972). Thus, along with coordinating group members' efforts and inputs, groups need to display a kind of "meta-coordination" to effectively switch between different kinds of group work.

To summarize, for team innovation to occur, several processes, ranging from the cognitive to the interpersonal, need to run smoothly. Poorly functioning teams may therefore reflect not only the existence of poorly functioning individual members, but also a collective failure to coordinate and align individual contributions (see Kozlowski & Ilgen, 2006). In the next section, we will discuss how leadership may be a crucial factor in managing team processes conducive to innovation.

LEADERSHIP AS A CRUCIAL FACTOR IN TEAM INNOVATION

As team leadership is often considered to be key in creating and changing teams' social and structural context, one would expect the link between leadership and team innovation to be strong. Indeed, leadership has been posited to be a key contextual factor in promoting team innovation (for a review, see Hughes et al., 2018). Notably, although team creativity and innovation pose different challenges than individual creativity and innovation, most research in this area has been done on the individual level. Although such individual-level influences will affect team performance, actual team-level research is necessary to help us understand processes such as coordination, conflict, or information exchange.

In short, to understand the role of leadership in facilitating team innovation, we need to focus on the specific functions that leaders have in the team context. This functional perspective on leadership conceptualizes team leadership as being fundamentally oriented towards satisfying critical team needs, with the ultimate goal of fostering team effectiveness (Fleishman et al., 1991; Morgeson et al., 2010; Zaccaro et al., 2001). In other words, the leadership role is "to do, or get done, whatever is not being adequately handled for group needs" (McGrath, 1962: 5, in Zaccaro et al., 2001: 453). This usually implies aligning and integrating team processes with the ultimate aim of ensuring team effectiveness. Leaders can engage in many different behaviors related to the team processes outlined above, such as creating a shared vision, setting goals, facilitating information sharing, creating psychological safety, providing support, influencing climate and norms, managing conflicts, managing material and immaterial resources, and so on (e.g., Fleishman et al., 1991; Morgeson et al., 2010; Zaccaro et al., 2001). One way to make sense of this cornucopia of different behaviors is to sort leader behaviors into two categories: behaviors dealing with task accomplishment (that is, task-focused behaviors), and those enabling team interaction and/or development (that is, person-focused behaviors; see Burke et al., 2006).

Task-focused leader behaviors generally consist of initiating structure by, for instance, providing direction, defining task roles, establishing interdependencies among team members, and setting as well as maintaining performance goals and standards. Thus, behaviors associated with, for example, transactional leadership, such as "contingent reward" and "management by exception active," as well as behaviors associated with structuring and directive leadership, would fall under this category.

Person-focused leader behaviors generally consist of inspiring employees, being considerate, showing respect and concern for individual team members, providing autonomy and empowerment, engaging members in decision-making, being open to input, providing support and coaching, and acting as a role model. Leader behaviors associated with transformational leadership, leader–member exchange (LMX), participative leadership, empowering leadership, servant leadership, and authentic leadership would fall under this category.

Although, as explained above, not every form of leadership or leader behavior will neatly fall into either of these categories, this global categorization will help us to make sense of the diverse literature on team leadership and team innovation. In the next section, we will present our review of the literature.

THREE ROLES OF LEADERSHIP

So far, the body of research investigating the impact of leadership on team creativity and innovation is relatively small, with the main body of existing work having been built only since the late 1990s. However, the diversity in this work is considerable. In the following sections, we first review studies on leadership as a predictor of team creativity and innovation, then we highlight work addressing leadership as a moderator of other effects, and finally we discuss work that has considered leadership as a creativity–innovation transition catalyst.

Leadership as a Predictor of Team Creativity and Innovation

It is almost a truism to state that leadership is crucial to team innovation. Leaders are in a position to provide (or withhold) access to material and immaterial resources, have political leverage within an organization, are (often) disproportionately influential in team decision-making, and have a strong influence on the team's goals and climate. In other words, one potential role of leadership is that of a predictor of team innovation by, for instance, providing a vision, setting goals, providing support, empowering team members, motivating them, and/or providing adequate rewards. In doing so, leaders could stimulate (or hinder) all facets of the innovation process in teams, such as creativity, idea development, or successful idea implementation. In fact, most existing research has investigated leadership as a predictor. We will first discuss studies falling into the task-focused leader behavior category, followed by studies falling into the person-focused leader behavior category.

Task-focused leader behavior as predictor
Looked at from a functional leadership perspective, surprisingly few studies have investigated the impact of task-focused leader behaviors on team creativity and/or innovation. Most of these studies focused on transactional leadership.

Transactional leadership
Transactional leadership emphasizes an exchange relationship between leader and subordinates, and consists of contingent rewards as well as management by excep-

tion (active and passive). This implies setting clear performance goals, monitoring employee performance, and intervening with corrective actions when necessary. Such transactional leader behaviors might, at first blush, not seem to be beneficial for creativity and innovation because they can detract from intrinsic motivation, a crucial predictor of creative and innovative performance at work. However, as long as rewards and other transactive behaviors provide team members with creativity-relevant information (for example, making it clear that creative performance is expected and will be rewarded) and are not perceived as controlling, they may actually be helpful (see e.g., Byron & Khazanchi, 2012; Cerasoli et al., 2014, for meta-analyses). Indeed, it appears that transactional leadership on the whole is positively related to team innovation, but this effect is contingent on other contextual variables (we will also address this in the section on leadership as a moderator), leading to some inconsistency in the literature.

For instance, Liu et al. (2011) found that transactional leadership was positively (versus negatively) related to team innovation (mediated by team efficacy) under conditions of low (versus high) task-induced emotional labor. Liu et al. reason that high emotional labor requires transactional leaders to emphasize the importance of emotional control, detracting from the autonomy necessary for innovative performance. Only under low emotional labor would teams have the necessary autonomy to focus on the innovative goals set by their transactional leader.

Other examples of contingent effects of transactional leadership come from computer-mediated experimental studies on group creativity. For example, Sosik et al. (1998) found that transactional goal setting (a dimension of transactional leadership) and inspirational leadership (a subcomponent of transformational leadership) were both positively related to group creativity. In contrast, intellectual stimulation and individualized consideration (two other components of transformational leadership) were negatively related to group creativity. Moreover, the aforementioned effects (except that of intellectual stimulation) were stronger under conditions of anonymity within the group. Sosik et al. argue that anonymity allows group members to focus primarily on the task (instead of, for example, each other), which in turn should strengthen the positive effects of transactional leadership on group creativity. Similarly, Kahai et al. (2003) combined manipulations of transformational/transactional leadership with reward structure (individual versus group reward). More or less in line with Sosik et al., they found a positive effect of transactional leader behavior on the originality of proposed ideas (but also see Jung, 2001, who found the opposite); however, they did not find a positive moderating effect of anonymity.

Structuring, directive, and ambidextrous leadership
Some other studies in this category have not looked at transactional leadership per se, but at other task-focused leader behaviors. For example, adopting a two-dimensional model of authoritarian leadership, Pei (2017) argued that one of these dimensions, "structuring leadership," setting high but realistic performance standards and focusing on continuous improvement (the other dimension being autocratic leadership), should positively predict team creativity. In a field study among Chinese high-tech

enterprises, Pei found that this indeed was the case; moreover, this effect was medi-ated by team innovation climate.

In a study among consulting project teams, Li et al. (2018) looked at the effects of directive versus participative leadership and found that the former decreased team creativity (but increased team efficiency); whereas the latter increased creativity (but did not affect efficiency). Moreover, directive and participative leadership interactively predicted team efficiency, leading the authors to theorize that leadership should not be seen as a choice between different styles or behaviors, because seem-ingly contradictory leadership behaviors may well co-occur.

A similar line of reasoning was also used by Zacher and Rosing (2015), who argued that team innovation should be positively predicted by ambidextrous lead-ership. Ambidextrous leadership combines two types of complementary behaviors: opening behaviors (that is, behaviors that encourage subordinates to engage in exploration by experimenting and challenging the status quo) and closing behaviors (that is, behaviors that encourage exploitation by setting specific guidelines, taking corrective action and monitoring goal achievement). The reasoning is that innova-tion, with its combination of divergent, creative activities and convergent selection and implementation activities, requires leader behaviors that stimulate both, rather than merely one or the other. Indeed, Zacher and Rosing (2015) found that team innovation was highest when both opening and closing leader behaviors were high.

Conclusion
On the whole, it seems that task-oriented leadership such as transactional leadership can contribute to creativity and innovation in teams. This may be somewhat counter-intuitive, given that creativity and innovation are commonly associated with auton-omy rather than transactional, structuring, or closing behaviors. However, important as autonomy is, team members also need to be able to work effectively within a set of constraints, and some degree of structuring, monitoring, and transactional reward may be indispensable (also see Byron & Khazanchi, 2012; Rietzschel, 2018).

Our review also suggests that task-focused leader behaviors have been studied substantially more often as predictors of team creativity than team innovation. It is not immediately clear why this is the case, but it might both stem from and perpetu-ate a common belief that creativity (in particular) is incompatible with task-focused behaviors such as structuring or monitoring behaviors (e.g., Ritter & Rietzschel, 2017), even though research on the individual level has shown that this need not be the case (e.g., Rietzschel et al., 2014). That being said, it appears that task-focused leadership has been studied more often as a predictor of innovation at the organiza-tional or business unit level (e.g., Berraies & El Abidine, 2019; Howell & Avolio, 1993). As a consequence, we lack an understanding of the ways in which leaders may help their teams to perform creatively and innovatively through task-focused behaviors. As we will see in the next section, person-focused leader behaviors have been studied more often as predictors of team creativity and innovation.

Person-focused leader behavior as predictor

Within the area of person-focused leadership as a predictor, the vast majority of articles look at the role of transformational leadership. A much smaller number of studies investigate the effects of other person-focused leadership behaviors and factors such as the quality of leader–member exchange (LMX), leader empowering and coaching behaviors, authentic and servant leadership.

Transformational leadership

The predominance of research on transformational leadership is not surprising, given the nature of the construct, and the fact that transformational leadership is also among the most frequently studied leader behaviors on the individual level; see Lee et al. (2019) for a recent meta-analysis on effects of transformational leadership on individual-level creativity and innovation. That said, the construct is not without its critics, and some researchers have argued that the construct actually needs to be abandoned for both theoretical and methodological reasons (see e.g., Van Knippenberg & Sitkin, 2013; Chapter 3 by Van Knippenberg and Hoever, this volume). Nevertheless, the fact remains that most research thus far on person-focused leader behaviors as predictors of team creativity and innovation has focused on transformational leadership.

Typically, transformational leader behaviors can be clustered into four components: idealized influence (the leader engages in charismatic role modeling behavior, which inspires trust, respect, and employee emulation behaviors); inspirational motivation (the leader provides a higher meaning by articulating an appealing vision for the team); intellectual stimulation (the leader encourages employees to challenge existing assumptions, reframe problems, and engage in exploratory behaviors); and individualized consideration (the leader engages in coaching and mentoring behaviors with individual employees). Overall, and in line with what is commonly assumed, many studies have demonstrated positive links between transformational leader behaviors and team creativity and innovation (e.g., Boies et al., 2015; Chen et al., 2013; Eisenbeiß & Boerner, 2010; Eisenbeiß et al., 2008; Feng et al., 2016; Jiang & Chen, 2018; Paulsen et al., 2013; Paulsen et al., 2009; Shin & Eom, 2014; Williams et al., 2010).

Beyond establishing relationships, some studies have also attempted to identify underlying processes explaining these correlations. For instance, Chen et al. (2013) found that transformational leadership had a positive effect on team innovation by increasing the extent to which the team developed a climate supportive of innovation (see also Eisenbeiß et al., 2008 for similar findings). Team climate (a shared perception within teams of the way the team works; e.g., Anderson & West, 1996) has been meta-analytically identified as one of the strongest predictors of team innovation (Hülsheger et al., 2009) and, as argued above, leaders are likely to be particularly influential in shaping a team's climate.

However, several other mediating variables have also been identified. Some of these are primarily relational or interpersonal in nature; for example, Paulsen et al. (2013) found that the effects of transformational leadership on team innovation were mediated by member identification with the group and perceived support for creativity; Boies et al. (2015) found that the effects of intellectual stimulation on group creativity were mediated by team communication, whereas the effects of inspirational motivation were mediated by increased trust; and Jiang and Chen (2018) found that transformational leadership was positively related to team innovation through both integrative and autonomous team behaviors, that is, under high transformational leadership there was more intra-team cooperation as well as higher team member autonomy, both of which positively predicted team innovation. However, not all of the identified mediators are relational in nature; some are also more task-oriented, such as team self-management (Williams et al., 2010) and team proactivity (Shin & Eom, 2014).

Although the relationship between transformational leadership and team innovation clearly is empirically well supported, some studies paint a more nuanced picture by showing that the benefits of transformational leadership on team creativity and innovation may be evident only under specific conditions. For instance, Eisenbeiß et al. (2008) found that the positive effects of transformational leadership on team innovation via support for innovation occurred only when climate for excellence was high. Further, Feng et al. (2016) found that transformational leadership was particularly strongly related to group innovative behavior when organizations scored high (versus low) on radical change, but not when organizations scored high on incremental change.

Moreover, one study has challenged the assumption that the relation between transformational leadership and team innovation need always be linear. In a study of research and development (R&D) teams, Eisenbeiß and Boerner (2010) found that team innovation was higher under both low and high levels of transformational leadership than under moderate levels. The authors argue that since R&D team members are typically characterized by a high need for autonomy and a low need for leadership, moderate levels of transformational leadership might endanger autonomy without fully realizing the potential benefits of transformational leadership.

Finally, some work has examined the simultaneous effects of transformational leadership and other person-focused leader behaviors, such as authoritarian leadership, on team creativity (e.g., Zhang et al., 2011). In a study of 163 Chinese work groups, Zhang et al. found that transformational leadership related positively, and authoritarian leadership related negatively, to team creativity. Moreover, these effects were mediated by collective efficacy and knowledge sharing.

Relational forms of leadership
Other studies on person-focused predictors of team innovation concern the quality of leader–member exchange (LMX); that is, the quality of the relationship between the leader and individual team members. On the whole, LMX seems to be favorable for team creativity and innovation. For example, Gajendran and Joshi (2012) found that high-quality LMX and high communication frequency with the leader jointly fostered team member inclusion in decision-making and subsequent team innovation in highly distributed teams. Further, Kahrobaei and Mortazavi (2016) found a posi-

tive relation between LMX quality and teams' creative work involvement, mediated by the teams' "collective energy"; that is, the degree to which group members felt energetic, were actively looking for opportunities, and worked at a fast pace. Going beyond LMX quality per se, Li et al. (2016) tested a curvilinear effect of LMX differentiation on team creativity. The authors argue that, given the dyadic nature of LMX, different subordinates may well need different relationships for their creativity to be maximally stimulated. Thus, developing differential relationships with team members may be required to create optimal fit on the level of individual team members and thereby stimulate team creativity. Beyond a certain point, however, this differentiation will be ineffective because it will lead to a perception of inequality and favoritism, and may prevent teams from coordinating their collective efforts. In a field study, Li et al. found support for this inverted U-shaped relation; however, this was only the case when the within-team median value of LMX was low.

Other more relational leadership behaviors, such as empowering, coaching, and inclusive leader behaviors (e.g., Burpitt & Bigoness, 1997; Hon & Chan, 2013; Rousseau et al., 2013; Schaubroeck et al., 2016; Ye et al., 2019), have also been found to have modest but positive relationships with team creativity and innovation. Central to these leader behaviors is that leaders try to contribute to teams' and team members' self-development into independently effective units or employees. For instance, Hon & Chan (2013) showed that teams were more creative when they had empowering leaders, and this effect was mediated by team self-concordance (Bono & Judge, 2003) and team creative efficacy, especially among highly interdependent teams. In yet another study, Schaubroeck et al. (2016) showed that leader coaching behaviors positively predicted team innovation through team learning, but only among teams with high levels of contentious interpersonal communication. In other words, and in line with the notion of helping teams develop into independently effective units, coaching leader behaviors helped teams to mitigate the potentially negative effects of internal disagreements on learning and innovation. Furthermore, Ye et al. (2019) found that inclusive leadership positively predicted team innovation, especially when performance pressure was high. Moreover, this relation was mediated by voice behaviors (speaking up) within the team.

Another relational form of leadership, albeit on the negative side of the interpersonal spectrum, is abusive leadership, where leaders are intentionally rude and degrading to their subordinates. Naturally, such behaviors can easily kill individual creativity and innovation (e.g., Liu et al., 2012), but their relation with team creativity and innovation have remained understudied. One recent exception is a study by Rousseau and Aubé (2018), who investigated the effects of abusive supervision among leaders and followers in a public safety organization, and found that abusive supervision negatively predicted team innovation (especially when team members and their leaders were highly interdependent); this relationship was mediated by team proactivity: abusive supervisors had teams where members were less proactive in sharing their ideas and opinions, and these teams in turn were less effective in coming up with, and implementing, creative ideas.

Positive forms of leadership

Finally, a very small number of studies have proposed and found positive relation-ships between specific "positive" forms of leadership, such as authentic (e.g., Černe et al., 2013), servant (e.g., Yang et al., 2017; Yoshida et al., 2014), and ethical lead-ership (Mo et al., 2019), and team creativity and innovation. For instance, Yoshida et al. (2014) found that servant leaders (showing a sustained and altruistic commitment to helping their subordinates grow) were more likely to be seen as prototypical (embodying the teams' norms, values, and beliefs) for the team, which in turn posi-tively predicted team innovation. Moreover, they found this effect to be enhanced by a favorable innovation climate within the team. Further, Mo et al. (2019) tested a cur-vilinear effect of ethical leadership, reasoning that ethical leadership in teams could lead to both trust (in a concave manner, with decreasing benefits) and conformity (in a convex manner, with increasing costs; cf. Grant & Schwartz, 2011). Together, these should yield an inverted U-shaped relation between ethical leadership and team creativity; which indeed was what the authors found. Moreover, this relationhip was moderated by the strength of team faultlines (that is, when differences between team members on multiple characteristics are aligned; for example, young female versus old male team members), such that the inverted U, with its peak at intermediate levels of ethical leadership, occurred only when team faultline strength was low.

Conclusion

In sum, person-related leader behaviors seem to be among the strongest and most consistent positive predictors of team innovation, possibly because these are often focused at (or mediated by) team-level or relational processes (as opposed to, for example, transactional leadership), and hence are more likely to stimulate favorable group processes that can contribute to team innovation, such as climate, trust, and effective communication (cf. Hülsheger et al., 2009). Compared to task-focused leadership, person-focused leadership (particularly transformational leadership) has clearly been studied more often as a predictor of both team creativity and (espe-cially) team innovation. This is perhaps not surprising, in that person-focused leader behaviors are deemed to be more relevant (that is, more visible and presumably more effective) in the context of smaller social units such as teams or dyadic interactions. Nevertheless, ambidextrous leadership theory (Rosing et al., 2011) would suggest that there is a clear role for task-focused leadership on the team level as well.

The recent trend in the leadership literature of studying the effects of negative forms of leadership (such as abusive leadership; see e.g., Mackey et al., 2017) does not yet seem to have gained a lot of momentum in the literature on team creativity and innovation. This may be because creativity and innovation research has long focused on the importance of supporting safe work environments (see e.g., Shalley & Zhou, 2008); as such, demonstrating the dangers of abusive supervision may seem superfluous. Then again, some research on abusive supervision and individual employee creativity has uncovered surprising effects; for example, Lee et al. (2013) found a curvilinear (inverted U-shaped) relation between abusive supervision and individual creativity in a South Korean sample, suggesting that, at least in high power distance cultures, moderate levels of abusive supervision may energize employees into performing creatively. Future research might address the way in which negative leader behaviors and cultural factors interactively shape team creativity and innovation.

Leadership as a Moderator of the Effect of Other Variables

Leader behaviors may also strengthen or weaken the influence of other variables on team innovation (for example, enabling teams to make the best use of available resources). Moreover, leader behavior can mitigate the negative effects of variables such as demands and constraints on team innovation (e.g., Stollberger et al., 2019), and may provide followers with the resources necessary for successful innovation (e.g., Škerlavaj et al., 2014). Indeed, a substantial portion of the literature has addressed this moderating role of leadership, either by looking at the way leaders may buffer (that is, mitigate) negative effects of other (often contextual) factors, or by addressing the way leaders may strengthen positive effects.

Task-focused leader behavior as moderator

Research directly focusing on how task-focused leader behavior can moderate the effect of other variables on team innovation is scarce. In general, the limited evidence seems to suggest that task-focused leadership can mitigate the negative effects of other variables on team creativity and innovation.

For instance, Chen and Agrawal (2017) studied whether dynamic leadership (that is, leaders acting autonomously, being risk-taking and proactive) could mitigate the potentially negative effects of communication barriers on knowledge sharing and team creativity in newly formed teams. They argued that dynamic leaders act as knowledge builders (developing the team's expertise, scanning the environment for new ideas, and so on) and are in a position to give teams access to resources (for example, through external communication). Indeed, they found that dynamic leadership mitigated the negative effects of communication barriers in teams on knowledge sharing which, in turn, positively predicted team creativity.

As discussed earlier, some studies on task-focused leadership as a predictor have also included moderators, suggesting that these effects could also be interpreted differently. For example, the work by Liu et al. (2011) on transactional leadership and emotional labor suggests that the effects of emotional labor on team innovation are mitigated by transactional leadership; similarly, the work by Sosik et al. (1998) might be reinterpreted as a study on the effects of group anonymity and the moderating role of leadership.

Conclusion

Task-focused leader behaviors appear to mitigate the negative effects of other variables (for example, communication barriers, emotional labor) on team creativity and innovation. This may be because such leadership – not surprisingly – brings the task back into focus and provides team members with task-relevant resources, thereby buffering effects that might otherwise detract from creative and innovative performance. One question that remains is whether task-focused leadership only mitigates the effects of other variables, or whether it can also strengthen them, as seems to be the case for person-focused leader behaviors. Further, and similarly to what we saw in the previous section, the amount of research here is very limited, suggesting that the literature on team creativity and innovation tends to neglect task-focused leadership (possibly because it tends to focus on larger units instead).

Person-focused leader behavior as moderator

Research investigating how person-focused leader behavior can moderate the effects of other variables on team innovation is more sizeable, with most of this work focusing on transformational leadership and some very limited work considering other forms of person-focused leadership (for example, participative leadership; Somech, 2006).

Transformational leadership

Generally, transformational leadership appears to strengthen the relationship between other predictor variables and team creativity or innovation. For example, while job-relevant team diversity is generally argued to be good for team innovation (Hülsheger et al., 2009), diversity in teams can bring its own challenges (for example, suboptimal communication, not knowing who knows what, decreased motivation and trust, outright tensions and conflicts). Transformational leadership behaviors can help teams to capitalize on their diversity by minimizing the negative effects of diversity, while keeping its benefits. For example, providing teams with a clear and appealing vision should help team members to align their goals (e.g., Mascareño et al., 2020), which might help them to overcome possible negative diversity effects. Further, individualized consideration might help team members to feel safe and appreciated in a diverse team.

In line with this reasoning, Shin and Zhou (2007) found that transformational leadership and educational specialization heterogeneity interacted to affect team creativity: under high transformational leadership, teams with greater educational specialization heterogeneity exhibited greater team creativity (mediated by creative efficacy). The authors argue that transformational leaders energize their teams by providing a compelling vision and serving as a role model, while also helping them better leverage their differences. Similarly, Wang et al. (2016) showed that transformational leadership moderated cognitive diversity's effect on team creativity (via team intrinsic motivation), such that the effects were positive when transformational leadership was high, but negative when transformational leadership was low. Further, a recent study by Zhang et al. (2019) showed that transformational leadership positively moderated (that is, strengthened) the relationship between personality diversity within teams (specifically, on openness to experience) and knowledge sharing, which in turn predicted teams' idea development. Interestingly, however, this moderation effect was not found for idea generation, suggesting that it is crucial to take different facets of the innovation process into account.

However, results are not completely consistent. For example, Reuveni and Vashdi (2015) found that transformational leadership weakened the relationship between teams' professional heterogeneity and team innovation (via the team's shared mental models). The authors argue that, normally, professional heterogeneity leads team members to try to get to know and understand each other's perspective better, but that this process can be hampered under transformational leadership, and may get replaced by within-team competition.

Other studies have looked at different predictors. For example, Peltokorpi and Hasu (2016) focused on the interactive effects of transactive memory systems (TMS; that is, knowing "who knows what" within a diverse team; Wegner, 1986) and transformational leadership on team innovation, finding that transformational leadership strengthened the positive effect of TMS on team innovation. Furthermore, Nijstad et al. (2014) argued that transformational leadership would strengthen the link between minority dissent and team innovation, reasoning that transformational leaders create a psychologically safe climate which would lead to the effective use of dissenting opinions. Indeed, in a study of top management teams, they showed that minority dissent was positively related to the total number of innovations implemented. However, they found that only with high levels of transformational leadership (mediated by safety) were these implemented innovations radical.

Some of the studies discussed before can also be fruitfully reinterpreted as studies on person-focused leadership as a moderator. For example, the interaction pattern found by Eisenbeiß et al. (2008) suggests that climate for excellence was positively related to team innovation only under conditions of high transformational leadership; the results reported by Schaubroeck et al. (2016) could also be seen as indicating that leader coaching behaviors mitigate the effects of contentious communication in teams; and the results by Yoshida et al. (2014) suggest that servant leadership strengthens the positive effect of climate for innovation.

Other person-focused leader behaviors
Although the majority of research in this cluster is on transformational leadership, some studies have addressed the moderating role of other person-focused leader behaviors. For example, Akgün et al. (2007) found that team stressors (crisis and anxiety) positively affected several aspects of new product development in teams (such as idea generation and product development), but only when management support was high (that is, when management created a supportive and helpful climate within teams). Somech (2006) found that team heterogeneity (the number of different functional roles within a team) predicted team innovation (mediated by team reflection), but only when participative leadership (involving team members in decision-making) was high. In an experiment, Jaussi and Dionne (2003) found that leaders who were perceived as creative role models stimulated the creative performance of team members, especially if this role modeling was accompanied by the leader displaying unconventional behaviors, such as standing on furniture or hanging ideas on clotheslines.

Although not behavior as such, leaders' affective presence has also been studied in the context of team creativity and innovation. Madrid et al. (2016a) found that the affective impact employees felt when interacting with their team leader moderated the relation between idea generation and "silence"; that is, the degree to which team members kept their ideas to themselves. Madrid et al. found a negative relation between idea generation and silence, but only when leaders' positive affective presence was high or their negative affective presence was low. Further, Madrid et al. (2016b) found that leader affective presence predicted team innovation, mediated by information sharing within teams.

Conclusion
In sum, most papers studying the moderating effect of person-focused leadership focus on transformational leadership, although some other variables have been studied as well. Most of these studies show positive, strengthening moderation effects, and factors such as team efficacy and safety appear to be particularly important mediators here. Most importantly, person-focused leadership seems to help teams turn challenges (such as diversity) into constructive team processes conducive to innovation. Further, both team creativity and team innovation have been studied far more often in the context of person-focused leadership than in the context of task-focused leadership, which – as discussed previously – may be due to an implicit assumption that person-focused leadership is more relevant in these small-scale social interactions. Findings on the importance of team climate and creative self-efficacy as mediating variables support this view. However, to the extent that person-focused leadership also seems to exert its effects by enabling teams to effectively coordinate their efforts and make use of the (for example, cognitive) resources they have at their disposal (for example, by developing a shared mental model), it is conceivable that task-focused leadership aimed directly at intra-team coordination processes would also stimulate team innovation.

Leadership as a Transition Catalyst in Moving from Creativity to Implementation

The biggest challenge to innovation does not lie in a lack of creative ideas, but in getting those ideas implemented (e.g., Baer, 2012; Rietzschel et al., 2006; Somech & Drach-Zahavy, 2013; West, 2002). However, if some of the categories of research discussed above were relatively sparsely populated, the "transition catalyst" category of team leadership research remains largely empty. In fact, we were able to uncover only one empirical paper directly addressing this issue. Beside this paper, two other studies address issues that are strongly related and therefore are discussed here as well.

Peralta et al. (2019) conducted two field studies on the relation between teamwork quality, team creativity, and idea implementation, focusing on the moderating role of leadership in this relation. Specifically, the focus was on leaders' moral courage to go beyond compliance, a construct related to empowerment. They found that creativity was only positively related to implementation when leader moral courage was high, suggesting that leaders need to help teams move beyond a focus on "efficiency, cost containment, and raised performance targets" (ibid.: 4) and to reconcile these kinds of practical requirements with the drive for innovation, novelty, and high-quality services.

Although this is the only study we were able to uncover that directly addressed the role of leadership as a catalyst in the creativity–implementation relation, a few other studies are relevant in this context. For example, Chen (2007) conducted a field study on leadership in entrepreneurial teams, and found that entrepreneurial leadership (measured as risk-taking, proactivity, and innovativeness in team leaders) predicted teams' innovative capability (measured as team's patent creation); moreover, leadership positively interacted with team creativity in predicting team innovative capability. Importantly, although Chen's (2007) conceptual model is one where creativity moderates the effects of leadership, the results are equally compatible with an interpretation where leadership strengthens the relation between team creativity and team innovative capability. Note that the dependent variable in this study, patent creation, does not reflect idea implementation in a literal sense. However, developing and defining an idea to the extent that it is clear and detailed enough to be patented could arguably be considered a measure of implementation as well; in fact, many organizational teams may not be involved with actual implementation of an idea in a tangible sense.

Similarly, not every creative behavior need lead to the implementation of a new product, idea, or novel procedure; often, creativity is required to solve more mundane problems that a team encounters as part of its day-to-day activities. As such, idea implementation may also be reflected in a team's ability to effectively solve the problems it encounters, and leadership may be a catalyst here as well. For example, Magni and Maruping (2013) addressed the role of leadership in the relation between team improvisation and team performance. In this study, team improvisation was operationalized as a combination of creative behaviors and dealing with unexpected events; whereas team performance revolved around teams' ability to deliver high-quality output and implement solutions. The authors found that the relation between team improvisation and team performance was moderated by, among other things, empowering leadership, such that the relation was positive when empowering leadership was high, but negative when empowering leadership was low.

In short, although the role of leadership as a transition catalyst clearly remains understudied, the results discussed in this brief section strongly suggest that there is a role for leadership in enabling teams to capitalize on their ideas and either turn these into innovations or use them to maintain high levels of performance. In line with most of the research discussed above, the three studies discussed here all focus on person-focused leader behaviors (moral courage, risk-taking and proactivity, and empowering leadership) rather than on task-focused behaviors. However, perspectives such as ambidextrous leadership theory (Rosing et al., 2011) would suggest that it is precisely in the transition from creativity to implementation that leaders

Table 7.1   *Overview of main research themes, gaps, and challenges*

Leadership as a …	Research emphasis	Notable gaps and challenges
predictor of team creativity and innovation	Person-focused leader behaviors, particularly transformational (versus transactional) leadership and LMX	Relatively little attention for task-focused leader behaviors
	Increasing attention for mediators and contingency factors	Few nonlinear effects tested
		Lack of experimental studies
		Need to move beyond "classic" leader behaviors and styles (e.g., transformational)
		Combining leader behaviors (e.g., ambidextrous leadership)
		Team-level effects of negative leadership behaviors
moderator of effects on team creativity and innovation	Person-focused behaviors, particularly transformational leadership	Very little attention for task-focused leader behaviors
	Mitigating effects of task-focused behaviors	Few nonlinear effects tested
		Lack of experimental studies
		Inconsistent results on transformational leaders and diversity
catalyst in the creativity–innovation relation	Person-focused behaviors, particularly moral courage	Lack of empirical studies
		Adequately measuring creativity and innovation separately
		Leader behavior shift when moving from creativity to innovation (e.g., ambidextrous leadership)

may need to shift their behaviors to more task-focused or "closing" behaviors. This remains an important open area for future research.

DISCUSSION

In this chapter, we reviewed the research on team leadership and team innovation. While this literature is nowhere near as extensive as that on individual-level leadership effects, our review shows several broad trends, as well as some glaring gaps (also see Table 7.1). We will discuss both, identifying some valuable avenues for future research.

Trends in the Literature

Person-focused and task-focused leadership
One very clear pattern is that person-focused leadership (especially transformational leadership) is studied much more widely than task-focused leadership. While transformational leadership is sometimes seen as "the" leadership style for innovation, our review suggests that task-focused leadership, like transactional and structuring leadership, can also be beneficial. Although the differences between these leader

behaviors would suggest that they might exert their effects through different processes (for example, task focus and efficacy for task-focused leadership; versus climate, perceived support, or trust for person-focused leadership), the results on these mediating variables are not entirely consistent (see e.g., Williams et al., 2010; Pei, 2017). This inconsistency may perhaps be partly explained by inconsistent operationalizations, or by the fact that effective leadership is always multidimensional, combining different styles or behaviors as the situation requires (e.g., Li et al., 2018; Zacher & Rosing, 2015). The implicit assumption of incompatibility underlying much leadership research (for example, pitting transactional against transformational leadership) does not do justice to the complexity of organizational reality.

Predictor or moderator
While most studies address leadership as a predictor, most of them do take moderating variables into account, clearly adopting an interactionist perspective on leadership and team innovation (e.g., Woodman et al., 1993). Importantly, whether leadership is framed as an independent variable or a moderator in these studies depends on one's metatheory of what leaders (should) do. If leadership is thought of as a kind of prime mover that creates visions, sets goals, defines and allocates tasks, and energizes employees into action, testing it as a predictor makes theoretical sense. In contrast, thinking of leadership more in terms of its regulatory function (such as managing resources, constraints, and contextual influences) implies more of a moderator role. Whichever perspective one adopts, it is important to realize that one's metatheory implicitly guides the theoretical and methodological choices one makes; for example, in terms of mediating processes studied.

Methodological trends
Diverse as the literature on leadership and team innovation is, there are some clear trends in the way researchers conduct their studies and analyze their results.

Correlational work
Not surprisingly, most of this research is correlational. Although leadership can be studied experimentally (Rietzschel et al., 2017), the field thus far remains dominated by survey studies. Obviously, this means that causal conclusions regarding leadership are difficult, if not impossible to draw. However, especially with a topic such as leadership, with its strong connotations of agency and influence (e.g., Meindl et al., 1985), the temptation to interpret research results in causal terms is very strong, even though alternative possibilities such as third variables or reverse causality should always be considered. Unless the field moves to more diverse methods, including experimental research, it will remain difficult to adequately gauge the meaning of the results obtained, let alone to derive practical recommendations from them.

Measurement issues
Some other striking trends have to do with measurement. Although the complex and multidimensional nature of both leadership and innovation are widely acknowledged,

researchers commonly use broad and aggregate measures of their core constructs. Importantly, the few studies that do distinguish between different dimensions or facets of leader behavior suggest that this makes a difference (e.g., Boies et al., 2015). Of course, different facets of a construct may be likely to co-occur in practice, which makes it difficult to isolate their individual effects. This is yet another reason why experimental research, allowing researchers to independently manipulate such facets (as was done by Boies et al.), is crucially important for the field to make progress. Similarly, team innovation is all too often measured as a unitary construct. This point is of interest partly because the transition from creativity to implementation is known to be particularly problematic, but also because when different aspects of innovation are distinguished, they may well show different results (e.g., Zhang et al., 2019). Ideally, the different behaviors that make up the innovation process would be measured as such; that is, idea generation would be measured as the actual number (and quality) of ideas proposed by a team, and implementation would be measured in terms of how many ideas were actually successfully implemented (e.g., Somech & Drach-Zahavy, 2013). Unfortunately, this is rarely feasible and most organizational studies will still have to rely on scales. Even when using such scales, however, it is often possible to take a more fine-grained approach, for example by distinguishing between subscales that capture different aspects (e.g., Rietzschel, 2011; Mascareño et al., 2020).

Linear versus curvilinear effects
One other trend that we noticed, although it could also be construed as a gap, is that most research focuses on linear effects of leadership behaviors (see Li et al., 2016; Mo et al., 2019, for exceptions). However, there are reasons to expect that leader behaviors should have nonmonotonic effects (Grant & Schwartz, 2011; Pierce & Aguinis, 2013), especially when multiple processes are at work simultaneously (as was the case in the work by Mo et al., 2019). Thus, rather than asking the question of whether leader behaviors predict innovation, a more specific question might be: Which levels of certain leader behaviors lead to the best outcomes (and through which processes)?

Two Gaps and Future Avenues

Although our review suggests some clear trends, there are some striking lacunas in the empirical literature. We will elaborate on the two most important ones below.

The transition from creativity to implementation
Most importantly, we were able to identify only one study that directly addressed the role of leadership as a transition catalyst. This is a striking lacuna in the research base that needs to be remedied. More and more attention is given to the transition from creativity to implementation (e.g., Baer, 2012; Somech & Drach-Zahavy, 2013; West, 2002; Oldham & Cummings, 1996; Perry-Smith & Coff, 2011; Rietzschel et

al., 2006; Rietzschel et al., 2019; Škerlavaj et al., 2014), and the team "leadership field" should, in our view, follow this development.

In fact, leadership is especially likely to be crucial in this transition, because, as Baer (2012: 1102) put it, "idea implementation, in contrast to creativity, is primarily a social-political process," and leaders are at the heart of teams' social-political maneuvering. Beside the previously mentioned ambidextrous leadership theory (Rosing et al., 2011), one particularly useful framework in this context is Perry-Smith and Mannucci's (2017) idea journey: analyzing the innovation process as a journey through idea generation, idea elaboration, idea championing, and finally idea implementation. Crucial to this model is that different stages imply different needs: idea generation mostly requires flexibility and the freedom to come up with creative ideas; idea elaboration requires support and feedback (in order to keep going and improve an idea); idea championing requires influence and legitimacy (to harvest resources for further development); and idea implementation, finally, requires a shared vision and understanding – that is, others have to get involved in the production or implementation process, and need to speak the creator's "language" and work towards a single goal. The implications for team leadership are clear: the further one moves in the idea journey, the more important team leaders are likely to become. Leaders can be a source of support and feedback during idea elaboration, although team members may also get these from each other. When it comes to idea championing, leaders can provide teams with legitimacy and, particularly, influence (for example, by bringing team members into contact with crucial decision-makers, or pitching the team's idea in crucial board meetings). Finally, leaders are primary drivers and creators of visions, and as such have a crucial role to play in the idea implementation stage, not to mention their formal role in making "go/no go" decisions. One of the most important avenues for future research, therefore, is to address the ways in which leaders contribute (or fail to do so) to their teams' innovative performance in different stages of the idea journey (also see Škerlavaj et al., 2014, for an example on the individual level).

Building a model of team leadership
Finally, the body of research on leadership and team innovation clearly is in dire need of theoretical integration. Whereas the variety of variables studied is encouraging, this also makes the literature relatively scattered; the choice of leadership variables appears, at times, almost haphazard. The field would benefit enormously from a theoretical framework to understand the current state of the art and guide future studies (see also e.g., Anderson et al., 2014; Hughes et al., 2018). Unfortunately, most existing leadership theories lack a team focus and have tended to ignore processes at the team level (see also Kozlowski & Ilgen, 2006). A true theory of team leadership would need to address crucial team-level processes such as information exchange, communication, decision-making, climate, and dissent. Moreover, a focus on "traditional" leader behaviors and leadership styles may not suffice. Not only are constructs such as transformational leadership open to criticism on theoretical and methodological grounds (e.g., Van Knippenberg & Sitkin, 2013), but the strong focus

on person-focused leader behaviors and styles also seems to be too narrow; to the extent that task-focused leadership has been studied, it seems to hold more potential for stimulating creativity and innovation than might perhaps be expected. Thus, we believe that it is time to move beyond establishing relations and effects, and to begin integrating these into a coherent framework.

CONCLUSION

Teams are complex units with processes operating on multiple levels, which makes research in this area interesting and challenging. In our view, the field now needs to move beyond correlational studies with broad and undifferentiated operational-izations, and towards more diverse methods using fine-grained operationalizations, eventually working towards a comprehensive framework of team leadership and team innovation.

REFERENCES

Akgün, A.E., Byrne, J.C., Lynn, G.S., & Keskin, H. 2007. Team stressors, management support, and project and process outcomes in new product development projects. *Technovation*, 27: 628–639.

Amabile, T.M. 1996. *Creativity in context: Update to "The Social Psychology of Creativity."* Boulder, CO: Westview Press.

Anderson, N., Potočnik, K., & Zhou, J. 2014. Innovation and creativity in organizations: A state-of-the-science review, prospective commentary, and guiding framework. *Journal of Management*, 40: 1297–1333.

Anderson, N., & West, M.A. 1996. The Team Climate Inventory: Development of the TCI and its applications in teambuilding for innovativeness. *European Journal of Work and Organizational Psychology*, 5(1): 53–66.

Anderson, N.R., & West, M.A. 1998. Measuring climate for work group innovation: development and validation of the team climate inventory. *Journal of Organizational Behavior*, 19: 235–258.

Baas, M., Koch, S., Nijstad, B.A., & De Dreu, C.K.W. 2015. Conceiving creativity: The nature and consequences of laypeople's beliefs about the realization of creativity. *Psychology of Aesthetics, Creativity, and the Arts*, 9: 340–354.

Baer, M. 2012. Putting creativity to work: The implementation of creative ideas in organizations. *Academy of Management Journal*, 55: 1102–1119.

Berraies, S., & El Abidine, S.Z. 2019. Do leadership styles promote ambidextrous innovation? Case of knowledge-intensive firms. *Journal of Knowledge Management*, 23(5), 836–859.

Boies, K., Fiset, J., & Gill, H. 2015. Communication and trust are key: Unlocking the relationship between leadership and team performance and creativity. *Leadership Quarterly*, 26: 1080–1094.

Bono, J.E., & Judge, T.A. 2003. Self-concordance at work: Toward understanding the motivational effects of transformational leaders. *Academy of Management Journal*, 46: 554–571.

Burke, C.S., Stagl, K.C., Klein, C., Goodwin, G.F., Salas, E., & Halpin, S.M. 2006. What type of leadership behaviors are functional in teams? A meta-analysis. *Leadership Quarterly*, 17(3): 288–307.

Burpitt, W.J., & Bigoness, W.J. 1997. Leadership and innovation among teams: The impact of empowerment. *Small Group Research*, 28: 414–423.

Byron, K., & Khazanchi, S. 2012. Rewards and creative performance: A meta-analytic test of theoretically derived hypotheses. *Psychological Bulletin*, 138: 809–830.

Cerasoli, C.P., Nicklin, J.M., & Ford, M.T. 2014. Intrinsic motivation and extrinsic incentives jointly predict performance: A 40-year meta-analysis. *Psychological Bulletin*, 140: 980–1008.

Chen, M.-H. 2007. Entrepreneurial leadership and new ventures: Creativity in entrepreneurial teams. *Creativity and Innovation Management*, 16: 239–249.

Chen, M.-H., & Agrawal, S. 2017. Do communication barriers in student teams impede creative behavior in the long run? A time-lagged perspective. *Thinking Skills and Creativity*, 26: 154–167.

Chen, G., Farh, J.-L., Campbell-Bush, E.M., Wu, Z., & Wu, X. 2013. Teams as innovative systems: Multilevel motivational antecedents of innovation in R&D teams. *Journal of Applied Psychology*, 98: 1018–1027.

Černe, M., Jaklič, M., & Škerlavaj, M. 2013. Authentic leadership, creativity, and innovation: A multilevel perspective. *Leadership*, 9: 63–85.

De Dreu, C.K.W., Nijstad, B.A., Bechtoldt, M.N., & Baas, M. 2011. Group creativity and innovation: A motivated information processing perspective. *Psychology of Aesthetics, Creativity, and the Arts*, 5: 81–89.

Diehl, M., & Stroebe, W. 1987. Productivity loss in brainstorming groups: Toward the solution of a riddle. *Journal of Personality and Social Psychology*, 53: 497–509.

Eisenbeiß, S.A., & Boerner, S. 2010. Transformational leadership and R&D innovation: Taking a curvilinear approach. *Creativity and Innovation Management*, 19: 364–372.

Eisenbeiß, S.A., van Knippenberg, D., & Boerner, S. 2008. Transformational leadership and team innovation: Integrating team climate principles. *Journal of Applied Psychology*, 93: 1438–1446.

Feng, C., Huang, X., & Zhang, L. 2016. A multilevel study of transformational leadership, dual organizational change and innovative behavior in groups. *Journal of Organizational Change Management*, 29: 855–877.

Fleishman, E.A., Mumford, M.D., Zaccaro, S.J., Levin, K.Y., Korotkin, A.L., & Hein, M.B. 1991. Taxonomic efforts in the description of leader behavior: A synthesis and functional interpretation. *Leadership Quarterly*, 2(4): 245–287.

Gajendran, R.S., & Joshi, A. 2012. Innovation in globally distributed teams: The role of LMX, communication frequency, and member influence on team decisions. *Journal of Applied Psychology*, 97: 1252–1261.

Grant, A.M., & Schwartz, B. 2011. Too much of a good thing: The challenge and opportunity of the inverted U. *Perspectives on Psychological Science*, 6: 61–76.

Hoch, J.E. 2013. Shared leadership and innovation: The role of vertical leadership and employee integrity. *Journal of Business and Psychology*, 28(2): 159–174.

Hon, A.H.Y., & Chan, W.W.H. 2013. Team creative performance: The roles of empowering leadership, creative-related motivation, and task interdependence. *Cornell Hospitality Quarterly*, 54: 199–210.

Howell, J.M., & Avolio, B.J. 1993. Transformational leadership, transactional leadership, locus of control, and support for innovation: Key predictors of consolidated-business-unit performance. *Journal of Applied Psychology*, 78(6): 891–902.

Hughes, D.J., Lee, A., Tian, A.W., Newman, A., & Legood, A. 2018. Leadership, creativity, and innovation: A critical review and practical recommendations. *Leadership Quarterly*, 29(5): 549–569.

Hülsheger, U.R., Anderson, N., & Salgado, J.F. 2009. Team-level predictors of innovation at work: A comprehensive meta-analysis spanning three decades of research. *Journal of Applied Psychology*, 94(5): 1128–1145.

Jaussi, K.S., & Dionne, S.D. 2003. Leading for creativity: The role of unconventional leader behavior. *Leadership Quarterly*, 14: 475–498.

Jiang, Y., & Chen, C.C. 2018. Integrating knowledge activities for team innovation: Effects of transformational leadership. *Journal of Management*, 44: 1819–1847.

Jung, D.I. 2001. Transformational and transactional leadership and their effects on creativity in groups. *Creativity Research Journal*, 13: 185–195.

Kahai, S.S., Sosik, J.J., & Avolio, B.J. 2003. Effects of leadership style, anonymity, and rewards on creativity-relevant processes and outcomes in an electronic meeting system context. *Leadership Quarterly*, 14: 499–524.

Kahrobaei, S., & Mortazavi, S. 2016. How leader–member exchange can uplift team's energy to increase creative work involvement. *Team Performance Management*, 22(1/2): 75–91.

Kakar, A.K. 2017. Investigating the prevalence and performance correlates of vertical versus shared leadership in emergent software development teams. *Information Systems Management*, 34: 172–184.

Kozlowski, S.W., & Ilgen, D.R. 2006. Enhancing the effectiveness of work groups and teams. *Psychological Science in the Public Interest*, 7(3): 77–124.

Lee, A., Legood, A., Hughes, D., Tian, A.W., Newman, A., & Knight, C. 2019. Leadership, creativity and innovation: A meta-analytic review. *European Journal of Work and Organizational Psychology*, 29: 1–35.

Lee, S., Yun, S., & Srivastava, A. 2013. Evidence for a curvilinear relationship between abusive supervision and creativity in South Korea. *Leadership Quarterly*, 24(5): 724–731.

Li, G., Liu, H., & Luo, Y. 2018. Directive versus participative leadership: Dispositional antecedents and team consequences. *Journal of Occupational and Organizational Psychology*, 91: 645–664.

Li, Y., Fu, F., Sun, J.-M., & Yang, B. 2016. Leader–member exchange differentiation and team creativity: An investigation of nonlinearity. *Human Relations*, 69: 1121–1138.

Litchfield, R.C. 2008. Brainstorming reconsidered: A goal-based view. *Academy of Management Review*, 33: 649–668.

Liu, D., Liao, H., & Loi, R. 2012. The dark side of leadership: A three-level investigation of the cascading effect of abusive supervision on employee creativity. *Academy of Management Journal*, 55: 1187–1212.

Liu, J., Liu, X., & Zeng, X. 2011. Does transactional leadership count for team innovativeness? The moderating role of emotional labor and the mediating role of team efficacy. *Journal of Organizational Change Management*, 24: 282–298.

Mackey, J.D., Frieder, R.E., Brees, J.R., & Martinko, M.J. 2017. Abusive supervision: A meta-analysis and empirical review. *Journal of Management*, 43(6): 1940–1965.

Madrid, H.P., Totterdell, P., & Niven, K. 2016a. Does leader-affective presence influence communication of creative ideas within work teams? *Emotion*, 16: 798–802.

Madrid, H.P., Totterdell, P., Niven, K., & Barros, E. 2016b. Leader affective presence and innovation in teams. *Journal of Applied Psychology*, 101: 673–686.

Magni, M., & Maruping, L.M. 2013. Sink or swim: Empowering leadership and overload in teams' ability to deal with the unexpected. *Human Resource Management*, 52: 715–739.

Marta, S., Leritz, L., & Mumford, M. 2005. Leadership skills and the group performance: Situational demands, behavioral requirements, and planning. *Leadership Quarterly*, 16(1): 97–120.

Mascareño, J.M., Rietzschel, E.F., & Wisse, B.M. 2020. Envisioning innovation: Does visionary leadership engender team innovative performance through goal alignment? *Creativity and Innovation Management*, 29: 33–48.

Meindl, J.R., Ehrlich, S.B., & Dukerich, J.M. 1985. The romance of leadership. *Administrative Science Quarterly*, 30: 78–102.

Mo, S., Ling, C.-D., & Xie, X.-Y. 2019. The curvilinear relationship between ethical leadership and team creativity: The moderating role of team faultlines. *Journal of Business Ethics*, 154: 229–242.

Morgeson, F.P., DeRue, D.S., & Karam, E.P. 2010. Leadership in teams: A functional approach to understanding leadership structures and processes. *Journal of Management*, 36(1): 5–39.

Nemeth, C.J., & O'Connor, A. 2019. Better than individuals? Dissent and group creativity. In P.B. Paulus & B.A. Nijstad (eds), *The Oxford handbook of group creativity and innovation*: 73–83. Oxford: Oxford University Press.

Nijstad, B., Berger-Selman, F., & De Dreu, C. 2014. Innovation in top management teams: Minority dissent, transformational leadership, and radical innovations. *European Journal of Work and Organizational Psychology*, 23(2): 310–322.

Nijstad, B.A., & Stroebe, W. 2006. How the group affects the mind: A cognitive model of idea generation in groups. *Personality and Social Psychology Review*, 10: 186–213.

Oldham, G.R., & Cummings, A. 1996. Employee creativity: Personal and contextual factors at work. *Academy of Management Journal*, 39: 607–634.

Paulsen, N., Callan, V.J., Ayoko, O., & Saunders, D. 2013. Transformational leadership and innovation in an R&D organization experiencing major change. *Journal of Organizational Change Management*, 26: 595–610.

Paulsen, N., Maldonado, D., Callan, V.J., & Ayoko, O. 2009. Charismatic leadership, change and innovation in an R&D organization. *Journal of Organizational Change Management*, 22: 511–523.

Paulus, P.B., & Nijstad, B.A. 2019. *The Oxford handbook of group creativity and innovation*. Oxford: Oxford University Press.

Pei, G. 2017. Structuring leadership and team creativity: The mediating role of team innovation climate. *Social Behavior and Personality: An International Journal*, 45: 369–376.

Peltokorpi, V., & Hasu, M. 2016. Transactive memory systems in research team innovation: A moderated mediation analysis. *Journal of Engineering and Technology Management*, 39: 1–12.

Peralta, C.F., Saldanha, M.F., Lopes, P.N., Lourenço, P.R., & Pais, L. 2019. Does supervisor's moral courage to go beyond compliance have a role in the relationships between teamwork quality, team creativity, and team idea implementation? *Journal of Business Ethics*. doi:10.1007/s10551-019-04175-y.

Perry-Smith, J.E., & Coff, R.W. 2011. In the mood for entrepreneurial creativity? How optimal group affect differs for generating and selecting ideas for new ventures. *Strategic Entrepreneurship Journal*, 5: 247–268.

Perry-Smith, J.E., & Mannucci, P.V. 2017. From creativity to innovation: The social network drivers of the four phases of the idea journey. *Academy of Management Review*, 42: 53–79.

Pierce, J.R., & Aguinis, H. 2013. The too-much-of-a-good-thing effect in management. *Journal of Management*, 39: 313–338.

Reuveni, Y., & Vashdi, D.R. 2015. Innovation in multidisciplinary teams: The moderating role of transformational leadership in the relationship between professional heterogeneity and shared mental models. *European Journal of Work and Organizational Psychology*, 24: 678–692.

Rietzschel, E.F. 2011. Collective regulatory focus predicts specific aspects of team innovation. *Group Processes and Intergroup Relations*, 14: 337–345.

Rietzschel, E.F. 2018. Freedom, structure, and creativity. In R. Reiter-Palmon, V.L. Kennel, & J.C. Kaufman (eds), *Individual creativity in the workplace*: 203–222. San Diego, CA: Elsevier Academic Press.

Rietzschel, E.F., Nijstad, B.A., & Stroebe, W. 2006. Productivity is not enough: A comparison of interactive and nominal brainstorming groups on idea generation and selection. *Journal of Experimental Social Psychology*, 42: 244–251.

Rietzschel, E.F., Nijstad, B.A., & Stroebe, W. 2019. Why great ideas are often overlooked. In P.B. Paulus & B.A. Nijstad (eds), *The Oxford handbook of group creativity and innovation*: 179–198. Oxford: Oxford University Press.

Rietzschel, E.F., & Ritter, S.M. 2018. Moving from creativity to innovation. In R. Reiter-Palmon, V.L. Kennel, & J.C. Kaufman (eds), *Individual creativity in the workplace*: 3–34. London: Elsevier Academic Press.

Rietzschel, E.F., Slijkhuis, M., & Van Yperen, N.W. 2014. Close monitoring as a contextual stimulator: How need for structure affects the relation between close monitoring and work outcomes. *European Journal of Work and Organizational Psychology*, 23: 394–404.

Rietzschel, E.F., Wisse, B., & Rus, D. 2017. Puppet masters in the lab: Experimental methods in leadership research. In B. Schyns, P. Neves, & R. Hall (eds), *Handbook of methods in leadership research*: 48–72. Cheltenham, UK and Northampton, MA, USA: Edward Elgar Publishing.

Ritter, S.M., & Rietzschel, E.F. 2017. Lay theories of creativity. In C.M. Zedelius, B.C.N. Müller, & J.W. Schooler (eds), *The science of lay theories: How beliefs shape our cognition, behavior, and health*: 95–126. Cham: Springer International Publishing.

Rosing, K., Frese, M., & Bausch, A. 2011. Explaining the heterogeneity of the leadership-innovation relationship: Ambidextrous leadership. *Leadership Quarterly*, 22: 956–974.

Rousseau, V., & Aubé, C. 2018. When leaders stifle innovation in work teams: The role of abusive supervision. *Journal of Business Ethics*, 151: 651–664.

Rousseau, V., Aubé, C., & Tremblay, S. (2013). Team coaching and innovation in work teams: An examination of the motivational and behavioral intervening mechanisms. *Leadership and Organization Development Journal*, 34(4): 344–364.

Schaubroeck, J., Carmeli, A., Bhatia, S., & Paz, E. 2016. Enabling team learning when members are prone to contentious communication: The role of team leader coaching. *Human Relations*, 69: 1709–1727.

Shalley, C.E., & Zhou, J. 2008. Organizational creativity research: A historical overview. In C. Shalley & J. Zhou (eds), *Handbook of organizational creativity*: 3–31. Mahwah, NJ: Lawrence Erlbaum.

Shin, Y., & Eom, C. 2014. Team proactivity as a linking mechanism between team creative efficacy, transformational leadership, and risk-taking norms and team creative performance. *Journal of Creative Behavior*, 48: 89–114.

Shin, S.J., & Zhou, J. 2007. When is educational specialization heterogeneity related to creativity in research and development teams? Transformational leadership as moderator. *Journal of Applied Psychology*, 92: 1709–1721.

Somech, A. 2006. The effects of leadership style and team process on performance and innovation in functionally heterogeneous teams. *Journal of Management*, 32(1): 132–157.

Somech, A., & Drach-Zahavy, A. 2013. Translating team creativity to innovation implementation: The role of team composition and climate for innovation. *Journal of Management*, 39: 684–708.

Sosik, J.J., Avolio, B.J., & Kahai, S.S. 1998. Inspiring group creativity: Comparing anonymous and identified electronic brainstorming. *Small Group Research*, 29: 3–31.

Steiner, I.D. 1972. *Group process and productivity*. New York: Academic Press.

Stollberger, J., West, M.A., & Sacramento, C.A. 2019. Innovation in work teams. In P.B. Paulus & B.A. Nijstad (eds), *The Oxford handbook of group creativity and innovation*: 231–252. Oxford: Oxford University Press.

Škerlavaj, M., Černe, M., & Dysvik, A. 2014. I get by with a little help from my supervisor: Creative-idea generation, idea implementation, and perceived supervisor support. *Leadership Quarterly*, 25: 987–1000.

Van Knippenberg, D., De Dreu, C.K.W., & Homan, A.C. 2004. Work group diversity and group performance: An integrative model and research agenda. *Journal of Applied Psychology*, 89: 1008–1022.

Van Knippenberg, D., & Sitkin, S.B. 2013. A critical assessment of charismatic–transformational leadership research: Back to the drawing board? *Academy of Management Annals*, 7: 1–60.

Wang, X., Kim, T., & Lee, D. 2016. Cognitive diversity and team creativity: Effects of team intrinsic motivation and transformational leadership. *Journal of Business Research*, 69(9): 3231–3239.

Wegner, D.M. 1986. Transactive memory: A contemporary analysis of the group mind. In B. Mullen & G.R. Goethals (eds), *Theories of group behavior*: 185–208. New York: Springer-Verlag.

West, M.A. 2002. Sparkling fountains or stagnant ponds: An integrative model of creativity and innovation implementation in work groups. *Applied Psychology: An International Review*, 51: 355–387.

West, M.A., & Farr, J.L. 1990. Innovation at work. In M.A. West & J.L. Farr (eds), *Innovation and creativity at work: Psychological and organizational strategies*: 3–13. Oxford: John Wiley & Sons.

Williams, H.M., Parker, S.K., & Turner, N. 2010. Proactively performing teams: The role of work design, transformational leadership, and team composition. *Journal of Occupational and Organizational Psychology*, 83: 301–324.

Woodman, R.W., Sawyer, J.E., & Griffin, R.W. 1993. Toward a theory of organizational creativity. *Academy of Management Review*, 18: 293–321.

Wu, Q., & Cormican, K. 2016. Shared leadership: An analysis of the evolvement process across the project life cycle. *International Journal of Innovation, Management and Technology*, 7: 299–309.

Yang, J., Liu, H., & Gu, J. 2017. A multi-level study of servant leadership on creativity: The roles of self-efficacy and power distance. *Leadership and Organization Development Journal*, 38: 610–629.

Ye, Q., Wang, D., & Guo, W. 2019. Inclusive leadership and team innovation: The role of team voice and performance pressure. *European Management Journal*, 37: 468–480.

Yoshida, D.T., Sendjaya, S., Hirst, G., & Cooper, B. 2014. Does servant leadership foster creativity and innovation? A multi-level mediation study of identification and prototypicality. *Journal of Business Research*, 67: 1395–1404.

Yukl, G.A. 2013. *Leadership in Organizations* (Global edn). Harlow: Pearson.

Zaccaro, S., Rittman, A., & Marks, M. 2001. Team leadership. *Leadership Quarterly*, 12(4): 451–483.

Zacher, H., & Rosing, K. 2015. Ambidextrous leadership and team innovation. *Leadership and Organization Development Journal*, 36: 54–68.

Zhang, A.Y., Tsui, A.S., & Wang, D.X. 2011. Leadership behaviors and group creativity in Chinese organizations: The role of group processes. *Leadership Quarterly*, 22: 851–862.

Zhang, W., Sun, S.L., Jiang, Y., & Zhang, W. 2019. Openness to experience and team creativity: Effects of knowledge sharing and transformational leadership. *Creativity Research Journal*, 31: 62–73.

Zhou, J., Wang, X.M., Bavato, D., Tasselli, S., & Wu, J. 2019. Understanding the receiving side of creativity: A multidisciplinary review and implications for management research. *Journal of Management*, 45: 2570–2595.

8.   Teams as synthesizers: the role of constraints in the process of creative synthesis

Sarah Harvey and Poornika Ananth

Teams are an important forum through which the otherwise dispersed expertise, per-spectives, and information necessary to develop new organizational products, pro-cesses, and strategies are brought together (Ancona & Caldwell, 1992; Dougherty, 1992; Hargadon & Sutton, 1996; Lovelace et al., 2001; Taylor & Greve, 2006). Teams are therefore often viewed as the engines that drive organizational innova-tion (Amabile, 1988; Woodman et al., 1993). From this perspective, the role of the team is to provide diverse information and a variety of viewpoints on the team's task (Osborn, 1953; Paulus & Yang, 2000), and the team's goal is to generate ideas (Amabile, 1988; Staw, 1990).

The assumption that divergence facilitates team creativity mirrors the lay view of creativity as an unconstrained, chaotic process. However, there is also evidence that an unbounded creative process makes it difficult for members of organizations to effectively utilize one another's diverse informational resources to produce novel output. Alternatively, Harvey (2014) proposes a model of creative synthesis, in which teams turn their collective attention to their similarities in order to combine their knowledge to develop new ideas. In that model, creativity is a process of interpreting and integrating ideas (Harvey, 2014; Drazin et al., 1999; Weick et al., 2005). From the perspective of creative synthesis, a wide and varied search area may increase the opportunity for original connections, but it may also inhibit the ability of groups to make sense of and combine information to develop creative outputs. The creative synthesis perspective emphasizes the importance of mechanisms through which inconsistencies between different understandings can be reconciled in unique ways (Harvey, 2014; Poole & Van de Ven, 1989).

We suggest that constraints on the creative process may be one mechanism that facilitates creative synthesis. Constraints are any factors that limit a team's range of possible action (Dougherty, 2008) and there is a growing recognition that some constraints can benefit creativity (Binyamin & Carmeli, 2010; Gilson et al., 2005; Goldenberg et al., 1999; Harrison & Rouse, 2014; Hoegl et al., 2008; Joyce, 2009; Mumford et al., 2001; Sagiv et al., 2010). The research shows that constraints can enable idea generation in groups by reducing ambiguity and providing focus, and that a balance of autonomy and constraint can benefit idea generation in groups (Harrison & Rouse, 2014). The process of creative synthesis, however, involves not only the generation of new ideas, but also the evolution of the synthesis or a new understanding around which to generate ideas, as well as the repeated reconstruction of the synthesis through newly generated ideas (Harvey, 2014). Synthesis therefore requires the repeated development of novel yet shared understandings between team members. The literature on teams suggests three ways in which constraints might pave a path for creative synthesis. Firstly, successfully combining individual contributions into a coherent new idea or product rests on shared assumptions, values, and rules (Dougherty, 1992; Hargadon & Bechky, 2006; Leavitt, 1996; Peplowski, 1998; Weick, 1998). Building common assumptions, values, and rules constrains the problem structure a team uses to interpret their task. The problem structure is a framework consisting of the assumptions, values, and rules underlying group members' understandings of the task (Gioia, 1986; Walsh, 1995), and it forms the basis for a new synthesis. Secondly, teams tend to be more creative when they work on structured problems with clear common goals (Baruah & Paulus, 2011; Gilson & Shalley, 2004). Clear goals constrain the solution space of the problem, which refers to the concrete elements created through the development of a novel synthesis (Czarnecki and Eisenecker, 2000). Finally, a tightly structured process that separates idea generation from evaluation and provides cognitive space for individual ideation enables teams to benefit from members' unique perspectives (Delbecq et al., 1975; Osborn, 1953; Paulus & Yang, 2000). This constrains the nature of team interaction.

Previous research has viewed the problem structure, solution space, and team interaction as separate from the core divergent activity of the team. For example, the team's problem structure is conceptualized as deriving from the composition of the team, which determines members' underlying knowledge and perspectives (Milliken & Martins, 1996; van Knippenberg & Schippers, 2007); the solution space is assumed to be defined before ideas are generated (Amabile, 1988; Gilson & Shalley, 2004); and teams are advised to minimize interaction during idea generation (Gallupe et al., 1991; Paulus & Yang, 2000). As a result, relatively little is known about the mechanisms through which these constraints influence creativity, or how they interact with one another. In the creative synthesis model, these elements interrelate to mutually influence the repeated generation of novel ideas over time. Exploring how constraint affects a team's creative process can reveal its potential benefit to team creativity, and provide a richer understanding of the dynamics of creative teams.

The purpose of this chapter is to provide such an exploration. Specifically, the chapter asks: how do constraints affect team creativity, and in particular, the process of creative synthesis? To explore this, we present a qualitative process analysis (Langley, 1999; Pentland, 1999) of creativity in four firms in the institutional asset management industry in the United Kingdom (UK). Firms in the institutional asset management industry routinely face the problem of how to beat the market; something that few investors are able to do on a consistent basis. We discovered that two firms in our study used mechanisms to constrain problem structure, solution space, and interactions across the creative process. We draw on this insight to build a model in which constraints that occur across the creative process lead teams to continuously solve and then reconstruct the fund management problem; that is, how to select investment opportunities that will beat the market. Creativity occurs through creative synthesis, when teams construct novel problems and consequently develop novel solutions. This provides new insights into the process of creative synthesis and challenges the notion that teams benefit organizational innovation by acting as idea generators.

TEAMS AS IDEA GENERATORS

Team creativity occurs when the team works to produce ideas, processes, products, or other outputs that are both novel and valuable within the context of the creation's domain (Amabile, 1988; Mumford & Gustafson, 1988). In particular, this involves four broad stages of activity (Amabile, 1988): identifying or constructing problems; gathering information and skills for problem solving; generating alternatives; and selecting an idea for implementation. The shared goal of a creative team is to generate novel and high-quality ideas, and members may depend on one another in different ways to achieve this outcome: they may work together to identify a problem, develop the knowledge to solve the problem, generate ideas, or collectively choose between the solutions they develop. The team's creative efforts may therefore be directed to different dimensions of the creative process.

The majority of research focuses on idea generation as the primary way that interdependent work benefits creativity (George, 2007). Because generating ideas involves divergent thinking (Guilford, 1950), teams are expected to have an advantage, as one group member can initiate this process in another by making an unexpected suggestion or by expressing a perspective that the other had not previously considered (Nemeth, 1986; Paulus, 2000). An implication is that a team's creative process should be unconstrained in several ways. Firstly, the more diverse a team is in terms of members' underlying perspectives, the more members should stimulate new perspectives and ways of thinking about the problem (Bantel & Jackson, 1989; Taylor & Greve, 2006; Woodman et al., 1993). Secondly, this diversity should also stimulate original associations between team members' ideas that enable the team to develop divergent solutions, widening the solution space (Woodman et al., 1993). Thirdly, interactions in which team members feel free to express their ideas and to disagree with one another are necessary for the team to benefit from their different knowledge and perspectives (Binyamin & Carmeli, 2010; Mannix & Neale, 2005).

Research on the idea generating potential of teams, however, has revealed that teams also encounter many problems that limit their creativity. For example, team members have difficulty generating ideas while others in the group are speaking, or while mentally holding onto an idea until their turn to speak (Diehl & Stroebe, 1991, 1987). As a result, on average, groups tend to generate fewer and lower-quality ideas than do individuals working alone (Diehl & Stroebe, 1991; McGrath, 1984). Similarly, research on the benefits of diversity to team creativity is not unequivocal: studies continue to find that some diverse teams fail to be creative (Ancona & Caldwell, 1992; Bercovitz & Feldman, 2010; Dougherty, 1992; Harvey, 2013; Lovelace et al., 2001). Teams also struggle to identify and select the creative ideas that they generate (Rietzschel et al., 2006). These results suggest that teams with unconstrained problems, solution spaces, and interactions may not have the highest level of creativity.

THE CREATIVE SYNTHESIS MODEL

In contrast to the view that divergent problem structures, solution spaces, and interactions promote team creativity, research on creative synthesis (Harvey, 2014) reveals the potential value of constraining these dimensions of the team creative process. Creative synthesis is based on a dialectic model in which diverse group resources are integrated into breakthrough creative output. The process of synthesis involves: (1) enacting ideas by making them concrete (for instance, drawing sketches or developing resources for implementation); (2) focusing collective attention on ideas; and (3) building on similarities and overlaps between diverse perspectives. Through the process of synthesis, group members' ideas, information, and perspectives form a shared understanding of the creative problem and the evaluation criteria for solving the problem. That understanding is novel, because it lies at the intersection of members' unique knowledge and ideas.

Critical to the theory of creative synthesis is the notion that the shared understanding of the problem developed by the group makes it easier for group members to converge around – and therefore, to select – a particular idea (Harvey, 2014, 2013). In the present chapter, we build from this point to suggest that constraints may aid that process in three ways, which we elaborate below.

The Role of Constraints on Team Creativity

Firstly, constraining the problem structure may help team members to make sense of and use one another's ideas to generate new alternatives. A problem structure is constraining in that it determines the ideas an individual is likely to generate and consider (Cropley, 2006; Walsh, 1995; Ward, 1994). Therefore, if members have a common problem structure, they may miss out on other perspectives. However, sharing a problem structure imposes meaning on the team members' collective knowledge (Ford, 1996; Gioia, 1986; Gioia & Chittipeddi, 1991; Weick et al., 2005). Indeed, diverse teams are more creative when group members have a strong organizational culture that emphasizes what members have in common rather than what makes them unique (Chatman et al., 1998). This helps teams to develop a shared system of meaning for understanding one another's unique information (Earley & Mosakowski, 2000).

Secondly, restricting the solution space that a team considers may also benefit creativity by limiting the number of variables considered, so that creative effort can follow the most promising associations between fewer ideas (Finke et al., 1992; Harrison & Rouse, 2014). Consistent with this view, team creativity is higher when team members have a relatively clear prescribed goal that is shared by team members

(Gilson & Shalley, 2004; Mumford et al., 2001), rather than when members are encouraged to develop their creative ideas in different directions (Baruah & Paulus, 2011). Goals direct the creative efforts of individuals on the team (Shalley, 1995). The creative performance of diverse teams therefore improves when the solution space is constrained by emphasizing a cooperative norm that prompts team members to focus on one another's ideas (Chatman & Flynn, 2001).

Thirdly, structuring to constrain team member interactions with one another within the creative process may facilitate creativity. For example, Osborn's (1953) rules advocate separating idea generation from idea evaluation to prevent group members from worrying about criticism of their ideas. Sequentially writing down ideas and contributions to others' ideas also improves creative outcomes (Delbecq et al., 1975; Van de Ven & Delbecq, 1971). Similarly, using technology to facilitate interaction helps members to keep track of their ideas and provides anonymity (Cooper et al., 1998; Gallupe et al., 1991; Gallupe et al., 1994). Teams also generate more ideas when participation rules ensure that all group members contribute their ideas (West & Anderson, 1996), or when the process provides additional time for group members to generate ideas alone after the group interaction (Paulus & Yang, 2000). Structuring team interactions gives members the cognitive space needed for idea generation (Diehl & Stroebe, 1987, 1991) and reduces social anxiety (Mullen et al., 1991). However, these structures are themselves constraints on the creative process.

These three streams of research raise the possibility that constraints can facilitate team creativity. What is less clear, however, is through what mechanisms and processes this occurs. The creative process can be constrained at any point (Finke et al., 1992); however, each stream of research discussed above suggests a different role for constraint. In addition, as these streams of research generally treat constraints as a characteristic of the team or task, empirical tests examine cross-sections of teams with different degrees of constraint. This approach demonstrates the importance of constraints, but is not designed to reveal the process through which constraint benefits team creativity or how they interact with divergence (Acar et al., 2019). The purpose of the present study is therefore to explicitly explore the process through which both divergence and constraint unfold within team creativity over time.

RESEARCH SETTING

To explore these issues, we present an inductive, qualitative exploration of the creative process in the active institutional asset management industry in the UK. Active asset managers attempt to construct portfolios of assets (for example, stocks, bonds, equities, currencies) that will outperform a passive benchmark performance level for those assets.

Creativity in the Asset Management Industry

The asset management industry provides an interesting setting in which to study team creativity, because outperformance of the benchmark in this industry requires creativity. Good investment decisions meet the criteria of creative ideas; that is, investments outperform the benchmark when they are both novel (that is, the investment has not been taken by many other investors, so that they can be made at a low price), but also valuable or high in quality (that is, the investment is ultimately taken by other investors, so that the price goes up). There is such a strong parallel between investment decisions and creativity that Sternberg & Lubart (1995) formulated an investment theory of creativity which argues that creative people are those willing and able to buy their ideas low, when they are unknown or unpopular, and sell them high, when they have gained favor. This is also what active asset managers attempt to do when making investment decisions. In other words, asset management is a somewhat unique context, in that good investment performance is also an indication of high levels of creativity.

The parallel between creativity and investment management is further supported by the nature of the fund management process. While asset selection can be described as a highly rational process, the stages involved match the idealized creative process described in the literature of moving from idea generation to idea evaluation and selection (Amabile, 1988; Osborn, 1953). Specifically, six stages are involved in making asset management decisions (see Figure 8.1). First, ideas are generated about assets that may be currently over- or undervalued by the market. This is fundamentally a creative task, because the set of possible investments is too large for all to be considered, and the best investments are those that are not obvious (that is, that others have not taken). Ideas are next analyzed in more detail by, for example, gathering data and inputting them into quantitative models or "testing" them through rigorous team discussions. This is similar to the evaluation and selection of creative ideas where deciding what information to focus on for evaluation is also a judgment call, and many firms emphasize the originality of their process for evaluating ideas. The third step in the process involves deciding which assets to buy or sell and then giving direction to traders. In the fourth and fifth steps, more specific additional decisions are made for those assets that will be bought or sold: what size of a position to take in that asset, and the timing of the buy or sell decision. In the final step, the risk implications for the new portfolio are reviewed. This review may be done by the portfolio manager alone, or in conjunction with a separate risk management team that builds a model to determine how much the risk profile of the portfolio will change due to an asset sale or purchase.

In addition to the need for creativity both in the process and in final investment decisions, asset management firms tend to have their own approach or proprietary model for fund selection. Developing this approach also involves creativity; there is no commonly accepted way to repeatedly identify high-performing investment decisions. Some of an investment's success may be attributable to cumulative advantage (Salganik et al., 2006); however, underlying differences in the quality of the invest-

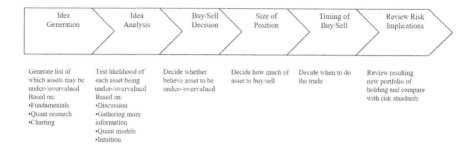

Figure 8.1   Overview of the asset management process

ment can still influence a decision's ultimate success (Salganik et al., 2006). Thus, firms that try to make decisions which reflect this underlying quality, or firms that try to make decisions to take advantage of the behavior of other investors, must still scan and assimilate a large and complex set of data and generate novel ways to make decisions based on this data. Different firms therefore focus on different information or integrate their information sources in different ways in order to generate a unique set of solutions.

In sum, while this process requires some rational analysis to eliminate bad investment decisions, just as any creative process does, there is no single good investment decision that can be identified through a rational problem-solving process alone; generation of novelty is required throughout the process.

The Role of Teams in the Asset Management Industry

Historically, asset management decisions were made by individual fund managers working alone. However, teams have increasingly been used in asset selection and allocation decisions.[1] Initially, the rationale for using teams was to limit the power and therefore risk associated with "star" managers. Furthermore, teams have the potential to generate novel understandings of the fund management task by integrating diverse understandings of factors such as asset diversification, liquidity, and valuation (Harvey, 2014). This is particularly important for firms in the asset management industry that need to distinguish themselves from platform-based investing (Treon, 2020). However, the integration of unique perspectives towards the development of a unique synthesis can be a challenging task, and indeed, diverse teams, which have the greatest potential for synthesis, are also those most likely to struggle to synthesise their inputs (Harvey, 2013). Interestingly, some firms appear to have found the team structure effective for making asset management decisions, reflected in the firm's success as a whole in terms of growth in assets under management and expert evaluations of the firm. In contrast, other firms have had less success using the team structure, with lower levels of firm performance. A further advantage of this setting is therefore that it allows a comparison of the conditions under which teams are used as an effective or ineffective mechanism for facilitating creativity.

METHODS

This study uses an inductive, qualitative approach to explore the role of divergence and constraint within the creative processes of teams in four asset management firms (Glaser & Strauss, 1967; Langley, 1999). We focused on four firms which used teams for fund management. The four firms were identified by an industry expert with over 20 years of experience in the asset management industry to be representative of firms using a team-based structure. All of the firms selected participated in the study. The firms are labelled Solid Rock, Theory Asset Management, Loyalty Asset Management, and Golden Touch (all pseudonyms). A firm may have multiple portfolio management teams, but firms had a consistent philosophy for how the teams should operate and their role in the investment process that carried across those teams. Our goal in the study was to understand the purpose of teamwork and the general process through which teams within each firm organized. We therefore assume some consistency across teams within a firm, and develop a picture of how teams are organized around the asset management task within a given firm.

Data Sources and Collection

Both qualitative and quantitative data were collected for the study in 2002 and 2003. Quantitative data supplemented and validated the qualitative data sources, rather than tested ideas (Eisenhardt & Bourgois, 1988; Sutton & Hargadon, 1996).

Archival materials
Company websites and corporate brochures of the four firms were analyzed for descriptions of firms' investment philosophy, goals, and fund management process. An industry report detailing assets under management, portfolio characteristics, and a qualitative assessment of performance for the firms, was also obtained for the two years prior to the study.

Industry experts
The first author attended an industry conference and consulted five professionals with at least ten years each of UK investment industry experience, who were surveyed for their perspective on the performance of firms in the study. Each expert was asked to provide a rating on a 9-point Likert-type scale of firms' outperformance of returns versus benchmark, and consistency of returns.

Semi-structured interviews
A total of 13 interviews were conducted with members of the four firms to identify and confirm the unique elements of their fund management process. We followed

Lincoln & Guba's (1985) strategy of purposeful sampling in first focusing data collection on the senior managers responsible for overseeing all portfolio managers within each firm. We label this person the Chief Investment Manager to distinguish him (all Chief Investment Managers in our study were male) from a portfolio manager. Chief Investment Managers differ from portfolio managers, who are responsible for taking decisions on whether or not specific assets should be included in (or excluded from) the portfolio. In contrast, the Chief Investment Manager is responsible for overseeing portfolio managers within their respective firm and is therefore ultimately responsible for the investment performance of the firm, including setting the investment strategy and managing individual portfolio managers and teams.

To ensure that the process espoused by the Chief Investment Manager was practiced as described within the organization, additional interviews were carried out with people working on portfolio teams at all levels within two of the organizations (one successful firm and one unsuccessful firm). Out of the 13 interviews, five were with Chief Investment Managers and eight were with other members of teams within the two firms. Interviews lasted one to two hours and were tape recorded and transcribed. Interviews focused on the asset selection process, form and structure of investment decision-making in the firm, the extent and role of teamwork in this process, and the informants' general attitude towards the use of teams in the industry. We stopped adding informants when doing so did not provide additional insights into the nature of the fund management process (Glaser & Strauss, 1967).

Surveys
During the semi-structured interviews, interviewees were also asked to complete a short survey that described the fund management process in their organization by indicating how individual thinking, informal teamwork, formal teamwork, and other in-house and external input contributed to the six subtasks involved in the stock selection process.

Observation
The final source of data collection was observation of a fund management meeting at one of the firms. This allowed us to further validate team members' descriptions of the decision process (Jick, 1979).

Analytic Strategy

The analysis of this data proceeded in four stages, described below.

Stage 1: Building the asset management process
The first stage of the analysis was to develop an understanding of the fund management process. To do this, we examined archival material and surveys for the stages of activity described by each of the firms, and abstracted the general stages that were common to all firms. The resulting process is illustrated in Figure 8.1.

Stage 2: Identifying mechanisms of divergence and constraint

The next stage was to identify divergence and constraint within the process of each firm in the study. To do this, we followed Miles & Huberman's (1984) principles for categorical analysis, moving from detailed coding of interview notes and archival material (Van Maanen, 1979), to identifying commonalities among phrases and relationships between concepts, to a higher level of more general abstraction. We focused on constructing meaningful interpretations of the data from which to develop theory (Gioia et al., 1994; Glaser & Strauss, 1967; Van Maanen, 1979). We used constant comparison techniques to assemble the first-order categories into more abstract, second-order theoretical categories (Van Maanen, 1979), iterating between theory and the data to develop an understanding of the phenomenon of interest.

Stage 3: Comparison of processes across each firm

Finally, we searched for commonalities between the processes used by the firms using the aggregate dimensions uncovered in stage 2. We present maps that summarize the two firms in each category in the 'Findings' section below. We then examined the differences between the categories.

FINDINGS

We categorized the mechanisms for making fund management decisions in terms of whether they encourage divergence in the creative process or constrain the process. In addition, mechanisms can be categorized according to which dimension of the creative process they affect: the team's problem structure, the solution space, or team interactions. The mechanisms are discussed in detail below.

Firms used two broad types of mechanisms to make creative investment decisions. Divergent mechanisms were designed to bring a variety of ideas, information, and inputs into fund management decisions. All of the firms used some mechanisms to facilitate divergence. For example, cognitive stimulation between team members with different perspectives was one of the primary mechanisms expected to generate new ideas. The Chief Investment Manager at Loyalty described the role of the team as: "flushing out potentially lots and lots of ideas and different people with diverse ways of looking at things, you know, ways of interpreting information, ideas and so on." He went on to describe the process: "start with the unconstrained, you put down unbounded ideas and then refine down to the final solution. All we want to do is try and come up with a solution. But that's the idea [of teamwork], it seems very good for idea regeneration."

The desire to improve decisions by exposing team members to others with different views was also reflected in team members' description of the decision-making process. A team member at Loyalty indicated that during the process of coming up with investment ideas, it was "good to have people to talk to, to bounce ideas off. It really opens your mind up to the decisions." The Chief Investment Manager at

Theory also described the process of evaluating investment decisions as involving divergent opinions over each investment:

> once an analyst's completed his or her research on a company we have what we call a research review. This research review is a group of analysts ... And in this discussion, the analyst is being challenged on each and every numbering ... Why did you assume this? Why is the margin going this way? Why is it different than the company's history? How consistent is it with other related industries? How consistent is it with other participants in the sector of competitors and so forth.

To support divergence of opinions and ideas, firms recruited people with different skills and perspectives, and used a laissez-faire management style that provided individuals with autonomy and support. The Chief Investment Manager at Golden Touch described this approach: "I think we trust people to get on with it and I think they generally do but we don't ask the question of whether we could do better by pushing it a bit." The asset management firms also used creativity-focused goals to stimulate divergence, encouraging team members to generate "lots and lots" of ideas and looking at opportunities from different perspectives. Solid Rock set formal objectives for fund managers to develop alternative views on money management.

A second set of mechanisms revealed through the categorical analysis were aimed at constraining decisions. As for divergent mechanisms, all of the firms used some mechanisms to constrain the process. Constraining mechanisms aimed to limit the variety of ideas and information considered in making asset management decisions. For example, at Solid Rock, people were recruited based on sharing a common perspective on the asset management task:

> the people we have here, they're attracted by that difference and see the very fact that they are coming to work with people who believe the same things about the way in which money should be run ... They'd all have a certain desire to try and capture the world in some way, in mathematical terms, which would be common throughout.

This limits the diversity of opinion available to the team. The Chief Investment Manager at Solid Rock stated this in perhaps the clearest way: "Diverse – the one thing that we don't want to be diverse in is an attitude towards investment philosophy." At Loyalty, this commonality of perspective was facilitated with an apprenticeship system in which new members of a fund management team were gradually socialized into a team's approach to making investment decisions:

> you don't have to sit someone in a room on their own to make that decision. They can do it in a public forum, right? But those present in a public forum have to understand where you've got to and had to witness how it happens, so that when the day comes that they're doing it, they'll [know how to].

Descriptions of the fund management process in practice suggested that these constraining mechanisms were effective in synthesizing diverse perspectives. For example, even divergent team discussions tended to end in convergence around investment ideas. At Theory, the Chief Investment Manager indicated that "by the end of this discussion you reach a consensus decision, whether this is an attractive investment or not," and suggested that "it actually rarely happens that we disagree whether a company is attractive or not … If we disagree, we usually seek more information."

The process of synthesis in these teams was also aided by the goals and objectives set for them. The Chief Investment Manager at Solid Rock played a role in constraining fund management decisions from the beginning by setting strict guidelines for the types of investments that should be made, including investment categories, risk parameters, and expected returns:

> I define the goals for each of those leaders of those teams in terms of what we're expecting by way of investment performance, by what we're expecting in terms of new product developments … So I'm defining those goals through a reasonably formal firm way, objective setting process, which cascades down through the firm globally.

Alternatively, constraints sometimes occurred at the end of the process, for example, when portfolio managers were responsible for making final investment decisions. The most obvious mechanism for constraining teams in the fund management process was the use of mathematical models in which the key decision-making criteria were quantified. All of the firms in the study used such a model to a greater or lesser extent, although they interacted with it in different ways. For example, Golden Touch described the final decision-making process as "effectively automated." Solid Rock describes using the quantitative tool "to … prioritize our work, so we'll take … its recommendation on what stocks within a sector are more attractive than others."

The examples above also illustrate that mechanisms for promoting divergence or constraint operated on different dimensions of a team's creative process: the problem structure, the solution space, or the team interaction. For example, recruiting people with diverse skills and perspectives (a divergent mechanism) influenced the teams' underlying problem structure, because the skills and perspectives available to the team provide the potential problem structure. Setting clear goals and objectives and team members' developing a common understanding of the task (a convergent mechanism), in contrast, influence the teams' solution space by determining the criteria for an idea's success. Finally, setting formal and managed team meetings during which newcomers were introduced to the investment philosophy at the firm (a convergent mechanism) guided the communication of ideas between team members.

Constraint-Focused Processes

Interestingly, there were commonalities in the sequence through which the mechanisms occurred in two of the firms in our study, Theory and Solid Rock. Figure 8.2 illustrates the way the mechanisms were ordered across the fund management process at these two firms.

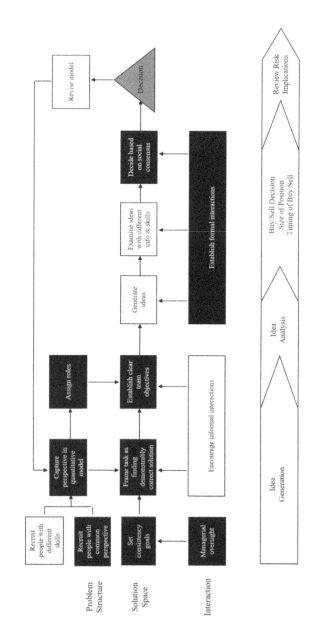

Figure 8.2   Fund management process for constraint-focused firms

In these firms, a significant amount of effort was devoted to constraining the problem structure. These firms developed a common approach to managing money and recruited others who shared that same vision. They then captured their approach in a quantitative model that was strictly adhered to. The role of individual team members was to generate and test ideas by drawing on their individual expertise. The problem structure and the role of each team member within that structure was so clear that the Chief Investment Manager at Solid Rock claimed that if one team member left, others could take over that individual's role with minimal disruption.

Team interactions were initially relatively free and unconstrained. However, as teams moved through the process, their interactions became more structured. For example, these firms held formal meetings in which one idea at a time was analyzed and discussed in detail, to examine and challenge each individual's suggestions with a variety of different perspectives. While interactions were constrained through structured meetings, therefore, the solution space – that is, the team's ideas about different investments – diverged.

These meetings ultimately resulted in decisions that synthesized the inputs of different members, supported by the analytic model. The drive for synthesis was also supported by constraining the team's solution space at the beginning and end of the fund management process. Initially, the firms set clear objectives and team members construed their task as finding the single best solution to meet these criteria. Many ideas were rejected for failing to meet these objectives. The need to achieve consensus at the end of the process then restricted the solution space because only a few ideas were accepted. At this point, however, the problem structure would sometimes diverge. That is, the team would revisit and revise the quantitative model in light of the decisions taken about investment ideas.

What is striking about this balance of divergence and constraint in the process illustrated in Figure 8.2 is that divergence occurred in only one type of mechanism at a time. Initially, divergence was promoted in the problem structure, while the task goals were firmly set by managers and team members' interactions were limited. Constraints on interaction were then relieved, while the problem structure and solution space were constrained. It was only towards the end of the process that divergence around the solution space occurred. Once it was constrained through decision-making, however, the problem structure diverged.

Divergence-Focused Processes

Figure 8.3 illustrates the fund management process at two other firms in the study, Golden Touch and Loyalty. Fund managers were recruited to these firms specifically for their different views on how to manage money, and these differences in perspective were encouraged throughout the fund management process. Although both firms did encapsulate decision criteria in a quantitative model, their attitude towards this model was much more flexible than at the more successful firms, and team members were expected and encouraged to interpret the model. The problem structure was therefore fluid throughout the fund management process at these firms. This was underscored by a goal of outperforming the market, and the consequent philosophy that the firm needed to make decisions that were fundamentally different from those of other firms. The firms believed that the best way to do this was to encourage diversity of perspectives and ideas. The solution space therefore also diverged across the process for these teams.

In contrast to the process followed in the convergence-focused process, constraints in this process occurred at only two points. The first was during the development of the model. However, the model itself was subsequently interpreted by individual team members. The second was when the final decision was made, usually by the most senior fund manager on a team, who decided which team member's opinion should be given the most weight. Weight was determined by who had the most relevant expertise and who seemed the most confident of their decision. The balance of the process was therefore focused on divergence with a small number of constraints. The only constraining mechanisms in these firms occurred at the very beginning of the process, when the problem structure moved towards consensus, and at the end of the process, when an individual fund manager took ultimate responsibility for decision-making.

AN EMERGENT MODEL OF CONSTRAINTS AND TEAM CREATIVITY

This study provides an empirically grounded model of how constraints in the team creative process can facilitate synthesis. The findings mirror those of a large body of research which suggests that both divergence and constraint are important to the generation of novel and useful ideas (Amabile, 1988; Cropley, 2006; Guilford, 1950). In addition, however, the findings also provide several surprising insights.

Firstly, while divergent idea generation is often described as the heart of the creative process (George, 2007), constraining mechanisms occurred at many points in the process for two of the firms. The balance of divergence and constraint in these firms was much more heavily tilted towards the latter. Interestingly, some data suggest that these firms were more successful not only in long-term profitability as measured by assets under management, but also in assessments of their investment performance by industry experts who evaluated them for our study.

A second surprising result is the timing of constraint within the creative process. Theoretical models of the creative process predict that constraint should occur towards the end of the process, as group members select between different ideas (Amabile, 1988). However, constraining mechanisms occurred early in the creative process of two of the firms in our study. This was particularly the case around the solution space, in which team members diverged only close to the point of decision-making, rather than at the beginning of idea generation. This finding is in line with Harrison & Rouse (2014) and Harvey & Kou (2013), who similarly observed evaluation early in the creative process. However, whereas those findings

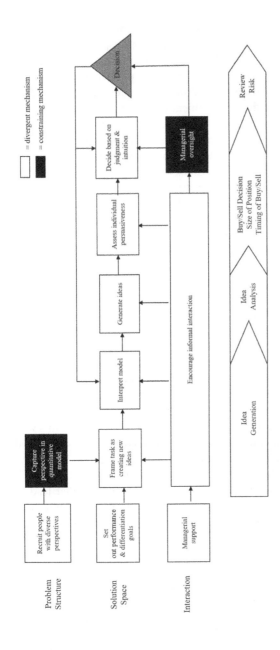

Figure 8.3   Fund management process for divergence-focused firms

focus on how solutions are shaped, the results of our investigation revealed that this further supported interactions, and the development of subsequent syntheses.

The third insight from these findings is that in other firms, both divergence and constraint occurred for each type of mechanism: the underlying problem structure, the solution space, and the team interaction. However, only one aspect of the process was allowed to diverge at any point in time. When the problem structure diverged at the beginning of the process, managers were clear in setting problem goals and limiting team interaction. In contrast, when team members had more freedom to interact informally, it was around a clearly defined problem based on shared assumptions about the underlying structure of knowledge. When team members' solutions and opinions diverged, team interactions were more tightly structured and the underlying problem structure was held firm by filtering ideas through the quantitative model.

We suggest that constraining different dimensions of the team creative process at different points in time fundamentally alters the nature of the creative task for teams. Specifically, we suggest that constraints facilitate the process of creative synthesis (Harvey, 2014), turning teams into synthesizers rather than idea generators. Creative synthesis is a process of combining different ways of understanding or interpreting a problem or situation. One path to creativity in the creative synthesis model is to continuously revise and reshape the synthesis itself. This is how constraints facilitated creativity in two of the firms in our study. We suggest that constraining one dimension of the creative process promotes the synthesis of divergent perspectives in another dimension. We elaborate three ways that this occurs below.

Firstly, constraints on problem structure promote divergence in team interactions. In the early stages of the constraint-focused process, team members' diverse skills and expertise were relatively quickly integrated into a quantitative model that captured their values for managing money. Imposing the constraint of the quantitative model forced a synthesis of individual knowledge (Harvey, 2014). However, group members interacted the most freely during this time, in the absence of tightly structured meetings. We propose that constraining the problem structure in this way provided a basis for team members to communicate effectively. Having a shared understanding of underlying beliefs and values improves communication by clarifying the relevance of information (Bunderson & Sutcliffe, 2002), enabling the smooth flow of interaction (Barrett, 1998), and preventing misunderstandings that lead to conflict (Cronin & Weingart, 2007). In addition, a shared problem structure may make team members feel more psychologically free to discuss ideas. People should feel the most interpersonally secure when their understanding of the organization's values and norms are clear (Binyamin & Carmeli, 2010; Lee et al., 2004). In this situation, they are less likely to believe that their behavior will be misinterpreted or rejected by others, and more likely to take risks and experiment.

Secondly, constraints on team interactions promote divergence in the solution space. The next stage of the constraint-focused process involved constraining interactions by establishing formal and structured meetings for discussing ideas. The underlying problem structure for solving the task, as captured in the quantitative model, also remained tightly defined during this period. What diverged, however, were specific investment ideas, opening up the solution space. It was at this stage that new ideas were generated and evaluated. We suggest that constraining interactions provided the cognitive space to enable team members to generate new solutions. This argument parallels the finding that simultaneously generating ideas and interacting with a team is challenging (Diehl & Stroebe, 1987, 1991). Structuring interactions helps to ensure that team members are exposed to one another's divergent information and ideas (Paulus & Yang, 2000; West & Anderson, 1996), but also helps to separate idea generation from evaluation (Osborn, 1953; Gallupe et al., 1991; Gallupe et al., 1994). In addition, structured interactions reduce the cognitive burden of mentally keeping track of new ideas, or generating ideas while others are speaking (Diehl & Stroebe, 1987; Paulus & Yang, 2000). What is interesting about the successful team process in the present study is that they diverged both by offering new solutions, and by evaluating those solutions from different perspectives. In doing so, they used one another's information to open up the solution space by creating, elaborating, and refining ideas.

Thirdly, constraints on solution space promote divergence in problem structure. In the later stages of the constraint-focused process, team interaction remained constrained, and task ideas were narrowed down once a final investment decision was made. At this point, however, the underlying problem structure was revised, diverging from the originally tightly constrained quantitative model. We propose that restricting the solution space by selecting an idea for implementation prompts a search for meaning that creates divergence in the underlying problem structure. For example, when final decisions are taken, some ideas that group members initially thought were good will be rejected because they do not fit within the model. This may cause team members to reflect on the underlying problem structure, adjusting that structure so that it more positively values such ideas in the future (Harvey, 2014). In other words, team members attempt to make sense of the idea in light of the problem structure. The construction of meaning is prompted by unexpected events like discrepancy or surprise (Dutton, 1993; Weick et al., 2005). Surprising events do not fit into existing cognitive schemas, creating cognitive dissonance that leads people to search for ways to make sense of their experience (Louis, 1980). These events block expected or anticipated paths and undermine existing routines (Barry & Meisiek, 2010). Exposure to diverse or inconsistent cues encourages problem-solvers to develop alternative ways of defining a problem (Reiter-Palmon et al., 1997). The resulting understanding is embedded in a previously unchartered, and therefore novel, perspective (Abolafia, 2010). A primary part of the creative act in this team process is therefore the construction of a new structure for understanding the problem.

Constraints are critical to the emergence of the team's new problem structure in two ways. Firstly, the problem structure must initially be constrained and shared by team members to create the synthesis. Otherwise, there is no opportunity for an idea to fall within or outside of the problem structure. Secondly, the solution space must be constrained by selecting an idea. If all ideas are considered to be viable, there is no stimulus to compare to the problem structure.

One potential boundary on the patterns described here is that the asset management firms in the present study had a high degree of underlying variety. Fund managers were individualistic and accustomed to a culture of acting as a "star manager" on the investment task. In addition, there was a strong flow of information throughout the investment process that may have countered pressures towards convergence and prevented the team from coming to decisions too early. Further, the successful teams explicitly prompted divergence later in the process, once they were beginning to come to consensus on an idea.

DISCUSSION

Teams are the forum through which expertise and ideas are combined to produce innovative new ideas, products, and processes. Previous research focuses on idea generation as the primary way that teams facilitate creativity and innovation (Amabile, 1988; Staw, 1990). From that perspective, team members draw on their diversity to follow divergent paths in creating new alternatives. By increasing the quantity of and variance in ideas, teams should be able to select novel and useful ideas to implement in the organization.

The present chapter builds on literature on an alternative process of creative synthesis (Harvey, 2014) to suggest that constraining the creative process turns teams into effective synthesizers of perspectives, information, and ideas. In the process uncovered here, constraints temporally separated the creative activities of problem construction, solution generation, and idea stimulation through team interactions, so that teams were divergent in only one dimension of the task at any point in time. In effect, constraints channeled the team's creative efforts, changing the nature of team creativity as they did so.

This contributes to research on the creative process in three ways. Firstly, it suggests a new way to conceptualize the role of teams in the creative process of organizations. In contrast to the dominant view of teams as idea generators (Amabile, 1988; Paulus, 2000; Woodman et al., 1993), we argue that in high-variability contexts, teams are more effective when they act like creative synthesizers, searching for the single best solution to a problem's constraints, and continually revising their shared framework for understanding that task over time. This perspective emphasizes creativity through problem construction rather than idea generation. Previous research suggests that creative individuals spend more time than others constructing the problem (Getzels & Csikszentmihalyi, 1976; Reiter-Palmon et al., 1997). In the present study, constraining the problem structure and the solution space created gaps or fissures that prompted teams to collectively revise their understanding of the problem. Their creativity therefore occurred in developing novel ways to view fund management.

The notion that teams can be more successful when they approach a creative task with a problem-solving framework is consistent with research on the relative advantages of working collectively rather than on one's own. Teams tend to be metfective at idea generation, producing fewer and less creative ideas than individuals working alone (Diehl & Stroebe, 1991), and fail to recognize the most creative ideas that they generate (Reitzschel et al., 2006). In contrast, teams generally outperform individuals on problem-solving tasks in which an answer can be demonstrated to be correct within the team's shared conceptual framework (Laughlin, 1988). Because it involves collectively constructing and revising the model that captured the team's values for money management, and following clearly defined rules for the task, creative synthesis creates the shared conceptual framework. This may allow team members to recognize good ideas that occur during group discussion (that is, those that fit within the shared problem structure), so that they are better able to select ideas that fit their shared understanding of the problem. A shared conceptual framework therefore improves the ability of a team to combine their knowledge (Taylor & Greve, 2006; Carmeli & Azeroual, 2009). If these teams also construct a novel synthesis by bringing together divergent perspectives on different investment metrics into a common understanding, their final solutions should differ from those of others in the industry; that is, they should end up with novel solutions. Synthesizers therefore derive their creativity from constructing novel problems and selecting the best ideas to fit the solution space. This is a different view of creativity than models in which divergent idea generation results in a large pool of ideas.

Secondly, the present study builds on research that is increasingly recasting constraint as a stimulator, rather than an inhibitor, of creativity and emphasizing the importance of convergence for creativity (e.g., Harvey, 2013). Previous studies have found that constraining a team's underlying problem structure, solution space, or interactions can improve creativity. The present study builds on these findings by providing an expanded role for constraint within the creative process and by elaborating three dimensions of constraint simultaneously and over time to explore the nature of their interaction with each other and with idea-generating processes. This allowed us to build theory about the mechanisms through which constraints benefited team creativity. In particular, we argue that constraints trigger a process that leads teams to synthesize ideas to construct and reconstruct the problem. We suggest that this is likely to lead to more novel problem constructions, which will result in higher levels of creativity (Getzels & Csiksentmihalyi, 1976).

A third implication of this study is that the creative process at one level – for example, at the level of the individual working alone – does not necessarily translate easily to other levels of analysis (Drazin et al., 1999). The creative process for teams in the present study, for example, did not strictly follow the model of divergence followed by idea selection of individual creators, because it began with convergence in the underlying problem structure which contributed to creativity through the process of synthesis (Harvey, 2014). In one sense, therefore, at the team level, the creative process may be reversed. However, it is also the case that these team-level processes are unnecessary at the individual level. For example, constraining the underlying problem structure used by individuals is not necessarily desirable, because individuals can integrate multiple perspectives. The present research therefore challenges the predominant assumption that the creative process operates in fundamentally the same way across levels of analysis.

CONCLUSION

This chapter provides a foundation for integrating our previously dispersed understanding of the role of constraint in the team creative process, specifically by linking it to the process of creative synthesis. Doing so has provided some insight into the value of structuring a team's problem structure, solution scope, and team interactions, and a roadmap for how these constraints interact with each other and with divergent processes. Future research to test the mechanisms proposed here can continue to build our understanding of the complex dynamic processes of team creativity.

NOTE

1. Although many firms continue to rely on individual portfolio managers, the present study sampled only those firms which use a team-based organizational structure.

REFERENCES

Abolafia, M.Y. (2010). Narrative construction as sensemaking: How a central bank thinks. *Organization Studies*, 31: 349–367.

Acar, O.A., Tarakci, M., & van Knippenberg, D. 2019. Creativity and innovation under constraints: A cross-disciplinary integrative review. *Journal of Management*, 45(1): 96–121.

Amabile, T.M. 1988. A model of creativity and innovation in organizations. In B.M. Staw & L.L. Cummings (eds), *Research in organizational behavior*, 10: 123–167. Greenwich, CT: JAI Press.

Ancona, D.G., & Caldwell, D.F. 1992. Demography and design: Predictors of new product team performance. *Organization Science*, 3: 321–343.

Bantel, K., & Jackson, S. 1989. Top management and innovations in banking: Does the composition of the team make a difference? *Strategic Management Journal*, 10: 107–124.

Barrett, F.J. 1998. Creativity and improvisation in jazz and organizations: Implications for organizational learning. *Organization Science*, 9: 605–623.

Barry, D., & Meisiek, S. 2010. Seeing more and seeing differently: Sensemaking, mindfulness, and the workarts. *Organization Studies*, 31: 1505–1530.

Baruah, J., & Paulus, P. 2011. Category assignment and relatedness in group ideation processes. *Journal of Experimental Social Psychology*, 47: 1070–1077.

Bercovitz, J., & Feldman, M. 2010. The mechanisms of collaboration in inventive teams: Composition, social networks, and geography. *Research Policy*, 40(1): 81–93.

Binyamin, G., & Carmeli, A. 2010. Does structuring of human resource management processes enhance employee creativity? The mediating role of psychological availability. *Human Resource Management*, 49(6): 999–1024.

Bunderson, J.S., & Sutcliffe, K.M. 2002. Comparing alternative conceptualizations of functional diversity in management teams: Process and performance effects. *Academy of Management Journal*, 45: 875–893.

Carmeli, A., & Azeroual, B. 2009. How relational capital and knowledge combination capability enhance the performance of work units in a high technology industry. *Strategic Entrepreneurship Journal*, 3: 85–103.

Chatman, J., & Flynn, F. 2001. The influence of demographic heterogeneity on the emergence and consequences of cooperative norms in work teams. *Academy of Management Journal*, 44: 956–975.

Chatman, J.A., Polzer, J.T., Barsade, S.G., & Neale, M.A. 1998. Being different yet feeling similar: The influence of demographic composition and organizational culture on work processes and outcomes. *Administrative Science Quarterly*, 43: 749–781.

Cooper, W.H., Gallupe, R.B., Pollard, S., & Cadsby, J. 1998. Some liberating effects of anonymous electronic brainstorming. *Small Group Research*, 29: 147–179.

Cronin, M.A., & Weingart, L.R. 2007. Representational gaps, information processing, and conflict in functionally diverse teams. *Academy of Management Review*, 32: 761–773.

Cropley, A.J. 2006. In praise of convergent thinking. *Creativity Research Journal*, 18(3): 391–404.

Czarnecki, K., & Eisenecker, U.W. 2000. *Generative programming: Methods, tools, and applications*. Boston, MA: Addison-Wesley.

Delbecq, A., Van de Ven, A., & Gustafson, D. 1975. *Group techniques for program planning*. Chicago, IL: Scott, Foresman, & Co.

Diehl, M., & Stroebe, W. 1987. Productivity loss in brainstorming groups: Toward the solution of a riddle. *Journal of Personality and Social Psychology*, 53(3): 497–509.

Diehl, M., & Stroebe, W. 1991. Productivity loss in brainstorming groups: Tracking down the blocking effect. *Journal of Personality and Social Psychology*, 61(3): 392–403.

Dougherty, D. 1992. Interpretive barriers to successful product innovation in large firms. *Organization Science*, 3: 179–202.

Dougherty, D. 2008. Bridging social constraint with social action to design organizations for innovation. *Organization Studies*, 29: 415–433.

Drazin, R., Glynn, M.A., & Kazanjian, R.K. 1999. Multilevel theorizing about creativity in organizations: A sensemaking perspective. *Academy of Management Review*, 24(2): 286–307.

Dutton, J. 1993. Interpretations on automatic: A different view of strategic issue diagnosis. *Journal of Management Studies*, 30(3): 339–358.

Earley, C.P., & Mosakowski, E. 2000. Creating hybrid team cultures: An empirical test of transnational team functioning. *Academy of Management Journal*, 43: 26–52.

Eisenhardt, K.M., & Bourgeois, L.J. 1988. Politics of strategic decision making in high-velocity environments: Toward a midrange theory. *Academy of Management Journal*, 31(4): 737–770.

Eisenhardt, K.M., & Graebner, M.E. 2007. Theory building from cases: Opportunities and challenges. *Academy of Management Journal*, 50(1): 25–32.

Finke, R.A., Ward, T.B., & Smith, S.M. 1992. *Creative cognition*. Cambridge, MA: Bradford/ MIT Press.

Ford, C.M. 1996. A theory of individual creative action in multiple social domains. *Academy of Management Review*, 21(4): 1112–1142.

Gallupe, R.B., Bastianutti, L.M., & Cooper, W.H. 1991. Unblocking brainstorming. *Journal of Applied Psychology*, 76: 137–142.

Gallupe, R.B., Cooper, W.H., Grise, M.L., & Bastianutti, L.M. 1994. Blocking electronic brainstorms. *Journal of Applied Psychology*, 79: 77–86.

George, J. 2007. Creativity in organizations. *Academy of Management Annals*, 1: 439–477.

Getzels, J.W., & Csikszentmihalyi, M. 1976. *The creative vision: A longitudinal study of problem finding in art*. New York: Wiley.

Gilson, L.L., Mathieu, J.E., Shalley, C.E., & Ruddy, T.M. 2005. Creativity and standardization: Complementary or conflicting drivers of team effectiveness? *Academy of Management Journal*, 48(3): 521–531.

Gilson, L.L., & Shalley, C.E. 2004. A little creativity goes a long way: An examination of teams' engagement in creative processes. *Journal of Management*, 30: 453–470.

Gioia, D.A. 1986. Symbols, scripts, and sensemaking. In H.P. Sims and D.A. Gioia (eds), *The thinking organization*: 49–74. San Francisco, CA: Jossey Bass Publishers.

Gioia, D.A., & Chittipeddi, K. 1991. Sensemaking and sensegiving in strategic change initiation. *Strategic Management Journal*, 12: 433–448.

Gioia, D.A., Thomas, J.B, Clark, S.M., & Chittipeddi, K. 1994. Symbolism and strategic change in academia: The dynamics of sensemaking and influence. *Organization Science*, 5: 363–383.

Glaser, B.G., & Strauss, A. 1967. *The discovery of grounded theory*. Chicago, IL: Aldine.

Goldenberg, J., Mazursky, D., & Solomon, S. 1999. The fundamental templates of quality ads. *Marketing Science*, 18(3): 333–351.

Guilford, J.P. 1950. Creativity. *American Psychologist*, 5: 444–454.

Hargadon, A.B., & Bechky, B.A. 2006. When collections of creatives become creative collectives: A field study of problem solving at work. *Organization Science*, 17(4): 484–500.

Harrison, S.H., & Rouse, E.D. 2014. Let's dance! Elastic coordination in creative group work: A qualitative study of modern dancers. *Academy of Management Journal*, 57(5): 1256–1283.

Harvey, S. 2013. A different perspective: The multiple effects of deep level diversity on group creativity. *Journal of Experimental Social Psychology*, 49(5): 822–832.

Harvey, S. 2014. Creative synthesis: Exploring the process of extraordinary group creativity. *Academy of Management Review*, 39(3): 324–343.

Harvey, S., & Kou, C.Y. 2013. Collective engagement in creative tasks: The role of evaluation in the creative process in groups. *Administrative Science Quarterly*, 58(3): 346–386.

Hoegl, M., Gibbert, M., & Mazursky, D. 2008. Financial constraints in innovation projects: When is less more? *Research Policy*, 37(8): 1382–1391.

Jick, T.D. 1979. Mixing qualitative and quantitative methods: Triangulation in action. *Administrative Science Quarterly*, 24(4): 602–611.

Joyce, C. 2009. *The blank page: Effects of constraint on creativity*. University of California, Berkley, Doctoral dissertation.

Langley, A. 1999. Strategies for theorizing from process data. *Academy of Management Review*, 24: 691–710.

Laughlin, P.R. 1988. Collective induction: Group performance, social combination processes, and mutual majority and minority influence. *Journal of Personality and Social Psychology*, 54: 254–267.

Leavitt, H.J. 1996. The old days, hot groups, and managers' lib. *Administrative Science Quarterly*, 41: 288–300.

Lee, F., Edmondson, A.C., Thomke, S., & Woline, M. 2004. The mixed effects of inconsistency on experimentation in organizations. *Organization Science*, 15(3): 310–326.

Lincoln, Y.S., & Guba, E.G. 1985. *Naturalistic Inquiry*. Beverly Hills, CA: SAGE Publications.

Louis, M.R. 1980. Surprise and sensemaking: What newcomers experience entering unfamiliar organizational settings. *Administrative Science Quarterly*, 25: 226–251.

Lovelace, K., Shapiro, D.L., & Weingart, L.R. 2001. Maximizing cross-functional new product teams' innovativeness and constraint adherence: A conflict communications perspective. *Academy of Management Journal*, 44: 779–793.

Mannix, E., & Neale, M.A. 2005. What differences make a difference? The promise and reality of diverse teams in organizations. *Psychological Science in the Public Interest*, 6: 2.

McGrath, J. 1984. *Groups: Interaction and performance*. Englewood Cliffs, NJ: Prentice Hall.

Miles, M.B., & Huberman, A.M. 1984. *Qualitative data analysis: A source book of new methods*. Beverly Hills, CA: SAGE.

Milliken, F.J., & Martins, L.L. 1996. Searching for common threads: Understanding the multiple effects of diversity in organizational groups. *Academy of Management Review*, 21: 402–434.

Mullen, B., Johnson, C., & Salas, E. 1991. Productivity loss in brainstorming groups: A meta-analytic integration. *Basic and Applied Social Psychology*, 12: 3–23.

Mumford, M.D., Feldman, J.M., Hein, M.B., & Nagao, D.J. 2001. Tradeoff between ideas and structure: Individual versus group performance in creative problem solving. *Journal of Creative Behavior*, 35: 1–23.

Mumford, M.D., & Gustafson, S.B. 1988. Creativity syndrome: Integration, application, and innovation. *Psychological Bulletin*, 103(1): 27–43.

Nemeth, C.J. 1986. Differential contributions of majority and minority influence. *Psychological Review*, 93: 23–32.

Osborn, A. 1953. *Applied imagination*. New York: C. Scribner.

Paulus, P.B. 2000. Groups, teams, and creativity: The creative potential of idea-generating groups. *Applied Psychology: An International Review*, 49(2): 237–262.

Paulus, P.B., & Yang, H. 2000. Idea generation in groups: A basis for creativity in organizations. *Organizational Behavior and Human Decision Processes*, 82: 76–87.

Pentland, B.T. 1999. Building process theory with narrative: From description to explanation. *Academy of Management Review*, 24(4): 711–724.

Peplowski, K. 1998. The process of improvisation. *Organization Science*, 9: 560–562.

Poole, M.S., & Van de Ven, A.H. 1989. Using paradox to build management and organization theories. *Academy of Management Review*, 14(4): 562–578.

Rietzschel, E.F., Nijstad, B.A., & Stroebe, W. 2006. Productivity is not enough: A comparison of interactive and nominal brainstorming groups on idea generation and selection. *Journal of Experimental and Social Psychology*, 42(2): 244–251.

Sagiv, L., Ariely, S., Goldenberg, J., & Goldschmidt, A. 2010. Structure and freedom in creativity: The interplay between externally imposed structure and personal cognitive style. *Journal of Organizational Behavior*, 31(8): 1086–1110.

Salganik, M.J., Dodds, P.S., & Watts, D.J. 2006. Experimental study of inequality and unpredictability in an artificial cultural market. *Science*, 311: 854–856.

Shalley, C.E. 1995. Effects of coaction, expected evaluation, and goal setting on creativity and productivity. *Academy of Management Journal*, 38: 483–503.

Staw, B.M. 1990. An evolutionary approach to creativity and innovation. In M. West and J.L. Farr (eds), *Innovation and creativity at work: Psychological and organizational strategies*: 287–308. Chicester: John Wiley & Sons.

Sternberg, R.J., & Lubart, T.I. 1995. *Defying the crowd: Cultivating creativity in culture of conformity*. New York: Free Press.

Sutton, R.I., & Hargadon, A. 1996. Brainstorming groups in context: Effectiveness in a product design firm. *Administrative Science Quarterly*, 41: 685–718.

Taylor, A. & Greve, H. 2006. Superman or the Fantastic Four? Knowledge combination and experience in innovative teams. *Academy of Management Journal*, 49(4): 723–740.

Treon, A. 2020. Creativity will pay for the next generation of asset managers. *Financial Times*. https://www.ft.com/content/2934f714-224c-11ea-92da-f0c92e957a96.

Van de Ven, A., & Delbecq, A.L. 1971. Nominal versus interacting group processes for committee decision making effectiveness. *Academy of Management Journal*, 14: 203–212.

van Knippenberg, D., & Schippers, M.C. 2007. Work group diversity. *Annual Review of Psychology*, 58: 515–541.

Van Maanen, J. 1979. The fact of fiction in organizational ethnography. *Administrative Science Quarterly*, 24: 539–550.

Walsh, J. 1995. Managerial and organizational cognition: Notes from a trip down memory lane. *Organization Science*, 6(3): 280–321.

Ward, T.B. 1994. Structured imagination: The role of category structure in exemplar generation. *Cognitive Psychology*, 27(1): 1–40.

Weick, K.E. 1998. Improvisation as a mindset for organizational analysis. *Organization Science*, 9: 543–556.

Weick, K., Sutcliffe, K., & Obsfeld, D. 2005. Organizing and the process of sensemaking. *Organization Science*, 16(4): 409–421.

West, M.A., & Anderson, N. 1996. Innovation in top management teams. *Journal of Applied Psychology*, 81: 680–693.

Woodman, R.W., Sawyer, J.E., & Griffin, J.E. 1993. Toward a theory of organizational creativity. *Academy of Management Review*, 18: 293–322.

9. Family and its influences on work creativity

Nora Madjar

Creativity at work, or the generation of novel and potentially useful ideas and solutions, is becoming increasingly important, both as a starting point for innovations and new initiatives, as well as a necessity for solving problems in challenging times (Amabile, 1996; Anderson et al., 2014), and research on the factors that influence employee creativity has exploded (Shalley et al., 2004; Zhou & Hoever, 2014). Initial studies on creativity centered on certain personality characteristics and examined it as a process that took place in the mind of a single individual (Simonton, 2000). However, the notion that creativity is largely a social phenomenon and that interactions with other individuals influence various aspects of creativity is now relatively well established (Amabile, 1996; Perry-Smith & Mannucci, 2017; Rouse, 2020).

In the last three decades, social relationships have been considered an important factor for organizational creativity (Baer, 2010; Perry-Smith & Shalley, 2003; Perry-Smith & Manucci, 2017; Tang et al., 2017). The impact of connections with diverse others and their contributions to creative outcomes is very well acknowledged (Perry-Smith & Shalley, 2003; Zhou et al., 2009), but with few exceptions (Madjar et al., 2002; Madjar, 2008; Tang et al., 2017) the focus has been mostly on co-workers and supervisors (Zhou et al., 2009; Perry-Smith, 2006) and not on nonwork individual connections.

However, previous studies on the work–family interface have long argued that employees' family lives and social relations outside the organizational boundaries can enrich or deplete their work lives (Greenhaus & Powell, 2006). As work has become increasingly virtual, it often blurs physical boundaries between work and nonwork lives (Golden et al., 2006). Lots of professionals face the challenge of managing the interface between their work and personal life roles. Famous people often publicly attribute their success to their spouses, and current popular wisdom proclaims that the most important career choice a person makes is whom to marry (Petriglieri & Obodaru, 2019; Sandberg, 2013). Moreover, people's work and nonwork lives are becoming both relevant to and affected by each other (Edwards & Rothbard, 2000; Rothbard, 2001).

It has been argued that we cannot always separate our family and work life, and a parent cannot close the door of their office and forget that their child is very sick while trying to generate creative ideas. Additionally, family events, even adverse family events such as death, have been discussed as triggers for specific thought processes and new meanings that may provide individuals with stronger motivation and new perspectives and facilitate creativity at work (Kessler, 2019). Some evidence also suggests that creative thoughts often do not stay in the office, and research demonstrates that family may provide the necessary support, resources, and motivation to be creative at work (Madjar, 2008; Tang et al., 2017). Earlier psychology research has recognized the family as one of the most important components in converting the potential for creativity into an actual skill and ability (Olszewski et al., 1987), and family relations could help individuals to develop certain personality characteristics, such as creative personality or openness to experience that may be beneficial for their creativity at work.

Therefore, this chapter attempts to expand the horizon of research on socio-relational sources of individual creativity by reviewing the effect of employees' family relationships on their workplace creativity. The goal is to review the literature on the role of family and delve into the different mechanisms through which family relations can influence creativity at work. The focus is on the current nuclear and extended family as social resources or barriers to creativity at work, and I consider the family connections both as a source of emotional support and as a source of cognitive resources or constraints for creativity. I also review what we know about the effect of family of origin as a significant factor for the development of creative abilities and personality characteristics that may later determine creativity at work. Based on the review and theorizing, I attempt to provide a more nuanced view of the effects of family on creativity at work and some of the factors that may determine the strength of these relations. I also discuss how individuals and organizations can take advantage of the positive influences and minimize the hindrances coming from these family relationships.

OVERVIEW

In contrast to the lone genius view, two fundamental theories of creativity propose that creativity is, in part, a social process (Amabile, 1996; Woodman et al., 1993) and that interactions with others influence various aspects of the creative endeavor. Individuals may develop creative ideas in isolation, but their interactions with others may also contribute to useful insights, motivation, support, or other necessary resources or barriers and constraints for creativity (Shalley et al., 2004; Zhou et al., 2009). More specifically, factors in the work environment, such as supervisory support (Madjar et al., 2002), social networks (Perry-Smith, 2006; Zhou et al., 2009), and other social influences resulting from social interactions, are proposed to be important antecedents to creativity. Besides, research evidence suggests that accolades for creativity tend to be bestowed on those who have been exposed to creative role models (Simonton, 1984). It has also been proposed that interactions with diverse individuals enhance creativity (e.g., Amabile, 1996; Woodman et al., 1993). All of these ideas provide an important start for understanding the social context for creativity. However, they fall short of reflecting the complex social environment that employees experience, both at the current moment and during their childhood, during a period when they were developing their creativity skills and potential for creativity at work. I start with what we know about the current nuclear and extended family as factors for creativity at work, and then review the literature on the effect of the family of origin as an important factor for developing creative personality. I also explore a variety of mechanisms that may explain the different effects of family on creativity, and try to reconcile some of the mixed findings.

CURRENT FAMILY AND CREATIVITY AT WORK

While the role of the family of origin for creative development has been investigated substantially in psychology, although with very mixed results, and without clear implications for adult creativity at work, less attention has been devoted to the effect of current family relations. These are actually the relations that mainly comprise individuals' social context outside of work. Relations with family often provide external stimulation and feedback, and may offer the most intense and meaningful experiences in life, and provide encouragement and excitement (Csikszentmihalyi, 1990). In addition, while not all the research on the role of the family is directly linked to creativity at work (e.g., Madjar et al., 2002), the family business and entrepreneurship literature, as well as research on the work–family interface, offer substantial insights (e.g., Aldrich & Cliff, 2003; Dumas & Perry-Smith, 2018; Graves et al., 2007; Powell & Eddleston, 2013; Rothbard, 2001). Collectively, this work suggests that creativity at work may be influenced by family relationships, as well as the more commonly studied factors of personality and work context.

Moreover, while relationships with spouse and children may define the primary family for some, these are not the only family types of relationships available to employees, and a focus only on the nuclear family has been criticized as not capturing the full picture of extended family relations and their impact on work (Gerstel, 2011). Thus, it is important to define the family broadly, to include relationships with siblings, parents, and many other relatives, together with the nuclear family (spouse and children). Family connections are unique in comparison to other kinds of relationships as they are found to be more stable and less prone to decay over time than friendships and other community ties (Burt, 2000). Kin relationships are usually associated with a higher level of helping and support (Stewart-Williams, 2007), and empirical evidence suggests that it is less costly to maintain communication and preserve emotional closeness with kin (Roberts & Dunbar, 2011). In particular, people rely mostly on family for emotional support (Klein & Milardo, 2000; Wellman & Wortley, 1990). While usually there is a high level of trust and it is easier to be vulnerable with family than with co-workers and supervisors, family members are also not so engaged in the problem or issue one is dealing with, so they may ask naive questions or provide useful novel information or hinder the individual's effort to be creative at work.

Family as a Source of Emotional Support and Psychological Resources for Creativity at Work

As engaging in creativity entails some risks and new ideas may not be approved or accepted, it has been suggested that in order to be creative, employees should feel safe and supported (Madjar et al., 2002; Oldham & Cummings, 1996). Creativity researchers have studied the extent to which various types of creativity-centered support facilitate or constrain work outcomes (Madjar et al., 2002; Madjar, 2008; Oldham & Cummings, 1996). When employees feel nurtured and encouraged to be creative, or they have a social group they comfortably belong to, they feel less tension and enjoy playing with ideas (Amabile, 1996). In this respect, family emotional support seems particularly important as it is likely to enable employees to spend more time and effort in the workplace, focus more on their roles, and take the necessary risks to carry out complex tasks successfully (Karatepe et al., 2008). Family support outside of work can also help people to either avoid or cope with negative influences arising from the workplace that might otherwise lead to burnout or turnover intentions (Kim & Choi, 2017). Family ties, characterized by unconditional loyalty and non-reciprocal social obligation, allowed creative entrepreneurs to receive financial and emotional support (Tsui & Farh, 1997). Koestner et al. (1999) found that family and friends' support had a direct impact on individuals' creative responses, and family support for creativity has predicted students' self-perceived creativity and entrepreneurial intentions (Zampetakis & Moustakis, 2006; Zampetakis et al., 2011).

The family-to-work enrichment perspective has also focused mainly on how positive affect and resources derived from the family role may positively influence the work role (Carlson et al., 2006; Greenhaus & Powell, 2006). Thus, it seems that one way through which family can influence creativity at work is through the emotional support, encouragement, and acceptance provided, and the psychological resources created and transferred. Psychological resources refer to personal resources, including positive emotions, motivation, and energy, self-esteem, and well-being that help people to deal actively with certain tasks (Hobfoll, 2002). These resources are transferable from family to work (Ten Brummelhuis & Bakker, 2012; Greenhaus & Powell, 2006). Madjar et al. (2002) provide valuable insights about the impact of family and friends on creative contributions within organizations by finding that support from the family domain facilitated creativity at work over and above support from supervisors and co-workers, especially for employees who had less creative personalities.

When family emotional support is high, individuals are more willing to be authentic and present their true self, including challenges, problems, and deficiencies (Reis, 2007). Instead of being distracted by worrying about the impact on the relationship, individuals who receive a high level of family support can focus on their interactions and the enrichment that they provide. As a result, they can attend to and play around with new ideas and thoughts, stimulated by interactions with family. High levels of emotional support provide important means for self-enhancement as well as motivation to engage in creative pursuits. A higher level of emotional support from family also frees more cognitive resources and allows the individual to take full advantage of the cognitive stimulation that additional familial roles could provide. For example, Chen et al. (2014) found that entrepreneurs with strong family ties, in addition to business ties, had a high level of individual creativity and firm creativity, which then had a positive influence on their happiness.

On the other hand, there is extensive research on family-to-work conflict and its negative impact on the employees' achievement at work (e.g., Greenhaus & Beutell, 1985; Perrewe et al., 1999), suggesting that family may not always positively influence creativity. When family emotional support is low, maintaining these family connections may involve higher personal costs of "giving" help without receiving it back from the family (Swartz, 2009). Pressures to address multiple, competing social role demands (mother, spouse, and creative writer) have been accompanied by internal conflicts in creative women (Labouvie-Vief, 1994; Pohlman, 1996). Given that family connections endure despite lack of reciprocity, this may be personally draining, and individuals may be more distracted and less able to attend to different ideas or perspectives. When people experience that their home situation negatively influences their work, they try to cope with these negative emotions (Carver & Scheier, 1981), and this effort depletes their available psychological resources (Rothbard, 2001), which may impair subsequent task performance, and especially creativity. Family can also create a normative order for conformity instead of support for creativity. For instance, family businesses in general discourage very radical and risky innovations, and research has indicated that family businesses tend to favor and support only exploitative innovations that are incremental and less uncertain in nature (De Massis et al., 2015).

Some of the main mechanisms through which emotional support from the family domain can influence creativity at work are its effect on employees' affect and the other psychological resources generated through positive spillover (Bowling et al., 2010; Greenhaus & Powell, 2006; Rothbard, 2001). A high level of marital satisfaction, for example, has been examined as an enjoyable and pleasant marriage experience that generates energy (Sonnentag et al., 2008) and positive emotions (Heller & Watson, 2005). People in satisfying marriages tend to have positive thinking, and more confidence (Fincham & Bradbury, 1993; Fincham et al., 2000), and Tang et al. (2017) demonstrated that a satisfying marriage boosted a spillover of psychological resources from family to work that enhanced employees' workplace creativity. Support from family has been positively related to work attitudes and outcomes (Barnett & Hyde, 2001; Barnett et al., 1992). It has been found to influence creativity at work through its effect on employees' positive mood (Madjar et al., 2002) or via a variety of skills, such as patience and interpersonal acumen (Ruderman et al., 2002), that individuals can acquire in the family as well.

According to broaden and build theory, positive emotions and psychological resources from the family can broaden an individual's momentary mindset and thought–action repertoire, enabling them to identify a wide range of possibilities (Fredrickson, 2001). These resources may help employees to recognize the relevance of seemingly irrelevant ideas (Fredrickson, 2013), which may increase cognitive flexibility (Dreisbach & Goschke, 2004) and openness to new information (Estrada et al., 1997), facilitating the generation of new ideas. All of these findings clearly suggest that family connections may indeed benefit creativity by offering more positive affect and psychological capital (Canavan & Dolan, 2006), creating a supportive and conducive context for individual creativity. At the same time, according to the resource allocation theory (Hobfoll, 2002), family conflict and a low level of support may stifle the necessary resources for creativity at work and not leave enough for engaging in the creative process.

It is important to point out that one of the primary sources of this emotional support and positive mood spillover is usually the nuclear family and one's significant other. However, these are not the only family connections, and according to the role accumulation perspective, commitment to multiple roles (for example, parent, sibling, spouse, cousin) is beneficial for the individual (Ruderman et al., 2002). It leads to positive outcomes such as higher self-esteem, self-complexity, increased job satisfaction, and social connections (Nordenmark, 2004; Pietromonaco et al., 1986; Ruderman et al., 2002; Sieber, 1974; Thoits, 1983), all of which should facilitate creativity. Nevertheless, these connections may present costs as well: costs in time and effort that may not be compensated with additional support or other psychological resources.

In summary, one way through which family may facilitate work creativity is by providing emotional support, opportunities for self-growth, positive affect, and other psychological resources as one of the mechanisms of this family-to-work spillover (Madjar et al., 2002; Rothbard, 2001). When people see that their family positively influences their work and supports, encourages, and accepts their creativity, they experience more positive emotions, which in turn makes them more likely to engage in the creative process. Of course, we have to be cognizant of the potential of the family context, through conflict, pressures, and lack of support or resources to have some adverse effects on the context and motivation for creativity as well.

Family as a Source of Informational Support and Cognitive Resources for Creativity at Work

In addition to providing supportive context for engagement in the creative process, anecdotal evidence and some initial empirical research shows that family and family roles have the potential to facilitate work creativity cognitively and more directly as well (Madjar, 2008). Assumptions about the need for others to have explicitly relevant knowledge are perhaps some of the reasons why much of the creativity literature has often ignored the family (e.g., Madjar et al., 2002). Understandably, using the logic of explicit usefulness, family relationships may be seen as less relevant due to their lack of expertise or context-specific knowledge. Most of the reviewed research has linked the effect of the current family to creativity at work through different indirect mechanisms, among which are motivation and positive affect (Madjar et al., 2002).

However, the family-to-work enrichment perspective has also discussed how instrumental resources derived from the family could positively influence the work role (Carlson et al., 2006; Greenhaus & Powell, 2006), and this may easily extend to creativity. Friedman and Greenhaus (2000), for example, suggest that informational support (advice) from one's spouse may be put to use in one's career, and social capital in one role can enhance performance in another (Greenhaus & Powell, 2006), and hence enhance cognitive variations and promote creativity (Isen, 2007). The theory of social capital and structural holes suggests that people (family) who are not directly involved in the problem will be more likely to provide unique perspectives (Burt, 2004). In addition, when an employee discusses a work-related problem with family, it may be necessary to clarify and elaborate to achieve understanding. In this process, in their attempt to offer help, the family members may reconstruct the problem and provide abstract, 'out-of-the-box' suggestions that might stimulate the employee's creativity. The family's questions or lack of understanding might force the individual to reframe and reconstruct the problem themselves. Alternatively, when observing how family members (for example, children struggling with distance learning during the COVID-19 pandemic) deal with an issue, individuals may come up with different perspectives and creative solutions for their own problems (managing telecommuting employees).

Moreover, when we talk about family, as suggested by research on role accumulation (Sieber, 1974; Thoits, 1983), it is important to consider multiple family roles with an emphasis on the full range of family relationships and not only the nuclear family, as this approach emphasizes the exposure to diverse information and resources that the family can potentially provide. That is, the employee may try to explain the burning problem they are working on to their spouse, who may have complementary expertise, in a different way than they will discuss it with their children or with their parents. In line with this, individuals involved in multiple family roles, who have a chance to interact with people from different environments who have different beliefs, competencies, and ideas, are expected to be more creative. These are unique connections as they represent close and enduring relationships (Bott, 1971), but at the same time they are to individuals who may not necessarily share the same organizational affiliation or profession. They may reflect varied and distinct work arenas and tend to be more heterogeneous in age and education than non-family (Marsden, 1987), but at the same time are emotionally close. Precisely this informal interpersonal communication with individuals from different life domains is expected to enhance creativity (Perry-Smith & Shalley, 2003), as it facilitates knowledge transfer and gives access to new insights (Ohly et al., 2010). In this respect, Madjar (2008) demonstrated that the informational support for creativity from family was as important as the informational support from work colleagues. Through the unique patterns of interactions with different family members, employees may develop more flexible ways of thinking and diverse perspectives for approaching a problem. For example, past research indicated that the presence of children at home might relate to creative performance at work (Tang et al., 2017), and some anecdotal evidence suggests that observing how children experiment and create new things may be insightful for adults. In addition, Graves et al. (2007) found that parental role commitment had a direct positive effect on managers' performance and overall functioning. These authors suggest that committed parents become less self-focused and develop an increased awareness of others' needs and perspectives; factors that may be critical for creativity.

Cognitive stimulation is defined as the extent to which individuals generate remote associations to a specific concept or category and show a high level of divergent thinking (Brown et al., 1998; Dugosh et al., 2000). Employees need a high level of cognitive involvement in order to be able to make remote associations, integrate, restructure available information, and create new solutions (Paulus & Dzindolet, 2008; Ward et al., 1999). Similar to other contextual characteristics, such as multi-tasking or team brainstorming (e.g., Madjar & Shalley, 2008; Paulus & Yang, 2000), family relations can provide individuals with cognitive stimulation that may enhance their creative contributions, especially when the family exposes the individual to diverse perspectives and attitudes. Role expansion theory (Greenhaus & Powell, 2006; Marks, 1977) posits that a variety of roles, suggested by relationships that cross family categories (for example, sibling, spouse, extended family) can affect how a person frames or interprets the world (Greenhaus & Powell, 2006; Seiber, 1974) and make them more cognitively flexible. For example, the more roles a person has, the more they may be able to take the perspective of others rather than hold rigid views (Sieber, 1974). As they move across different expectations and norms from one role to another, potentially having to reconcile them, they become accustomed to flexible and divergent thinking. For example, the same issue may be seen differently from the perspective of a child of an elderly parent, and the position of a sibling or parent of their own children. Moreover, compared to colleagues, family members are often "outsiders" and may lack expertise in the problem being solved. In some ways, they represent the newcomer, who poses naïve questions and alternative views that insiders miss (Levine et al., 2003), and interactions and relations with family may influence creativity by providing "input" for creativity, sometimes accidentally delivering the remote connections to a novel solution or the different perspectives.

Although family relationships have the potential to provide informational support and cognitive stimulation, this may also come at a cost. Instead of facilitating cre-ativity, at some point too many family roles may be detrimental instead of helpful. Creativity requires focus of attention, and complex cognitive processing (Finke et al., 1992; Howard-Jones & Murray, 2003), while numerous family connections and commitment to family may be associated with more intrusions and distractions. This, in turn, may interrupt the flow of thinking or hinder the complex cognitive thoughts necessary for new idea generation (Leroy et al., 2020). It may result in cognitive overload and minimize the potential for creative cognition. As the number of family roles increases, it becomes more difficult to reconcile different needs and expecta-tions. Thoits (1983) argued that beyond some optimal number, too many roles might be associated with too much conflict and stress that can undermine the expected positive effect of a larger number of roles on well-being. Information overload and cognitive complexity may stifle instead of facilitate creative idea generation.

In summary, family members, both nuclear and extended family, as outsiders to work problems, may be a good sounding board or a useful resource for insights. In addition to providing social context and support for engagement in creativity, they may offer additional information resources or influence employee creativity by providing cognitive stimulation and diverse perspectives, but they may also present more conflicting demands for the resources necessary for creativity.

FAMILY OF ORIGIN AND CREATIVITY AT WORK

While so far this chapter has provided a review of the influence of the current nuclear and extended family on work creativity through certain emotional and cognitive mechanisms, the role of the family of origin in the development of a creative personality cannot be ignored, and has been examined extensively in earlier research in developmental psychology. These personality characteristics and experiences might also play a significant role in shaping the potential of employees to contribute creatively at work. While organizational behavior research has focused on the relationship between work and the current family, entrepreneurship research has focused on the family of origin, and it seems likely that employees' original family system might affect attitudes and behaviors as well as later work creativity (Jaskiewicz et al., 2017). Certain family socialization practices or family structures (large family, an only child, authoritarian parenting) may determine the best context for employees to be creative or the projects where their creativity will flourish. For example, employees originally from highly enmeshed and rigid families (Olson, 2000) might find it challenging to embrace the creative process and see entrepreneurial opportunities. Alternatively, a competitive context or high level of risk and uncertainty might be more conducive for individuals with certain family backgrounds (for example, secondborn) but not others, as competition might not stimulate creativity for all (e.g., Baer et al., 2014). It may also be important to understand the family dynamics that shaped a person's creative personality or motivations for creativity or triggers that may represent certain constraints, so organizations may provide training and help individuals to learn or "unlearn" certain practices from their childhood in order to increase their creative potential.

Many authors recognize the influence of parents, teachers, and other caregivers on the maximization of creative potential (Gruber & Wallace, 1999; Olszewski-Kubilius, 2002; Runco, 2007). Past research has explored a lot of different aspects of the family, starting with structural variables such as family configuration, size, stability, birth order, and socio-economic status, as well as the education level of the parents and parenting style, among others (Runco & Albert, 2005; Runco et al., 1999; Subotnik et al., 2003). For example, past research has identified the socio-economic status of the parents as well as birth order or number of siblings as important factors for creativity (Dai et al., 2012; Yang et al., 2017). Unfortunately, results are somewhat mixed and inconclusive. For example, family size and birth order seem to be good predictors of creative potential (Runco, 2007), but the results on the direction of these effects on creativity have been inconsistent. In addition, Baer et al. (2005) found that the relations between birth order and creativity may not be universal and may depend on the sibling group size, gender, and age difference with the other siblings. That is, only firstborns with a large group of siblings relatively close in age exhibited more creativity, as well as firstborns with opposite-sex siblings. These findings paint a quite complex picture of the relations between birth order and sibling structure and creativity (Baer et al., 2005).

A big controversy in the family–creativity relation is the role of traumatic events in the family. In general, research has discussed an intact family with both parents in the house, higher socio-economic status, and higher educational level of the parents as associated with more resources, both emotional and cognitive, and hence higher creativity (Csikszentmihalyi, 1990; Kerr & Chopp, 1999). In a study of over 200 talented teenagers, Csikszentmihalyi et al. (1997) found that 88 per cent of the teens' parents were married, suggesting that a large proportion of talented teens thrive in families where both parents are present in the home. Throughout history, there are examples of close family members who not only played a role in shaping the child but who also played a role in the creative process itself (Miller & Cohen, 2012). Gardner (1993), in his study of the lives of Sigmund Freud, Albert Einstein, Pablo Picasso, Igor Stravinsky, T.S. Eliot, Martha Graham, and Mahatma Gandhi, mentioned that each had a strong personal support system at the time of their breakthrough. These relationships seemed to provide both unconditional emotional support and cognitive stimulation in the form of feedback and intellectual stimulation.

At the same time, past inquiries have identified stress, experienced during childhood, as a contributing factor to the development of creative skills (Ochse, 1991); and a big controversy in the literature on eminent creatives often discusses the loss of a parent or other traumatic family event as associated with higher creativity. In contrast to the intact family effects on creativity (Csikszentmihalyi, 1990), in other research, losing a parent of the same gender seemed to play a role in the development of creativity. Research has indicated that boys who lose their fathers and girls who lose their mothers may be freed of typical gender roles or achievement expectations, and this may have enhanced their creativity (Kerr & Chopp, 1999). In a study of genius cited by Simonton (1996), more than one-quarter of the subjects had lost a parent by age 10, more than two-thirds by 15, almost half by 21. Simonton (1998) also found ambiguity in family backgrounds in his study of world-class achievers. The family backgrounds were varied and diverse. While organizations might not have control over the upbringing of their employees, it may be important to know what contexts stimulate their creativity or how to counteract the negative influences from the family of origin. The findings demonstrate that sometimes there are family settings where children are constrained by strict rules and rigid structures and still thrive and are creative; while there are settings and parental values which support a high level of autonomy, enabling children to experiment with new things, to express themselves and have the freedom to create (Deng et al., 2016).

Also, most of the research on the effects of family of origin has centered on describing families in terms of certain demographic and family characteristics and structures (birth order, family dynamics, parents' educational level), rather than on the psychological processes underlying them (Dai et al., 2012; Deng et al., 2016). At the same time, it is the psychological processes within the family, connected with the nature of parent–child relationships and the environment created by parents, that may have a stronger influence on creativity. It may be that family values related to creativity such as freedom, autonomy, encouragement for originality, nonconformity, and modeling of creativity may be more important than the family configuration or characteristics (Amabile, 1996; Runco, 1994). Family members can provide extra resources and additional learning opportunities for a child, or compete for them (Steelman et al., 2002); and in different family configurations, different psychological and motivational mechanisms may play a role. For example, Runco explained that middle children are more likely to be rebellious and creative to avoid competition with the eldest child. At the same time, some research has found a higher level of creativity for firstborns (e.g., Eisenman, 1987; Schubert et al., 1977), arguing that firstborns have more interaction with adults than later-born children, resulting in receiving more resources from their parents and the parents being better role models. Baer et al. (2005) discuss the importance of sibling age differences and gender as moderators of the birth order–creativity effects. They suggest that in certain family configurations, firstborns feel more constrained, as they are expected and required to be their siblings' caretakers, which makes them grow up faster and follow more conventional rules instead of playing freely and experimenting with creative ideas as children. On the other hand, when firstborns are competing for attention among many other siblings close in age, this may motivate them to be creative in order to stand out.

All of the reviewed inconsistent findings paint a mixed picture of the effect of the family of origin on the development of creative ability, personality, or potential. It seems that there is no clear pattern, but there are multiple possible explanations for these mixed results: (1) like the current family, the family of origin might influence creativity through different psychological mechanisms; (2) they may influence different types of creativity; and (3) they may provide more cognitive or more emotional or motivational resources for creativity or, as Csikszentmihalyi (1990) suggests, both intact homes and homes that have experienced trauma, loss, or separation of parents may foster creative achievements but through different modes. More specifically, Kerr and Chopp (1999) propose that disturbed families give rise to fiery creativity that burns out quickly, and happy families give rise to sustained, moderate everyday creativity. Where family configurations are concerned, it may be that individuals with stable families indeed may receive more emotional and cognitive support to be creative. Individuals who experience a parental loss may not have the same amount of family support, but may have a very different context or motivation for creativity: they may experience less requirement to conform and model the same-sex parent, which may free their creativity. Creativity for them may also be seen as an outlet or refuge from difficult circumstances (Feldman, 1994). It seems that under the right circumstances, both individuals with intact families and those with family traumas may excel in creativity later in life; but again, knowing the factors that shaped their personality and creative abilities might be helpful for both the employees and the organizations involved.

As mentioned earlier, this research on the influence of the family of origin is important for understanding the social context for creativity at work and the influence of the current family in multiple ways. Firstly, it may provide many insights for the socialization processes of these employees and what are the most critical factors for their creativity at work. For instance, it may be imperative for organizations to provide more emotional support and encouragement for creativity for some individuals who are used to stable encouraging families. At the same time, for others who may have been successful by just conforming to an authoritarian parent, it may be important to gain experience and become comfortable with uncertainty, experimentation, and play at work, to be exposed to different perspectives in order to improve their creative abilities. In addition, some employees may show a high level of resilience and grit based on their childhood experiences and may be very well suited for creativity in times of crisis. Others, who are risk-takers but need more stable environments, may thrive only when they have the space and time for radical new ideas and innovations in peaceful times. More research needs to explore how the family of origin can influence one's creative potential at work, and how individuals can use this information to become more creative.

MODERATORS OF THE INFLUENCE OF FAMILY ON CREATIVITY AT WORK

While the reviewed research reveals the potential for family (both nuclear and extended) to influence work creativity, the mechanisms through which this influence may happen are multiple, and the results seem not always positive or consistent. Moreover, some of the positive and negative effects of family on creativity may happen simultaneously. In essence, a large extended family may provide family-to-work conflict and a low level of emotional support, but at the same time boost cognitive stimulation and access to diverse perspectives. Some of the effects may also depend on the type of creativity necessary (radical versus incremental), the interaction between family of origin and background and the social context created by the current family, or some other characteristics of the individual and the family or the job. I will try to highlight a few that are likely to affect the family-to-work creativity influences.

Openness to Experience

One of the most frequently studied personality characteristics in connection to creativity is openness to experience: a broad preference for variety and a tendency for intellectual curiosity (McCrae & Costa, 1997). High openness to experience is characterized by more flexibility in thinking, more imagination, and curiosity. People who are high on openness have greater access to a variety of perspectives and ideas

(McCrae & Costa, 1997). In addition, McCrae (1996) suggested that openness is a determining factor for social interactions. Findings about the effects of openness to experience on creativity have not always been consistent (Baer & Oldham, 2006; George & Zhou, 2001; Madjar, 2008), but one possible explanation for these mixed results may be that the research may have captured different aspects of the context. Specifically, Madjar (2008) found differential effects of openness on emotional and informational support for creativity. Following these findings, it seems reasonable to believe that both low-openness and high-openness individuals may benefit from the family influences, but in different ways. For example, it seems natural that people with a high openness will seek the extra stimulation from family, while low-openness individuals may need the extra encouragement and emotional support from family to engage in the creative process. While different perspectives and diverse information may be available around them, they may benefit from their family connections and cognitive resources only if there is a high level of emotional support from the family as well.

Gender

Gender is widely emphasized in research on family and work (e.g., Eby et al., 2005) and has been proposed to differentially affect "spillover" from family to work (Greenhaus & Powell, 2006; Powell & Greenhaus, 2010). Social network research also suggests that men's and women's work and nonwork networks differ. For example, men in general report a higher number of co-workers within their social circle than women (Marsden, 1987; Moore, 1990), while women are more centrally involved in family-based relationships (e.g., Marsden, 1990) and may have more family connections than men (Marsden, 1987; Moore, 1990). Similarly, the effects of family might also differ based on gender. For example, according to social role theory, women assume additional responsibilities for managing family, including elder care and children, while often working full-time. These additional obligations mean that familial relationships will play a different role for them (Ajrouch et al., 2005). If this is the case, although women may have a more diverse and larger number of family connections than men, with more people they consider close (Antonucci et al., 1998), these familial relationships across a higher number of categories may be more distracting and come with higher personal costs for women than for men. As demonstrated by Rothbard and Edwards (2003), women's investment in family relations has a significant negative effect on their work investment, while this effect is not present for men. At the same time, women may acquire more resources from the family that they can bring to work. Consistent with this, Rothbard (2001) also found that spillover from family to work was more significant for women than for men. So, women may experience higher costs, together with the potential benefits of family connections, or they seem to be more sensitive to the family influences on their work creativity. For women, the higher cost of maintaining multiple role relationships is likely to attenuate their benefits relative to men. Individuals have limited time to focus attention and be creative, and it is possible that family may reduce time, cognitive focus, and ability to be creative instead of providing the necessary support for it. It may be that women may respond more positively to support from family than male entrepreneurs, for example (Powell & Eddleston, 2013), but the lack of family support will also have a stronger effect on women than on male employees' engagement in creativity. Moreover, without a high level of emotional support, women may not be able to benefit from the diverse perspectives and cognitive stimulation coming from the family. Men, on the other hand, are not burdened so much with family responsibilities and may easily benefit from the additional informational support and cognitive stimulation provided outside of work.

CONCLUSIONS, IMPLICATIONS, AND FUTURE DIRECTIONS

This chapter reviews the research on the effect of current nuclear and extended family, as well as the family of origin, on work creativity. The reviewed literature provides enough evidence that family members, as part of the individual's social context, can both facilitate and, at the same time, hinder creativity at work through multiple different mechanisms. They can provide encouragement, support, and positive emotions, and have the capacity to be a sounding board or a source of insights for new ideas. They can also provide distractions, take away resources, create frustrations, and diminish motivation for creativity.

While the review reveals numerous advances in understanding the effect of family on creativity at work, it also highlights substantial inconsistencies and mixed results that future research with strong theoretical foundations should try to reconcile. That is, we have just touched the surface and need to expand substantially our grasp of how family relations may influence work creativity. Family relationships have seldom been studied as part of the social context for work creativity, even though there has been a substantial history of research on the interdependence between family and work (e.g., Greenhaus & Powell, 2006). There are some empirical studies directly exploring the link between support and affect, originating from the family, and creativity at work (Madjar et al., 2002; Madjar, 2008; Tang et al., 2017). But with few exceptions (e.g., Madjar, 2008), the evidence linking family members to creativity through informational insights and cognitive stimulation is more anecdotal and less well established. Future research should focus on this informational and cognitive side of the family-to-work spillover.

Moreover, while the work–family relations literature has mentioned potential implications for creativity and entrepreneurship (Greenhaus & Powell, 2006; Powell & Greenhaus, 2010), its focus has been mostly on routine work performance and work–family and family–work conflict and enrichment. It is crucial to focus more on creativity and the different stages of the creative process, and to examine how family can influence the idea generation as well as the idea evaluation and verification stage of the creative process. In addition, we cannot ignore the effect of creative work on the family. Recent research (Harrison & Wagner, 2016) found that engaging in creative behaviors may be too cognitively taxing and have adverse effects on the individual's family, while being beneficial for their work and organization. Thus, to make engaging in creativity at work sustainable, we need more research on the consequences of creativity for the individual and how to balance its effect on individuals and their family's well-being.

This chapter also expands the notion of family. It explores the potential effects of both the nuclear family as well as the extended family or a broader set of family relations, as a resource for work creativity. However, future research needs to examine further the potential effects of different family relationships (children and siblings, for example) on work creativity. Family relationships differ from work relationships in significant ways, and future research needs to explore their different impact more. With the current trend of telecommuting, the effects of nonwork relationships may be becoming even more critical, and a better understanding of how they compare with the impact of support and cognitive stimulation from work relationships is important (Golden et al., 2006). For example, we still do not know whether family relations can offer support and information as a substitute for the lack of work connections for certain individuals (for example, sole entrepreneurs). Or whether their emotional and informational support is complementary and beneficial only after a certain level of work support, or only for people with certain personality characteristics.

In the context of the COVID-19 pandemic, when much work moved mostly from home, with family members around us, family is often becoming the primary social context for work, which calls for even more research on the intersection of family and creativity. Future research needs to explore the effects on creativity of this "forced" work–family integration due to COVID-19 or other events leading to remote work arrangements. It is critical to examine how the interruptions and intrusions originating from family members in this context may differ from the interruptions and intrusions related to the work context. Future research also needs to investigate new methods for managing these interruptions to protect one's ability to experience flow and be creative at work, even when working from home (Leroy et al., 2020).

The current COVID-19 situation presents a unique opportunity to examine how certain work and family demands, as well as work and family supports, may provide opportunities for individuals to craft or modify their jobs and in turn handle the new situation better (with more creative engagement and less distress). Creativity may be necessary for successful remote work and work–family integration; it may be essential for the long-term sustainability of remote work arrangements and future research needs to focus on the factors that may motivate and facilitate even more engagement in these creative processes, as well as the role of family in them. Moreover, creativity may be a potential buffer to the stress created by the COVID-19 pandemic and working from home, where there is no clear break or boundary between work and personal life; it may be an essential aspect of the work–family interface and serve as a stress relief mechanism that may improve employees' well-being. More research is needed along these lines of inquiry.

We need a better understanding of how connections with family, both as a source of support and as a source of information, may impact an employee's creativity at work. These are unique connections which, unlike work ones, are often characterized by very strong emotional ties and, at the same time, very weak advice or expertise ties. In this respect, some more research on ego-centered networks, including the specific connections with family, their frequency, and their impact as sources of both emotional and informational support, may be beneficial. It is also essential to understand whether it is the depth (emotional strength) of these family relations or their breadth (number or diversity) that has a more significant impact on creativity at work. In addition, more longitudinal research or qualitative studies that explore the antecedents as well as the different work and nonwork contexts, which facilitate the development of family relations as influential for creativity at work, may be invaluable.

It seems that creativity research can learn a lot from family research, and especially from the family of origin research, for the factors and conditions that organizations may explore to stimulate creativity and increase employees' creative potential (Jaskiewicz et al., 2017). For example, researchers have widely acknowledged that behaviors in organizations are imprinted during an individual's youth (Jaskiewicz et al., 2015). Family system theory shows that family structure, communication, and relationships affect how people view challenges, interact with others, and respond to stress (Broderick, 1993). If employees' original family system might affect attitudes and behavior at work and the way employees respond to changes in it, researchers may leverage family systems to better explain attitudes and behaviors at work and designs that are more conducive for employees' creativity. Family systems theory may inform theorizing about person–organization fit and creativity that goes beyond the well-established interactionist models of creativity (Woodman et al., 1993).

The family–work dynamics research often uses boundary theory to explain and predict boundary-crossing activities that individuals engaged in when transitioning between work and family roles (Ashforth et al., 2000). In this respect, to understand better the conditions as well as the mechanisms that facilitate family–work spill-over and integration of insights from multiple roles, the creativity literature may also benefit from integrating boundary theory. Individuals' tendencies to integrate or separate multiple roles, both inside and outside of work, may be examined as a critical factor in their ability to make remote associations and integrate different perspectives.

Substantial research in developmental psychology has examined the effects of parenting style, together with parental communications and parental values (Jaskiewicz et al., 2017; Murphy & Johnson, 2011) on leadership (Olson, 2000), creative development, and other work-related outcomes. The theorizing and findings from these previous studies on the family of origin influences on the development of creativity may also provide valuable insights for research and practice on the effects of leadership, supervision, and mechanisms for training for higher creativity now, in an organizational context.

By looking separately at the emotional support and its effects on affect and psychological resources, as well as on the informational resources and their impact on cognitive stimulation, this chapter is an attempt to provide a more nuanced view of the effects of family on creativity, through both emotional as well as cognitive mechanisms (Madjar, 2008). Future research may examine additional mechanisms, such as motivation for example, through which family may influence work creativity. As described so far, the family-to-work creativity relations and influence seem complex, with potential for opposite effects through different mechanisms. For example, while positive family experiences are expected to influence work creativity positively, while negative experiences are detrimental for creativity, some negative family experiences, or family ambivalence, may actually have positive effects on creativity as well. For instance, individuals often have examples where criticism or lack of appreciation of one's action from a family member may actually provide a different perspective or just a higher motivation to persevere and develop the creative idea further. A broad investigation of the factors and moderators that may change the direction or the effect of these relationships is clearly needed. The effects of family ambivalence, family communication patterns, and the potential mechanisms for their effects on creativity at work, deserve both more theorizing and more empirical research.

One of the main implications of this review is that individuals and organizations need to be aware of the potential effects of family on work creativity. Organizations, on the other hand, need to establish policies that allow employees to attend to their family relationships or minimize the adverse effects that exist in the family–work interface. If families are indeed an essential part of the social context for creativity, creativity research needs to understand better their role, in order to take advantage of the positive influences and minimize the hindrances from the family for work creativity.

REFERENCES

Ajrouch, K.J., Blandon, A.Y. & Antonucci, T.C. 2005. Social networks among men and women: The effects of age and socioeconomic status. *Journal of Gerontology*, 60: 311–317.

Aldrich, H.E., & Cliff, J.E. 2003. The pervasive effects of family on entrepreneurship: Toward a family embeddedness perspective. *Journal of Business Venturing*, 18(5): 573–596.

Amabile, T.M. 1996. *Creativity in context*. Boulder, CO: Westview Press.

Anderson, N., Potočnik, K., & Zhou, J. 2014. Innovation and creativity in organizations: A state-of-the-science review, prospective commentary, and guiding framework, *Journal of Management*, 40: 1297–1333.

Antonucci, T.C., Akiyama, H., & Lansford, J.E. 1998. Negative effects of close social relations. *Family Relations: An Interdisciplinary Journal of Applied Family Studies*, 474: 379–384.

Ashforth, B.E., Kreiner, G.E., & Fugate, M. 2000. All in a day's work: Boundaries and micro role transitions. *Academy of Management Review*, 25: 472–491.

Baer, M. 2010. The strength-of-weak-ties perspective on creativity: A comprehensive examination and extension. *Journal of Applied Psychology*, 95: 592–601.

Baer, M., & Oldham, G.R. 2006. The curvilinear relation between experienced creative time pressure and creativity: Moderating effects of openness to experience and support for creativity. *Journal of Applied Psychology*, 91: 963–970.

Baer, M., Oldham, G.R., Hollingshead, A.B., & Jacobsohn, G.C. 2005. Revisiting the birth order–creativity connection: The role of sibling constellation. *Creativity Research Journal*, 17: 67–77.

Baer, M., Vadera, A.K., Leenders, R.T., & Oldham, G.R. 2014. Intergroup competition as a double-edged sword: How sex composition regulates the effects of competition on group creativity. *Organization Science*, 25: 892–908.

Barnett, R.C., & Hyde, J.S. 2001. Women, men, work, and family: An expansionist theory. *American Psychologist*, 56: 781–796.

Barnett, R.C., Marshall, N.L., & Singer, J.D. 1992. Job experiences over time, multiple roles, and women's mental health: A longitudinal study. *Journal of Personality and Social Psychology*, 62: 634–644.

Bott, E. 1971. *Family and social network: Roles, norms and external relationships in ordinary urban families*. New York: Free Press.

Bowling, NA., Eschleman, K.J., & Wang, Q. 2010. A meta-analytic examination of the relationship between job satisfaction and subjective well-being. *Journal of Occupational and Organizational Psychology*, 83: 915–934.

Broderick, C.B. (1993). *Understanding family process: Basics of family systems theory*. Newbury Park, CA: SAGE.

Brown, V., Tumeo, M., Larey, T.S., & Paulus, P.B. 1998. Modeling cognitive interactions during group brainstorming. *Small Group Research*, 29: 495–526.

Burt, R.S. 2000. Decay functions. *Social Networks*, 22: 1–28.

Burt, R.S. 2004. Structural holes and good ideas. *American Journal of Sociology*, 110: 349–399.

Canavan, J., & Dolan P. 2006. *Family Support as Reflective Practice*. London: Jessica Kingsley.

Carlson, D.S., Kacmar, K.M., Wayne, J.H., & Grzywacz, J.G., 2006. Measuring the positive side of the work–family interface. *Journal of Vocational Behavior*, 68: 131–164.

Carver, C.S., & Scheier, N.F. 1981. *Attention and self-regulation: A control theory approach to human behavior*. New York: Springer-Verlag.

Chen, Z., Powell, G.N., & Cui, W. 2014. Dynamics of the relationships among work and family resource gain and loss, enrichment, and conflict over time. *Journal of Vocational Behavior*, 843: 293–302.

Csikszentmihalyi, M. 1990. *Flow: The psychology of optimal experience*. New York: Harper & Row.

Csikszentmihalyi, M., Rathunde, K., & Whalen, S. 1997. *Talented teenagers: The roots of success and failure*. Cambridge: Cambridge University Press.

Dai, D.Y., Tan, X., Marathe, D., Valtcheva, A., Pruzek, R.M., & Shen, J. 2012. Influences of social and educational environments on creativity during adolescence: Does SES matter? *Creativity Research Journal*, 24(2–3): 191–199.

De Massis, A., Frattini, F., Pizzurno, E., & Cassia, L. 2015. Product innovation in family versus nonfamily firms: An exploratory analysis. *Journal of Small Business Management*, 53: 1–36.

Deng, L., Wang, L., & Zhao, Y. 2016. How creativity was affected by environmental factors and Individual characteristics: A cross-cultural comparison perspective. *Creativity Research Journal*, 283: 357–366.

Dreisbach, G., & Goschke, T. 2004. How positive affect modulates cognitive control: Reduced perseveration at the cost of increased distractibility. *Journal of Experimental Psychology: Learning, Memory, and Cognition*, 30: 343–353.

Dugosh, K.L., Paulus, P.B., Roland, E.J., & Yang, H. 2000. Cognitive stimulation in brainstorming. *Journal of Personality and Social Psychology*, 79: 722–735.

Dumas, T.L., & Perry-Smith, J.E. 2018. The paradox of family structure and plans after work: Why single childless employees may be the least absorbed at work. *Academy of Management Journal*, 614: 1231–1252.

Eby, L., Casper, W., Lockwood, A., Bordeaux, C., & Brinley, A. 2005. Work and family research in IO/OB: Content analysis and review of the literature 1980–2002. *Journal of Vocational Behavior*, 66: 124–197.

Edwards, J.R., & Rothbard, N.P. 2000. Mechanisms linking work and family: Clarifying the relationship between work and family constructs. *Academy of Management Review*, 25: 178–199.

Eisenman, R. 1987. Creativity, birth order, and risk-taking. *Bulletin of the Psychonomic Society*, 25: 87–88.

Estrada, C.A., Isen, A.M., & Young, M.J. 1997. Positive affect facilitates integration of information and decreases anchoring in reasoning among physicians. *Organizational Behavior and Human Decision Processes*, 721: 117–135.

Feldman, D.H. 1994. *Beyond universals in cognitive development*, 2nd edn. Norwood, NJ: Ablex.

Fincham, F.D., & Bradbury, T.N. 1993. Marital satisfaction, depression, and attributions: A longitudinal analysis. *Journal of Personality and Social Psychology*, 64: 442–452.

Fincham, F.D., Harold, G.T., & Gano-Phillips, S. 2000. The longitudinal association between attributions and marital satisfaction: Direction of effects and role of efficacy expectations. *Journal of Family Psychology*, 142: 267–285.

Finke, R.A., Ward, T.B., & Smith, S.M. 1992. *Creative cognition: Theory, research, and applications*. Cambridge, MA: MIT Press.

Fredrickson, B.L. 2001. The role of positive emotions in positive psychology: The broaden-and-build theory of positive emotions. *American Psychologist*, 56: 218.

Fredrickson, B.L. 2013. Positive emotions broaden and build. In E. Ashby Plant & P.G. Devine (eds), *Advances in experimental social psychology*: 1–53. Burlington, VT: Academic Press.

Friedman, S.D., & Greenhaus, J.H. 2000. *Work and family – Allies or enemies? What happens when business professionals confront life choices*. New York: Oxford University Press.

Gardner, H. 1993. *Creating minds: An anatomy of creativity seen through the lives of Freud, Einstein, Picasso, Stravinsky, Eliot, Graham, and Gandhi*. New York: Basic Books.

George, J.M., & Zhou, J. 2001. When openness to experience and conscientiousness are related to creative behavior: An interactional approach. *Journal of Applied Psychology*, 86: 513–524.

Gerstel, N. 2011. Rethinking families and community: The color, class, and centrality of extended kin ties. *Sociological Forum*, 26(1): 1–20.

Golden, T.D., Veiga, J.F., & Simsek, Z. 2006. Telecommuting's differential impact on work–family conflict: Is there no place like home? *Journal of Applied Psychology*, 91: 1340–1350.

Graves, L.M., Ohlott, P.J., & Ruderman, M.N. 2007. Commitment to family roles: Effects on managers' attitudes and performance. *Journal of Applied Psychology*, 92: 44–56.

Greenhaus, J.H., & Beutell, N.J. 1985. Sources of conflict between work and family roles. *Academy of Management Review*, 10: 76–88.

Greenhaus, J.H., & Powell, G.N. 2006. When work and family are allies: A theory of work–family enrichment. *Academy of Management Review*, 31: 72–92.

Gruber, H.E., & Wallace, D.B. (1999). The case study method and evolving systems approach for understanding unique creative people at work. In R.J. Sternberg (ed.), *Handbook of Creativity*, 93–115. New York: Cambridge University Press.

Harrison, S.H., & Wagner, D.T. 2016. Spilling outside the box: The effects of individuals' creative behaviors at work on time spent with their spouses at home. *Academy of Management Journal*, 59: 841–859.

Heller, D., & Watson, D. 2005. The dynamic spillover of satisfaction between work and marriage: The role of time and mood. *Journal of Applied Psychology*, 90: 1273–1279.

Hobfoll, S.E. 2002. Social and psychological resources and adaptation. *Review of General Psychology*, 64: 307–324.

Howard-Jones, P.A., & Murray, S. 2003. Ideational productivity, focus of attention and context. *Creativity Research Journal*, 15: 153–166.

Isen, A.M. 2007. Positive affect, cognitive flexibility, and self-control. *Persons in Context: Building a Science of the Individual*, 48: 130–147.

Jaskiewicz, P., Combs, J.G., & Rau, S.B. 2015. Entrepreneurial legacy: Toward a theory of how some family firms nurture transgenerational entrepreneurship. *Journal of Business Venturing*, 30: 29–49.

Jaskiewicz, P., Combs, J.G., Shanine, K.K., & Kacmar, K.M. 2017. Introducing the family: A review of family science with implications for management research. *Academy of Management Annals*, 11: 309–340.

Karatepe, O.M., Kilic, H., & Isiksel, B. 2008. An examination of the selected antecedents and outcomes of work–family conflict and family–work conflict in frontline service jobs. *Services Marketing Quarterly*, 29: 1–24.

Kerr, B., & Chopp, C. 1999. Families and creativity. In M. Runco & S. Pritzker (eds), *Encyclopedia of creativity*: 709–715. New York: Academic Press.

Kessler, D. 2019. *Finding meaning: The sixth stage of grief*. New York: Scribner.

Kim, K., & Choi, S.B. 2017. Influences of creative personality and working environment on the research productivity of business school faculty. *Creativity Research Journal*, 29: 10–20.

Klein, R.C.A., & Milardo, R.M. 2000. The social context of couple conflict: Support and criticism from informal third parties. *Journal of Social and Personal Relationships*, 17: 618–637.

Koestner, R., Walker, M., & Fichman, L. 1999. Childhood parenting experiences and adult creativity. *Journal of Research in Personality*, 33: 92–107.

Labouvie-Vief, G. 1994. Women's creativity and images of gender. In B. Turner & L.E. Troll (eds), *Women growing older: Psychological perspectives*: 140–168. Thousand Oaks, CA: SAGE.

Leroy, S.A., Schmidt, A.M., & Madjar, N. 2020. Interruptions and task transitions: understanding their characteristics, processes, and consequences. *Academy of Management Annals*, 14(2): 661–694.

Levine, J.M., Choi, H.S., & Moreland, R.L. 2003. Newcomer innovation in work teams. In P.B. Paulus & B.A. Nijstad (eds). *Group creativity: Innovation through collaboration*: 202–224. New York: Oxford University Press.

Madjar, N. 2008. Emotional and informational support from different sources and employee creativity. *Journal of Organizational and Occupational Psychology*, 81: 83–100.

Madjar, N., Oldham, G.R., & Pratt, M.G. 2002. There's no place like home? The contributions of work and nonwork creativity support to employees' creative performance. *Academy of Management Journal*, 45(4): 757–767.

Madjar, N. & Shalley, C.E. 2008. Multiple tasks and multiple goals effect on creativity: Forced incubation or just a distraction? *Journal of Management*, 34: 786–805.

Marks, S.R. 1977. Multiple roles and role strain: Some notes on human energy, time and commitment. *American Sociological Review*, 42: 921–936.

Marsden, P.V. 1987. Core discussion networks of Americans. *American Sociological Review*, 53: 122–131.

Marsden, P.V. 1990. Network data and measurement. *Annual Review of Sociology*, 16: 435–463.

McCrae, R.R. 1996. Social consequences of experiential openness. *Psychological Bulletin*, 120: 323–337.

McCrae, R.R., & Costa Jr, P.T. 1997. Conceptions and correlates of openness to experience. In R. Hogan, J. Johnson, & S. Briggs (eds), *Handbook of personality psychology*: 825–847. San Diego, CA: Academic Press.

Miller, E.M., & Cohen, L.M. 2012. Engendering talent in others: expanding domains of giftedness and creativity. *Roeper Review*, 34: 104–113.

Moore, G. 1990. Structural determinants of men's and women's personal networks. *American Sociological Review*, 1: 726–735.

Murphy, S.E., & Johnson, S.K. 2011. The benefits of a long-lens approach to leader development: Understanding the seeds of leadership. *Leadership Quarterly*, 22: 459–470.

Nordenmark, M. 2004. Multiple social roles and well-being: A longitudinal test of the role stress theory and the role expansion theory. *Acta Sociologica*, 47: 115–126.

Ochse, R. 1991. The relation between creative genius and psychopathology: A historical perspective and a new explanation. *South African Journal of Psychology*, 21: 45–53.

Ohly, S., Kase, R., & Škerlavaj, M. 2010. Networks for generating and for validating ideas: The social side of creativity. *Innovation*, 12: 41–52.

Oldham, G.R., & Cummings, A. 1996. Employee creativity: Personal and contextual factors at work. *Academy of Management Journal*, 39: 607–634.

Olson, D.H. 2000. Circumplex model of marital and family systems. *Journal of Family Therapy*, 22: 144–167.

Olszewski, P., Kulieke, M., & Buescher, T. 1987. The influence of the family environment on the development of talent: A literature review. *Journal for the Education of the Gifted*, 11: 6–28.

Olszewski-Kubilius, P. 2002. A summary of research regarding early entrance to college. *Roeper Review*, 24: 152–157.

Paulus, P.B., & Dzindolet, M. 2008. Social influence, creativity and innovation. *Social Influence*, 3: 228–247.

Paulus, P.B., & Yang, H. 2000. The psychological foundations of knowledge transfer in organizations – Idea generation in groups: A basis for creativity in organizations. *Organizational Behavior and Human Decision Processes*, 82: 76–87.

Perrewe, P.L., Hochwarter, W.A., & Kiewitz, C. (1999). Value attainment: An explanation for the negative effects of work–family conflict on job and life satisfaction. *Journal of Occupational Health Psychology*, 4: 318.

Perry-Smith, J.E. 2006. Social yet creative: The role of social relationships in facilitating individual creativity. *Academy of Management Journal*, 49: 85–101.

Perry-Smith, J.E., & Mannucci, P.V. 2017. From creativity to innovation: The social network drivers of the four phases of the idea journey. *Academy of Management Review*, 42: 53–79.

Perry-Smith, J.E., & Shalley, C.E. 2003. The social side of creativity: A static and dynamic social network perspective. *Academy of Management Review*, 28: 89–106.

Petriglieri, J. L., & Obodaru, O. 2019. Secure-base relationships as drivers of professional identity development in dual-career couples. *Administrative Science Quarterly*, 64: 694–736.

Pietromonaco, P.R., Manis, J., & Frohardt-Lane, K. 1986. Psychological consequences of multiple social roles. *Psychology of Women Quarterly*, 10: 373–382.

Pohlman, L. 1996. Creativity, gender and the family: A study of creative writers. *Journal of Creative Behavior*, 30: 1–24.

Powell, G.N., & Eddleston, K.A. 2013. Linking family-to-business enrichment and support to entrepreneurial success: do female and male entrepreneurs experience different outcomes? *Journal of Business Venturing*, 28: 261–280.

Powell, G.N., & Greenhaus, J.H. 2010. Sex, gender, and the work-to-family interface: Exploring negative and positive interdependencies. *Academy of Management Journal*, 53: 513–534.

Reis, H.T. 2007. Steps toward the ripening of relationship science. *Personal Relationships*, 14: 1–23.

Roberts, S.G., & Dunbar, R.I. 2011. Communication in social networks: Effects of kinship, network size, and emotional closeness. *Personal Relationships*, 18: 439–452.

Rothbard, N.P. 2001. Enriching or depleting? The dynamics of engagement in work and family roles. *Administrative Science Quarterly*, 46: 655–684.

Rothbard, N.P., & Edwards, J.R. 2003. Investment in work and family roles: A test of identity and utilitarian motives. *Personnel Psychology*, 56: 699–729.

Rouse, E.D. 2020. Where you end and I begin: Understanding intimate co-creation. *Academy of Management Review*, 451: 181–204.

Ruderman, M.N., Ohlott, P.J., Panzer, K., & King, S.N. 2002. Benefits of multiple roles for managerial women. *Academy of Management Journal*, 45: 369–386.

Runco, M.A. 1994. *Problem finding, problem solving, and creativity*. Norwood, NJ: Greenwood Publishing Group.

Runco, M.A. 2007. *Creativity: Theories and themes: Research, development, and practice*. San Diego, CA: Elsevier Academic Press.

Runco, M.A., & Albert, R.S. 2005. Parents' personality and the creative potential of exceptionally gifted boys, *Creativity Research Journal*, 17: 355–368.

Runco, M.A., Johnson, D., & Gaynor, J.R. 1999. The judgmental bases of creativity and implications for the study of gifted youth. In A. Fishkin, B. Cramond, & P. Olszewski-Kubilius (eds), *Investigating creativity in youth: Research and methods*: 113–141. Cresskill, NJ: Hampton Press.

Sandberg, S. 2013 *Lean in: Women, work, and the will to lead*. New York: Random House.

Schubert, D.S., Wagner, M.E., & Schubert, H.J. 1977. Family constellation and creativity: Firstborn predominance among classical music composers. *Journal of Psychology*, 95: 147–149.

Shalley, C.E., Zhou, J., & Oldham, G.R. 2004. The effects of personal and contextual characteristics on creativity: Where should we go from here? *Journal of Management*, 306: 933–958.

Sieber, S.D. 1974. Toward a theory of role accumulation. *American Sociological Review*, 39: 567–578.

Simonton, D.K. 1984. Artistic creativity and interpersonal relationships across and within generations. *Journal of Personality and Social Psychology*, 46: 1273–1286.

Simonton, D.K. 1996. Creative expertise: A life-span developmental perspective. In K.A. Ericsson (ed.), *The road to excellence: The acquisition of expert performance in the arts and sciences, sports, and games*: 227–253. New York: Lawrence Erlbaum Associates.

Simonton, D.K. 1998. Achieved eminence in minority and majority cultures: Convergence versus divergence in the assessments of 294 African Americans. *Journal of Personality and Social Psychology*, 74: 804–817.

Simonton, D.K. 2000. Creativity: Cognitive, personal, developmental and social aspects. *American Psychologist*, 55: 151–158.

Sonnentag, S., Mojza, E., Binnewies, C., & Scholl, A. 2008. Being engaged at work and detached at home: A week-level study on work engagement, psychological detachment, and affect. *Work and Stress*, 22: 257–276.

Steelman, L.C., Powell, B., Werum, R., & Carter, S. 2002. Reconsidering the effects of sibling configuration: Recent advances and challenges. *Annual Review of Sociology*, 28: 243–269.

Stewart-Williams, S. 2007. Altruism among kin vs. nonkin: Effects of cost of help and reciprocal exchange. *Evolution and Human Behavior*, 28: 193–198.

Subotnik, R.F., Olszewski-Kubilius, P., & Arnold, K.D. 2003. Beyond bloom: Revisiting environmental factors that enhance or impede talent development. In J.H. Borland (ed.), *Rethinking gifted education*: 227–272. Washington, DC: American Psychological Association.

Swartz, T.T. 2009. Intergenerational family: Relations in adulthood: Patterns, variations and implications in the contemporary United States. *Annual Review of Sociology*, 35: 191–212.

Tang, Y., Huang, X., & Wang, Y. 2017. Good marriage at home, creativity at work: Family–work enrichment effect on workplace creativity. *Journal of Organizational Behavior*, 38: 749–766.

Ten Brummelhuis, L.L., & Bakker, A.B. 2012. A resource perspective on the work–home interface: The work–home resources model. *American Psychologist*, 677: 545.

Thoits, P.A. 1983. Multiple identities and psychological well-being: A reformulation and test of the social isolation hypothesis. *American Sociological Review*, 48: 174–187.

Tsui, A.S., & Farh, J.L. 1997. Where guanxi matters: Relational demography and guanxi in the Chinese context. *Work and Occupations*, 241: 56–79.

Ward, T.B., Smith, S.M., & Finke, R.A. 1999. Creative cognition. In R.J. Sternberg (ed.), *Handbook of creativity*: 189–213. Cambridge: Cambridge University Press.

Wellman, B., & Wortley, S. 1990. Different strokes from different folks: Community ties and social support. *American Journal of Sociology*, 96: 558–588.

Woodman, R.W., Sawyer, J.E., & Griffin, R.W. 1993. Toward a theory of organizational creativity. *Academy of Management Review*, 18: 293–321.

Yang, J., Hou, X., Wei, D., Wang, K., Li, Y., & Qiu, J. 2017. Only-child and non-only-child exhibit differences in creativity and agreeableness: Evidence from behavioral and anatomical structural studies. *Brain Imaging and Behavior*, 112: 493–502.

Zampetakis, L.A., Gotsi, M., Andriopoulos, C., & Moustakis, V. 2011. Creativity and entrepreneurial intention in young people: Empirical insights from business school students. *International Journal of Entrepreneurship and Innovation*, 123: 189–199.

Zampetakis, L.A., & Moustakis, V. 2006. Linking creativity with entrepreneurial intentions: A structural approach. *International Entrepreneurship and Management Journal*, 23: 413–428.

Zhou, J., & Hoever, I.J. 2014. Workplace creativity: A review and redirection. *Annual Review of Organizational Psychology and Organizational Behavior*, 1: 333–359.

Zhou, J., Shin, S.J., Brass, D.J., Choi, J., & Zhang, Z.X. 2009. Social networks, personal values, and creativity: Evidence for curvilinear and interaction effects. *Journal of Applied Psychology*, 94: 1544–1552.

10. Creativity connects: how the creative process fosters social connection and combats loneliness at work

Jack A. Goncalo, Joshua H. Katz, Lynne C. Vincent, Verena Krause, and Shiyu Yang

INTRODUCTION

Scholarly interest in creativity has spiked over the last decade, with creativity being the subject of edited volumes (Glover et al., 2013; Feist et al., 2017) and special issues of major journals (for example, *Journal of Organizational Behavior* and *Organizational Behavior and Human Decision Processes*). The fascination with creativity in management circles is in no small part because creative ideas can be wildly profitable (Audia & Goncalo, 2007). For example, the creative technology behind Gore-tex has been widely applied to a range of products from medical implants to clothing.[1] Hotmail introduced the idea of web-based email in July 1996, and it sold in December of 1997 to Microsoft for $400 million (Pelline, 1998). Web email has now become completely ubiquitous, and Microsoft Outlook, based on Hotmail's technology, is one of Microsoft's core offerings.

With these success stories in mind, most management research on creativity has focused on the antecedents of creative output (Khessina et al., 2018). What is the process that leads up to the emergence of ideas like these? Decades of research has investigated the thought processes, personality traits, and social contexts that foster creative work performance. In this chapter, we advance a different view of creativity: one that moves beyond the narrow focus on creativity as a mere output to consider the consequences of creativity for well-being at work. We suggest that engaging in the creative process can foster employee well-being by facilitating social connections and lifting psychological burdens. A great deal of research has investigated how social relationships such as social networks (Burt, 2004; Perry-Smith, 2006; Fleming et al., 2007; Baer et al., 2015) or team norms (Hirst et al., 2009; Goncalo & Duguid, 2012; Goncalo et al., 2019) facilitate creative output, but we turn the tables to consider how engaging in the creative process might in and of itself shape the frequency, quality, and depth of personal relationships at work. In doing so, we urge managers to consider the broader consequences of pursuing creativity: consequences that might be positive in ways that are unrelated to profit. We focus in particular on two kinds of psychological burdens that are prevalent in organizations: the burden of social isolation and the burden of keeping secrets. We show how engaging in the creative process can reduce loneliness by connecting people who might otherwise feel isolated. We theorize that these positive consequences are most likely to emerge in organizations with strong norms promoting openness and acceptance of new ideas. Finally, we conclude by calling for a broader view of the consequences of creativity: a view that extends beyond the typical focus on profitable outcomes.

LONELINESS AND ISOLATION AT WORK

Feelings of loneliness and isolation are a serious problem in the modern workplace (Ozcelik & Barsade, 2018). Loneliness is a negative emotional experience that results when an individual's network of social connections at work is deficient in some critical way (Perlman & Peplau, 1981). Loneliness is an individual's subjective experience rather than some easily detectible or objective feature of their social network (VanderWeele et al., 2012). In other words, it is possible for a person to have many social connections, even close ones, and to feel lonely if they perceive a discrepancy between their desired and actual social relationship quantity and, especially, quality (VanderWeele et al., 2012). Conversely, an employee can have very few or no social connections and not be lonely. It depends on how an individual's everyday experiences align with their desired experiences and relationships at work. Though it might be hard to predict who feels lonely and why, there is growing evidence pointing to the immensity and seriousness of the problem. One large-scale survey showed that 53 percent of Americans felt intensely lonely in their public life (McPherson et al., 2006). Loneliness can cause a wide range of problems, from chronic pain to depression, fatigue (Jaremka et al., 2014), and reduced job performance (Ozcelik & Barsade, 2018). Though research on the consequences of loneliness is somewhat limited, loneliness is linked to increased mortality among the elderly (Steptoe et al., 2013). Moreover, a meta-analysis shows that loneliness leads to as much as a 30 percent increased chance of mortality in the broader population (Holt-Lunstad et al., 2015). Disturbingly, both perceived and actual isolation had similar effects on mortality. In other words, thinking that you are alone and isolated is just as dangerous as actually being isolated. In sum, lonely people are sadder, sicker, and in more pain than their socially connected peers.

Is loneliness a problem at work? There is a growing consensus that it is. One recent survey showed that 42 percent of the respondents do not have a close friend at work.[2] This is important at least in part because employees who do not have a single friend at work might be lonely, but they might also be less engaged and less willing to do anything more than the bare minimum to get by on the job. Indeed, one study showed that loneliness not only had a direct impact on an employee's task performance, but it also had a negative impact on how their colleagues viewed their working relationship (Ozcelik & Barsade, 2018). Admitting to others that you are lonely might actually make matters even worse. Individuals who perceive that others are lonely may withdraw from these lonely co-workers, which provides a negative cue that further reinforces the perception that one's working relationships are deficient in some way (Ozcelik & Barsade, 2018).

Building social connections at work is an important tool to fight social isolation and the negative consequences that follow. We use the term "social connection" broadly to refer to a wide range of forms of social interactions, ranging from momentary contacts between two people in a single context to more meaningful and enduring interpersonal relationships (Dutton & Heaphy, 2003). In the sections that follow, we argue that the creative process provides the opportunities for building connections by not only forging new relationships that may not otherwise exist, but also increasing the strength of existing relationships. Moreover, when the creative process allows for or encourages repeated interactions between individuals, it is possible that the once momentary contacts without prior history may later develop into reoccurring and long-lasting relationships with high levels of closeness and intimacy (Dutton & Heaphy, 2003). Therefore, we believe the creative process may contribute to connection-building across the range of different forms of social interactions.

More specifically, we argue that giving employees the opportunity to do creative work can foster social connections and reduce loneliness in three ways. Firstly, a salient goal to be creative at work can motivate the formation of new connections. Secondly, engaging in creative work can build social bonds by providing the opportunity for mutual self-disclosure. Thirdly, the opportunity to be creative might help people who are burdened by the psychological weight of secrecy by making people who engage in the creative exploration feel liberated from constraints. Taken together, these three avenues suggest ways that the creative process can boost the well-being of employees who choose to undertake it.

CREATIVITY MOTIVATES THE FORMATION OF SOCIAL CONNECTIONS

Creativity refers to solving a problem in a new way (Woodman et al., 1993), and the creative process involves changing one's perspective (Cronin & Loewenstein, 2018). Creative products are typically defined as being both novel and useful (Amabile, 1983). For example, Gore-tex resulted from a novel technology: a polymer that was newly discovered. That new discovery became creative when it was applied to solve a wide range of different problems such as weatherproofing clothing. In other words, creativity does not mean being different for the sake of being different; creative ideas are not simply bizarre, they must also solve a problem. Conversely, the defining characteristic of a creative idea over one that is merely practical is that it departs from what is known: it introduces something new (Amabile, 1996).

Much research on creativity would suggest that the path of the creative individual is a rather lonely one. Creative people must break with the status quo to pursue unique ideas that might not be readily accepted (Simonton, 1999; Dollinger, 2007). Many creative ideas originate as a minority point of view, at least in the initial stages (Nemeth, 1997). Because creative ideas are initially risky, untested, and unproven, they are frequently rejected (Mueller et al., 2012). In fact, simply expressing an idea at work can make the idea pitcher seem quirky and unpredictable; traits that are incompatible with leadership positions (Mueller et al., 2011). Forming a team to generate creative ideas would seem to be almost inherently social, but the most creative teams are not necessarily the most collectivistic; in fact, creative teams may be individualistic and competitive (Goncalo & Staw, 2006; Goncalo & Krause, 2010). In sum, it would seem that creativity is best left to the loners, the outsiders, and the rejects (Kim et al., 2013).

Yet, this "loner" view of creativity may not be complete and may actually exclude the potential for the creative process to forge rather than break social connections. We recognize the long stream of research demonstrating how certain social network configurations (Burt, 2004; Perry-Smith, 2006) and social interactions (Hargadon & Bechky, 2006) can help to stimulate the creative process. Rather, our focus here is on how the goal of being creative can motivate people to seek out and form social ties with others, with the perhaps unintended positive side-effect of reducing loneliness and social isolation.

Creativity is a long process that unfolds over time across many different stages (Perry-Smith & Mannuci, 2017; Cronin & Loewenstein, 2018). One might begin at the idea generation stage by coming up with a wide range of potential solutions that diverge in many different directions (Paulus & Yang, 2000). However, generating ideas is not enough: it may also be necessary to share these ideas with others (West et al., 2003). Through communication and interaction with others, individuals can gain a greater and more varied range of information from which to generate creative solutions (e.g., Woodman et al., 1993; Amabile, 1996). Finally, from a wide range of potential solutions, individuals must select a subset of ideas or even one idea to pursue to fruition (Rietzschel et al., 2006, 2010). Below we trace the process through each of these stages to demonstrate how the creative process can provide opportunities for social connectedness and reduce feelings of social isolation.

How the Goal to be Creative can Motivate the Formation of Social Connection

Organizations often form teams to share creative ideas because teams provide the opportunity to build upon, combine, and improve on their ideas (Paulus & Yang, 2000; Goncalo et al., 2019). Indeed, people overwhelmingly believe that interactive face-to-face groups outperform groups that work independently (Stroebe et al., 1992; Paulus et al., 1993). This deeply held belief in the superiority of teams for creative output, whether it is accurate or not, leads individuals who are looking to solve a problem creatively to seek out others to tackle problems conjointly. For example, a majority of entrepreneurs choose to form a team to start a new venture rather than going at it alone (Lechler, 2001; Chowdhury, 2005).

Not only do people believe that the quality of the ideas generated in an interactive group is superior, but group members are also more satisfied and optimistic when they have worked in an interactive group rather than individually, suggesting that the interaction itself has psychological benefits (Paulus et al., 1993; Larey & Paulus, 1995; Paulus et al., 1995). Team creativity makes people happier than working alone, for several reasons. Firstly, idea generation in a group allows for social comparison such that group members are able to compare their own performance with other members' performance (Paulus et al., 1993). Since this comparison usually leads people to realize that they perform as well as or even better than others, they are happier (Paulus & Dzindolet, 1993; Lyubomirsky & Ross, 1997). Secondly, group brainstorming allows for memory confusion such that group members attribute others' ideas to themselves, making them believe they performed better than they actually did, again leading to greater satisfaction (Stroebe et al., 1992). Thirdly, group brainstorming allows for a reduction in perceived cognitive failures such that there are fewer occurrences in which there is a complete block and no ideas are being produced (Nijstad et al., 2006). Aside from the objective productivity of the team, the interaction itself provides an opportunity to connect with others. The positive emotions engendered in creative teams may allow group members to feel connected to one another, to want to work together in the future, and potentially to form relationships with others at work; all of which should increase an individual's feeling of belongingness and reduce loneliness (see Lawler, 2001).

The creative process, however, does not stop at the idea generation phase. Idea elaboration, championing and implementation need to follow in order to bring the initial creative idea to fruition (Perry-Smith & Mannucci, 2017). Just as the idea generation stage seems to foster social connections, so do the other phases of the creative process also require reaching out to others. Whether an individual came up with a potentially creative idea themself or as part of a team, the idea needs to be elaborated upon. The idea needs to be thought through, potential problems need to be discovered and resolved, and the idea's usefulness needs to be determined. In other words, the initial, raw idea needs to be further developed, which requires emotional support from others (Perry-Smith & Mannucci, 2017). At this vulnerable stage that is characterized by uncertainty over whether the novel idea is in fact feasible, people are likely to turn to close others who they can trust for constructive feedback (Harrison & Rouse, 2015). The social support at this stage is particularly important because many creative ideas seem like bad ideas initially, but elaboration can aid in illuminating their potential (Catmull & Wallace, 2014; Harvey, 2014). Ideally, a cyclical process of discussion with others, comparison, and revision of the idea ensues, which is thought of as the backbone of particularly successful creative organizations (Harvey, 2014). Reaching out to well-known others is thus paramount at this stage.

Once the idea has taken full shape and potential kinks have been worked out, the idea needs to be presented to "gatekeepers" in order to receive approval for its ultimate implementation (Perry-Smith & Mannucci, 2017). In other words, some form of validation that the idea is indeed creative and worthy of pursuit generally needs to occur (Campbell, 1960; Staw, 1990; Ford, 1996; Harvey, 2014). For this purpose, the idea generators again have to seek out and form connections with others. For example, entrepreneurs who have an idea for a new venture might look to acquaintances, people they know less well, for input. Particularly when looking for potential collaborators and investors for the venture, it might be necessary to reach out into the far corners of one's social connections. Often, those one knows less well have the information and further connections one seeks (Perry-Smith, 2006; Zhou et al.,

2009). For employees in organizations, too, in order to move the idea through the organization, to get it accepted and supported, people need to utilize a wide range of connections (Anand et al., 2007; Cattani & Farriani, 2008). Influence tactics and strong as well as weak relationships play a major role in getting support for an idea (Howell & Higgins, 1990). It is not just in the activation of these networks that relationships could be strengthened or formed to advance an idea, but also those in creative positions or those likely to seek creative influence may develop networks and broader connections in anticipation of aiding their creative ideas in the future.

Finally, implementing the creative idea represents another significant hurdle, one that might motivate individuals to form social connections (Klein & Sorra, 1996). Finding support within an immediate work group can aid in idea implementation (West, 2002). However, creating and effectively using a broad social network within an organization can greatly improve the chances that creative ideas will be successfully implemented (Baer, 2012). Thus, once again, implementation necessitates the creator to reach out to others. For example, the creator requires help with the production process because an altogether different skillset is needed to turn the idea into a finished product, service, or process. Thus, throughout the different stages of the creative process, the creator needs to reach out to well- or less well-known people within their social network, but also to create new connections with formerly unknown others.

In sum, the entire creative process, from idea generation to implementation, is ripe with opportunities to connect people who might not have formed relationships absent a salient goal to be creative. The social connections formed in the process of being creative might not only lead to innovation (Burt, 2004; Perry-Smith, 2006), but in the process might also have the side-effect of forging new relationships at work.

HOW THE CREATIVE PROCESS CAN DEEPEN RELATIONSHIPS AT WORK VIA SELF-DISCLOSURE

The Benefits of Creative Self-Disclosure

The creative process motivates individuals to connect with others with whom they might not ordinarily interact; but can these relationships deepen into longer-lasting and intimate creative collaborations (Rouse, 2020)? Here we address the underlying psychological process through which engaging in the creative process can strengthen social bonds: through the act of self-disclosure.

Most existing research on collaborative creativity has focused on how to boost creative output: how can we reduce process loss so that people can generate a wide range of creative ideas together? More recently, scholars have begun to investigate the interpersonal consequences of engaging in the creative process, and research is beginning to discover that being creative has some unintended side-effects (Khessina et al., 2018). For instance, expressing a creative idea can trigger biases that, if left unchecked, can undermine the adoption of new ideas (Mueller et al., 2012). People who express creative ideas also run the risk of being passed over for leadership positions because the creative prototype includes traits such as risk-taking and impulsiveness that most would consider a poor fit for a leadership position (Mueller et al., 2011). For these reasons, a more nuanced view of the consequences of creativity, including the possibility that being creative can have unintended positive and negative side-effects, might be fruitful (Khessina et al., 2018).

One potentially positive consequence of expressing creative ideas is that doing so can reveal our inner selves to others (Goncalo & Katz, 2020). This idea might seem somewhat counterintuitive in light of evolutionary theories that depict the creative process as a quasi-random combination of knowledge that gives rise to novel combinations through blind variation and selective retention (Campbell, 1960; Staw, 1995; Simonton, 1999, 2003). In other words, the creative process can be rather detached and dispassionate. Yet, there is recent evidence to suggest the creative act may be much more personal.

Indeed, scholars have argued that being creative can actually be a personally meaningful activity (Amabile & Pratt, 2016). As people engage in the creative process, they have a great deal of choice; choices that can be revealing of the self. For instance, people can choose which problems to pursue based on decisions as to what is personally meaningful and worthy of time and attention (Lepisto & Pratt, 2017). Amabile & Pratt (2016) identify perceived meaningfulness of the creative task as a significant component of the individual-level psychological processes implicated in creativity. They argue that the sense of meaningfulness of creative work can cause persistence in the task and support the individual during failure or rejection. Even when individuals face setbacks or even failure, if individuals believe that their creative endeavors are meaningful, they can justify continuing with the idea (Amabile & Pratt, 2016). Being creative can, in and of itself, represent a vital part of one's identity (Farmer et al., 2003). Actively engaging in creative work allows people to express, validate, and maintain that creative identity (McCall & Simmons, 1978). By engaging in creative behaviors, individuals can proactively shape their identity and others' perceptions of them. In this way, doing creative work allows individuals to express valuable aspects of themselves; an opportunity that other behaviors at work may not provide.

Prior research also suggests that when people are asked to be creative they draw on their own unique perspectives, idiosyncratic preferences, and aspects of themselves that make them unique and distinguishable from others (Beersma & De Dreu, 2005; Goncalo & Staw, 2006; Cheng et al., 2008; Leung et al., 2008; Kim et al., 2013; Zitek & Vincent, 2015). This self-expression in the creative process not only produces more original ideas by virtue of the fact that they are derived from unique personal experience, but sharing ideas that emerge from this process will also reveal aspects of oneself that might not have surfaced otherwise.

Goncalo and Katz (2020) tested this prediction in a series of studies in which people were asked to generate either creative ideas (novel and unique) or uncreative ideas (generic, conventional, typical). Participants were then asked to rate the extent to which the ideas they shared were personally revealing. The results of several studies showed, across two different brainstorming topics, that people who generated creative ideas believed they disclosed significantly more personal information compared to participants who generated uncreative ideas.

We were also curious as to whether feelings of self-disclosure might extend to a partner. Does hearing another person's creative ideas make one feel as though one's partner has revealed something personal, and does that in turn make one more confident that one can predict a partner's personality? We asked people to generate ideas in pairs and again varied the instructions to elicit ideas that were either creative or relatively uncreative. We then asked each person to rate their partner's personality on several dimensions, and asked them to rate their confidence in their judgment of their partner's personality. The results echoed our findings from the individual-level studies. The results showed that, when asked to be creative, both partners: (1) believed that they self-disclosed; (2) believed that their partner also disclosed something personal to them; and (3) were more confident that their estimates of their partner's personality traits were accurate. In other words, being creative together made both partners feel more known to one another. This finding fits neatly with the notion that dyadic co-creation is one that involves intimacy between partners who are jointly engaged in the creative process (Rouse, 2020).

Creative self-disclosure can, in turn, foster the formation of meaningful relationships at work. There is a strong link between self-disclosure and social connection for three reasons. Firstly, people who disclose more are also more liked by others. Secondly, people tend to disclose more about themselves to those whom they like more. Thirdly, people like those to whom they disclose more (Collins & Miller, 1994). Through this process, self-disclosure can lead to an upward cycle of relationship building. A person begins to disclose to another, which causes them to like that other person more, which then causes them to disclose more to that person, and so on. Because people who do creative work reveal their personal identities, interests, and passions, other people might be emboldened to respond in kind; a process that can strengthen relationships over time. In other words, self-disclosure is not simply a way to develop intimacy in and increase the strength of existing relationships, but it can also form the basis for and even strengthen new relationships that previously did not exist at all. Self-disclosure can decrease loneliness, by supporting the formation of new relationships with others. One person discloses more to others, which then causes those others to disclose back, which generally increases liking between people at a variety of different stages and strengthens the relationship. Self-disclosure is not a one-way street. Indeed, self-disclosure from one party encourages self-disclosure from the other (Jourard, 1971). Different disclosure levels from one partner directly predict disclosure levels of the other partner, regardless of initial levels of liking (Derlega et al., 1973). These cycles of reciprocal self-disclosure can gradually increase liking of even previously unacquainted partners (Sprecher et al., 2013).

In sum, engaging in the creative process not only brings people into contact with one another as people seek out novel inputs and perspectives into their own work; but also being creative together can strengthen these social bonds because the creative act involves self-disclosure. Thus, being creative with a partner can provide the foundation for bonding and connectedness at work (Collins & Miller, 1994; Laurenceau et al., 1998; Reis & Shaver, 1988; Phillips et al., 2009; Polzer et al., 2002). Creative work is personal. Because the motivation to engage in the tasks often derives from the enjoyment and love of the creative task itself in addition to some kinds of extrinsic rewards, creative tasks are uniquely revealing by indicating what is personally important and valuable. By engaging in creativity for the love of the creative idea itself, an individual clearly indicates what they find important, thus revealing their own true self and deeply held values. The creative process provides an avenue through which people purposefully or perhaps inadvertently disclose their true selves through their work. While it may be inappropriate or even bizarre to share deeply personal information in a work setting, doing so in the context of creative work might allow personal information to be shared within the context of a professional relationship. As people share their passion through their work, they reveal themselves to others, and doing so can build meaningful bonds that reduce feelings of loneliness.

The Dark Side of Creative Self-Disclosure: Accounting for the Possibility of Rejection

It is important to acknowledge that the positive effect of creative self-disclosure is not inevitable. Indeed, sharing creative ideas can be a socially risky endeavor: individuals who share creative ideas risk criticism and rejection, at least initially (Mueller et al., 2012). We have argued that the creative process can combat loneliness at work by fostering social connections. However, how the audience reacts may also influence whether connections can be successfully established. Creative ideas are not always recognized or well received (Mueller, 2017). Creative ideas are often unconventional, deviant, and unorthodox (Nemeth & Staw, 1989). Indeed, there is empirical evidence that sharing creative ideas can lead to negative impressions of the idea generator (Cropley, 2009; Mueller et al., 2011). More directly, people reported experiencing negative emotional reactions (for example, anger, frustration, and disappointment) to their ideas being rejected or ignored (Amabile et al., 2005). To the extent that acceptance and validation from others are important for cultivating social connections (Phillips et al., 2009), creative self-disclosure that is greeted by rejection might exacerbate rather than relieve feelings of loneliness and isolation.

Some individuals might be able to harness this experience of rejection to fuel rather than stunt their creativity. Being rejected or ostracized may serve as catalyst for creativity among individuals with an independent self-concept (Kim et al., 2013). For individuals with an independent self-concept, the experience of rejection is interpreted as a signal that they are unique and distinct: "I'm not strange, I'm just different." This differentiation mindset, in turn, can motivate problem-solvers to share creative ideas that stand out from the rest (Förster et al., 2005; Galinsky et al., 2008). Because creative self-disclosure can be risky for many, innovative organizations institute norms to reduce criticism and rejection of new ideas (Goncalo et al., 2019). Norms that promote an open and safe atmosphere for sharing ideas will provide a context in which creative self-disclosure will lead to feelings of acceptance and higher-quality relationships within creative teams (Goncalo et al., 2015a).

Creativity, Self-Disclosure, and Connectedness Online

Creativity can reduce loneliness by connecting people and providing opportunities for self-disclosure; but do these benefits require face-to-face interaction? This is an important question to address because, in modern organizations, collaborating across geography (Nemeth & Goncalo, 2005) and even national boundaries (Chua et al., 2012; Chua et al., 2015) has become commonplace. At the time of writing in June 2020, the 2020 COVID-19 global pandemic has brought this issue into sharp focus for millions of working people across the globe. In order to facilitate these diverse collaborations, organizations rely upon computer-mediated communication, which can be synchronous such as chat, or asynchronous such as email (Derks et al., 2008). Employees halfway across the world from each other are now able to instantaneously collaborate on a work project or share knowledge about how to solve problems that may arise. Even for those who are collocated, email and chat serve as a consistent basis of communication and collaboration. Corporations are even beginning to take advantage of other forms of computer-mediated communication, such as social media, to keep in touch with their customers (Mangold & Faulds, 2009). Social media use can be a key factor in determining the relationship between an organiza-tion and its stakeholders (Saffer et al., 2013). Even executives often communicate through a wide range of social media platforms to stay in touch with their broad base of both employees and customers (Gaines-Ross, 2013). This allows them to forge a more direct and personal connection to those with whom they are communicating, as well as affording them more direct control over their relationship with others.

Previously, most of these connections took place in person, but new research on social media and other computer-mediated communication shows how even digital self-disclosure can help to build relationships. Recent work found that even non-intimate self-disclosure through social media strengthened liking and increased relationship strength (Utz, 2015). In this case, these increases in the strength of the relationship took place regardless of the responsiveness of the partner. Indeed, increased self-disclosure on social media increased social support and online social well-being (Huang, 2016). In an experimental design, Deters and Mehl (2013) showed a direct link between increased status posting on Facebook (a form of self-disclosure) and decreased loneliness. This effect was not dependent on responses from others in the network; those who posted more felt more connected to others regardless of how their status was responded to.

Other recent communications work showed that self-disclosure through computer-mediated communication (usually chat programs employed to communi-cate in lab dyads) will still elicit liking from the other party, though it may not have the same effect of encouraging reciprocal communication (Kashian et al., 2017). In computer-mediated communication, like regular communication, the response of the person being disclosed to can shape the relationship between disclosure and liking. Even in computer-mediated communication, a person who responded to self-disclosure with self-disclosure of their own, or compliments, strengthened their relationship with the disclosure and increased liking much more than a person who responded with deflections (Dai et al., 2016). In sum, even if the creative process unfolds via computer-mediated communication, the potential for social connection remains and the personal interactions that ensue can provide opportunities for self-disclosure and feelings of liking and connectedness.

CREATIVITY CAN LIFT THE BURDEN AND ISOLATION OF SECRECY

There are many causes for loneliness and social isolation at work. In the previous section, we suggested that allowing people to be creative could address these problems by providing opportunities for self-disclosure and social connection. Yet, sometimes employees can feel isolated because they must actively maintain secrets that prevent them from openly communicating with others. Many employees keep secrets from their colleagues at work at the expense of their health and well-being (Kelly, 2002; Pennebaker, 1989). Maintaining a secret, particularly a big secret, can have significant consequences such as increased stress, reduced cognitive resources, and a reduced ability to complete work tasks (Lane & Wegner, 1995; Critcher & Ferguson, 2014).

While directly revealing the secret itself may be the most obvious way to reduce the burden of secrecy (Slepian et al., 2014), there are many circumstances in which revealing a secret might have significant negative consequences for the individual and the organization. For instance, at work, employees are aware of potential consequences of disclosing secrets related to sexual orientation (Michael et al., 1994), chronic illness (Vickers, 2002), or even a mixed-race heritage (Jones & Smith, 2001). By withholding these significant aspects of one's identity, individuals may feel as if they are not valued or welcomed in that organization, which may cause additional distress due to a sense of disconnection from the organization. Choosing to maintain these secrets may emerge from a desire to avoid shame or embarrassment (Maas et al., 2012). Furthermore, some professions require individuals to maintain secrecy as a moral and ethical obligation (Cramton & Knowles, 1998). For instance, doctors and other medical professionals must maintain the privacy of their patients. Failing to maintain patients' privacy can cause individuals not only to lose their job but also to lose their license to practice medicine. Similarly, lawyers are charged with keeping their clients' counsel and are forbidden from revealing certain information. Keeping secrets may be necessary, but doing so may leave people feeling disconnected and isolated at work. Self-disclosure might be helpful under these circumstances, but it might not be possible, depending on the secret being concealed. Here we build on recent research suggesting that creative work functions to liberate burdens and promote well-being by reconnecting people with others and by allowing a way to disclose something personal about oneself while not disclosing the secret directly (Goncalo et al., 2015b).

The Burden of Secrecy

Maintaining a secret is not only experienced as a psychological burden; individuals can experience maintaining a secret as a physical burden as well (Slepian et al., 2012). Secrets can literally feel like one is carrying a heavy weight (Slepian et al., 2012). This is because abstract concepts such as secrecy can become intertwined with physical experiences such as physical burdens, and eventually attain a reality of their own (Barsalou, 2008). There are many other examples of this psychological phenomenon. Take, for instance, the notion that people can be either "cold" or "warm." "Cold" and "warm" refer to both physical experiences and to psychologically potent metaphors for personality. Because the metaphor and the physical experience are meshed together, people can actually rate a stranger's personality as warmer when holding a warm as opposed to a cold beverage (Williams & Bargh, 2008). Similarly, walking backwards can cue memories of the past, while walking forward can cue thoughts about the future (Miles et al., 2010). Through this process, keeping a secret can have real physical consequences. For instance, people keeping a big secret think and behave as though they are shouldering a physical burden. Secret-keepers can overestimate the steepness of a hill (because hills seems steeper when you are feeling weighed down) or the weight of a common object (because objects also feel heavier when you are feeling weighed down) (Slepian et al., 2012). Thus, secrecy, like loneliness, has physical consequences. Engaging in creative work may provide a way to overcome those burdens of secrecy without disclosing information that one cannot disclose or chooses not to disclose.

Doing Creative Work Feels Liberating and Lifts the Burden of Secrecy

The burden of keeping a big secret may be lifted by giving individuals the opportunity to work on a creative task, even if that task does not afford the opportunity to confess. People who keep a big secret may be forced to actively suppress thoughts that are unwelcome and intrusive (Slepian et al., 2014). In other words, keeping a big secret constrains people to a ruminative focus on suppressing unwanted thoughts (Gold & Wegener, 1995). The expectation to be creative, by priming the expectation to "think differently" helps individuals to break away from the constraining effects of existing knowledge to generate a wider range of ideas (Sassenberg & Moskowitz, 2005). Less creative thinkers tend to focus their thoughts narrowly around one theme or category, generating many ideas that are highly similar to each other; while more creative thinkers feel free to jump around between categories, generating many ideas that are distinct from each other (Brown & Paulus, 2002; Goncalo & Staw, 2006). Being creative might relieve the burden of secrecy by permitting uninhibited exploration – roaming freely across the boundaries between different types of ideas rather than being constrained to consider a narrow set of ideas within only one category or theme – a process that is likely to feel liberating. Thus, one psychological benefit of engaging in the creative process is that it triggers positive emotion, including feelings of liberation (Goncalo et al., 2015b).

There is very little research on the unburdening effects of creative work, but there is some empirical evidence to suggest that engaging in the creative process can lift the burden of secrecy. Though directly revealing a secret is often impractical or impossible, this burden may be relieved by providing people with the opportunity to do creative work. In a laboratory experiment, participants were asked to think of a big or small secret they keep, and they were then assigned a brainstorming task with the instruction to generate either "creative" or "practical" solutions depending on the condition to which they were randomly assigned (Goncalo et al., 2015b). After completing the brainstorming task, participants were asked to help carry heavy book stacks. Ostensibly, the lab was moving into a new location and so the experimenter supposedly needed help moving the books. People who feel physically burdened should be expected to offer to help move fewer stacks of books. Indeed, the participants who were asked to keep a big secret but did not have a creative outlet offered to move significantly fewer books than the secret-keepers who were given a creative outlet. The latter participants offered to move as many books as the participants who were not keeping a big secret. In other words, holding a big secret causes physical labor to seem more effortful, but this burden was lifted after doing creative work (Goncalo et al., 2015b). The findings of this experiment also pointed to the underlying process that explains why creative work lifts the burden of secrecy. The unburdening effect of doing creative work was fully mediated by self-reported feelings of liberation. In other words, people who kept a big secret reported that generating creative ideas gave them a general feeling of being liberated, and those feelings of liberation, in turn, predicted their willingness to help on tasks that would otherwise be too physically taxing.

Keeping secrets can make people feel socially isolated and may even exact a physical toll. The challenge in managing the consequences of secrecy is that employees cannot always be expected to simply confess. Some secrets are too personal to share. However, doing creative work, because it permits free and uninhibited exploration, can offer psychological refuge to employees who are constrained to withhold their true selves from others, thus offering another avenue through creative work can boost employee well-being.

THE CONSEQUENCES OF CREATIVITY: IMPLICATIONS FOR WORK PRACTICE

Thinking about the creative process as a source of employee well-being leads to a number of implications for practice.

Think more Broadly about the Creative Process

The creative process leads to creative ideas. One would hope so, yet this narrow focus on creativity as an output variable comes at the expense of recognizing the potentially wide range of other consequences. We have suggested that creative work connects people through their personal passions and intrinsic interests. Employees with the goal of being creative often reach out to others, build teams, and share ideas. This process might lead to more creative outcomes (or not) but the process itself should be recognized as a source of well-being at work. Therefore, policies and practices intended to foster creativity, and innovation can be justified not only by their potential for profit but also for their role in improving quality of life in the workplace. The potential for creativity to reduce loneliness is likely to be enhanced in organizations that emphasize acceptance and institute strong norms to avoid criticism (Goncalo et al., 2019).

Look for Benefits of Creativity in Surprising Places

Even though we focused specifically on the consequences of creativity for employee well-being, our analysis highlighted an array of outcomes not commonly associated with creative work. For example, by lifting the burden of secrecy, people might be more willing to lend others a hand. Creative work can also have an emotional impact on people who might be weighed down, giving people an outlet through which to deal with burdens. Indeed, creative work might be particular appealing to individuals who feel rejected, isolated, and lonely, because it serves as a refuge from these negative feelings. Being creative can also feel like self-disclosure. Creative work is not impersonal; we share some of ourselves when we offer ideas that are rooted in our personal interests and reflect our own unique point of view on the world. There may be more benefits to the creative process that may become apparent once we start looking for them.

Consider the Implications for Work–Life Balance

The consequences of creativity are not inevitably positive. Indeed, there might be a dark side that should be considered. Recent research suggests that creativity can be negatively associated with work–life balance, leading people who do creative work to spend less time with their spouse (Harrison & Wagner, 2016). One reason might be that creative work is so absorbing that it saps resources that could be directed toward building relationships with other people. Another possibility is that doing creative work builds relationships at work at the expense of non-work relationships. Indeed, strong culture organizations encourage these workplace bonds because the more time people spend at work, they more easily they are socialized to workplace norms, and the easier it is to influence and control employee behavior (O'Reilly & Chatman, 1996). Employees might be deriving their happiness from work at the expense of outside social ties.

CONCLUSION

We began by suggesting that the prevailing view of creativity has been narrowly focused on creativity as a potentially profitable output variable, while largely ignoring the many byproducts of the creative process. We hope to shift this perspective toward a broader view of creativity: one that includes the possibility that being creative can drive a wide range of outcomes with important implications for employee well-being. Doing creative work can connect people, permit the sharing of one's deepest passions, and even lift the burden of keeping secrets. From our perspective, creativity is not only profitable, but it may also be a key element of a happy and productive workplace.

NOTES

1. https://www.gore.com/about/technologies.
2. https://www.relate.org.uk/about-us/media-centre/press-releases/2014/8/20/way-we-are
   -now-new-study-reveals-our-couple-family-friendships-sex-and-work-secrets.

REFERENCES

Amabile, T.M. 1983. The social psychology of creativity: A componential conceptualization. *Journal of Personality and Social Psychology*, 45(2): 357.

Amabile T.M. 1996. *Creativity in context*. Boulder, CO: Westview.

Amabile, T.M., Barsade, S.G., Mueller, J.S., & Staw, B.M. 2005. Affect and creativity at work. *Administrative Science Quarterly*, 50(3): 367–403.

Amabile, T.M., & Pratt, M.G. 2016. The dynamic componential model of creativity and innovation in organizations: Making progress, making meaning. *Research in Organizational Behavior*, 36: 157–183.

Anand, N., Gardner, H.K., & Morris, T. 2007. Knowledge-based innovation: Emergence and embedding of new practice areas in management consulting firms. *Academy of Management Journal*, 50(2): 406–428.

Audia, P.G., & Goncalo, J.A. 2007. Past success and creativity over time: A study of inventors in the hard disk drive industry. *Management Science*, 53(1): 1–15.

Baer, M. 2012. Putting creativity to work: The implementation of creative ideas in organizations. *Academy of Management Journal*, 55(5): 1102–1119.

Baer, M., Evans, K., Oldham, G.R., & Boasso, A. 2015. The social network side of individual innovation: A meta-analysis and path-analytic integration. *Organizational Psychology Review*, 5(3): 191–223.

Barsalou, L.W. 2008. Grounded cognition. *Annual Review of Psychology*, 59: 617–645.

Beersma, B., & De Dreu, C.K. 2005. Conflict's consequences: Effects of social motives on post negotiation creative and convergent group functioning and performance. *Journal of Personality and Social Psychology*, 89(3): 358.

Brown, V.R., & Paulus, P.B. (2002). Making group brainstorming more effective: Recommendations from an associative memory perspective. *Current Directions in Psychological Science*, 11(6): 208–212.

Burt, R.S. 2004. Structural holes and good ideas. *American Journal of Sociology*, 110(2): 349–399.

Campbell, D.T. 1960. Blind variation and selective retentions in creative thought as in other knowledge processes. *Psychological Review*, 67(6): 380–400.

Catmull, E., & Wallace, A. 2014. *Creativity, Inc: overcoming the unseen forces that stand in the way of true inspiration*. New York: Random House.

Cattani, G., & Ferriani, S. 2008. A core/periphery perspective on individual creative performance: Social networks and cinematic achievements in the Hollywood film industry. *Organization Science*, 19: 824–844.

Cheng, C.Y., Sanchez-Burks, J., & Lee, F. 2008. Connecting the dots within: Creative performance and identity integration. *Psychological Science*, 19(11): 1178–1184.

Chowdhury, S. 2005. Demographic diversity for building an effective entrepreneurial team: Is it important? *Journal of Business Venturing*, 20(6): 727–746.

Chua, R.Y., Morris, M.W., & Mor, S. 2012. Collaborating across cultures: Cultural metacognition and affect-based trust in creative collaboration. *Organizational Behavior and Human Decision Processes*, 118(2): 116–131.

Chua, R.Y., Roth, Y., & Lemoine, J.F. 2015. The impact of culture on creativity: How cultural tightness and cultural distance affect global innovation crowdsourcing work. *Administrative Science Quarterly*, 60(2): 189–227.

Collins, N.L., & Miller, L.C. 1994. Self-disclosure and liking: a meta-analytic review. *Psychological Bulletin*, 116(3), 457–475.

Cramton, R.C., & Knowles, L.P. 1998. Professional secrecy and its exceptions: Spaulding v. Zimmerman revisited. *Minnesota Law Review*, 83(63): 63–127.

Critcher, C.R., & Ferguson, M.J. 2014. The cost of keeping it hidden: Decomposing concealment reveals what makes it depleting. *Journal of Experimental Psychology: General*, 143(2): 721.

Cronin, M.A., & Loewenstein, J. 2018. *The craft of creativity*. Palo Alto, CA: Stanford University Press.

Cropley, A.J. 2009. Teachers' antipathy to creative students: Some implications for teacher training. *Baltic Journal of Psychology*, 10: 86–93.

Dai, Y., Shin, S.Y., Kashian, N., Jang, J.W., & Walther, J.B. 2016. The influence of responses to self-disclosure on liking in computer-mediated communication. *Journal of Language and Social Psychology*, 35(4): 394–411.

Derks, D., Fischer, A.H., & Bos, A.E. 2008. The role of emotion in computer-mediated communication: A review. *Computers in Human Behavior*, 24(3): 766–785.

Derlega, V.J., Harris, M.S., & Chaikin, A.L. 1973. Self-disclosure reciprocity, liking and the deviant. *Journal of Experimental Social Psychology*, 9(4): 277–284.

Deters, F.G., & Mehl, M.R. 2013. Does posting Facebook status updates increase or decrease loneliness? An online social networking experiment. *Social Psychological and Personality Science*, 4(5): 579–586.

Dollinger, S.J. 2007. Creativity and conservatism. *Personality and Individual Differences*, 43: 1025–1035.

Dutton, J.E., & Heaphy, E.D. 2003. The power of high-quality connections. In K.E. Cameron, J.E. Dutton, & R.E. Quinn (eds), *Positive organizational scholarship*: 263–278. San Francisco, CA: Berrett Koehler.

Farmer, S., Tierney, P., & Kung-McIntyre, K. 2003. Employee creativity in Taiwan: An application of role identity theory. *Academy of Management Journal*, 46: 618–630.

Feist, G.J., Reiter-Palmon, R., & Kaufman, J.C. (eds). 2017. *The Cambridge handbook of creativity and personality research*. Cambridge: Cambridge University Press.

Fleming, L., Mingo, S., & Chen, D. 2007. Collaborative brokerage, generative creativity, and creative success. *Administrative Science Quarterly*, 52(3): 443–475.

Ford, C.M. 1996. A theory of individual creative action in multiple social domains. *Academy of Management Review*, 21(4): 1112–1142.

Förster, J., Friedman, R.S., Butterbach, E.B., & Sassenberg, K. 2005. Automatic effects of deviancy cues on creative cognition. *European Journal of Social Psychology*, 35(3): 345–359.

Gaines-Ross, L. 2013. Get social: a mandate for new CEOs. *MIT Sloan Management Review*, 54(3): 1.

Galinsky, A.D., Magee, J.C., Gruenfeld, D.H., Whitson, J.A., & Liljenquist, K.A. 2008. Power reduces the press of the situation: Implications for creativity, conformity, and dissonance. *Journal of Personality and Social Psychology*, 95(6): 1450.

Glover, J.A., Ronning, R.R., & Reynolds, C. (eds). 2013. *Handbook of creativity*. New York: Springer Science & Business Media.

Gold, D.B., & Wegner, D.M. 1995. Origins of ruminative thought: Trauma, incompleteness, nondisclosure, and suppression. *Journal of Applied Social Psychology*, 25(14): 1245–1261.

Goncalo, J.A., Chatman, J.A., Duguid, M.M., & Kennedy, J.A. 2015a. Creativity from constraint? How the political correctness norm influences creativity in mixed-sex work groups. *Administrative Science Quarterly*, 60(1): 1–30.

Goncalo, J.A. & Duguid, M.M. 2012. Follow the crowd in a new direction: When conformity pressure facilitates group creativity (and when it does not). *Organizational Behavior and Human Decision Processes*, 18(1): 14–23.

Goncalo, J.A., & Katz, J.H. 2020. Your soul spills out: The creative act feels self-disclosing. *Personality and Social Psychology Bulletin*, 46(5): 679–692.

Goncalo, J.A., Katz, J.H., & Ellis, L.M. 2019. PIECE Together. In Paul B. Paulus and Bernard A. Nijstad (eds), *The Oxford handbook of group creativity and innovation*: 217–230. Oxford: Oxford University Press.

Goncalo, J.A., & Krause, V. 2010. Being different or being better? Disentangling the effects of independence and competition on group creativity. In *Advances in group processes*: 129–157. Bingley: Emerald Group Publishing.

Goncalo, J.A., & Staw, B.M. 2006. Individualism–collectivism and group creativity. *Organizational Behavior and Human Decision Processes*, 100(1): 96–109.

Goncalo, J.A., Vincent, L.C., & Krause, V. 2015b. The liberating consequences of creative work: How a creative outlet lifts the physical burden of secrecy. *Journal of Experimental Social Psychology*, 59: 32–39.

Hargadon, A.B., & Bechky, B.A. 2006. When collections of creatives become creative collectives: A field study of problem solving at work. *Organization Science*, 17(4): 484–500.

Harrison, S.H., & Rouse, E.D. 2015. An inductive study of feedback interactions over the course of creative projects. *Academy of Management Journal*, 58(2): 375–404.

Harrison, S.H., & Wagner, D.T. 2016. Spilling outside the box: The effects of individuals' creative behaviors at work on time spent with their spouses at home. *Academy of Management Journal*, 59(3): 841–859.

Harvey, S. 2014. Creative synthesis: Exploring the process of extraordinary group creativity. *Academy of Management Review*, 39(3): 324–343.

Hirst, G., Van Knippenberg, D., & Zhou, J. 2009. A cross-level perspective on employee creativity: Goal orientation, team learning behavior, and individual creativity. *Academy of Management Journal*, 52(2): 280–293.

Holt-Lunstad, J., Smith, T.B., Baker, M., Harris, T., & Stephenson, D. 2015. Loneliness and social isolation as risk factors for mortality: A meta-analytic review. *Perspectives on Psychological Science*, 10(2): 227–237.

Howell, J.M., & Higgins, C.A. 1990. Champions of technological innovation. *Administrative Science Quarterly*, 35(2): 317–341.

Huang, H.Y. 2016. Examining the beneficial effects of individual's self-disclosure on the social network site. *Computers in Human Behavior*, 57: 122–132.

Jaremka, L.M., Andridge, R.R., Fagundes, C.P., Alfano, C.M., Povoski, S.P., et al. 2014. Pain, depression, and fatigue: Loneliness as a longitudinal risk factor. *Health Psychology*, 33(9): 948–957.

Jones, N.A., & Smith, A.S. 2001. *The two or more races population: 2000*. Census brief No. C2KBR/01-6. Washington, DC: US Census Bureau.

Jourard, S.M. 1971. *Self-disclosure: An experimental analysis of the transparent self*. New York: Wiley.

Kashian, N., Jang, J.W., Shin, S.Y., Dai, Y., & Walther, J.B. 2017. Self-disclosure and liking in computer-mediated communication. *Computers in Human Behavior*, 71: 275–283.

Kelly, A.E. 2002. *The psychology of secrets*. Seacaucus, NJ: Springer Science & Business Media.

Khessina, O.M., Goncalo, J.A., & Krause, V. 2018. It's time to sober up: The direct costs, side effects and long-term consequences of creativity and innovation. *Research in Organizational Behavior*, 38: 107–135.

Kim, S.H., Vincent, L.C., & Goncalo, J. A. (2013). Outside advantage: Can social rejection fuel creative thought? *Journal of Experimental Psychology: General*, 142(3): 605.

Klein, K.J., & Sorra, J.S. 1996. The challenge of innovation implementation. *Academy of Management Review*, 21(4): 1055–1080.

Lane, J.D., & Wegner, D.M. 1995. The cognitive consequences of secrecy. *Journal of Personality and Social Psychology*, 69(2): 237.

Larey, T.S., & Paulus, P.B. 1995. Social comparison and goal setting in brainstorming groups. *Journal of Applied Social Psychology*, 25(18): 1579–1596.

Laurenceau, J.P., Barrett, L.F., & Pietromonaco, P.R. 1998. Intimacy as an interpersonal process: The importance of self-disclosure, partner disclosure, and perceived partner responsiveness in interpersonal exchanges. *Journal of Personality and Social Psychology*, 74(5): 1238.

Lawler, E.J. 2001. An affect theory of social exchange. *American Journal of Sociology*, 107(2): 321–352.

Lechler, T. 2001. Social interaction: A determinant of entrepreneurial team venture success. *Small Business Economics*, 16(4): 263–278.

Lepisto, D.A., & Pratt, M.G. 2017. Meaningful work as realization and justification: Toward a dual conceptualization. *Organizational Psychology Review*, 7(2): 99–121.

Leung, A.K.Y., Maddux, W.W., Galinsky, A.D., & Chiu, C.Y. 2008. Multicultural experience enhances creativity: The when and how. *American Psychologist*, 63(3): 169.

Lyubomirsky, S., & Ross, L. 1997. Hedonic consequences of social comparison: A contrast of happy and unhappy people. *Journal of Personality and Social Psychology*, 73(6): 1141.

Maas, J., Wismeijer, A.A., Van Assen, M.A., & Aquarius, A.E. 2012. Is it bad to have secrets? Cognitive preoccupation as a toxic element of secrecy. *International Journal of Clinical and Health Psychology*, 12(1): 23.

Mangold, W.G., & Faulds, D.J. 2009. Social media: The new hybrid element of the promotion mix. *Business Horizons*, 52(4): 357–365.

McCall, G., & Simmons, J.L. 1978. *Identities and interaction*. New York: Free Press.

McPherson, M., Smith-Lovin, L., & Brashears, M.E. 2006. Social isolation in America: Changes in core discussion networks over two decades. *American Sociological Review*, 71(3): 353–375.

Michael, R.T., Gagnon, J.H., Laumann, E.O., & Kolata, G. 1994. *Sex in America: A definitive survey*. Boston, MA: Little, Brown.

Miles, L.K., Nind, L.K., & Macrae, C.N. 2010. Moving through time. *Psychological Science*, 21(2): 222–223.

Mueller, J. 2017. *Creative change: Why we resist it… how to embrace it*. Boston, MA: Houghton Mifflin Harcourt.

Mueller, J.S., Goncalo, J.A., & Kamdar, D. 2011. Recognizing creative leadership: Can creative idea expression negatively relate to perceptions of leadership potential? *Journal of Experimental Social Psychology*, 47(2): 494–498.

Mueller, J.S., Melwani, S., & Goncalo, J.A. 2012. The bias against creativity: Why people desire but reject creative ideas. *Psychological Science*, 23(1): 13–17.

Nemeth, C.J. 1997. Managing innovation: When less is more. *California Management Review*, 40(1): 59–74.

Nemeth, C.J., & Goncalo, J.A. 2005. Creative collaborations from afar: The benefits of independent authors. *Creativity Research Journal*, 17(1): 1–8.

Nemeth, C.J., & Staw, B.M. 1989. The tradeoffs of social control and innovation in groups and organizations. In L. Berkowitz (ed.), *Advances in experimental social psychology*, Vol. 22: 175–210. New York: Academic Press.

Nijstad, B.A., Stroebe, W., & Lodewijkx, H.F. 2006. The illusion of group productivity: A reduction of failures explanation. *European Journal of Social Psychology*, 36(1): 31–48.

O'Reilly, C.A., & Chatman, J. A. 1996. Culture as social control: Corporations, cults, and commitment. *Research in Organizational Behavior*, 18: 157–200.

Ozcelik, H., & Barsade, S.G. 2018. No employee an island: Workplace loneliness and job performance. *Academy of Management Journal*, 61(6): 2343–2366.

Paulus, P.B., & Dzindolet, M.T. 1993. Social influence processes in group brainstorming. *Journal of Personality and Social Psychology*, 64(4): 575.

Paulus, P.B., Dzindolet, M.T., Poletes, G., & Camacho, L.M. 1993. Perception of performance in group brainstorming: The illusion of group productivity. *Personality and Social Psychology Bulletin*, 19(1): 78–89.

Paulus, P.B., Larey, T.S., & Ortega, A.H. 1995. Performance and perceptions of brainstormers in an organizational setting. *Basic and Applied Social Psychology*, 17(1–2): 249–265.

Paulus, P.B., & Yang, H.C. 2000. Idea generation in groups: A basis for creativity in organizations. *Organizational Behavior and Human Decision Processes*, 82(1): 76–87.

Pelline, J. 1998. *Microsoft buys Hotmail*. CNET, January 3. Retrieved from https://www.cnet.com/news/microsoft-buys-hotmail/.

Pennebaker, J.W. 1989. Confession, inhibition, and disease. In L. Berkowitz (ed.), *Advances in experimental social psychology*, Vol. 22: 211–244. New York: Academic Press.

Perlman, D., & Peplau, L.A. 1981. Toward a social psychology of loneliness. In R. Gilmour & S. Duck (eds), *Personal relationships in disorder*: 31–56. London: Academic Press.

Perry-Smith, J.E. 2006. Social yet creative: The role of social relationships in facilitating individual creativity. *Academy of Management Journal*, 49(1): 85–101.

Perry-Smith, J.E., & Mannucci, P.V. 2017. From creativity to innovation: The social network drivers of the four phases of the idea journey. *Academy of Management Review*, 42(1): 53–79.

Phillips, K.W., Rothbard, N.P., & Dumas, T.L. 2009. To disclose or not to disclose? Status distance and self-disclosure in diverse environments. *Academy of Management Review*, 34(4): 710–732.

Polzer, J.T., Milton, L.P., & Swann Jr, W.B. 2002. Capitalizing on diversity: Interpersonal congruence in small work groups. *Administrative Science Quarterly*, 47(2): 296–324.

Reis, H.T., & Shaver, P. 1988. Intimacy as an interpersonal process. In S. Duck, D.F. Hay, S.E. Hobfoll, W. Ickes, & B.M. Montgomery (eds), *Handbook of personal relationships: Theory, research and interventions*: 367–389. Hoboken, NJ: John Wiley & Sons.

Rietzschel, E.F., Nijstad, B.A., & Stroebe, W. 2006. Productivity is not enough: A comparison of interactive and nominal brainstorming groups on idea generation and selection. *Journal of Experimental Social Psychology*, 42(2): 244–251.

Rietzschel, E.F., Nijstad, B.A., & Stroebe, W. 2010. The selection of creative ideas after individual idea generation: Choosing between creativity and impact. *British Journal of Psychology*, 101(1): 47–68.

Rouse, E.D. 2020. Where you end and I begin: Understanding intimate co-creation. *Academy of Management Review*, 45(1): 181–204.

Saffer, A.J., Sommerfeldt, E.J., & Taylor, M. 2013. The effects of organizational Twitter interactivity on organization–public relationships. *Public Relations Review*, 39(3): 213–215.

Sassenberg, K., & Moskowitz, G.B. 2005. Don't stereotype, think different! Overcoming automatic stereotype activation by mindset priming. *Journal of Experimental Social Psychology*, 41(5), 506–514.

Slepian, M.L., Masicampo, E.J., & Ambady, N. 2014. Relieving the burdens of secrecy: Revealing secrets influences judgments of hill slant and distance. *Social Psychological and Personality Science*, 5(3): 293–300.

Slepian, M.L., Masicampo, E.J., Toosi, N.R., & Ambady, N. 2012. The physical burdens of secrecy. *Journal of Experimental Psychology: General*, 141(4): 619–624.

Simonton, D.K. 1999. Creativity as blind variation and selective retention: Is the creative process Darwinian? *Psychological Inquiry*, 10: 309–328.

Simonton, D.K. 2003. Scientific creativity as constrained stochastic behavior: The integration of product, person, and process perspectives. *Psychological Bulletin*, 129(4): 475–494.

Sprecher, S., Treger, S., Wondra, J.D., Hilaire, N., & Wallpe, K. 2013. Taking turns: Reciprocal self-disclosure promotes liking in initial interactions. *Journal of Experimental Social Psychology*, 49(5): 860–866.

Staw, B.M. 1990. An evolutionary approach to creativity and innovation. In M.A. West & J.L. Farr (eds), *Innovation and creativity at work: Psychological and organizational strategies*: 287–308. Hoboken, NJ: John Wiley & Sons.

Staw, B.M. 1995. Why no one really wants creativity. In C.M. Ford & D.A. Gioia (eds), *Creative action in organizations: Ivory tower visions and real world voices*: 161–172. Thousand Oaks, CA: SAGE.

Steptoe, A., Shankar, A., Demakakos, P., & Wardle, J. 2013. Social isolation, loneliness, and all-cause mortality in older men and women. *Proceedings of the National Academy of Sciences*, 110(15): 5797–5801.

Stroebe, W., Diehl, M., & Abakoumkin, G. 1992. The illusion of group effectivity. *Personality and Social Psychology Bulletin*, 18(5): 643–650.

Utz, S. 2015. The function of self-disclosure on social network sites: Not only intimate, but also positive and entertaining self-disclosures increase the feeling of connection. *Computers in Human Behavior*, 45: 1–10.

VanderWeele, T.J., Hawkley, L.C., & Cacioppo, J.T. 2012. On the reciprocal association between loneliness and subjective well-being. *American Journal of Epidemiology*, 176(9): 777–784.

Vickers, M. 2002. *Work and unseen chronic illness: Silent voices*. Abingdon: Routledge.

West, M.A. 2002. Sparkling fountains or stagnant ponds: An integrative model of creativity and innovation implementation in work groups. *Applied Psychology*, 51(3): 355–387.

West, M., Smith, K.G., & Tjosvold, D. 2003. Past, present, and future perspectives on organizational cooperation. In M. West, K.G. Smith, & D. Tjosvold (eds), *International handbook of organizational teamwork and cooperative working*: 575–597. Hoboken, NJ: John Wiley & Sons.

Williams, L.E., & Bargh, J.A. 2008. Experiencing physical warmth promotes interpersonal warmth. *Science*, 322(5901): 606–607.

Woodman, R.W., Sawyer, J.E., & Griffin, R.W. 1993. Toward a theory of organizational creativity. *Academy of Management Review*, 18(2): 293–321.

Zhou, J., Shin, S.J., Brass, D.J., Choi, J., & Zhang, Z.X. 2009. Social networks, personal values, and creativity: evidence for curvilinear and interaction effects. *Journal of Applied Psychology*, 94(6): 1544.

Zitek, E.M., & Vincent, L.C. 2015. Deserve and diverge: Feeling entitled makes people more creative. *Journal of Experimental Social Psychology*, 56: 242–248.

PART III

STRETCHING HOW WE MAKE SENSE OF AND STUDY CREATIVITY AND INNOVATION

11. Creative spirals: when ideas beget ideas
Andrew Hargadon

Within the past few decades, a systems view has emerged to study the creative process within its broader social context. The systems model of creativity attempts to locate individuals and their actions relative to the cultural context from which their knowledge, tools, values, and practices derived and to the field, as gatekeepers, whose judgment determines which actions are deemed creative. As Csikszentmihalyi (2014: xxiii) argues, "the systems model is a first step toward a demystified, scientific understanding of how certain actions, and the individuals who act them out, end up being considered creative." Hennessey (2015: 1) notes that, "with the exception of research examining the productivity of teams, the empirical study of creativity was until recently almost exclusively focused at the level of the individual creator." In their 2010 review of the creativity research, Hennessey & Amabile (2010: 571) called for more research that follows this systems view, suggesting: "progress will be made when more researchers recognize that creativity arises through a system of interrelated forces operating at multiple levels, often requiring interdisciplinary investigation."

However, while recent papers have adopted more ecological approaches to studying creativity, they have largely treated the environment as a static backdrop for creative actors and their actions. As Hennessey (2015: 197) notes, the majority of the recent works on systems models of creativity, "like most of the smaller-scale investigations upon which they have been based, have been grounded in a focus on the individual's largely impersonal interaction with their environment." So while Csikszentmihalyi (1999) has demonstrated that social and cultural as well as cognitive or psychological factors shape the creative act, the effects of prior creative acts on subsequent ones remain largely ignored.

This chapter begins with a question: Under what conditions does having one creative idea make it more (or less) likely to have more? This question is motivated by an empirical phenomenon, an ephemeral but distinct period when local creative activities produce a rapid series of novel, valuable, and related ideas. I label this phenomenon a "creative spiral" and, in the next section, describe and illustrate it with evidence from previous microhistorical research on the creative efforts of Thomas Edison in the development of his system of electric lighting. I then define creative spirals as a theoretical construct and develop a causal model integrating recent work on the systems model of creativity with work on sociomateriality and temporality to explain how, under particular conditions, such spirals emerge. Finally, I consider three implications of this phenomenon: formalizing a theory of creative spirals, defining future research questions, and considering alternative methodologies for its study.

CREATIVE SPIRALS

Before delving into the case of Edison, I offer a brief definition of creative spirals which I expand upon later in the chapter. Creative spirals describe an ephemeral but distinct empirical phenomenon during which individuals or collectives generate multiple, interdependent creative ideas. The focus on interdependence distinguishes creative spirals from the observation of creative ideas that appear to be, or are treated as, independent of one another. The theoretical significance of such a phenomenon lies in recognizing how creative ideas produce the conditions for further creativity. Understanding what conditions foster such creative spirals requires recognizing the context in which problems and their creative solution emerge and through which each new creative act is shaped by and in turn shapes others.

To illustrate the phenomenon of creative spirals, I describe the interactions between creative ideas generated by Edison and his colleagues during the development of their system of electric lighting. While the popular image of Edison is as a lone inventor of technological artifacts – the electric light, the phonograph, and a variety of other electromechanical devices – the volume of inventions that emerged from the Menlo Park research lab, the recombinant nature of those artifacts, and the collective nature of the process have been well researched (for example, Hughes, 1983, 1989; Conot, 1979; Freidel & Israel, 1986; Millard, 1990; Hargadon & Sutton, 1997; Hargadon, 2003). However, less attention has been devoted to exploring the interdependent and causal relationships between the numerous creative ideas generated in the process. In the two years beginning in the summer of 1878 and running through the summer of 1880, Edison (representing the collective work of the lab)[1] explored the technical and commercial potential of the electric light. In 1878 and 1879, the laboratory executed 14 successful patents on electric lighting.[2] In 1880, they executed 50 successful patents, and in the four subsequent years of 1881–84, after forming the Edison Electric Company and during the construction of the first electric generating plant at 255–257 Pearl Street in Manhattan, the laboratory generated an additional 267 patents associated with Edison's system of electric lighting. See Figure 11.1 for the distribution of patents associated with electric lighting from 1978 to 1889.

While patents are an imperfect measure of creativity, the interactions inherent in such concentrated bursts of creative activity are difficult to ignore. Yet the evolutionary model underlying many approaches to creativity presumes a process of variation, selection, and retention of independent ideas (Campbell, 1960; Staw, 1990; Simonton, 1999). Campbell (1960) first invoked this perspective in developing his model of evolutionary epistemology, with creativity as a special case of knowledge production; Simonton (1988) and Staw (1990, 2009) further developed the model to frame individual and collective creativity as a similar process. Csikszentmihalyi's Systems Model of Creativity applies the evolutionary model at the level of communities and cultures, defining the creative process as involving "the generation of a novel creative product, the selection of the product by others in the field, and the retention of selected products that the field adds to the domain" (Csikszentmihalyi, 2014: 68).

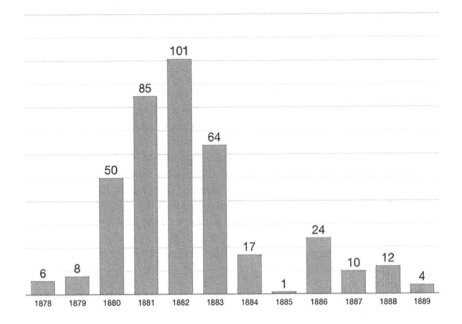

Figure 11.1   *Executed patents by Edison associated with electric lighting, United States Patent and Trademark Office (USPTO)*

This assumption of independence overlooks potential interactions between prior creative ideas and subsequent ones.

To explore the interdependence of creative ideas and any enabling conditions and processes, it becomes necessary to engage with the sociomaterial and temporal nature of the particular creative ideas and actions involved. Sociomateriality is a theoretical perspective that "focuses on how meanings and materialities are enacted together in everyday practices" (Orlikowski, 2010: 135; see also Suchman, 2007). This perspective emerged in response to the relative absence of explanations involving how social processes and outcomes are inextricably connected with the material environment within, through, and with which humans act and interact (Orlikowski, 2007; Suchman, 2007). Of particular interest to understanding creative spirals is the concept of sociomaterial affordances, which recognizes how a material object or artifact "favors, shapes, or invites, and at the same time constrains, a set of specific uses" (Orlikowski & Scott, 2008: 453). Indeed, the term "sociomaterial" reflects an acknowledgement that all material objects are intrinsically bound by the perceptions, beliefs, and values surrounding their use as well as their relationships to other socially embedded material objects in a particular social context.

Temporality also plays an implicit role in process studies of creativity, but has often played a more explicit analytical role in studies of organizations and organizing. In both the creativity literature and organizational studies, process theories acknowledge events as taking place over time, but pay less attention to how processes and their outcomes also take place in time, that is to say, how processes and events are products of particular moments in time and how they in turn shape subsequent moments (Wadwhani, 2016). Because creative outcomes are defined as "novel and useful ideas" (Amabile & Pratt, 2016), one effect of such creative outcomes is to demonstrate that something is possible which was not considered so before. What the lenses of sociomateriality and temporality offer to a systems model of creativity in general and creative spirals in particular is a means to recognize how a particular material and temporal context both enables and constrains these possibilities.

The next section uses a sociomaterial and temporal lens to describe the context and creative activities of Edison's Menlo Park research team from the summer of 1878, when they turned their attention to developing their system of electric lighting, through to the summer of 1880, when their work moved from the New Jersey laboratory to constructing the Pearl Street Station in New York City. Once construction began at Pearl Street, creative output continued to grow (see Figure 11.1), but so too did the number of people involved and the number of technical challenges that emerged and had to be resolved.

CREATIVE SPIRALS IN THE EDISON LAB, 1878–80

To set the stage, Edison's contribution was not the invention of any generic component of this system, but rather the development of a technologically and commercially viable system of electric lighting. This usage of the term "system" draws from general systems theory (Bertalanffy, 1969), and particularly its use by historian Thomas Hughes (1983) to understand and compare the growth of different electric systems in the United States (US), United Kingdom (UK), and Germany from 1880 to 1930. This usage defines systems as constituted of heterogenous (social and material) elements, interconnected through a configuration that describes their roles and relationships and directed by an overarching function or goal. The elements are interconnected, in that changes in one element's role (its state or performance) affects the state or performance of other elements in the system. As Hughes (1983: 21) notes:

> Edison is most widely known for his invention of the incandescent lamps but it was only one component in his electric lighting system and was no more critical to its effective functioning then the Edison jumbo generator, the Edison main and feeder, or the parallel distribution system. Other inventors with generators and incandescent lamps and comparable ingenuity have been forgotten because they did not carry the process further and introduce a system of lighting.

This chapter considers the emergence of Edison's system of electric lighting from 1878 to 1880, the years immediately preceding Hughes's study. While the individual elements of Edison's system already existed before Edison began, each had to be modified from its original form to work best with the other elements and in service of the objectives of the larger system. Edison himself once described this aspect of his inventive activities around electric lighting:

> It was not only necessary that the lamps should give light and the dynamos generate current, but the lamps must be adapted to the current of the dynamos, and the dynamos must be constructed to give the character of current required by the lamps, and likewise all parts of the system must be constructed with reference to all other parts, since, in one sense, all the parts form one machine, and the connections between the parts being electrical instead of mechanical. Like any other machine the failure of one part to cooperate properly with the other part disorganizes the whole and renders it inoperative for the purpose intended. (Edison, in Hughes, 1983: 21)

From this perspective, Edison's development of a system of electric lighting reflects multiple creative ideas shaping the design of the individual elements in that system as well as the interactions between them.

To recognize the causal links between such ideas and how they may generate creative spirals, it is necessary to describe both the material improvements that Edison and his colleagues made in any one element and, from a temporal perspective, how the problems they faced and the solutions they developed in that effort led to novel problems and their solution in other elements of the system. In the case of Edison's development of the system of electric lighting, I consider the co-evolution of three core elements of the system: the incandescent lamp (mainly its filament and related vacuum technology), the network circuit, and the dynamo. These core elements co-evolved in response to the objectives of the overall system, to the material affordances and constraints of the individual elements, and to the temporal sequence of their development.[3] As creative ideas were conceived and enacted to solve problems in one element, they generated new problems and potential solutions in other elements. The interdependent nature of the creative output that emerged during this period suggests that this recursive dynamic drives the creative spiral observed. To explore this, I offer a brief history of Edison's efforts and their outcomes.

The original opportunities and challenges of electric lighting emerged in the early 1800s with the development of chemical batteries. Scientists and inventors quickly recognized two material pathways for generating light: as the arc created between two electrodes from an electric discharge produces a plasma emitting light in the visible range, or as the heat generated as electricity passes through a conductor reaches temperatures at which it emits light in the visible range. These phenomena remained scientific curiosities until the 1850s, when advances in the chemistry of batteries and dynamos afforded arc lighting systems that demonstrated commercial value. Battery-powered arc lights were first introduced in the 1840s (in 1844, such a series of arc lamps was used in a production of the Paris Opera). The first commercially viable dynamos (electric generators that produce direct current) also emerged in the 1840s and were used for electroplating metals. Through the 1850s and 1860s, lighting systems based on arc lamps and dynamos continued to improve. During that time, incandescent lighting remained limited due mainly to material constraints: the heat required to incandesce a filament quickly fused, or melted, the material.[4] By the early 1870s, developing and manufacturing commercial arc lamps and arc lighting systems had become profitable ventures, and their success was driving related innovations in automated controls for regulating the rate at which carbon rods were consumed during the arcing process (and automatically replacing spent rods).

Seeing these automated electromechanical controls, and their material similarities to his work in early telegraph and telephone systems, Edison believed he could develop similar controls for incandescent lamps that would prevent their overheating. He also recognized that while arc lights were limited to large spaces, a greater and still untapped market seemed to await practical incandescent lamps. In the summer of 1878, Edison began to experiment with various materials to thermally regulate incandescent bulbs by disconnecting the circuit before fusing occurred.[5]

In the first week of September, Edison visited the factory of William Wallace, who with Moses Farmer produced the first viable dynamo in the US.[6] In Wallace's factory, Edison saw not only the Wallace–Farmer dynamo but also how it powered ten arc lamps wired in series. Though Edison was nowhere near perfecting his own incandescent lamp, he recognized the implications of Wallace's subdivision of arc lights for a similar system using incandescent bulbs.[7] The next week, Edison told a *New York Sun* reporter his new vision:

> When ten lights have been produced by a single electric machine, it has been thought to be a great triumph of scientific skill, with the process I have just discovered I can produce a thousand – ten thousand – from one machine. Indeed the number may be said to be infinite. Illumination by carburetted hydrogen gas will be discarded. With 15 or 20 of these dynamo-electric machines recently perfected by Mr. Wallace I can light the entire lower part of New York City, using a 500 horsepower engine. (*New York Sun*, 1878)

While this newspaper article contains more marketing hyperbole than technical achievement, it demonstrates how quickly Edison's vision moved from building an improved lamp to building an entire system of incandescent electric lighting. Edison drafted his first caveat for an electric light patent that envisioned both subdivided light and the use of a thermoregulated switch that would turn individual lamps off as they overheated and on again when they cooled:

> The object of this invention is to produce light for illuminating purposes by metals heated to incandescence by the passage of an electric current through them, a great number of pieces of such metals forming part of an electric circuit and distributed at various parts of the same. (Edison, in Freidel & Israel, 1986: 8)

The work of the lab then broadened its focus from the incandescent bulb to accumulating and combining the elements: the bulbs, the dynamos, and the network of wires connecting them together.

That fall, it quickly became apparent to Edison that the vision of a subdivided lighting system necessitated wiring the lamps in parallel rather than in series, in order that each lamp could turn on and off without affecting the others. To accomplish this, the lamps would require a high resistance, or the electric current would fluctuate each time a lamp was disconnected from the circuit. When Edison began working on the electric light in the fall of 1878, they initially believed the Wallace–Farmer dynamo would be capable of powering their system of incandescent lamps. Yet Edison's vision of the broader network required miles of copper lines conducting the electricity throughout buildings in parallel circuits. The resistance in the wiring alone would make the system uneconomical (indeed, the cost of the copper alone would be prohibitive). As Edison reflected in an interview with the *New York World* in 1879 (in Freidel & Israel, 1986: 75):

> When I first started out on this thing, I took into consideration only the lamp, but I soon became convinced that it was necessary to have a more powerful generator [dynamo] and feasible plan of sub-dividing the light. The generator was the last fact accomplished, and you will soon see for yourself how it works.

These material constraints of parallel circuits and high-resistance lamps created new problems that Edison had to address in the winter and spring of 1879: the dynamos would need to provide high and constant voltage (rather than current) and the incandescent filaments would have to be high-resistance (instead of low).[8] This revealed a new problem: the existing dynamos, designed to power arc lights, would not work for incandescents. So, in the winter of 1879, Edison began developing a wholly new generator tuned to the material needs of their system. The most efficient dynamo on the market, a constant-current, variable-voltage machine made by Siemens and designed for arc lighting systems, converted 55 percent of the horsepower provided by a steam engine into electricity. Edison's constant-voltage, variable-current dynamo designed for their parallel circuit system converted more than 80 percent. Improvements in this new dynamo continued rapidly through spring until efficiencies reached around 90 percent.[9] Also that winter, after experimenting with a range of ultimately unsuccessful ideas for durable filaments, Edison recognized that the air in the bulbs was volatizing the platinum. This framed another new problem: how to create a vacuum sufficient to slow, if not eliminate, fusing. Edison acquired the latest vacuum technology, a Sprengel pump, and hired a skilled glass blower to oversee the construction of evacuated lamps. This in turn created yet another problem: the slow nature of Sprengel pumps made it difficult to iterate and test new designs, leading them to acquire a second, faster but less precise Geissler vacuum pump. At the same time, the prospect of a working lamp based on a platinum filament started to weaken: it remained prohibitively expensive for commercial use and, because the metal filament had a low resistance, it would not match the needs of the distributed circuit.

By the summer of 1979, Edison developed a novel pump design that combined elements of both existing pumps. The new Sprengel–Geissler pump immediately produced a platinum-filament bulb that burned for 13 hours, a clear breakthrough. Meanwhile, Edison attempted to put together a small-scale version of the entire system: 30 thermoregulated platinum-filament lamps wired in a parallel series, to be powered by electricity generated from their improved dynamo (itself powered by a steam engine). But when the system was connected and the steam engine opened up, first one and then all the bulbs glowed, brightened, and then sparked and exploded. Edison's first response was to improve the thermoregulator (until it became a more complicated mechanism than the bulb itself).

Early that fall, when their Sprengel–Geissler combination pump broke, the Edison team created a more sophisticated pump that achieved bulbs with a vacuum of one-millionth of an atmosphere (better than any known pump).[10] This improved pump produced platinum-filament lamps that burned for 24–36 hours, replacing the need for a thermoregulator altogether. The near-perfect vacuum, they discovered, fundamentally changed how materials behaved as they incandesced. Materials that had proven unsatisfactory in previous incandescent lamps became potentially viable again when used in a near-perfect vacuum. Carbon, which fused quickly when incandesced in air, remained stable and even burned brighter than the platinum in the near-perfect vacuum. Further experiments with different forms of carbon (carbonized thread, cardboard, paper, and so on) proved even better, as the thinner the carbon filaments, the greater the resistance of the lamp. A design that cut carbonized card-board into a slender horseshoe shape had a resistance of roughly 100 Ohms, sufficient to work technically and economically within Edison's evolving system of parallel circuits. In December of 1879, the first public "exhibition" of Edison's subdivision of incandescent lamps was built in the grounds of the Menlo Park laboratory. The demonstration was a public success and, in the winter of 1880, Edison turned next to building out a complete model of his system.

Their first advance was a constant-current "tree" circuit that involved a trunk and branches, main and branching conductors running out to and returning from strings of lamps. In this configuration, the size of the copper mains running from and returning to the "trunk" had to equal the combined size of all the branch conductors. However, calculations showed that this circuit, at the envisioned scale of nine city-blocks, was infeasible as it would require over 800 000 pounds of copper and cost over $200 000. Soon afterwards, they developed a "multiple-arc distribution" circuit that entailed using multiple dynamos to power multiple parallel circuits (or arcs) by common main lines; this was developed and a patent filed in January 1880.

Meanwhile, Edison continued to improve the electric lamps, generators, and circuits. In addition, until then the need for underground conductors, insulation, junctions, electric meters, and other elements had taken a back seat to the development and validation of the lamps, generators, and circuit design. Now they had to turn their attention to designing and building the balance of the system. Each of these elements presented new problems that had not existed before and now needed to be solved. In addition, the lamps and generators (and the other elements of the system) needed to be adapted for large-scale production; creating yet more problems in need of solutions. By May of 1880, Edison had found that carbonized bamboo filaments used readily available materials and produced lamps which burned for 1200 hours. Later that summer, they further developed the multiple-arc system into a "feeder and main" circuit, in which feeder wires delivered power to smaller circuits, dramatically reducing the current requirements (and waste heat) of the main lines. These changes reduced the copper requirements by 85 percent (and the capital costs from $200 000 to $30 000).[11] All the while, they were experimenting with high-resistance filaments and improved lamps, which required changes in the voltage and current of the dynamos, resulting in a variety of smaller improvements.

Each creative act in the development of Edison's system of electric lighting shaped subsequent problems and the relative value of their solution. Many of the advances in lamps, dynamos, and circuits required corresponding changes in the other elements. Failures in the development of thermoregulation and platinum filaments drove Edison to view the existing vacuum pump technologies as inadequate and make dramatic improvements. Those improvements in turn obviated the need for thermoregulation altogether, and made the design of carbon filaments both a critical problem and a technical and commercially viable solution. Their design of the parallel circuit created the need for high-resistant lamps as well as constant-voltage dynamos, which in turn drove major improvements in the dynamo. The viability of these core elements of Edison's system of electric lighting in turn generated a range of new problems in the design and manufacture of the balance of the system: the meters, conductors, insulation, control systems, and much more, associated with the emerging electric lighting industry. Over the course of almost two years, from the summer of 1878 to the spring of 1880, the work of the lab defined the problems they faced and developed tentative solutions for them, some of which worked and some failed. Both surfaced new problems to be addressed next. Successful solutions generated novel problems that had not existed before.

CREATIVE SPIRALS AS A THEORETICAL CONSTRUCT

Creative spirals present a novel theoretical construct in the field of creativity generally and within the systems model of creativity specifically (Csikszentmihalyi, 2006, 2014; Hennessey, 2015; McIntyre, 2016a). Theoretical constructs are "conceptual abstractions of phenomena that cannot be directly observed" and have been established for purposes of scientific observation and explanation (Suddaby, 2010: 346; MacCorquodale & Meehl, 1948; Kerlinger, 1973).[12] While clear constructs are not a substitute for theory (Sutton and Staw, 1995), they are the building blocks of strong theory and a vital early step in theory construction. The construct of creative spirals represents an abstraction not of the quantity of creative output but rather of its quality, as multiple, interdependent, and endogenously driven creative output. Clear constructs require a precise yet parsimonious definition that allows categorical distinctions between concepts and well-articulated scope conditions, or contextual circumstances within which a construct applies (or not). This section explicates each with regard to creative spirals.

Creative spirals are defined here as an ephemeral but distinct empirical phenomenon in which individuals or collectives generate an exceptional amount of independent yet inherently related creative ideas. By "ephemeral but distinct" I mean that temporal and spatial boundaries can be drawn around the phenomenon that includes the relevant participants, their ideas, and the enactment of those ideas. For example, the temporal boundaries surrounding Edison's development of his system of electric lighting might be drawn around the exceptional number of patents that were executed (and ultimately granted) from 1878 to 1884, as shown in Figure 11.1; arguments could be made to consider the activities and events beginning in 1878 and extending through 1889 as theoretically relevant. The spatial boundaries during this time period include the Menlo Park research laboratory, where most of the development work took place in a single room 100 feet long and 30 feet wide with four shared workbenches in the center. In 1881, Edison began construction of the first electric generating plant at the Pearl Street Station in Manhattan, at which point much of the creative output relocated there. The term "individuals or collectives" describe conditions in which participants are interacting intensively with one another, with their ideas, and with the enactment of those ideas throughout the period defined. In this case, returning to Jehl's comment that Edison was in reality a collective noun, and to the historical evidence, we can bound the interactions to a small set of individuals working closely together in Menlo Park, New Jersey, and then in New York City at the Pearl Street Station being constructed. By "exceptional amount" of creative ideas, I recognize the need for a justifiable difference between the rate of idea generation during this phenomenon relative to the same collective at different places and times, or different groups at the same time. As shown in Figure 11.1, I have made the claim that this output of patentable ideas related to the development of Edison's system of electric lighting reflects a rate and amount outside the norm. Finally, the description of "independent yet inherently related creative ideas" reflects the recognition that each idea generated is itself novel, valuable, and non-obvious. This excludes, then, the generation of an exceptional amount of unrelated creative ideas, or a consistent production of derivative ideas.

In addition to a clear definition, the scope conditions of a theoretical construct are the parameters that define which empirical phenomena fit within the construct and which do not (Harris, 1997; Walker & Cohen, 1985). For creative spirals to serve as a useful construct in identifying and investigating a particular empirical phenomenon, the conditions under which this construct applies must be clarified. I offer here some provisional conditions covering levels of analysis, sociomateriality, and temporality. The construct of creative spirals applies primarily at the meso level of analysis, where it is possible to study the actions and interactions of individuals and collectives within a particular context. This condition reflects the necessity of discerning both the generation of discrete creative actions and their effects on subsequent ones. Studies of individual creativity may not provide empirical access to the distinctions between ideas, their enactment, and subsequent ideas and actions. Conversely, macro-level analysis often obfuscates the particular interactions between individuals and creative output. As a construct, creative spirals also requires accounting for the sociomaterial nature of the context such that the interdependence of problems, their solution, and the resulting effects on subsequent problems and solutions, can be analyzed. For example, the problems and solutions involved in developing the incandescent lamp were nested within and defined by the material affordances and constraints of not only the lamp but also the dynamo and electric circuit. Temporal conditions are also essential to the study of creative spirals; the relationship between ideas occurring over time becomes critical to understanding the nature of observable spirals. Again, the illustrations suggest that temporality should be bound to a period during which the participants, ideas, and interactions remain relatively insulated from exogenous events unfolding in the field. Creativity assessments such as artwork, essays, and work products (Amabile, 1996), or problem-solving exercises such as the nine-dot problem (Scheerer, 1963) or castle-and-bridges (Gick & Holyoak, 1983), have long been structured as independent socially, materially, and temporally. This reflects some creative situations but neglects other more embedded situations where initial problems and solutions shape the rate and direction of subsequent creative output.

ADVANCING THE SYSTEMS MODEL

Creative spirals extend the systems model of creativity by describing how, in extreme cases, participants become simultaneously the creators, gatekeepers, and constituents of the domain in which novel ideas are generated, validated, and enacted. The singular contribution of Csikszentmihalyi's (2006, 2014) systems model of creativity is to recognize that creativity takes place only within social systems. Creative acts are "as much a product of social and cultural influences as [they are] cognitive or psychological" (Hennessey, 2015: 198). Further, as Csikszentmihalyi (2006: 7) argues:

> The stronger claim made here is that there is no way, even in principle, to separate the reaction of society from the person's contribution. The two are inseparable. As long as the idea or product has not been validated [by the field], we might have originality, but not creativity.

As shown in Figure 11.2, the systems model of creativity focuses on the interactions between three dominant but largely independent elements: the person (comprising their genetic makeup, talents, and experience), the domain (the cultural system constituting the available knowledge, tools, values, and practices), and the field (the community of practice, or gatekeepers having the power to determine what is to be included in the larger cultural domain). Within this model, creativity occurs when a person makes a change in a particular domain that is sanctioned by a field. McIntyre (2016b) illustrates the explanatory value of a systems model of creativity in his description of the interactions among the domain, field, and individual songwriters within contemporary Western popular music. He shows how these three interrelated elements – rather than simply the artists alone – constitute a system that produces creative songs. Hargadon & Bechky (2006), following Farrell (1982), extend the systems model in their empirical study of design teams by recognizing how creative acts, and the conditions that support them, reflect a collective, rather than individual, process. Rouse (2020) develops a similar but distinct model of intimate co-creation that emerges from dyads. Hennessey (2015) elaborates the systems model by recognizing how domains may have multiple levels that differentially effect the creative

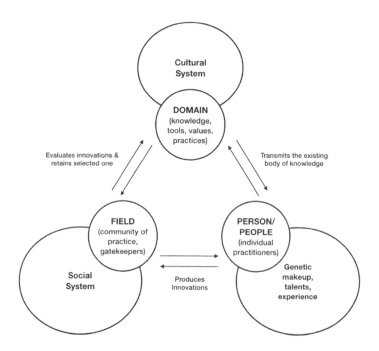

Source: Adapted from Csikszentmihalyi (2006: 4).

Figure 11.2   Systems model of creativity

process. In one study, she examines the effects of both "Big-C" culture (at the societal level) and "little-c" culture (as experiences in the workplace or classroom) on the intrinsic motivation of individual students. These studies demonstrate that the potential of the systems model for contextualizing creativity as both a process and an outcome remains both a rich subject and relatively underexplored.

However, beyond recognizing the steady accumulation of creative output in domains, the systems model does not consider the interdependence of individual creative acts and how this interdependence shapes the conditions supporting creative spirals. As Edison and his colleagues progressed with their system of electric lighting, the cumulative adaptations to dynamos, lights, circuits, and other elements moved them further away from the material arrangements and conceptual understandings of the existing field. A schism emerged between their collective understandings of what worked, what did not, and why, and the collective understandings of the broader field of engineers and scientists. A schism that could be seen when a UK parliamentary committee, after lengthy consultations with the UK's leading scientists, insisted that Edison's proposed system demonstrated "the most airy ignorance of the fundamental principles both of electricity and dynamics" (Conot, 1979: 129–133). American scientists expressed similar beliefs, and arc light inventors and manufacturers described Edison's plans as "so manifestly absurd as to indicate a positive want of knowledge of the electrical circuit and the principle governing the construction and operation of electric machines" (Conot, 1979: 162). As Conot (1979: 164) explained: "Platinum lamps and carbon burners had all been tried before and failed. The crucial elements, the perfect vacuum and the slender filament whose existence depended on it, were not perceived [by those outside Edison's lab]."

The construct of creative spirals extends the systems model of creativity by accounting for moments when collectives construct and sustain conditions in which they serve not only as creators but also as the local gatekeepers (field) and the practioners constituting a domain (culture). Such moments reflect an emergent phenomenon in which the collective have jointly created a relatively unique new system of knowledge, tools, or practices – their own domain – and through their shared knowledge and values also constitute the field, as the same individuals determine what novel ideas are deemed valuable and retained. As Figure 11.3 illustrates, over time their creative output builds upon itself. The collective further differentiate their shared knowledge and values from the extant domain and field, reinforcing the new domain and assuming their role as its gatekeepers. The work of the Edison lab in this way constructed a radically different system of electric light involving novel incandescent lamps, dynamos, circuits, and other elements, enabling them to rapidly diverge from the existing scientific and commercial gatekeepers and domains surrounding electric light.

Finally, the example of Edison's development of electric lighting suggests an additional aspect of the creative process that extends the systems model. A dominant characteristic of creative spirals is that a novel solution in one element of a system changes the performance requirements of the elements it interacts with, precipitating nascent problems requiring recognition and solution, which in turn ripple through the system. Csikszentmihalyi (2014: 118) notes that problem definition has long been recognized as a critical first step in the creative process:

> As Einstein and many others have observed, the solution of problems is a much simpler affair than their formulation. Anyone who is technically proficient can solve a problem that is already formulated, but it takes true originality to formulate a problem in the first place. (Einstein and Infeld, 1938)

Yet this observation does not distinguish between latent problems and nascent ones. Creative spirals involve not only the definition and solution of existing problems but also the generation of new problems that either did not exist before or had lacked compelling reasons to solve them. While this may happen without spirals, the phenomenon of creative spirals reflects moments when problem generation occurs repeatedly within a sociomaterially and temporally bounded setting. As importantly, these emergent problems are not necessarily difficult to recognize or solve. In the case of Edison's work, new problems often presented themselves, sometimes dramatically, and solutions could easily be developed.

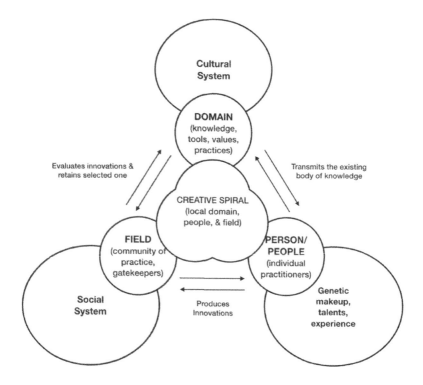

*Figure 11.3   Creative spirals phenomenon within Csikszentmihalyi's systems
model of creativity*

DISCUSSION

The phenomenon of creative spirals suggests three implications for future research:
the need for a formal theory of creative spirals, the opportunity to pursue several
foundational research questions, and alternative research methodologies to support
the theory and research.

Formalizing a Theory of Creative Spirals

This chapter has introduced creative spirals as an empirical phenomenon and a theoretical construct. However, its explanatory power as a theory of creativity remains
undeveloped. As a phenomenon, creative spirals can be most easily seen in retro-
spect, in those historical moments when individuals or small groups have generated
exceptional quantities of creative output. As a novel theoretical construct in the field
of creativity generally and within the systems model of creativity specifically, creative spirals represent an abstraction of a set of interdependent and causal relationships

between ideas generated during moments of exceptional creative output. While theoretical constructs are not themselves theory, they are an essential step towards the development of novel theory as they establish conceptual abstractions of phenomena enabling future observation and explanation (Suddaby, 2010). For example, they enable us to identify other potential instances of creative spirals beyond Edison, such as the seven-year development of Ford's system of mass production, during which automobile production increased from just over 1700 cars in 1907 to over 260 000 in 1914, while the price fell from $950 to $490 (Hounshell, 1984; Hargadon, 2003). By looking more closely at particular instances in which Ford and his engineers developed advances in mass production, we can see when an initial idea begets other ideas that have equal or greater impact. The first application of the assembly line was for the manufacture of magneto assemblies, a manufacturing department in which individuals assembled magnetos at the rate of three per hour, or 20 man-minutes each. When Ford engineers installed a first iteration of the assembly line in that department, the time required per magneto assembly immediately fell to 13 man-minutes. Over the next year, subsequent adaptions – each representing a nascent idea – reduced the time required to five man-minutes. Rabinow (1996) describes a similar chain of emergent problems and their solution in the development of PCR at Cetus Corporation as it progressed from a concept envisioned by Cary Mullis to a commercial system developed by two teams of scientists over the next five years. To develop a theory of creative spirals, much empirical and theoretical research remains to explain when and how creative ideas produce the conditions for further creativity.

Promising Research Questions

The development of a theory of creative spirals suggests a set of new research questions, of which I note several here. Firstly, because the interdependence between prior creative solutions, the new problems resulting, and their solutions rests in the objectives and attributes of a given sociotechnical system both as a whole and as individual elements, it becomes necessary to capture the sociomaterial and temporal particulars of creative spirals. Edison's system of electric lighting built on advances in commercial dynamos, lighting, and electric circuits, but was driven by the need to adapt them in particular ways to his unique vision for a large-scale, subdivided system, driving incandescent lamps for which these existing elements were materially insufficient. Future research must ask: What generalizable attributes can be found to explain such particular conditions shaping individual creative spirals?

While creative spirals are an ephemeral phenomenon, it is not clear what gives rise to these moments or affects their lifespan. Edison's work on the initial system of electric lighting at the Menlo Park labs lasted approximately two years, at which point the work transitioned to New York City and the focus shifted to building the first commercial electric plant at the Pearl Street Station. There, a second wave of creativity can be seen as problems emerged, and were solved, around installing power mains in city streets and wiring office buildings, metering electric use, and maintaining large-scale power plants. Future research might explore the precipitating events that affect the start, continuance, and end of creative spirals.

Finally, problem generation represents a central mechanism in creative spirals as this phenomenon produces problems that are related, significant, and familiar to the individuals involved in the moment. Moreover, these individuals are both the creators and the gatekeepers of any potential solution, and thus able to continually assess and pursue promising alternatives. Little is known about the nature and lifecycle of problems. While creativity research recognizes the importance of both defining and solving problems, more research is needed to understand the differences between old problems, which are likely persistent, and nascent ones, which are likely easier to solve or to understand the lifecycle of problems themselves and their embeddedness in particular contexts.

Alternative Methodologies

Creative spirals represent an empirical phenomenon shaped by factors at the level of individuals and collectives, where sociomateriality and temporality shape the nature of the problems and solutions. Microhistorical research may be well suited for capturing the context and the experiences and actions of the individuals involved. Replicating such conditions in laboratory settings would be difficult. Relying on ethnography or case study methods with the intention of seeing in real time the emergence of a creative spiral is equally problematic, as such outcomes and their impact on larger domains are difficult to predict. Quantitative analysis may help in recognizing and measuring aberrations in creative output, but often requires generic measures of creativity such as patents or citations that strip away the contextual attributes and interdependencies central to understanding the phenomenon. Historical methods offer the opportunity to investigate observed periods of exceptional creative output, but may not be able to capture the experiences and actions of the individual involved or the material and temporal nature of their work. Microhistorical methods present a variant of historical methods closely aligned to grounded theory (Glaser & Strauss, 1967; Suddaby, 2006) that locate the intensive study of individual experience and action within both a local setting and a broader historical context (Decker, 2015; Magnusson & Szíjártó, 2013; Hargadon, 2015). This methodology is well suited to study individual and collective processes that are both contextually embedded and made meaningful by their outcomes, such as creativity, innovation, and decision-making. Microhistory relies on rich sources of primary historical evidence to focus on the experiences and actions of individuals in a particular time and place, while at the same time locating that evidence within a broader historical context anchored around and informed by the outcome of interest. For example, the development of Edison's system of electric lighting offers a rich source of primary materials in the notebooks, diaries, interviews, and artifacts that recorded the development of dynamos, bulbs, and electric circuits in the Edison lab from 1878 to 1880, as well as primary and secondary records describing the larger context surrounding the evolution of the electric lighting industry during the 1870s and 1880s. Additionally, temporal distance provides researchers the opportunity to define the outcome of Edison's actions and their impact on the larger context.

CONCLUSION

This chapter began by asking: Under what conditions does having one creative idea make it more likely to have others? The short answer, presented here, is that creative spirals represent one such condition because, when individuals and collectives adapt existing elements to construct a novel system (Usher, 1929; Basalla, 1988), each adaptation not only represents a creative solution but also requires corresponding adaptations from interdependent elements. As Edison (1926, in Hughes, 1983: 22) noted, "The problem then that I undertook to solve was stated generally, the production of the multifarious apparatus, methods and devices, each adapted for use with every other, and all forming a comprehensive system."

The initial vision of the system and each subsequent advance toward that system contributes to the creative spiral as each new idea that works – and some that do not – generates new problems that, in turn, require definition and solution.

Edison's creative output began with the combination of existing technologies for electric lighting, power generation, and distribution. His early attempts to develop novel incandescent lamps failed, but not before manifesting the larger problem (and commercial potential) of constructing an integrated system of electric lighting involving lamps, dynamos, power circuits, and other elements. The resulting inventions reflected the collective efforts of his company to adapt each of these elements to the needs of the others and in service of the overall system. As the system came together in early models, prototypes, and initial projects, imbalances in the system became apparent which drove further creativity. The systems model of creativity recognizes the interplay between the individuals involved in generating creative outputs; the domain from which they draw their knowledge, tools, practices, and values; and the field-level gatekeepers that judge which new ideas should add to that domain. The phenomenon of creative spirals suggests that under certain conditions collectives may form in the pursuit of a novel system, and through their objectives and actions become simultaneously the relevant creators, gatekeepers, and domain of that system. To recognize these conditions requires accounting for the sociomaterial and temporal context shaping them, where ideas enacted create local problems that enable and drive yet more ideas.

NOTES

1. Note that, following the view of Francis Jehl, one of Edison's long-time assistants, Edison was "in reality a collective noun and [meant] the work of many men" (Jehl, in Hargadon, 2003: 93), and any references to Edison reflect this understanding of the collective nature

of their creative process. For simplicity and accuracy, I use the term "Edison" while using the pronouns they/them/their.

2.   The execution date refers to the date that an inventor signs a patent application in preparation for its filing with the United States Patent and Trademark Office. I have used the execution date of ultimately successful patents rather than the application or issued date, because the execution date is most closely associated with the actual invention process, as inventors may delay for months to file the patent (for example, avoiding the necessary attorney or filing fees or removing certain claims) and issuance may take years.

3.   These elements in Edison's larger system of electric lighting were themselves subsystems, representing configurations of elements performing a shared function. Moreover, the subsystems involved included the element itself functioning within the larger system (for example, the lamp) as well as the subsystem for manufacturing that element (the manufacture, distribution, and sale of incandescent lamps at commercial scale), and the subsystem that was necessary to develop that element (fund, procure material, design, prototype, and experiment).

4.   According to Hughes (1983), records indicate that 20 types of incandescent lamps were invented between 1809 to 1878, during what has been called the pre-commercial period ending with Edison's successful version.

5.   This approach would occupy the next year and was far from the final solution. Edison's thermoregulating device started as a hard rubber rod whose expansion broke a circuit, then an air chamber that expanded to break the circuit, then a magnetic circuit breaker timed to provide current intermittently. It was based on these ideas that Edison filed his first caveats on electric lighting; however, both physics and and economics made these solutions impossible.

6.   In the late 1860s, the first commercial dynamos came from European manufacturers and William Wallace and Moses Farmer had developed and began producing their own version in 1874.

7.   With these ideas and his recent public success with the phonograph, he was able to convince the Vanderbilt family to invest $30 000 in a new company to develop the subdivided incandescent light. After several months of negotiations as well as technical efforts, the Edison Electric Light Company was incorporated, valued at $300 000 with Edison personally owning $250 000 worth of stock and the Vanderbilts owning the remaining $50 000 (of which only the original $30 000 paid out until later).

8.   See Conot (1979: 144) and Josephson (1959: 210).

9.   It is possible this achievement was due to the lack of prior motivations to build the best vacuum pump. In other words, Edison's efforts to build a system of incandescent lighting generated the problem of building a better vacuum pump.

10.   Edison himself was originally mistaken in his specifications of the new generator (Edison's understanding of young field of electronics was limited). Francis Upton, one of the team, was forced to radically redesign the dynamo, which was famously known as the "Long-legged Mary Ann" for the unique design of its armatures.

11.   The last major development in the design of the circuit during this period happened in the November of 1882, when they developed the now common "three-wire" system. This improvement reduced the capital costs of the conductors by an additional 62.5 percent (Conot, 1979: 232).

12.   Note that this chapter does not address construct validity, which describes the plausability of inferences based on particular operationalization and measurement of an intended construct within a given study.

REFERENCES

Amabile, T. 1996. *Creativity in context*. Boulder, CO: Westview Press.
Amabile T.M., & Pratt, M.G. 2016. The dynamic componential model of creativity and innovation in organizations: Making progress, making meaning. *Research in Organizational Behavior*, 36: 157–183.
Basalla, G. 1988. *The evolution of technology*. New York: Cambridge University Press.
Bertalanffy, L. v. 1969. *General system theory foundations, development, applications*. New York: G. Braziller. http://books.google.com/books?id=yepEAAAAIAAJ.
Campbell, D.T. 1960. Blind variation and selective retention in creative thought as in other thought processes. *Psychological Review*, 67: 380–400.
Conot, R.E. 1979. *A streak of luck*. New York: Seaview Books.
Csikszentmihalyi, M. 1999. Implications of a systems perspective for the study of creativity. In R.J. Sternberg (ed.), *Handbook of creativity*: 313–335. New York: Cambridge University Press.
Csikszentmihalyi, M. 2006. A systems perspective on creativity. In J. Henry (ed.), *Creative management and development*: 3–17. Thousand Oaks, CA: SAGE Publications.
Csikszentmihalyi, M. 2014. *The systems model of creativity: The collected works of Mihaly Csikszentmihalyi*. Dordrecht: Springer. http://site.ebrary.com/id/11016432.
Decker, S. 2015. Mothership reconnection: Microhistory and institutional work compared. In P. Genoe MacLaren, A.J. Mills, & T. Weatherbee (eds), *The Routledge companion to management and organizational history*. New York: Routledge.
Einstein, A., & Infeld, L. 1938. *The evolution of physics from early concepts to relativity and quanta*. New York: Simon & Schuster.
Farrell, M.P. 1982. Artists' circles and the development of artists. *Journal of Small Group Behavior*, 13(4): 451–474.
Freidel, R., & Israel, P. 1986. *Edison's electric light: Biography of an invention*. New Brunswick, NJ: Rutgers University Press.
Gick, M.L., & Holyoak, K.J. 1983. Schema induction and analogic transfer. *Cognitive Psychology*, 15: 1–38.
Glaser, B.G., & Strauss, A.L. 1967. *The discovery of grounded theory: Strategies for qualitative research*. Chicago, IL: Aldine.
Hargadon, A. 2003. *How breakthroughs happen: The surprising truth about how companies innovate*. Boston, MA: Harvard Business School Press.
Hargadon, A. 2015. From what happened to what happens: Using microhistorical case studies to build grounded theory in organization studies. In K.D. Elsbach & R.M. Kramer (eds), *Handbook of qualitative organizational research: Innovative pathways and ideas*: 122–133. New York: Routledge.
Hargadon, A.B., & Bechky, B.A. 2006. When collections of creatives become creative collectives: A field study of problem solving at work. *Organization Science*, 17(4): 484–500.
Hargadon, A.B., & Sutton, R.I. 1997. Technology brokering and innovation in a product development firm. *Administrative Science Quarterly*, 42(4): 716–749.
Harris, W.A. 1997. On "scope conditions" in sociological theories. *Social and Economic Studies*, 46(4): 123–127.
Hennessey, B.A. 2015. Creative behavior, motivation, environment and culture: The building of a systems model. *Journal of Creative Behavior*, 49(3): 194–210.
Hennessey, B.A., & Amabile, T.M. 2010. Creativity. *Annual Review of Psychology*, 61: 569.
Hounshell, D.A. 1984. *From the American system to mass production*. Baltimore, MD: Johns Hopkins University Press.
Hughes, T.P. 1983. *Networks of power*. Baltimore, MD: Johns Hopkins University Press.
Hughes, T.P. 1989. *American genesis: A century of invention and technological enthusiasm*. New York: Viking.

Josephson, M. 1959. *Edison: A biography*. New York: McGraw-Hill.
Kerlinger, F.N. 1973. *Foundations of behavioral research*. Fort Worth, TX: Holt, Rinehart & Winston.
MacCorquodale, K., & Meehl, P.E. 1948. On a distinction between hypothetical constructs and intervening variables. *Psychological Review Psychological Review*, 55(2): 95–107.
Magnusson, S.G., & Szíjártó, I. 2013. *What is microhistory? Theory and practice*. London, UK and New York, USA: Routledge.
McIntyre, P. 2016a. General systems theory and creativity. In P. McIntyre, J. Fulton, & E. Paton (eds), *The creative system in action*: 13–26. London: Palgrave Macmillan UK.
McIntyre, P. 2016b. Songwriting as a creative system in action. In P. McIntyre, J. Fulton, & E. Paton (eds), *The creative system in action*: 47–59. London: Palgrave Macmillan UK.
Millard, A. 1990. *Edison and the business of innovation*. Baltimore, MD: Johns Hopkins University Press.
New York Sun. 1878. Invention's big triumph: An electric machine that will transmit power by wire. September 16. http://edison.rutgers.edu/yearofinno/EL/NYSun_Highlight_9-10-78.pdf.
Orlikowski, W.J. 2007. Sociomaterial practices: Exploring technology at work. *Organization Studies*, 28(9): 1435–1448.
Orlikowski, W.J. 2010. The sociomateriality of organisational life: Considering technology in management research. *Cambridge Journal of Economics*, 34(1): 125–141.
Orlikowski, W.J., & Scott, S.V. 2008. Sociomateriality: Challenging the separation of technology, work and organization. *Academy of Management Annals*, 2(1): 433–474.
Rabinow, P. 1996. *Making PCR: A story of biotechnology*. Chicago, IL: University of Chicago Press.
Rouse, E.D. 2020. Where you end and I begin: Understanding intimate co-creation. *AMR Academy of Management Review*, 45(1): 181–204.
Scheerer, M. 1963. Problem-solving. *Scientific American*, 208: 118–128.
Simonton, D.K. 1988. *Scientific genius*. Cambridge: Cambridge University Press.
Simonton, D.K. 1999. *Origins of genius: Darwinian perspectives on creativity*. New York: Oxford University Press.
Staw, B.M. 1990. An evolutionary approach to creativity and innovation. In J.L. Farr and M.W. West (eds), *Innovation and creativity at work: Psychological and organizational strategies*: 287–308. New York: Wiley.
Staw, B.M. 2009. Is group creativity really an oxymoron? Some thoughts on bridging the cohesion–creativity divide. In E.A. Mannix, J.A. Goncalo, & M.A. Neale (eds), *Research on managing groups and teams*, Vol. 12: 311–323. Bingley: Emerald Group Publishing.
Suchman, L.A. 2007. *Human–machine reconfigurations: Plans and situated actions*. New York: Cambridge University Press.
Suddaby, R. 2006. What grounded theory is not. *Academy of Management Journal*, 49(4): 633–642.
Suddaby, R. 2010. Editor's comments: Construct clarity in theories of management and organization. *Academy of Management Review*, 35(3): 346–357.
Sutton, R.I., & Staw, B.M. 1995. What theory is not. *Administrative Science Quarterly*, 40: 371–384.
Usher, A.P. 1929. *History of Mechanical Invention*. Cambridge, MA: Harvard University Press.
Walker, H.A., & Cohen, B.P. 1985. Scope statements: Imperatives for evaluating theory. *American Sociological Review*, 50(3): 288–301.
Wadhwani, R.D. 2016. Historical methods for contextualizing entrepreneurship research. In F. Welter & W.B. Gartner (eds), *A research agenda for entrepreneurship and context*: 134–145. Cheltenham, UK and Northampton, MA, USA: Edward Elgar Publishing.

12. Creativity over the career

Pier Vittorio Mannucci

"How can I sustain creativity over time?" This question is one of the most pressing ones for creative workers in every field. Some individuals who have been consistently successful in developing novel and useful ideas suddenly lose the "magic touch" that differentiated them from others; conversely, individuals who have never displayed any creative talent before, all of a sudden achieve creative success. In short, creativity varies over an individual's career. This variation can be highly problematic for creative workers and organizations alike. Organizations in fact rely more and more on the regularity of their employees' creativity to ensure a steady firm innovation and, thus, financial performance (Amabile & Pratt, 2016; Ahuja & Lampert, 2001; Zhou & Hoever, 2014). Creative workers who are not able to avoid bumpy dynamics in their creativity might end up being penalized in terms of career opportunities.

Given the centrality of this issue, it is not surprising that it represents one of the oldest topics in behavioral sciences. The first study dates back to Adolphe Quetelet's (1968 [1835]) pioneering work in 1835, where he looked at the career productivity of English and French playwrights. In the 20th century several researchers, such as Wayne Dennis, Harvey C. Lehman, and Dean Keith Simonton, devoted much attention and even entire research programs to understanding how individuals' ability to produce creative outcomes varies over their career. Yet, despite this intense scrutiny, there are still many unanswered questions that limit our ability to sustain creativity over the career. The field is in fact fragmented, with different research traditions that each provide pieces of the puzzle without coalescing into a clear theoretical understanding of why creativity varies and what, if anything, we can do to limit its variations.

The purpose of this chapter is to provide a multidisciplinary review of the rich research tradition that has focused on creativity over the career, looking beyond management literature to provide more precise insights into the key themes that have historically characterized this vast area of inquiry as well as into the most recent trends. The objective in adopting a multidisciplinary angle is to provide a more precise overview of the field, since the large majority of key contributions have come from outside the management realm. In so doing, I also aim to point out how this research can inform and stimulate research on creativity over the career in organizational settings. This topic is in fact becoming increasingly relevant due to both the growing importance of creativity in organizations (Amabile & Pratt, 2016) and the increasing duration of lifespan and professional careers (Kulik et al., 2014; Mainemelis et al., 2016).

Early research focused mostly on mapping career trajectories – that is, maps of creative output over the career – in order to understand how creativity varies over the career. We have thus gained a rich amount of knowledge of the average creative trajectories followed by creators over their career. Specifically, research has shown increasing theoretical and empirical support for the idea that creativity is "young," with career age having a direct, curvilinear effect on individual creativity (see Simonton, 1988a, 1997, for reviews). As a consequence, the myth of the young genius making critical breakthroughs is iconic in both arts and sciences (Galenson, 2005; Jones & Weinberg, 2011).

However, these average trajectories are hardly representative of individual creators, as they exhibit dramatic differences in the distribution of creative outcomes over their careers, both within and across fields (Simonton, 1997). Building on this observation, scholars have tried to explain why we observe these differences by focusing on factors at different levels of analysis. Specifically, scholars have focused on personal (e.g., Feist, 1993; Simonton, 1991), process (e.g., Galenson & Weinberg, 2001; Weinberg & Galenson, 2019), and product characteristics (e.g., Hargadon & Douglas, 2001; Simonton, 1980) to explain why individuals differ in their creative trajectories.

While insightful, these contributions offer little insight into what fosters creativity at different stages of the career. In other words, while we know how creativity varies, we do not know whether what fosters creativity at one point in the career will also foster it at a later point. The assumption of extant literature has been that creativity antecedents are career-neutral. However, this assumption hardly seems realistic: a newcomer has totally different cognitive, emotional, and motivational needs compared to an accomplished veteran. This gap has motivated a small yet vibrant area of research that has shifted the focus from career age as a predictor to career age as a moderator that shapes the effectiveness of different antecedents in fostering creativity (e.g., Cirillo et al., 2014; Mannucci & Yong, 2018).

The review proceeds as follows. Firstly, I provide an overview of the "classic" research that has looked at how creativity varies, both within and across fields. Secondly, I present the literature that has attempted to explain why individuals differ in their creative trajectories. I disentangle this literature by separating studies according to the three perspectives identified by Simonton (2003): person, product, process. Thirdly, I review more recent work that has looked at career age as a moderator, trying to understand what fosters creativity at different stages of the career. Finally, I present possibilities for future research.

HOW DOES CREATIVITY VARY?

Mapping Creative Trajectories

Early scholarly work on variation of an individual's creativity has focused on answering a simple question: Does creativity vary over time, and if so, how? Many developmental and cognitive psychologists have devoted significant effort to answering these questions. Two scholars in particular stand out for the quantity and richness of work dedicated to this topic: Harvey C. Lehman and Dean Keith Simonton. Lehman (e.g., Lehman, 1942, 1953, 1954, 1958, 1960) investigated the creative productivity and quality of eminent creatives across a variety of fields, such as mathematics, medicine, novel writing, poetry, and composing (see Simonton, 1988a, for a complete review). In an extensive body of work, Simonton (e.g., Simonton, 1975a, 1975b, 1977, 2000a, 2000b) further explored creativity variation, increasing the sophistication of Lehman's analysis. While other scholars have made significant contributions to this field (e.g., Dennis, 1958, 1966; Roe, 1972), the systematic focus displayed by Lehman and Simonton is such that the field can be summarized by describing their work.

The general pattern of creativity variation follows a curvilinear trajectory and displays a single peak, situated between young adulthood and middle age, followed by a decline. This decline is steeper for major contributions (that is, the most important and impactful contributions), with their number declining very fast after the peak, and is more gradual and regular for productivity (that is, the sheer number of outcomes generated, regardless of their importance and impact). While this relationship was long believed to be an inverted U-shape, it is actually better described by an inverted-backward J-curve, as the slope leading to the peak is steeper than the slope after the peak (Simonton, 1988a): creativity tends to rise fairly rapidly to the peak and thereafter decline gradually. This body of research has shown that the strongest factor explaining differences in trajectories, and particularly in the peak age, is the field a creator operates in: for example, creators working in poetry and mathematics tend to peak earlier, whereas novel writing and medicine tend to peak later (e.g., Lehman, 1953; Simonton, 1975a). While the archival nature of these studies does not allow us to directly measure the mechanisms, Simonton has argued that this is due to the different nature of work across fields: poetry and mathematics entail faster rates of ideation and elaboration than do novel writing and medicine, and thus exhibit a faster progression to the peak.

Building on these findings, Simonton identified different phases in the creative trajectories of eminent creators that represent the key moments of their creative careers (Simonton, 1975b). The first phase is named the "developmental period," and corresponds to the initial years of an individual's life and career. During this stage the individual does not really produce creative outcomes, but builds up an "initial creative potential" due to a variety of early experiences. This creative potential is defined as the maximum number of ideational combinations a creator is capable of conceiving, assuming they had an unlimited life span. This phase is followed by the "productive period," during which the creator produces the majority of the works for which they achieve eminence. The last phase is the "consolidative period," during which eminent individuals have already realized most of their creative contributions. In this phase they either attempt to reorganize and give coherence to their previous work, or engage in vigorous defense and advocacy of their past accomplishments (Simonton, 1975b).

Most importantly, Simonton developed a theoretical model that represents the first systematic attempt (and, to date, the only one) to explain the variation of creativity over the career (Simonton, 1997). According to the model, creativity is a dynamic ability, whose level is dependent on individual factors. In particular, creative ability at any given point in time is a function of the individual's initial creative potential, ideation rate, and elaboration rate. The initial creative potential is transformed into actual products through a two-step process. Firstly, the individual generates ideas through a combinatory mechanism; secondly, the creator develops these ideas into finished products. These two phases – generation and elaboration – happen mainly at the individual level (Perry-Smith & Mannucci, 2017) and are dependent on the initial creative potential. This implies that, at any given time of the career, the maximum number of potential creative ideas a creator is capable of conceiving can be divided into: (1) ideas neither generated or developed, still in the "potential" stage; (2) ideas generated but yet to be developed; and (3) ideas generated and already developed into completed outcomes. While (1) decreases over time, (3) tends to increase, with (2) first increasing and then decreasing. The rate at which ideas are converted from potential to generated is called the ideation rate, while the rate at which ideas are developed after having being generated is called the elaboration rate. Along with creative potential, these two parameters affect how creativity evolves through a creator's career, and are argued to economically explain individual differences in trajectories.

Problems with Descriptive Models of Creativity Variation

While pioneering and insightful, research focusing on the description and explanation of average creative trajectories has revealed theoretical and empirical limitations when it comes to explaining creativity variation. Firstly, Simonton himself underlines that the observed trajectories and theoretical models emerging from these studies are purely descriptive (Simonton, 1997). They cannot be estimated until the career is over, and thus can be used only for post-hoc analysis (Simonton, 1997) and not for predicting how and why the creativity of a given individual will vary over their career. Moreover, these curves might even have limited descriptive utility. On the one side, they seem to be unstable over time. Recent longitudinal studies in fact show that shifts in the age of peak creativity over time are extremely large, increasing by between seven and 13 years depending on the field. These shifts within fields are much larger (between two and four times) than the differences across fields that have usually been used to explain differences in creative trajectories (Jones & Weinberg, 2011). On the other side, these models might suffer from oversimplification: the creativity and the career of an individual are influenced by many factors at different levels of analysis (Amabile & Pratt, 2016; Anderson & Bidwell, 2019; Mannucci & Yong, 2018) that cannot be reduced to the three parameters identified by these models, or to career age alone. These factors can positively or negatively affect creativity, thus making performance significantly deviate from what the models would predict. For example, changing industry or interacting with new people might renew and replenish the "initial creative potential" (Cirillo et al., 2014; Perry-Smith, 2006); whereas being embedded in an unsupportive work environment might reduce the elaboration rate and lead individuals to disengage from creativity entirely (Perry-Smith &

Mannucci, 2017; Rouse, 2020). This problem is indeed acknowledged also by the proponents of these models: Simonton states that external factors can "defect the observed performance from what would be predicted according to existing theory" (Simonton, 1997: 84).

A second problem affecting existing models is that they might suffer from compositional fallacy: an artifact that occurs when individual attributes are aggregated in such a way that observed relationships among the variables reflect the manner of aggregation more than the actual correlations occurring at the individual level of analysis (Simonton, 1997). This problem occurs because these studies try to predict individual trajectories based on statistics aggregated across a multitude of individuals. While the adoption of longitudinal designs, as much of extant research has done, mitigates this risk compared to cross-sectional data, the issue cannot be completely ruled out, and can result in biased estimates, particularly when it comes to the decline in creativity after the peak age (Simonton, 1988a).

Thirdly, the large majority of these studies distinguish between creative productivity and quality, operationalizing the former as the total number of creative products generated by an individual, and the latter as the number of most creative works. This distinction, however, does not account for the continuous nature of creativity. Creativity scholars have repeatedly emphasized that creativity is not a binary concept but a continuous one (e.g., Amabile, 1996; Amabile & Mueller, 2008; Cattani & Ferriani, 2008; Shalley et al., 2004): each product is characterized by a different level of creativity, and contributions of average creativity can still be impactful. Moreover, what is a "minor" contribution for one creator could be a major one for another one. By separating the creativity of the product and the number of products, scholars focusing on creative trajectories have generated an artificial distinction between the number of total products and the number of major products that does not account for this continuous nature. The few studies on creative trajectories that account for the continuous nature of creativity, giving to each product a creativity score based on its impact (for example, citations, mentions in reviews and books) report that career age has neither a linear nor a curvilinear direct effect on creativity (Dennis, 1958, 1966; Simonton, 1977). This suggests that, without the intervention of external factors, the average creativity of generated outcomes would remain constant over the career, and is thus not influenced in any way by career age. This further impairs our ability to use these curves to derive meaningful conclusions on how and why creativity actually varies.

As a consequence of these limitations, two separate research perspectives have emerged. The first, more established, one has tried to address the issues related to compositional fallacy and oversimplification of existing models by identifying factors that explain individual differences in trajectories. The second, more recent, has sought to move away from descriptive models to develop prescriptions on how to foster creativity at different stages of the career. I present each of these traditions in the next two sections.

WHY ARE INDIVIDUAL TRAJECTORIES DIFFERENT?

That certain individuals are more creative than others can easily be observed by taking a closer look at the trajectories of eminent creators. Consider these examples of literary creativity: William Shakespeare conceived seven of his most creative works, including *Hamlet, As You Like It, Macbeth,* and *King Lear,* in two distinct years, 1599 and 1606, with many of his most problematic, less creative plays conceived between these two years (Shapiro, 2005, 2015). Wolfgang Goethe displayed a longer creative trajectory, writing a critically acclaimed novel, *The Sorrows of Young Werther,* in his mid-twenties, composing a series of successful plays in his thirties and forties, and completing Parts I and II of *Faust* at ages 59 and 83, respectively (Simonton, 1997). Finally, Harper Lee's novel *To Kill a Mockingbird* remains the only work she published during her lifetime, but it won the Pulitzer Prize in 1960 and is widely regarded as one of the cornerstones of American literature.

It is thus not surprising that research seeking to understand individual differences in trajectories has been rather rich, spanning a series of disciplines and approaches. With richness, however, came also disjoint and lack of systematicity: scholars have approached this line of research by looking at very diverse factors at different levels. Over time, three perspectives have emerged as more prominent: (1) the person perspective, focusing on the individual characteristics and skills that shape creativity over time; (2) the product perspective, focusing on how product characteristics shape the likelihood that different audiences over time consecrate the outcome as creative; and (3) the process perspective, looking at how differences in the way individuals approach the creative process might explain differences in trajectories.

Person

The person perspective on creativity has its roots in the work of Francis Galton. In his book *Hereditary Genius,* Francis Galton (1869) suggested that individuals vary deeply in inherent characteristics that he dubs "natural ability" (the G factor), and that this natural ability is inherited, rather than nurtured. In turn, this ability translates into higher, more constant levels of creativity over the career.

Subsequent research has put into question the first part of the equation, showing that ability and the G factor are also a function of nurture, and not just of nature (Kroeber, 1944; Simonton, 1988b). However, research has corroborated and extended the second part, showing that creators who are able to be constantly creative over time can do so thanks to inherent characteristics and exceptional skills such as personality, cognitive styles, and training (Feist, 1993, 1998; Simonton, 1991).

Simonton (1991) provided the first convincing evidence in support of Galton's theory by investigating creative achievement in a variety of fields such as philosophy, music, and visual arts. He found that a single-factor model has a robust explanatory power across all these samples, suggesting that prolonged creative success is indeed a function of a special set of individual characteristics. In 1993, Gregory Feist conducted the first systematic study of individual-level factors that predict continued creativity over the career, integrating different factors into a single structural model rather than looking at factors in isolation. By focusing on accomplished academics in the fields of biology, chemistry, and physics, he found that factors such as parents' occupation, age, and political and religious orientations did not have any effect on creativity over the career. Creators who were more creative over the career tended to be competitive and high in epistemic curiosity, need for autonomy, and intrinsic motivation. Feist (1998) corroborated and extended these findings by conducting a meta-analysis on the effect of personality on artistic and scientific creativity. Findings show that the traits that predict creativity early in the career also predict it late in the career. These traits include openness to experience and a disposition toward independence and autonomy. As these traits are temporally stable, people with these traits seem to be able to sustain creativity for prolonged periods of time.

One limitation of this line of research is that, for the most part, it relies on samples of exceptional individuals. Unsurprisingly, no studies using this approach have been conducted in organizational settings, thus limiting our ability to derive meaningful conclusions on how they translate to organizational contexts. However, one can observe parallels between these findings and well-established antecedents of creativity at work: the findings on autonomy, curiosity, and intrinsic motivation mirror their well-known importance for employees to be creative at work (Amabile & Pratt, 2016; Hagvedt et al., 2019; Shalley et al., 2004; Yong et al., 2020). One logical conclusion could therefore be that, while certain exceptional individuals can autonomously find their own sources of motivation and curiosity when they are working independently, within organizations it is up to the management to create an environment that stimulates these factors (Amabile et al., 1996).

Product

Another line of inquiry has focused on the characteristics of the products that individuals generate. This area is rooted on research on creative consecration – that is, the recognition and celebration of an individual's creativity by relevant field members and gatekeepers – which in turn is premised on a systems view of creativity, and in particular on the idea that creativity is not an objective property, but is socially constructed (Amabile, 1996; Csikszentmihályi, 1999). What is considered creative by one audience can be considered uncreative by another: while *Crouching Tiger, Hidden Dragon* was consecrated as a creative success in the United States, in China it was received as Ang Lee's least creative movie (Niu & Sternberg, 2002). Similarly, and more relevant for this chapter, what is considered creative at one point in time might not be considered creative later: Salieri was more celebrated than Mozart during their time; and Van Gogh, now celebrated as one of the greatest artists of his time, did not sell a single painting in his lifetime.

While research on creative consecration is very broad (e.g., Cattani et al., 2017; Cattani et al., 2014; Sgourev, 2013), only a few studies have looked at the robustness of creative consecration over time. Studies in this tradition have mainly explored whether product originality and differentiation lead to creative consecration over time. At a first glance, the answer to this question might appear tautological: novelty and originality are key ingredients of creativity, and consequently they should lead to creative consecration. However, research has shown that individuals often have a bias against novelty, with novel ideas being rejected rather than consecrated (Mueller et al., 2012; Mueller et al., 2018; see Perry-Smith & Mannucci, 2020, for a review). The issue becomes even more pressing when one considers it over the span of a career, as dynamism adds shifting audiences' tastes and preferences to an already complicated picture. Consistently, many studies have shown that, while creative reputation over time exhibits a good amount of transhistorical consistency, shifts in field characteristics and audience preferences make this consistency far from perfect (Over, 1982; Rosengren, 1985; Simonton, 1991).

Findings emerging from studies adopting a dynamic angle paint a more complicated picture: while a novelty bias seems indeed to be present, it plays out differently at different points in time. In a study focusing on classical music, Simonton (1980) found that melodies and themes that are judged to be creative by both contemporary and posthumous audiences tend to be those that are of moderate originality with respect to the entire repertoire; the most original themes tend to be the least consecrated ones. Interestingly, the story is different when one assesses originality with respect to the repertoire of the time during which the melody was composed (the "musical Zeitgeist"). When this "Zeitgeist originality" increases, creative fame first declines, and thereafter increases, with the most consecrated and famous melodies being very atypical for their time. In other words, best-known creative melodies tend to be highly atypical and original as compared to the repertoire to their time, and of average originality when compared to the overall repertoire. This pattern suggests a field-level assimilation process of originality that has relevant implications for maintaining creativity over time. Original products that are consecrated as creative at a certain point in time need to be integrated in the "field standards" in order to be still consecrated as creative over time. Products that are atypical for their time but get assimilated, cited, and diffused, at least up to a certain degree, enjoy everlasting creative fame. On the contrary, products that are atypical for their time but remain atypical over time, staying at the margins of field production, tend to be forgotten.

In a recent study conducted in the fashion industry, Godart and Galunic (2019) corroborate and extend this finding, suggesting that whether an original element is consecrated over time depends on its field embeddedness and visibility. They find that the popularity of creative elements such as color, fabric, and pattern is fostered by being more deeply connected and embedded with other elements: the more interconnected an element is, the higher its creative popularity because of increased visibility and acceptance. However, this "visibility" benefit can be accrued only with moderate levels of visibility, and is bounded in time: original elements that receive high media exposure see their creative recognition decline over time even if they are highly interconnected. Excessive levels of visibility, in fact, can diminish the appearance of exclusivity and originality of a product, and thus hurt its perceived creativity.

These findings suggest that creative consecration over time is a delicate balance between being original and atypical, and being popular and embedded within the field: while originality and popularity help in the short run, excessive levels of both can hurt creativity over time. The question then becomes how to achieve this delicate balance: in other words, is it possible to design a product whose characteristics lead to creative consecration when the product comes out, but are also robust to shifting visibility and audience standards? A historical case study on the invention of the electric light (Hargadon & Douglas, 2001) provides a potential answer: the study suggests that Edison was able to gain increasing acceptance for his ideas by cloaking the radical novelty of his new system "in the mantle of established institutions" (ibid.: 479), such as the gas industry. Through this "robust design," Edison strategically blended some features of his idea with the familiar, presented others as new, and kept other potentially more problematic ones hidden from sight. These latter features then became celebrated as the truly novel innovations he introduced. The case study suggests that the balance between originality and popularity can be achieved through the strategic presentation of the features of the idea. A robust design, in fact, results in an idea that is effective both in the short run and in the long run. Its arrangement of concrete details is effective in "locating the novel product or process in the familiar world" (Hargadon & Douglas, 2001: 480), but at the same time preserves the flexibility necessary to adapt to the evolution of understanding and meaning. In so doing, it makes the idea robust to the evolving tastes of audiences and ensures its enduring creative consecration.

Process

A third line of inquiry has focused on the characteristics of individuals' creative process. The underlying idea is that different creatives approach creative tasks differently, and that these differences can affect their creative trajectories. The champion of this theory has been David Galenson, an economist of the University of Chicago. Galenson distinguishes between two ways of approaching the creative process, which he defines as "conceptual" and "experimental" (Galenson, 2005; Galenson & Weinberg, 2001; Weinberg & Galenson, 2019). These two approaches are not dichotomous, but represent the opposite ends of a continuum. Creators who approach their work conceptually are guided by precise goals, and plan their work carefully in advance before executing it systematically. In contrast, experimental creators have ambitious but vague goals, and work by trial and error, arriving gradually and incrementally at their desired outcome. According to Galenson, these differences in the creative process result in differences in creative trajectories. Specifically, conceptual creators tend to produce their best work early in their career, whereas experimental creators need more time to produce their more significant work, which tends to emerge late in their career. Although the theory was originally conceived for painting, Galenson later extended and found support for it in different fields of artistic and scientific creativity (Galenson, 2005). Purely conceptual creators, who Galenson dubs "young geniuses," include the likes of Picasso, Orson Welles, T.H. Eliot, and F. Scott Fitzgerald. Purely experimental creators – the "old masters" – include Cézanne, Alfred Hitchcock, Virgina Woolf, and Mark Twain.

Importantly, Galenson argues that the creative process an artist adopts impacts not only when an artist will conceive her/his best work, but also whether he/she will be able to maintain a steady flow of creative outcomes over time. Conceptual artists seem to be less likely to keep up their creative productivity over time (Galenson, 2005; Weinberg & Galenson, 2019). Their inventions and creative products are often radically new, game-changers that differ dramatically not only from other creators' work, but also from the creator's own previous work. At the same time, the majority of these artists seem unable to keep the creative fire going over time, and many of them end up producing one or very few creative outcomes. On the contrary, experimental creators' trial and error approach ensures that they are constantly on the lookout for something new, never satisfied, slowly building their contribution to the field which emerges gradually through their work. This results in a more constant flow of creative ideas over time.

While intriguing and intuitively appealing, scholars have pointed out some problems with Galenson's theory. Critics have questioned the validity of the distinction between conceptual and experimental creators, arguing that it is vague and at times even contradictory (Winner, 2004). For example, creators who are classified as purely conceptual, such as Picasso, seem to have followed a more experimental approach at some stages of their career (see Simonton, 2007b), thus putting the distinction under question. That said, it must be noted that Galenson's findings have been replicated in independent studies, sometimes even conducted before he elaborated his theory (e.g., Feist, 1993; Simonton, 2007a). For example, in the aforementioned study on scientific eminence, Feist (1993) found that creators working with an intuitive approach and with no clear goals tended to be more productive over their career. This is consistent with Galenson's theory and findings on experimental creators.

When it comes to its organizational applicability, Galenson's research suffers from the same problems of the "mapping" tradition, in that it focuses on the accomplishments of exceptional creators working in artistic and, in a few cases, scientific fields. Notwithstanding this problem, there is reason to believe that Galenson's theory and findings could have relevant organizational implications. Firstly, by underlining that different types of processes exist, Galenson is the first to highlight that there are different paths through which creativity can be achieved. This intuition is likely to be particularly relevant in organizations, where the tendency to adopt a "one-size-fits-all" approach is always tempting: failing to recognize the differences in creative processes can have nefarious consequences, as they reflect differences in goals, methods, and vision that need to be accounted for in order to properly motivate and stimulate employees (Amabile & Pratt, 2016). Secondly, as the cycles for innovation are shortening (Ahuja & Lampert, 2001), the pressure on employees to produce new ideas quickly is increasing. This could engender problems for creatives who have a more experimental approach, as they might need more time to produce creative outcomes, leading to them burning out or leaving the organization, and consequently to the loss of potentially valuable ideas. As Galenson himself underlines (Galenson & Weinberg, 2016), the "myth of the young genius" is also perpetuated by the fact that conceptual innovations are easier to recognize, as they appear suddenly and conspicuously, whereas experimental innovations emerge gradually, almost imperceptibly, over time. In other words, the failure to recognize these differences in processes could be one of the causes of the ageism that characterizes creative professions (Mannucci & Yong, 2018).

WHAT FOSTERS CREATIVITY AT DIFFERENT CAREER STAGES? CAREER AGE AS A MODERATOR

Prompted by the limitations of the two approaches presented above, in recent years organizational scholars have started to approach the career–creativity relationship from a different angle. Instead of looking at the direct effect of career age on creativity, these scholars have explored whether career age could be a moderating factor; that is, whether it could shape the effectiveness of other factors in fostering creativity.

While different in terms of target and scope, these papers share an underlying theoretical framework in that they build on research traditions in organization theory and applied psychology (Feldman, 1989; Frensch & Sternberg, 1989; March, 1991; McCrae et al., 1987) to argue that career age affects individuals' cognitive complexity and flexibility. Specifically, as individuals become more socialized with the rules and norms of a field, complexity increases, whereas flexibility declines (Dane, 2010; March, 1991). Early-career individuals have flexible mental structures, characterized by loose links between concepts and thus open to modifications. Over time, however, socialization causes individuals to become increasingly reliant on established linkages, focusing only on those mental pathways and associations that they have already used in the past (Bartlett, 1958). As a consequence, mental structures become rigid and resistant to modification (Dane, 2010). From this reasoning, scholars derive the prediction that factors which foster complexity will benefit creativity early in the career, when individuals need to master the field and accumulate knowledge to be able to generate novel and meaningful associations. On the contrary, factors which foster flexibility should yield stronger benefits late in the career, when they can prevent and counterbalance the cognitive rigidity induced by increasing career age.

This theoretical prediction has been supported by findings in a variety of settings. Some studies focused on factors at the organizational and team level. Cirillo et al. (2014) studied inventors employed by Xerox and found that older inventors benefited more than young ones by joining corporate spinouts (that is, new ventures founded by employees with the support of the original organization). In particular, joining a corporate spinout improves older inventors' explorative behaviors and reduces the degree to which they rely on their pre-existing knowledge to generate new patents, thus fostering their innovativeness and creativity. In a study focusing on 59 Nobel Prize winners, Eubanks et al. (2016) found that being embedded in a team that encourages constructive task conflict and participative decision-making was more important late in the career rather than early in the career. The study is exploratory, and thus does not delve into the mechanisms. However, task conflict and participative decision-making are likely to encourage the expression of dissent, thus exposing the creator to diverging opinions and diverse views (e.g., Yong et al., 2014). The fact that individuals benefit more from this type of climate when they are late in their career is thus consistent with the general idea that factors which foster flexibility are particularly effective at this stage.

Other studies have focused on factors at the individual level, and in particular on knowledge characteristics and collaboration patterns. In a longitudinal study on creative workers in the Hollywood animation industry, Mannucci and Yong (2018) found that individuals benefit from increasing knowledge depth early in their career, while knowledge breadth is more beneficial in later stages. On the contrary, knowledge depth becomes detrimental in later stages, as it exacerbates the cognitive entrenchment engendered by increasing career age; and knowledge breadth does not yield benefits early in the career, as spending some time in the field is necessary in order to appropriately recombine diverse knowledge into meaningful permutations. In a study on project managers, Guillén and Kunze (2019) show that older managers benefit more than younger ones by working with people from different departments in terms of both actual and perceived innovative behavior. Not only does interdepartmental collaboration increase creativity for older employees (but not for younger ones), but it also reduces negative stereotypes towards older managers by showing that they are flexible and willing to work with diverse people.

Finally, Belkhouja and Yoon (2018) focused simultaneously on individuals' knowledge characteristics and collaboration patterns. In a study of management and business scholars, they found that knowledge breadth and collaborating with individuals outside one's institution yield different benefits in terms of research impact depending on the career stage. Young scholars' citations are impaired by very high levels of knowledge breadth, with moderate levels leading to higher citations; whereas older scholars' impact increases when their knowledge breadth is high. Also, young scholars derive creative benefits from working with a moderate number of individuals outside their own institution, whereas older scholars' impact is hindered by collaborating with co-authors at institutions other than their own.

This line of research is still at the early stages, and it thus represents a fruitful path for further inquiries, particularly when it comes to potential boundary conditions. It must be noted that, unlike some of the paradigms presented in prior sections, scholars working in this area have not adopted a reductionist approach, and have derived their conclusions after controlling for potential confounding factors such as prior success, collaboration networks, and firm characteristics. That said, it is of course possible, and even desirable, that with more research more contradictions will become apparent, allowing us to gain a more fine-grained understanding of what fosters creativity at different points of the career.

FUTURE RESEARCH DIRECTIONS

While the research tradition on creativity over the career is long and rich, a variety of unanswered questions remain. In particular, the second and third research streams presented above are in need of further exploration and better theoretical integration to truly capture the depth and complexity of the career–creativity relationship. In this section, I present a few possible avenues for future research to help move the field forward. These avenues not only represent a potential extension of each research tradition, but also offer the opportunity to integrate and bridge different traditions, providing us with a more comprehensive understanding of creativity over the career.

Individual Characteristics

Extant research centered on the individual has focused on intrapersonal character-istics such as personality and curiosity (e.g., Feist, 1993; Simonton, 1991). More research would be needed to understand how other individual-level factors shape individuals' ability to stay creative over time. For example, research on the effect of interpersonal factors such as personal networks could yield interesting insights. Social networks are a powerful driver of creativity (see Perry-Smith & Mannucci, 2015, and Burt, Chapter 5 in this volume, for recent reviews), and there is reason to believe that their dynamics could have considerable effects on creative trajectories. Research in this area, however, is still in its infancy. For example, in a working paper on the British television industry, Soda and colleagues focus on how social networks can shape an individual's creativity over their career. They find that creators who maintain open networks, connecting many disconnected others, tend to be more creative over their career. However, the ability to be constantly creative is contingent not only on maintaining an open network, but also on regularly "rejuvenating" the network by adding new collaborators (Soda et al., 2018).

Another entirely neglected, yet potentially insightful, individual-level factor lies in how individuals perceive, frame, and make sense of their own career. Most of extant research on creative careers has in fact adopted a rather mechanistic view, neglecting the active roles that individuals' actions and cognition play in determining the shape of their career trajectories. While there is yet no published work in the area, the field is starting to recognize the importance of considering sensemaking processes in creative careers. For example, in a recent working paper, Fetzer et al. (2019) con-ducted an inductive study of employees of the Eames Office and Arthur Andersen to understand how individuals make sense of their creative careers. Findings suggest that individuals' early organizational experiences shape the career stories they tell, and that over time these stories shape decisions regarding collaboration, engagement in the creative process, and professional decisions on where to work and where not to work.

Process Characteristics

Galenson's work on the creative process suffers from a reductionist approach in that it reduces all variance in creative trajectories to a single factor (the creative process) without accounting for other potential alternative explanations. Future research could test the robustness of this theory when other potentially relevant alternative explanations are accounted for. For example, the fact that some artists produce more creative work early in their career whereas others produce it later could be endogenously caused by this early success, which has been shown to negatively affect subsequent creativity (Audia & Goncalo, 2007). Consequently, early achievers' creativity decline might not be due to their creative process, as argued by Galenson, but precisely to that early success, which constrains their ability to come up with novel ideas. Similarly, Galenson's findings could be alternatively explained also by field-level differences. By choosing to focus on creators within fields rather than across fields, in fact, Galenson has neglected the fact that field-level and individual-level factors might actually be interdependent, rather than mutually exclusive. Consistently, Simonton (2007a) has shown that the two dimensions are orthogonal: in a study focusing on poets and novelists, he has found support for a fourfold typology of creative career trajectories: conceptual poets, conceptual novelists, experimental poets, and experimental novelists.

Another potentially interesting avenue for future research is to consider how the creative process evolves over time. As Galenson (2005) himself acknowledges, individuals' creative process and mode of work might change over time, thus changing the nature of their outcomes and potentially their creative trajectories. There is much anecdotal evidence corroborating this idea. Bob Dylan provides a perfect illustration: while recalling the period between 1965 and 1966, when he recorded three of his most creative and groundbreaking albums (*Bringing It All Back Home*, *Highway 61 Revisited*, and *Blonde on Blonde*), he said that

> Those early songs were almost magically written. Try to sit down and write something like that. There's a magic to that … And, you know, I did it. I did it at one time. You can't do something forever. I did it once, and I can do other things now. But I can't do that. (Remnick, 2015)

While there is no empirical work on the subject, in 1955 Elliott Jaques wrote an insightful and thought provoking article on the topic that could act as the basis for further empirical enquiry. He argued that early in the career, the creative process is "intense and spontaneous" (Jaques, 1955: 503). This "hot-from-the-fire" creative process is characterized by an extremely fast pace, with ideas spurring almost ready-made out of the creator's mind. On the contrary, the creative process late in the career is "sculpted," with a lot of thinking and reworking occurring before the idea is actually executed (Jaques, 1955). Sudden bursts of inspiration still occur, but they are only the beginning of the process, which then proceeds to many cycles of reworking the initial idea. Jaques saw this evolution as a consequence of aging and maturity, and provided many examples of artists who went through this evolution. Future research could build on Jacques's ideas to develop and test a model of how the creative process evolves over time.

Contextual Characteristics

Another potentially fruitful avenue of research resides in exploring more in-depth the organizational context and the field where individual creators are embedded. This would entail explicitly acknowledging the interdependency between an individual's career and what is happening in the organization or field they are embedded in. For example, external shocks can completely reshape organizational functioning and the configuration of a field, and are thus likely to affect the career trajectories of individuals working in that field. External shocks such as financial crises or pandemics could induce companies to downsize, thus reducing perceived support for creativity and leading people to disengage from creative endeavors or to change career (Amabile & Conti, 1999). Similarly, unexpected failures and financial shortages can induce people to change company or even switch professions, in the short term or in the long term (Mainemelis et al., 2016).

At the field level, external shocks can actually open up opportunities for new people to enter the field. Consider the example of John Harrison, the inventor of the maritime chronometer: he would probably not have been able to present and implement his invention if it was not for the Isles of Scilly naval shipwrecks in 1707, the worst maritime disaster in the United Kingdom's (UK) history. The disaster induced the UK Parliament to put out three very large rewards for anyone who could solve the so-called "longitude problems." This opened up an opportunity for an outsider such as Harrison, a self-taught craftsman of humble origins, allowing him to enter into a pursuit that would have usually been reserved to academics (Cattani et al., 2017). Similarly, the collapse of the Soviet Union completely reshaped the field of theoretical mathematics. As all the research conducted in the Soviet Union used to be kept secret from the rest of the world, its release after the Soviet collapse caused a sudden and unexpected increase in the pace of change in theoretical mathematics, making entire subfields and lines of research obsolete and accelerating the development of others (Agrawal et al., 2016). As a result, some Western scholars flourished after the collapse, while others experienced a decline in creativity (Teodoridis et al., 2019). Finally, in their study of Nobel laureates, Jones and Weinberg (2011) observed that creative career trajectories in the field of physics experienced more significant shifts after the development of quantum mechanics, one of the biggest, paradigm-shifting revolutions in the field (Kuhn, 1962). Understanding how external shocks interact with individual characteristics to shape career trajectories would provide us with a better understanding of both individual differences in trajectories and the moderating role of career age. Extreme shocks might in fact also change the way in which career age shapes cognition and motivation, thus altering its moderating effect and the factors that are more or less effective in fostering creativity at different career stages.

Career Interdependency

Another relevant contextual factor that has been largely ignored by extant creativity research (see Simonton, 1984, for a partial exception) is the interdependence of careers. Careers do not happen in a vacuum, but are entangled in an interconnected web of careers: one's career is shaped by the careers of colleagues, managers, and competitors (Anderson & Bidwell, 2019; Barnett & Miner, 1992). As a consequence, the creative trajectory of a creator is likely to be influenced by others' career trajectories. For example, a co-worker moving to another company or retiring could have negative consequences on one's ability to stay creative. Consistently, Azoulay and colleagues have found that the death of very prolific academics negatively affects the creativity of their co-authors in subsequent years (Azoulay et al., 2010). Similarly, different individuals might have different reactions to the fact that a "creative rival" is experiencing momentum: some might be challenged, and thus inspired to produce more creative work; some might feel threatened, and thus disengage from creativity entirely or engage in safer, less novel work (Kakkar et al., 2019). More research is needed to understand how this interdependence in trajectories might affect a focal individual's trajectory and ability to stay creative over time. More broadly, the field could benefit by paying closer attention to research on careers and career management (see Dokko et al., 2019, for a recent review), as it could provide valuable insights into how and why creativity varies over the career as a consequence of human resources choices such as hiring, promotions, and job rotation.

"Forever Creative": Bridging the Different Perspectives

The Holy Grail of the research in creativity over time is to understand the recipe to stay forever creative. So far, this task has eluded scholars. One reason for this lack of understanding is that "forever creative" individuals are rare. Another reason is that the ability to stay constantly creative over time is likely the byproduct of factors at different levels, ranging from actors' personal characteristics to the work environment to societal forces. Considering these two problems suggests that answering the question on how to stay "forever" creative, or at least getting closer to it, would require the in-depth, multi-level exploration of the careers of few individuals, rather than the quantitative analysis of large number of individuals. This would entail the use of qualitative methodologies that so far have been vastly neglected by current research on creative careers, such as grounded theory and historical case-studies. In particular, the latter seem perfectly suited for this task, as they can provide the necessary distance to observe how a creative career longitudinally unfolds through the interaction between complex individual-level factors and context-specific meaning and needs (Cattani et al., 2017; Hargadon & Douglas, 2001; Sgourev, 2013).

Career Age as a Moderator: Alternative Mechanisms and Theoretical Modeling

The research tradition looking at career age as a moderator is relatively recent. As such, there are plenty of opportunities to enrich it by expanding and strengthening both its scope and its theoretical foundations. A relevant avenue for further research lies in the exploration of alternative theoretical mechanisms. Currently scholars have focused exclusively on how career age shapes individuals' cognition, to explain its moderating effects. However, career age is likely to shape not only cognition, but also other fundamental individual processes such as motivation and emotional experience. Research has shown that intrinsic motivation tends to decline as the time spent within a given field increases (Gottfried et al., 2001; Otis et al., 2005), due to the attainment of mastery goals (Dweck & Leggett, 1988). Similarly, there is evidence that the way individuals experience emotions changes consistently over their lifespan (e.g., Magai et al., 2006). Given the importance of motivation (e.g., Amabile, 1983; Liu et al., 2016) and emotions (e.g., Amabile et al., 2005; Parke et al., 2015) for creativity, these shifts can result in different needs compared to those engendered by changes in cognitive structures. Exploring the moderating role of career age by adopting a motivational or emotional lens thus constitutes a promising avenue for future research, as it could provide insights into factors that promote creativity at different stages of the career that have so far gone overlooked.

More broadly, this area of research would benefit from the creation of a comprehensive theoretical model. This model should take into account the evolution of fundamental individual-level processes such as cognition, motivation, and emotions (Amabile & Kramer, 2011), and how these different evolutions engender different and potentially competing needs. Focusing on just one mechanism without considering the others could in fact lead to misleading conclusions: while in some cases the needs engendered by the evolution of cognitive structures are the same as those engendered by motivation, in other cases they might diverge significantly (Mannucci & Yong, 2018). This means that a factor that should foster creativity by fulfilling a cognitive need (for example, increasing flexibility at later stages) might hinder it by frustrating a motivational need (for example, decreasing creative self-efficacy). A comprehensive theory on the moderating role of career age is thus warranted in order to gain a better understanding of why a creator either is able to be consistently creative over the career or exhibits fluctuations in creativity, following a more or less predictable trajectory.

CONCLUSION

The objective of this chapter was to review the existing body of literature on creativity over the career. Despite being one of the oldest topics in behavioral sciences, research in management and organizations has started to explore it only relatively recently. I thus conducted a multidisciplinary review with the twofold objective of presenting not only the empirical efforts conducted so far, but also the historical evolution of the field. To this end, I classified this research based on three different traditions that have focused on three different questions: (1) How does creativity vary? (2) Why do individuals differ in their creative trajectories? and (3) What fosters creativity at different stages of the career? After having pointed out the findings and shortcomings of each tradition, I sought to point out promising future lines of inquiry. I proposed that future research on creativity over the career should focus on investigating currently neglected individual-level, process-level, organization-level, and field-level factors, and on integrating these perspectives by exploring the lives of "forever creative" individuals. This would entail the use of so-far neglected methodologies, such as grounded theory and historical case studies. Finally, scholars should explore different theoretical mechanisms underlying the moderating effect of career age, with the objective of developing a more comprehensive theoretical framework.

REFERENCES

Agrawal, A., Goldfarb, A., & Teodoridis, F. 2016. Understanding the changing structure of scientific inquiry. *American Economic Journal: Applied Economics*, 8: 100–128.

Ahuja, G., & Lampert, C.M. 2001. Entrepreneurship in the large corporation: A longitudinal study of how established firms create breakthrough inventions. *Strategic Management Journal*, 22: 521–543.

Amabile, T.M. 1983. The social psychology of creativity: A componential conceptualization. *Journal of Personality and Social Psychology*, 45: 357–376.

Amabile, T.M. 1996. *Creativity in context*. Boulder, CO: Westview Press.

Amabile, T.M., Barsade, S.G., Mueller, J.S., & Staw, B.M. 2005. Affect and creativity at work. *Administrative Science Quarterly*, 50: 367–403.

Amabile, T.M., & Conti, R. 1999. Changes in the work environment for creativity during downsizing. *Academy of Management Journal*, 42: 630–640.

Amabile, T.M., Conti, R., Coon, H., Lazenby, J., & Herron, M. 1996. Assessing the work environment for creativity. *Academy of Management Journal*, 39: 1154–1184.

Amabile, T., & Kramer, S. 2011. *The progress principle: Using small wins to ignite joy, engagement, and creativity at work*. Boston, MA: Harvard Business Press.

Amabile, T.M. & Mueller, J.S. 2008. Studying creativity, its processes, and its antecedents: An exploration of the componential theory of creativity. In J. Zhou & C.E. Shalley (eds), *Handbook of organizational creativity*: 33–64. New York: Lawrence Erlbaum.

Amabile, T.M., & Pratt, M.G. 2016. The dynamic componential model of creativity and innovation in organizations: Making progress, making meaning. *Research in Organizational Behavior*, 36: 157–183.

Anderson, T., & Bidwell, M. 2019. Outside insiders: understanding the role of contracting in the careers of managerial workers. *Organization Science*, 30: 1000–1029.

Audia, P.G., & Goncalo, J.A. 2007. Past success and creativity over time: A study of inventors in the hard disk drive industry. *Management Science*, 53: 1–15.

Azoulay, P., Graff Zivin, J.S., & Wang, J. 2010. Superstar extinction. *Quarterly Journal of Economics*, 125: 549–589.

Barnett, W.P., & Miner, A.S. 1992. Standing on the shoulders of others: Career interdependence in job mobility. *Administrative Science Quarterly*, 37: 262–281.

Bartlett, F.C. 1958. *Thinking*. London: Allen & Unwin.

Belkhouja, M., & Yoon, H.D. 2018. How does openness influence the impact of a scholar's research? An analysis of business scholars' citations over their careers. *Research Policy*, 47: 2037–2047.

Cattani, G., & Ferriani, S. 2008. A core/periphery perspective on individual creative performance: Social networks and cinematic achievement in the Hollywood film industry. *Organization Science*, 19: 824–844.

Cattani, G., Ferriani, S., & Allison, P.D. 2014. Insiders, outsiders, and the struggle for consecration in cultural fields: A core–periphery perspective. *American Sociological Review*, 79: 258–281.

Cattani, G., Ferriani, S., & Lanza, A. 2017. Deconstructing the outsider puzzle: The legitimation journey of novelty. *Organization Science*, 28: 965–992.

Cirillo, B., Brusoni, S., & Valentini, G. 2014. The rejuvenation of inventors through corporate spinouts. *Organization Science*, 25: 1764–1784.

Csikszentmihályi, M. 1999. Implications of a systems perspective for the study of creativity. In R.J. Sternberg (ed.), *Handbook of creativity*: 313–335. New York: Cambridge University Press.

Dane, E. 2010. Reconsidering the trade-off between expertise and flexibility: A cognitive entrenchment perspective. *Academy of Management Review*, 35: 579–603.

Dennis, W. 1958. The age decrement in outstanding scientific contributions: Fact or artifact? *American Psychologist*, 13: 457–460.

Dennis, W. 1966. Creative productivity between the ages of 20 and 80 years. *Journal of Gerontology*, 21: 1–8.

Dokko, G., Tosti-Kharas, J., & Barbulescu, R. 2019. An interdisciplinary review of theories used in career studies. In H. Gunz, M. Lazarova, & W. Meinhofer (eds), *The Routledge companion to career studies*: 25–41. London: Routledge.

Dweck, C.S., & Leggett, E.L. 1988. A social-cognitive approach to motivation and personality. *Psychological Review*, 95: 256–273.

Eubanks, D.L., Palanski, M.E., Swart, J., Hammond, M.M., & Oguntebi, J. 2016. Creativity in early and established career: Insights into multi-level drivers from Nobel Prize winners. *Journal of Creative Behavior*, 50: 229–251.

Feist, G.J. 1993. A structural model of scientific eminence. *Psychological Science*, 4: 366–371.

Feist, G.J. 1998. A meta-analysis of personality in scientific and artistic creativity. *Personality and Social Psychology Review*, 2: 290–309.

Feldman D.C. 1989. Socialization, resocialization, and training: Reframing the research agenda. In I.L. Goldstein (ed.), *Training and development in organizations*: 376–416. San Francisco, CA: Jossey-Bass.

Fetzer, G., Harrison, S., Rouse, B., & Innis, B. (2019). The story of my life: Interpretations of early experiences and creativity over the career. *Academy of Management Proceedings*, 2019(1): 19217.

Frensch, P.A., & Sternberg, R.J. 1989. Expertise and intelligent thinking: When is it worse to know better. *Advances in the Psychology of Human Intelligence*, 5: 157–188.

Galenson, D.W. (2005). *Old masters and young geniuses: The two life cycles of artistic creativity*. Princeton, NJ: Princeton University Press.

Galenson, D.W., & Weinberg, B.A. 2001. Creating modern art: The changing careers of painters in France from impressionism to cubism. *American Economic Review*, 91: 1063–1071.

Galton, F. 1869. *Hereditary genius*, 2nd edn. London: Macmillan.

Godart, F.C., & Galunic, C. 2019. Explaining the popularity of cultural elements: Networks, culture, and the structural embeddedness of high fashion trends. *Organization Science*, 30: 151–168.

Gottfried, A.E., Fleming, J.S., & Gottfried, A.W. 2001. Continuity of academic intrinsic motivation from childhood through late adolescence: A longitudinal study. *Journal of Educational Psychology*, 93: 3–13.

Guillén, L., & Kunze, F. 2019. When age does not harm innovative behavior and perceptions of competence: Testing interdepartmental collaboration as a social buffer. *Human Resource Management*, 58: 301–316.

Hagtvedt, L.P., Dossinger, K., Harrison, S.H., & Huang, L. 2019. Curiosity made the cat more creative: Specific curiosity as a driver of creativity. *Organizational Behavior and Human Decision Processes*, 150: 1–13.

Hargadon, A.B., & Douglas, Y. 2001. When innovations meet institutions: Edison and the design of the electric light. *Administrative Science Quarterly*, 46: 476–501.

Jaques, E. 1955. Death and the mid-life crisis. *International Journal of Psychoanalysis*, 46: 502–514.

Jones, B.F., & Weinberg, B.A. 2011. Age dynamics in scientific creativity. *Proceedings of the National Academy of Sciences*, 108: 18910–18914.

Kakkar, H., Sivanathan, N., & Pettit, N.C. 2019. The impact of dynamic status changes within competitive rank-ordered hierarchies. *Proceedings of the National Academy of Sciences*, 116: 23011–23020.

Kroeber, A.L. 1944. *Configurations of culture growth*. Berkeley, CA: University of California Press.

Kuhn, T.S. 1962. *The structure of scientific revolutions*. Chicago, IL: University of Chicago.

Kulik, C.T., Ryan, S., Harper, S., & George, G. 2014. Aging populations and management. *Academy of Management Journal*, 57: 929–935.

Lehman, H.C. 1942. The creative years: oil paintings, etchings, and architectural works. *Psychological Review*, 49: 19–42.

Lehman, H.C. 1953. *Age and achievement*. Princeton, NJ: Princeton University Press.

Lehman, H.C. 1954. Men's creative production rate at different ages and in different countries. *Scientific Monthly*, 78: 321–326.

Lehman, H.C. 1958. The chemist's most creative years. *Science*, 127: 1213–1222.

Lehman, H.C. 1960. The age decrement in outstanding scientific creativity. *American Psychologist*, 15: 128–134.

Liu, D., Jiang, K., Shalley, C.E., Keem, S., & Zhou, J. (2016). Motivational mechanisms of employee creativity: A meta-analytic examination and theoretical extension of the creativity literature. *Organizational Behavior and Human Decision Processes*, 137: 236–263.

Magai, C., Consedine, N.S., Krivoshekova, Y.S., Kudadjie-Gyamfi, E., & McPherson, R. 2006. Emotion experience and expression across the adult life span: Insights from a multimodal assessment study. *Psychology and Aging*, 21: 303–317.

Mainemelis, C., Nolas, S.M., & Tsirogianni, S. 2016. Surviving a boundaryless creative career: The case of Oscar-nominated film directors, 1967–2014. *Journal of Management Inquiry*, 25: 262–285.

Mannucci, P.V., & Yong, K. 2018. The differential impact of knowledge depth and knowledge breadth on creativity over individual careers. *Academy of Management Journal*, 61: 1741–1763.

March, J.G. 1991. Exploration and exploitation in organizational learning. *Organization Science*, 2: 71–87.

McCrae, R.R., Arenberg, D., & Costa, P.T. 1987. Declines in divergent thinking with age: Cross-sectional, longitudinal, and cross-sequential analyses. *Psychology and Aging*, 2: 130–137.

Mueller, J., Melwani, S., & Goncalo, J.A. 2012. The bias against creativity: Why people desire but reject creative ideas. *Psychological Science*, 23: 13–17.

Mueller, J., Melwani, S., Loewenstein, J., & Deal, J.J. (2018). Reframing the decision-makers' dilemma: Towards a social context model of creative idea recognition. *Academy of Management Journal*, 61: 94–110.

Niu, W., & Sternberg, R. 2002. Contemporary studies on the concept of creativity: The East and the West. *Journal of Creative Behavior*, 36(4): 269–288.

Otis, N., Grouzet, F.M., & Pelletier, L.G. 2005. Latent motivational change in an academic setting: A 3-year longitudinal study. *Journal of Educational Psychology*, 97: 170–183.

Over, R. 1982. The durability of scientific reputation. *Journal of the History of the Behavioral Sciences*, 18, 53–61.

Parke, M.R., Seo, M.G., & Sherf, E.N. 2015. Regulating and facilitating: The role of emotional intelligence in maintaining and using positive affect for creativity. *Journal of Applied Psychology*, 100: 917–934.

Perry-Smith, J.E. 2006. Social yet creative: The role of social relationships in facilitating individual creativity. *Academy of Management Journal*, 49: 85–101.

Perry-Smith, J.E., & Mannucci, P.V. 2015. Social networks, creativity, and entrepreneurship. In C.E. Shalley, M.A. Hitt, & J. Zhou (eds), *The Oxford handbook of creativity, innovation, and entrepreneurship*: 205–224. New York: Oxford University Press.

Perry-Smith, J.E., & Mannucci, P.V. 2017. From creativity to innovation: The social network drivers of the four phases of the idea journey. *Academy of Management Review*, 42: 53–79.

Perry-Smith, J., & Mannucci, P.V. 2020. From ugly duckling to swan: a social network perspective on novelty recognition and creativity. In D.J. Brass & S. Borgatti (eds), *Social networks at work*: 177–199. London: Routledge.

Quetelet, A. 1968 [1835]. *A treatise on man and the development of his faculties*. New York: Franklin.

Remnick, D. 2015. Bob Dylan and the "hot hand." *New Yorker*, November 9. http://www.newyorker.com/culture/cultural-comment/bob-dylan-and-the-hot-hand. Retrieved December 2019.

Roe, A. 1972. Patterns of productivity of scientists. *Science*, 176: 940–941.

Rosengren, K.E. 1985. Time and literary fame. *Poetics*, 14: 157–172.

Rouse, E.D. 2020. Where you end and I begin: Understanding intimate co-creation. *Academy of Management Review*, 45(1), 181–204.

Sgourev, S.V. 2013. How Paris gave rise to Cubism (and Picasso): Ambiguity and fragmentation in radical innovation. *Organization Science*, 24: 1601–1617.

Shalley, C.E., Zhou, J., & Oldham, G.R. 2004. The effects of personal and contextual characteristics on creativity: where should we go from here? *Journal of Management*, 30: 933–958.

Shapiro, J.S. 2005. *1599: A year in the life of William Shakespeare*. London: Faber & Faber.

Shapiro, J.S. 2015. *The year of Lear: Shakespeare in 1606*. New York: Simon & Schuster.

Simonton, D.K. 1975a. Age and literary creativity: A cross-cultural and transhistorical survey. *Journal of Cross-Cultural Psychology*, 6: 259–277.

Simonton, D.K. 1975b. Sociocultural context of individual creativity: A transhistorical time-series analysis. *Journal of Personality and Social Psychology*, 32: 1119–1133.

Simonton, D.K. 1977. Creative productivity, age, and stress: A biographical time-series analysis of 10 classical composers. *Journal of Personality and Social Psychology*, 35: 791–804.

Simonton, D.K. 1980. Thematic fame, melodic originality, and musical zeitgeist: A biographical and transhistorical content analysis. *Journal of Personality and Social Psychology*, 38: 972–983.

Simonton, D.K. 1984. Artistic creativity and interpersonal relationships across and within generations. *Journal of Personality and Social Psychology*, 46: 1273–1286.

Simonton, D.K. 1988a. Age and outstanding achievement: What do we know after a century of research? *Psychological Bulletin*, 104: 251–267.

Simonton, D.K. 1988b. Galtonian genius, Kroeberian configurations, and emulation: A generational time-series analysis of Chinese civilization. *Journal of Personality and Social Psychology*, 55: 230–238.

Simonton, D.K. 1991. Latent-variable models of posthumous reputation: A quest for Galton's G. *Journal of Personality and Social Psychology*, 60: 607–619.

Simonton, D.K. 1997. Creative productivity: A predictive and explanatory model of career trajectories and landmarks. *Psychological Review*, 104: 66–89.

Simonton, D.K. 2000a. Creative development as acquired expertise: Theoretical issues and an empirical test. *Developmental Review*, 20: 283–318.

Simonton, D.K. 2000b. Creativity: Cognitive, personal, developmental, and social aspects. *American Psychologist*, 55: 151–158.

Simonton, D.K. 2003. Scientific creativity as constrained stochastic behavior: The integration of product, person, and process perspectives. *Psychological Bulletin*, 129: 475–494.

Simonton, D.K. 2007a. Creative life cycles in literature: Poets versus novelists or conceptualists versus experimentalists? *Psychology of Aesthetics, Creativity, and the Arts*, 1(3): 133–139.

Simonton, D.K. 2007b. The Creative Process in Picasso's Guernica Sketches: Monotonic Improvements versus Nonmonotonic Variants. *Creativity Research Journal*, 19: 329–344.

Soda, G., Mannucci, P.V., & Burt, R.S. 2018. *Networks, creativity, and time: Staying creative through time and space.* Paper presented at the annual meetings of the Academy of Management, Chicago, IL.

Teodoridis, F., Bikard, M., & Vakili, K. 2019. Creativity at the knowledge frontier: The impact of specialization in fast-and slow-paced domains. *Administrative Science Quarterly*, 64: 894–927.

Weinberg, B.A., & Galenson, D.W. 2019. Creative careers: The life cycles of Nobel laureates in economics. *De Economist*, 167: 221–239.

Winner, E. 2004. Art history can trade insights with the sciences. *Chronicle of Higher Education*, 50(43): B10–B10.

Yong, K., Mannucci, P.V., & Lander, M.W. 2020. Fostering creativity across countries: The moderating effect of cultural bundles on creativity. *Organizational Behavior and Human Decision Processes*, 157: 1–45.

Yong, K., Sauer, S.J., & Mannix, E.A. 2014. Conflict and creativity in interdisciplinary teams. *Small Group Research*, 45: 266–289.

Zhou, J., & Hoever, I.J. 2014. Research on workplace creativity: A review and redirection. *Annual Review of Organizational Psychology and Organizational Behavior*, 1: 333–359.

13. Unraveling the bias against novelty: guiding the study of our tendency to desire but reject the new

Jennifer Mueller and Yidan Yin

Novel ideas – ideas that depart from the status quo – fuel organizations' ability to differentiate, improve and compete (Amabile & Pratt, 2016). Yet, rising evidence shows that organizational decision-makers, those with responsibility to determine or recommend which ideas should remain in an organization (Csikszentmihalyi, 1999), in a host of domains, reject novel ideas even when novelty is prized (Mueller et al., 2018). For example, one study found that after crowdsourcing ideas to solve a problem, gatekeepers rejected ideas requiring them to employ distant knowledge to assess and instead embraced familiar solutions (thus negating the need to crowdsource in the first place) (Piezunka & Dahlander, 2015). Patent officers were more likely to reject patents that spanned technological domains (Ferguson & Carnabuci, 2017). Grant reviewers rejected novel proposals controlling for proposal quality (Boudreau et al., 2016). Criscuolo et al. (2017) identified that selection panels were more likely to reject research and development (R&D) projects with high levels of novelty. Siler et al. (2015) showed that 12 of 14 breakthrough papers were desk rejected by editors from elite medical journals, only to be published later in lower-tier journals. In sum, an ever-increasing body of research is showing that decision-makers (for example, editors, reviewers, patent officers, gatekeepers) chronically reject the most novel ideas even when novel ideas are desired and high in technical quality. This suggests that decision-makers, who are often experts in a given domain, can chronically reject novel ideas even in contexts where the primary aim is to cultivate them.

This bias against novelty presents a puzzle that has only recently received research attention. Prior creativity research has largely been focused on factors which aid the generation of creative (novel and useful) ideas (Anderson et al., 2014), with relatively less focus on how organizations can improve the evaluative tactics enacted by those with decision-making responsibility; those who determine which employees' ideas to advance and further develop (Mueller et al., 2018; Zhou et al., 2019). The literature on idea evaluation has focused on how a person might assess their own ideas (Licuanan et al., 2007) or how people might assess others' ideas (Berg, 2016), without necessarily examining how the process of evaluation might change when a person has responsibility for determining whether that very idea should be retained by the organization and accountability for whether the idea achieves a specific goal (for example, makes a profit, addresses a problem). Further, research has not examined what it means for a decision-making role to be intertwined with the leadership role. Leadership roles often include responsibility for evaluating subordinates' new ideas, and so require that leaders enact the decision-making role in this interpersonal context where relationship development with the subordinate is part of the evaluation process. On the one hand, this omission is surprising, as one study found that the activities of those with decision-making responsibility (for example, suits) contributed to a far greater percentage of variance in organizational performance than those without decision-making responsibility (for example, innovators) (Mollick, 2012). On the other hand, this omission makes sense from a practical perspective as it is very difficult to gain access to and collect data from organizational decision-makers whose activities are seen as proprietary and whose time is highly guarded (Knudsen & Levinthal, 2007).

Importantly, recent research has unveiled that participants in decision-making roles, roles with responsibility for determining which ideas to resource, evaluate ideas differently because they experience a stronger sense of accountability and responsibility during evaluation relative to participants who were not assigned decision-making roles (Mueller et al., 2018). Decision-making responsibility (for example, decision-making roles) can evoke accountability pressures that alter the goals and subsequent evaluative processes in ways that increase the likelihood of decision-makers rejecting creative ideas (Mueller et al., 2018). However, no research to date has examined how those in decision-making roles overcome a bias against novelty when they are accountable for the success or failure of the ideas they are evaluating. Studying how those with decision-making responsibility evaluate ideas they are accountable for is key to building a broader understanding of how creative ideas make an impact in organizations. Further, because prior research suggests that the decision-making role bridges the creative idea generation and idea implementation stages (Kanter, 1988) – two key stages of the innovation process – examining how decision-makers overcome a bias against novelty can provide an important lens linking the literatures on creativity and innovation, which have largely remained separate (Perry-Smith & Mannucci, 2017).

Critically, this chapter discusses the bias against novelty (not creativity). Focusing on novelty as opposed to creativity allows us to achieve three objectives. Firstly, it allows us to more seamlessly integrate the literatures on innovation and creativity, since both discuss novelty and how novelty is evaluated, but from very different perspectives which have not been well integrated to date. Secondly, scholars have identified that novelty is the distinguishing characteristic of a creative idea beyond whether an idea is useful (Diedrich et al., 2015); research has shown that people sometimes exhibit an aversion to novelty, but has not provided evidence that people exhibit an aversion to usefulness. Hence, we wish to focus on the "novelty" aspect of creativity which is most likely to evoke negative evaluations of ideas. Thirdly, we seek to understand the early-phase evaluations enacted by decision-makers as this is when the bias against novelty is most likely to happen (Harvey & Mueller, 2021) and when the usefulness of ideas (hence the true creativity of ideas) is relatively unknown. By focusing on why people might exhibit a bias against novelty (rather than creativity) and how they can overcome it, we provide one avenue towards understanding this early-phase evaluative process that might inform the downstream creativity of a product.

The goal of this chapter is to integrate perspectives from the creativity, innovation, entrepreneurship, and behavioral decision-making literatures to more deeply explore what the bias against novelty is, why and when it happens, and what people can do to overcome it. To approach this question, we first explain why and when people have a bias against novelty, and then review two distinct approaches to studying and thinking about the bias against novelty: the outcome- and process-based approaches. We then follow with a discussion of what the prior literature says about how decision-makers (that is, those with gatekeeping responsibility to determine which ideas are retained by the organization) can overcome this tendency to reject novel ideas. The chapter concludes with a call for more research to help unveil the mechanisms explaining when and why those in decision-making roles exhibit a bias against novelty, and how to overcome it. We also provide recommendations for future researchers to employ when attempting to understand and ultimately help those in decision-making roles to overcome a bias against novelty.

DEFINING NOVELTY

Novelty has been defined as a change from current practice or the status quo (Amabile, 1988). In the innovation literature, novelty is identified as a product of recombination (Lee, 2001) and described as a prerequisite for innovation as well as organizational learning and change (Rosenkopf & McGrath, 2011). Critically, novelty is different from creativity, which is defined as a change from the status quo that is inherently useful. While people implicitly believe labeling an idea "new" or novel has an inherently positive connotation (for example, people do not colloquially say an idea is "new" to mean it is potentially bad) (Loewenstein & Mueller, 2016), the scholarly theories propose that novelty is a dimension that is separate and distinct from usefulness. Creativity is said to happen when novelty has met a threshold for usefulness, and novelty is more diagnostic than usefulness of whether an idea is creative (Diedrich et al., 2015).

One of the first hints that people held a bias against novelty started to emerge in the creativity literature when researchers noticed that the novelty and usefulness dimensions were sometimes negatively correlated, especially when usefulness was operationalized as feasibility (Rietzschel et al., 2010). The theme that novel ideas are sometimes viewed to be less useful was first articulated by Staw (1995) in his classic article, "Why no one really wants creativity," who pointed out that novelty is largely a nuisance for managers, offering little upside. Staw argued that novelty can disrupt cultural norms and coordination efforts that are carefully planned, and place managers in unsafe political territory. Indeed, work in the innovation domain has noted that relative to proven ideas with little novelty, novel ideas are more likely to produce errors and fail in the short term (Klein & Knight, 2005). Classic articles have long noted that if new ideas fail, those with decision-making responsibility who endorsed them face the risk of losing status, reputation, and job security (Ford & Gioia, 2000). So, while novel ideas allow for a host of long-term positive outcomes including corporate renewal and competitive advantage, in the short term, novel ideas can also bring a host of negative outcomes for those who embrace them.

EVALUATING NOVELTY

Idea Evaluation

Idea evaluation, the assessment of an idea by individuals and groups, is the underlying process that people engage in to determine whether an idea is valuable, creative, and can solve the problem at hand. In the creativity literature, idea evaluation is described as a process whereby people focus on the properties of the idea; noting that when ideas have features which match problem requirements, people will evaluate the idea positively (McIntosh et al., 2019). For this reason, classic scholarship in the creativity domain has identified cognitive aspects of evaluation most closely linked to whether an idea is perceived to be useful, viable, and feasible (Campbell, 1960; Mumford, 1999; Runco & Smith, 1992). From an idea evaluation perspective, the extent to which an idea is novel may be relevant to evaluation only if the novelty itself is perceived to be useful. For example, in an advertising context, novelty may be seen as useful if the novelty comes in the form of a surprise, which grabs consumer attention (Loewenstein et al., 2011). In a product development context, novelty may be seen as useful to the extent it differentiates a product and provides consumers with a unique reason to buy a product (Schilling & Hill, 1998). In a medical context, novelty may be seen as useful to the extent that it provides a new pathway where the path of least resistance or common approach will likely fail (Edmondson, 1999). In each of these contexts, novelty can be evaluated positively when the novelty itself is seen to enhance an idea's usefulness.

A key assumption of the literature on idea evaluation is that an idea's usefulness is knowable, so the goal of idea evaluation is to accurately identify the true level of usefulness for each idea in a consideration set. For this reason, theories in creativity and innovation have described the process of evaluation as involving uncertainty reduction: reducing uncertainty around whether the idea will work in the intended way (Drazin et al., 1999; Ford et al., 2008). Importantly, a large body of research from a diverse range of fields has shown that uncertainty is an aversive state that people strive to avoid (Berger, 1986; Weary et al., 2001; Whitson & Galinsky, 2008). Taken together, the theory of idea evaluation proposes that, on average, people will value ideas that have highly certain use, and reject ideas with uncertain use because uncertainty is a state that people attempt to avoid.

Evaluating Novelty in Organizational Contexts

Work in the creativity domain also briefly describes how evaluation is structured within the broader organizational context where the task of evaluation is assigned to specific individuals with decision-making roles. In his systems model of creativity, Csikszentmihalyi (1988) discusses the role of decision-makers or gatekeepers: those who determine which ideas are retained by the organizational system. At the organizational level, evaluation is commonly structured hierarchically by allocating decision-making roles to a small number of organizational members. Decision-making roles are pervasive throughout the creative process in the form of "catchers" (Elsbach & Kramer, 2003), search consortia and R&D selection panels (e.g., Criscuolo et al., 2017), c-suite executives and boards of directors (e.g., Bantel & Jackson, 1989; Forbes & Milliken, 1999; West & Anderson, 1996), leaders who assess subordinate ideas (Murnighan & Conlon, 1991), and other members tasked to recommend a course of action (e.g., De Dreu & West, 2001; Van de Ven & Delbecq, 1974). Indeed, the innovation literature identifies that those in decision-making roles are the critical bridge between creative idea generation and implementation efforts (Kanter, 1988). Other work shows that decisions made by those with decision-making responsibility account for a large percentage of variance in organizational performance, substantially larger than the percentage of variance in organizational performance accounted for by those in creative idea generation roles (Mollick, 2012).

Importantly, the evaluative processes enacted by those in decision-making roles may differ significantly from the evaluative process often studied in the creativity literature, where laboratory participants are prompted to evaluate ideas with the aim of "selecting" the best idea to implement in a single evaluative session. Critically, real-world decision-makers assess the same ideas over time, whereas most laboratory studies examine one-shot evaluation of ideas where evaluators do not have formal decision-making authority. The innovation literature provides some insights into how the process of evaluation unfolds for those in decision-making roles in the field. For example, in a stage-gate context, an idea necessarily goes through many stages of evaluation and gates before it has developed sufficiently to warrant a decision-maker's recommendation towards implementation or mass production (Cooper, 2006). In the context of a journal, papers often go through many rounds of revision and resubmission before associate editors recommend that the journal publishes a paper. In R&D contexts, those with decision-making authority engage in many phases of evaluating a project over many years before an idea is green-lighted for mass production (Criscuolo et al., 2017). This is especially true for complex ideas aimed to solve messy and ill-defined problems that may take many iterations to evaluate and understand (Harvey & Mueller, 2021). In sum, the evaluation process that decision-makers undergo does ultimately result in a selection decision to implement an idea or a recommendation for evaluation by a higher level of decision-makers; however, this decision often occurs after many earlier-phase decisions have already been made to keep the idea alive.

There are two additional differences between the idea evaluation process in the field where decision-makers evaluate ideas over time, and the process in laboratory contexts where the evaluation occurs in a single instance. Firstly, unlike a one-shot act of evaluation in the laboratory, evaluating ideas in the field often involves interpersonal activities such as giving feedback and providing recommendations. Field studies have shown that ideas being considered during later-phase evaluation are higher in quality than those considered at an earlier phase (Siler et al., 2015). The quality of ideas tends to improve over time, because decision-makers not only winnow out low-quality ideas but also make recommendations and provide feedback to those who generated the idea (Ford & Gioia, 2000; Harrison & Rouse, 2015). Secondly, because decision-makers in the field provide feedback for ideas, the ideas themselves change over time, often in ways that decision-makers cannot predict at first. This means that the quality of ideas initially assessed may be quite different from the quality of ideas after prolonged development. One study confirmed that experts' assessments of idea quality early on did not reliably predict objective assessments of idea quality later on, presumably because the ideas themselves had changed and morphed over the course of development (Huang & Pearce, 2015). Hence, while laboratory studies have provided many fruitful insights into the process of creative idea evaluation, this process may have limited applicability to evaluation enacted by decision-makers in the field, where interpersonal activities are likely involved and an idea's ultimate level of quality cannot be accurately determined with an initial assessment.

The process of evaluation enacted by decision-makers in the field also shows a troubling trend. Research shows that an initial set of ideas is likely to have the highest range of novelty, because decision-makers tend to winnow out the most novel ideas in the consideration set over time even when novelty is desired (Kornish & Ulrich, 2011; Siler et al., 2015; Siler & Strang, 2017). This pattern may signal that decision-makers exhibit a bias against novelty: decision-makers reject novel ideas during the initial phases of consideration and give preference for ideas with relatively low levels of novelty. Thus, to understand when and why decision-makers exhibit a bias against novelty, it may not make sense to study later-phase evaluations that veer towards implementation, as this is when the most novel ideas have already been winnowed out of the idea set. Instead, it makes more sense to study early phases of idea evaluation, when plentiful novel ideas face the highest likelihood of rejection.

UNDERSTANDING BIAS AGAINST NOVELTY

Why do People Exhibit a Bias Against Novelty?

The creativity literature has identified a central tension between novelty and usefulness: the more novel an idea, the more uncertainty exists about whether the idea is useful and will solve the problem in predictable ways (Ford & Sullivan, 2005; Miron-Spektor & Beenen, 2015; Mueller et al., 2012). This central tension between novelty and the predictability of an idea's use lies at the heart of why people often reject novel ideas.

When a person has a goal around accurately diagnosing an idea's usefulness in the moment, they often prioritize predictability and sidestep the tension between novelty and predictability of idea usefulness to choose ideas that they are more confident will indeed be useful. There are three reasons why people prioritize predictability of idea use over novelty. Firstly, decades of research in the domain of social cognition has identified that people often behave like "cognitive misers" and exhibit a desire for cognitive economy, processing information quickly and efficiently in ways that allow them to navigate the world with relative ease (Fiske & Taylor, 1991). Schema incongruity theory notes that assessing novel ideas takes significantly more time and effort relative to assessing ideas that are already proven and so lacking in novelty, thereby suggesting that people are more likely to choose an idea with relatively low novelty because low-novelty ideas take less cognitive effort to assess. Secondly, Tversky & Kahneman (1991) identified that people give more weight to losses than to equal gains, tend to regret action relative to inaction (Kahneman et al., 1982), and experience more regret when a decision changes the status quo than when maintaining the status quo (Ritov & Baron, 1992). Because the perceived cost of implementing a novel idea and changing from standard practice can carry more weight than the potential benefits of the change (Moshinsky & Bar-Hillel, 2010), people prefer ideas that are currently in use and so have high predictability, to novel ideas that are less predictable. Finally, a large literature has found that people generally consider uncertainty to be an aversive state and strive to avoid it (Hogg & Mullin, 1999; Weary et al., 2001; Whitson & Galinsky, 2008). Choosing an idea that is novel but less predictable can evoke anxiety and feelings of conflict (Miron-Spektor & Beenen, 2015). Hence, evaluators may be motivated to reduce their feelings of anxiety and conflict by choosing ideas that are less novel but are more predictable.

In support of people prioritizing predictability over novelty, the idea evaluation literature has identified that when first evaluating an idea, evaluators tend to focus exclusively on whether ideas are of high quality and useful (McIntosh et al., 2019), assuming that idea novelty is mainly relevant to the earlier idea generation phase of the creative process (Paulus & Yang, 2000). This view suggests that if evaluators focus only on accurately evaluating idea usefulness, they will end up choosing proven ideas with lower novelty, because they will downgrade ideas whose usefulness is unproven or unknown and prioritize ideas whose usefulness is known (Blair & Mumford, 2007; Licuanan et al., 2007; Rietzschel et al., 2010). Indeed, research shows that, left to their own devices, groups and individuals tend to prefer ideas with relatively low novelty and high usefulness (Blair & Mumford, 2007; Putman & Paulus, 2009; Rietzschel et al., 2010). In one study, when experimenters told participants in brainstorming groups to select the best idea, they chose ideas with high usefulness and low novelty (Rietzschel et al., 2010). But even when experimenters told participants to select an idea that was both novel and useful, participants still chose ideas with a moderate level of novelty over ideas with a high level of novelty.

If perceived predictability of an idea's use – or the extent to which a person views a product as safe and likely to work – is powerfully related to whether people will choose an idea, then understanding what makes an idea seem "predictable" can provide one lens through which to understand when novel ideas are likely to be rejected. Research suggests that one key attribute people look to in determining whether an idea is "predictable" is whether the product is also familiar: the more familiar an idea, the more a person will view the idea as likely to work and provide value (Fox & Levav, 2000). Schema congruity theory unveils the cognitive process underlying how people determine their familiarity with and subsequent liking for an idea (Mandler, 1982). Schemas are mental representations that a person has about the cues and features relevant to a given category (for example, product or idea). An established schema is one that a person has already been exposed to and is familiar with. An idea or product that matches with a person's existing schema is likely to evoke a moderately positive evaluation; an idea inconsistent with a person's pre-existing schema is likely to evoke arousal; an idea that is radically inconsistent with an existing schema is likely to evoke a negative evaluation because it is difficult to understand and process.

Another key attribute that people look to when determining whether an idea is predictable, and thus safe to use, is whether the idea is currently in use. While actual (or mere) exposure can increase perceived familiarity with something and corresponding liking of the familiar (Zajonc, 2001), work on the status quo bias has found that liking can occur even when a person has not necessarily been exposed to the idea before. That is, people can prefer an idea merely because they are told it currently exists, in that others have used the idea before and are continuing to use it now (Eidelman et al., 2009). And the longer an idea has existed and been in use, the more people will like the idea (Eidelman et al., 2010). One reason why people prefer product features that are already in use is that these features fit with the widely held implicit theory of "survival of the fittest" (Eidelman & Crandall, 2012). That is, if ideas have existed for a long time, they must have stood the test of time because they have proven value.

Another way in which people determine whether something is safe and predictable is whether the idea conforms to a standard reference point. People may use standard practice as a reference point and exhibit loss aversion when considering whether to deviate from standard practice to implement new ideas (Ritov & Baron, 1992). This notion that reference points can shift how people perceive a change from standard practice can partially explain why expertise can sometimes evoke a bias against novelty. Deep expertise in a single domain may prompt those evaluating ideas to focus on how new ideas differ from reference points (for example, film) in ways that emphasize whether the new idea will fail when assessed on traditional criteria; criteria that are safe, proven, and vetted, but often less relevant when assessing the viability of new ideas. Research shows that domain experts can downgrade new products relative to consumers (Escoffier & McKelvey, 2015; Kornish & Ulrich, 2014), and so inaccurately predict the market. In a now classic study, Paige Moreau and colleagues examined how experts and novices in film assessed the digital camera, finding that experts in film assessed the digital camera as having significantly lower product viability relative to novices in film (Moreau et al., 2001). Importantly, they found that experts downgraded the viability of the digital camera because it performed poorly on a traditional criterion: picture quality. While experts were correct in the short term that the earliest digital cameras have significantly lower picture quality relative to film, novices were also correct; and more importantly, correct in the long term, because they assessed the viability of the digital camera in terms of immediacy and low cost of film development, two non-traditional criteria of the day that were prioritized by consumers in the long run. Importantly, though, Moreau and colleagues found in a second study that expertise in both film and scanner technology increased expert assessment of the digital camera's viability. Other studies in the domain of entrepreneurship have also found that the use of traditional criteria can also contribute to experts devaluing the unique capabilities of new ideas that differ from the capabilities of older technologies (Grégoire et al., 2010).

A fourth attribute contributing to when people view a product as safe and predictable is whether an idea has social approval cues: cues that provide evidence of social acceptability (Cialdini, 1998), widely viewed legitimacy (Rao et al., 2008), and potential for success (Salganik & Watts, 2009). Social approval cues convey not only that an idea is in use, but also that the idea is widely used, liked, and endorsed, thereby providing the veneer that an idea will solve a problem in a predictable way. Prior work has shown that social approval is "most influential when decision-makers are uncertain about the value of a course of action, and when able to observe the actions of similar others" (Rao et al., 2001: 504). This perspective suggests that when evaluating novel ideas – ideas with uncertain use – social approval cues may be weighted heavily in assessments. The problem arises because novel ideas often lack social approval as they are often too early-stage (Schilling & Hill, 1998); further, social approval cues are "fool's gold" or noisy indicators of idea quality when ideas are new (Rao et al., 2001). For that matter, novel ideas, by definition, have not been in use for a long period of time and are unlikely to have existed before. Whether or not an idea is used and approved by a wide range of people is relevant not only to decisions to select the idea, but also to assessments of whether the idea is creative.

Taken together, when people are confronted with the tension between novelty and predictability of an idea's use, they often decide to avoid the tension and choose the predictable option with lower novelty because of their desire for cognitive economy, and aversion to loss and uncertainty. Social approval cues, existence, familiarity, and the length of time an idea has existed, are features that indicate ideas are predictably safe, useful, and viable, but they are features that novel ideas tend to lack.

When do People Experience a Bias Against Novelty?

If the central tension between novelty and predictability of an idea's use is at the heart of why people can reject novel ideas, then unveiling contexts where this tension is especially acute and difficult to resolve can help us to pinpoint when people might be most likely to exhibit a bias against novelty. Importantly, the tension between novelty and predictability of an idea's use may not be felt as acutely in all contexts.

Indeed, in some contexts, even though both novelty and predictability of idea usefulness are highly desired, people have an opportunity to confront and reduce their uncertainty around idea use. One such context is when people can both generate and implement ideas. For example, hackers can quickly and rapidly implement multiple novel solutions to see which best solves a problem (Flowers, 2008). R&D employees with responsibility to implement ideas can quickly develop and test prototypes to determine whether an idea will work (Lifshitz-Assaf, 2017). Entrepreneurs can "fail fast" and implement potential products that they can quickly test with consumers (Tahirsylaj, 2012). Most real-world teams studied in the organizational creativity literature (for example, R&D teams, dance troupes, information technology service projects) are responsible for implementing the ideas they generate (Amabile et al., 1996; Farh et al., 2010; Harrison & Rouse, 2014). To our knowledge, the organizational creativity literature has largely examined employees engaging in tasks where idea generation and idea implementation are both possible, and has not found evidence of a systematic bias against novelty in these contexts.

Individuals and groups may experience a greater sense of tension and stress during idea evaluation when they desire both novel and useful solutions but cannot rapidly prototype novel ideas to reduce the uncertainty around idea use. Research has long noted that when a goal is unattainable – such as reducing uncertainty about whether a novel idea is useful – this creates feelings of stress and negative affect (Lazarus & Folkman, 1984). Importantly, decision-makers are often responsible for evaluating, not implementing ideas. For example, Mueller et al. (2018) identified that individuals in decision-making roles – roles emphasizing responsibility and accountability around identifying which ideas should remain in the organization – were more likely to downgrade the same creative idea if it had low versus high social approval. Critically, individuals who engaged in evaluation but were not in decision-making roles did not assess the same creative idea with high or low social approval differently. Mueller et al. (2018) identified that decision-making roles evoked feelings of responsibility for making accurate decisions, as well as accountability to justify decisions in a context where implementing and testing were not possible; these pressures contributed to those in a decision-making role downgrading creative ideas with low social approval.

Following this logic, the earliest phases of idea evaluation, before ideas have been vetted and tested over time, are when uncertainty is highest around whether an idea is useful. If people have an automatic negative reaction to uncertainty, then the earliest phases of evaluation for novel ideas are when ideas are the most likely to be rejected. This suggests that examining a bias against novelty necessarily requires examining the initial moments of evaluation, as the most novel ideas are likely to be winnowed out at an early point in the evaluation process.

Taken together, research suggests that the tension between novelty and predictability of idea use is most acute when idea implementation is not possible, but people have accountability and responsibility for making correct decisions during the earliest phases of idea evaluation. These conditions perfectly describe the structure and design of decision-making roles, gatekeepers responsible for determining which ideas should remain in the organization. If those in decision-making roles are more likely to experience a bias against novelty relative to others in the organization, then this predicts doom for many organizations that desire novelty, as research shows a negative relationship between employee creativity and organizational performance when those in decision-making roles are characterized as avoiding risk and uncertainty (Gong et al., 2013). Thus, a critical domain to study a bias against novelty is not within the ranks of those generating ideas, but within the ranks of those with responsibility for deciding which ideas the organization should endorse.

This view that managerial decision-making is of key importance is not new and has long been discussed in the literature on innovation (Li et al., 2013; Van de Ven, 1986), idea selling (Dutton et al., 2001), and employee voice (Detert & Burris, 2007). A critical point is that managerial attention is a highly valuable but limited resource, and is crucial for pushing through initiatives. Research has shown that failure to gain managerial attention for a given initiative often results in failing to gain endorsement for the initiative (Dutton et al., 2001). To make matters worse, as people rise in a hierarchy, they spend a higher percentage of time in a decision-making role and have more demands on their time and attention (Li et al., 2013). If understanding and assessing novel ideas takes more time and attention relative to understanding and assessing ideas low in novelty, then on average those with the highest level of decision-making responsibility are most likely to reject novel ideas, because they lack the time and attentional resources to appropriately assess novel ideas.

HOW TO STUDY BIAS AGAINST NOVELTY

There are at least two approaches to studying the bias against novelty: the outcome-based and process-based approaches. This section provides an in-depth description of these two approaches to studying the bias against novelty. We will first discuss the outcome-based approach taken by the broader literature examining the bias against novelty, then provide a summation of the emerging literature on the process-based approach.

The Outcome-Based Approach to Studying a Bias Against Novelty

The outcome-based approach focuses on the outcome or discrete decision to reject or accept an idea. It defines the bias against novelty as a discrete decision to reject a novel idea in favor of an idea with less novelty, when the novel idea is objectively useful or valuable and novelty is needed to solve the problem (Boudreau et al., 2016; Criscuolo et al., 2017; Ferguson & Carnabuci, 2017; Piezunka & Dahlander, 2015; Siler et al., 2015; Siler & Strang, 2017). From this perspective, if a decision-maker rejected a novel idea that was not useful in favor of a useful idea that was not novel, this person would have made a correct decision; however, if a decision-maker rejected a novel idea that was useful (and presumably novelty was needed to solve the problem) in favor of a useful idea with low novelty, then the decision would be biased. This framework focuses on the extent to which decision-makers are susceptible to making false negative errors in judgment: rejecting ideas due to an underestimation of their potential success (Berg, 2016). For example, in examining how gatekeepers who aimed to fund innovative medical approaches assessed research grant proposals, Boudreau et al. (2016) found that one standard deviation increase in the novelty of a proposal decreased the rank of a proposal by 4.5 points; this effect held even after controlling for proposal quality. Boudreau et al. (2016) showed that gatekeepers were "biased against novelty" because they discounted novel ideas regardless of proposal quality, in a context where novelty was desired. The key assumption of the outcome-based approach is that whether or not a decision to reject an idea is an error can be determined, because the quality of the idea can be assessed in a way that is objective and not prone to error.

This outcome-based approach to studying the bias against novelty has yielded a host of fruitful papers which have helped to build a mass of research demonstrating that this bias is pervasive and costly for organizations (Berg, 2016; Boudreau et al., 2016; Siler et al., 2015). While intriguing, the outcome-based approach to studying the bias against novelty has several limitations. Most importantly, the outcome-based approach assumes that you can measure the usefulness of an early-phase novel idea. However, for novel ideas that have uncertain usefulness, it is much harder to quantify errors in assessing the usefulness of those ideas before they have been fully implemented. For example, in the Boudreau et al. study cited above, proposal quality was measured in many ways, including the number and kinds of citations the proposal involved, as well as how highly cited the proposal authors were. While clever, inventive, and objective, these measurements of proposal quality do not consider the actual effectiveness (for example, cost/benefit for patient outcomes) of the medical advance. This approach is understandable, because to develop an objective measure of the quality of the medical advance proposed, one would need to fully implement each proposal and assess the cost/benefit of the advance for patients and physicians.

Even though it is not possible in the moment to know whether a new idea that has never been implemented before is truly useful in the long term, it is still possible to employ the outcome method of assessing the bias against novelty, if you can assess a set of ideas and track their development and corresponding decisions to accept or reject them over time and after implementation. For example, Siler et al. (2015) tracked 1008 papers submitted to one of three elite medical journals, of which 772 were desk-rejected from one of the medical journals and 808 were eventually published. This allowed the authors to employ an objective assessment of paper quality: article citations after publication. The authors found that of the 14 most highly cited papers in the set, 12 were initially desk-rejected and eventually published in journals with lower impact factors. The authors suggested that this might reflect editors' difficulty assessing exceptional or unconventional work in the desk-rejection (early) phase of evaluation. However, this approach is still not ironclad. Although Siler and colleagues were able to obtain article citations for nearly every paper in the initial consideration set, it is still difficult to ascertain whether the initial editorial decision to reject the 12 breakthrough papers was biased. This is because a decision to desk-reject a paper may have spurred the authors to dramatically improve their papers' quality in ways that would eventually increase the papers' ultimate impact when later published in a different journal.

In sum, even when scholars can obtain objective data indicating the quality of each idea in the consideration set after implementation, it is still difficult to know whether the initial decision to reject an idea was "biased," because the idea itself may have changed and dramatically improved after the initial decision was made. Even if ideas do not change or improve after initial decisions are made, research suggests that ideas can sometimes succeed based on random factors, unrelated to idea quality or novelty (Salganik et al., 2006). Further, the outcome-based approach to identifying a bias against novelty may not be a feasible one to employ in many organizational contexts where it is not possible to fully implement all ideas in a consideration set. Finally, because the outcome-based approach is focused on identifying whether a given decision was biased or not, it is not well suited to examining processes underlying when and why people reject novel ideas early on. As a result, the outcome-based method has not yet illuminated the processes underlying how people might overcome a bias against novelty.

The Process-Based Approach to Studying a Bias Against Novelty

Recent research has seen the rise of a second approach to studying the bias against novelty. While the outcome-based approach focuses on whether a given decision to accept or retain a novel idea was characterized by bias, a process-based approach focuses on whether the processes enacted to reject an idea were characterized by bias. The process-based approach defines the bias against novelty as prematurely rejecting ideas and failing to fully consider positive and negative aspects of ideas (Harvey & Mueller, 2021). The process perspective takes into account the form and nature of the evaluation taking place, focusing on the initial assessment of an idea and a decision to retain an idea for further discussion or vetting, but places less focus on the outcome of the evaluation, whether a novel idea was implemented or selected, or even whether the novel idea was high quality. The theoretical reason why the process-based approach does not consider decision-making outcomes is because it acknowledges that novel ideas are inherently uncertain (Miron-Spektor & Beenen, 2015; Mueller et al., 2012). The more novel an idea, the less is known about whether that idea will solve a problem. Further, an idea's true usefulness may be incredibly complex to assess in an organizational setting. George (2007) noted that usefulness can mean different things to different organizational actors because each may have different goals (for example, short term versus long term) and so focus on different aspects of the idea when assessing usefulness. Finally, it is not possible to accurately assess the usefulness of an early-stage novel idea before the idea has been implemented. Van de Ven noted that: "Objectively, of course, the usefulness of an idea can only be determined after the innovation process is completed and implemented" (Van de Ven, 1986: 592). This is because the process of implementation itself can change an idea, how it is used, and who uses it in ways that are not known at the start. Indeed, one study found that expert assessments of the viability of early-stage new ventures were not at all related to how well the ventures performed years later after initial implementation (Huang & Pearce, 2015). Because the usefulness of a novel idea is difficult, if not impossible, to quantify until after the idea has been implemented, it is difficult to know with any accuracy whether the decision to reject the novel idea before it has been implemented is an error.

This focus on studying bias as a process versus an outcome can be understood by examining an analogous phenomenon studied in the group decision-making litera-ture. Early on, Janis (1982) identified that groups could exhibit groupthink: bias in decision-making characterized by poor group performance due to rapid agreement without considering minority or divergent viewpoints. Interestingly, scholars quickly observed that groupthink measured retrospectively showed positive correlations with group performance (Choi & Kim, 1999) and, as defined, was indistinguishable from positive group processes such as group cohesion (McCauley, 1998). Further, the outcome of group decision-making – group performance – was often influenced by factors outside the group's control, such as market forces, luck, or a change in man-agement. If scholars relied on the outcome of group decision-making to determine whether the group exhibited bias, it was not possible to know whether the success or failure was completely due to a biased group process or some other random factor outside the group's control. For these reasons, scholars began to focus less on group outcomes to determine whether a group engaged in biased decision-making, and more on the process the group enacted to develop the outcome (Aldag & Fuller, 1993; Brownstein, 2003; Goncalo et al., 2010). From a process perspective, if a group had a good group process, even if the group subsequently failed in the short term, it would likely exhibit higher performance over multiple trials relative to a group with a poor group process. In contrast, if a group made complex decisions quickly and without rigorous discussion that included opposing views, this group would have exhibited bias irrespective of performance, and so was likely to perform worse over multiple trials. In sum, a process perspective does not employ the outcome of the decision-making process to infer any quality of the process itself, but instead focuses on the process (for example, earlier-phase practices and motivations) that contributes to the outcome to determine whether or not a bias occurred.

Prior work that has taken a process-based approach to studying the bias against novelty has focused largely on the factors contributing to creative idea recognition: an early-phase assessment of whether an idea is indeed creative. For example, one study operationalized bias as a difference between implicit and explicit associa-tions with novelty, and linked these associations to assessments of idea creativity. Specifically, borrowing from the literature on racial bias, Mueller et al. (2012) proposed that: "Just as people have deeply rooted biases against people of a certain age, race, or gender that are not necessarily overt (Greenwald & Banaji, 1995: 13), so too can people hold deeply rooted negative views of creativity that are not openly acknowledged." Mueller et al. (2012) employed the Implicit Attitude Test, a reaction time test, to identify whether participants exhibit an implicit preference for creativity or practicality. For example, an implicit preference for creativity would be indicated if participants exhibited faster reaction times when pairing positive words (for example, "sunshine") with words like "creativity" relative to words like "practicality" and when pairing negative words (for example, "vomit") with words like "practicality" relative to words like "creativity." Explicit preferences were assessed as the extent to which a participant self-reported valuing creativity versus practicality. Importantly, the authors found that participants always exhibited an explicit preference for creativity relative to practicality. The authors also showed that in the control condition, participants exhibited an implicit preference for creativity relative to practicality. However, when primed with uncertainty intolerance, participants exhibited an explicit preference for creativity relative to practicality, but an implicit preference for practicality relative to creativity; they also subsequently rated an idea as having lower creativity relative to a group primed to tolerate uncertainty.

The Mueller et al. (2012) study on the bias against creativity offers a process-based approach because it examined when and why bias might unfold over the course of evaluating a creative idea. Firstly, the study identified that the bias could be implicit or automatic, and so can occur at the earliest moments of evaluating an idea. This suggests that one way to examine the process of engaging in a bias against novelty is to identify whether individuals or groups reject ideas quickly with little deliberation or discussion. Secondly, the study identified that this process might occur even when participants explicitly say they desire creative ideas. This suggests that the bias against creativity can occur even in contexts where creativity is desired and potentially even required to solve the problem at hand. Thirdly, the study provided initial evidence that this bias might depend on whether a person experiences an intolerance to uncertainty. While this study examined the bias against creativity, it provides one way to conceptualize a process-based approach to studying the bias against novelty (a key precursor to creativity). That is, the process of exhibiting a bias against novelty is likely to occur when people rapidly reject new ideas in contexts where tolerance for uncertainty is discouraged, irrespective of whether that context purports to support creativity.

In sum, initial work employing this process-based approach examines the earliest phases of evaluation as well as the contextual factors that affect the uncertainty intolerance of those evaluating ideas. Further, a process perspective is necessarily agnostic about whether novel ideas are high quality in actuality, as the quality of a novel idea can be determined only after implementation. Instead, the process perspective focuses on how individuals and groups determine whether a novel idea has the potential to be high quality, given that the quality is unknown in the moment, and likely to change as the idea develops over time. Hence, when it comes to studying a bias against novelty, a process perspective focuses on the early-phase processes, when people first encounter ideas, that result in an assessment or decision to retain a novel idea or not.

The process-based approach to studying the bias against novelty has many strengths. Firstly, identifying the reason why individuals and groups exhibit a bias against novelty helps researchers to identify situations where novel ideas are most likely to be rejected, thus offering opportunities for early intervention. For example, decision-makers in organizations where the cost of error is high (for example, hospitals, military contexts) are more likely to reject novel ideas due to experiencing an acute tension between novelty and predictability of idea use. Secondly, examining the practices that people enact when exhibiting a bias against novelty can help researchers to learn how individuals and groups can overcome this bias. For example, if the process governing a bias against novelty is characterized by automatic rejection, then an evaluation process not characterized by bias would likely involve refraining from automatically rejecting an idea, retaining the idea in a consideration set, and evaluating that idea over some period of time (McIntosh et al., 2019). Further, if a tendency to automatically reject novel ideas is governed by employing implicit and easily accessible and conventional evaluation criteria, then it is possible that those who overcome this tendency to automatically reject ideas necessarily question whether the conventional evaluation criteria are appropriate to employ when assessing a novel idea (Harvey & Mueller, 2021). Taken together, the process of overcoming a bias against novelty is likely to be dynamic and unfolding over time (Chia, 1994), and a process perspective can open up new pathways to understanding how people might overcome a bias against novelty.

Because a process-based approach to studying a bias against novelty assumes that the true quality of a novel idea is unknowable, a downside of this process-based approach is that it does not address whether ideas that are retained are objectively useful. Unfortunately, the outcome-based approach has this same downside and one can only assess the true usefulness of ideas after they have been fully implemented. Hence, neither the process nor the outcome approach can distinguish whether early-phase novel ideas are objectively useful in the long term at the moment they were initially accepted or rejected. However, if we can unveil rigorous and good evaluation practices that help people to overcome a bias against novelty, these practices should have the advantage of helping people to make better and non-biased decisions on average in the long run. This still remains an open question for future research to address.

GUIDING FUTURE RESEARCH ON HOW TO OVERCOME THE BIAS AGAINST NOVELTY

Prior work has focused on mindsets, identifying that prevention focus (Zhou et al., 2017), low-level construal (Mueller et al., 2014), and uncertainty intolerance (Mueller et al., 2012) increase people's bias against novelty by diminishing the extent to which people can recognize and value novel ideas relative to those in a control condition. While this body of work on mindsets provides a useful examination of the processes which might increase the extent to which people exhibit a bias against novelty, it has not necessarily unveiled the processes through which people might overcome this bias. For example, research has shown that those who were tolerant to uncertainty (Mueller et al., 2012) and exhibited high-level construal (Mueller et al., 2014) assessed idea creativity no differently than participants in a control condition. Further, the question remains as to whether people can switch their mindsets in the real world to better detect novel ideas and embrace novelty (Mueller, 2017). Preliminary findings suggest that mindsets evoked by decision-making roles may be habitual and sticky, and thus difficult to change. Specifically, Mueller et al. (2018) noted that employees who dedicated a higher percentage of time to the role of decision-maker in their organization exhibited higher levels of economic mindset. Hence, while it is clearly possible to switch a person's mindset by priming it in the laboratory, future research needs to examine how to switch mindsets evoked by chronic exposure to certain roles.

Another intriguing study found that people in managerial roles were less accurate in predicting the online popularity of short videos relative to those in idea generation roles, theorizing that the act of generating ideas might inoculate people against a bias against novelty (Berg, 2016). However, this study did not examine managers with responsibility for deciding whether to pursue the specific videos they evaluated. Further, prior work has shown that managers (for example, decision-makers) are often accountable for providing feedback and suggestions to help develop subordinates' ideas, an activity often involving managerial idea generation efforts during idea evaluation (Harrison & Rouse, 2015). Hence, it raises two questions. Firstly, if both managers and idea generators often generate ideas as part of their roles, what aspects of the managerial versus idea generator role actually harmed managers' ability to accurately assess creative ideas? Secondly, since Berg (2016) never examined whether idea generation actually aided evaluation for those in a managerial (that is, decision-making) role, it begs the question of how do managers overcome a bias against novel ideas when they have responsibility for determining whether those ideas should be pursued by the organization, and accountability if those ideas should fail? Illuminating the form and nature of how people in managerial roles might embrace the tension between novelty and predictability of idea use is an open question in need of further research.

This question of how mid-level managers or leaders assess ideas in ways that allow them to keep novel ideas alive is another important one for future research to consider. In organizations, innovation is often structured such that mid-level managers and leaders are the initial "gatekeepers" who determine whether their subordinates' ideas move forward for other organizational decision-makers to consider (Day, 1994). This suggests that middle managers, or mid-level leaders with decision-making authority over whether subordinate ideas move forward, may be important stewards of innovation, as they are likely to encounter ideas at the earliest phases of development when ideas have the highest potential to develop but the actual feasibility and use of these ideas is relatively difficult to predict. Further, mid-level managers and leaders may experience strong pressures to succeed and avoid failure, as there is an increasing amount of competition to move up towards the top of the hierarchy. If so, then middle managers or mid-level leaders with decision-making responsibility over subordinates' ideas may experience this tension between novelty and predictably of ideas use most acutely, and so are more likely to reject novel ideas. Moreover, evaluation in this context is not strictly cognitive, but interpersonal, as it involves communicating and interacting with subordinates over time. Hence, mid-level leaders may engage in evaluation practices beyond those described in the classical creativity literature which focuses on cognitive aspects of evaluation. Because it is not possible to determine the true value of an idea that was rejected early on and never implemented (as organizations often place rejected ideas in the proverbial file drawer), it is not possible to employ the outcome-based method to study the bias against novelty within an organizational context; instead, future research should adopt a process-based approach to examining how mid-level leaders deal with the tension between novelty and predictability of idea use in ways that allow them to keep subordinates' novel ideas alive.

Most of the research examining a bias against novelty addresses affective experience only tangentially, usually by describing people's aversion to uncertainty and preference for predictability. However, a burgeoning body of literature in the domain of affect and organizations has begun to propose some promising new directions of studying how to overcome a bias against novelty. Emotions have appraisal tendencies that predispose individuals to appraise the environment in specific ways towards certain functional ends (Frijda, 1986). Some emotions may guide people towards choosing ideas with a moderate to low level of predictability, because they orient a person either towards risk-taking, or towards reframing uncertainty and complexity as a challenge to be met. For example, anger has an appraisal tendency towards orienting people to experience a sense of control and certainty, whereas fear has an appraisal tendency towards orienting people to experience a lack of control and uncertainty. As a result, people who experienced anger relative to fear exhibited more optimistic risk assessments and risk-seeking choices (Lerner & Keltner, 2001). Hence, it is possible that people who feel angry in the course of evaluating a novel idea might evaluate novel ideas as having a higher likelihood of successfully solving a problem relative to those who feel fearful. Similarly, curiosity, an approach-oriented motivational state associated with exploration, has an appraisal tendency that views challenging events as positive and likely to evoke growth and increased learning (Silvia, 2006). In contrast, people who experience confusion approach novelty as a challenge that is unlikely to be met with success (Silvia, 2009). Hence, it is possible that evaluators who experience feelings of curiosity during idea evaluation may be more likely to tolerate the fact that novel ideas lack predictable use, and so engage in experimentation and information search to attempt to reduce the uncertainty associated with novel ideas, rather than rejecting them outright. Either way, future research should examine the extent to which discrete emotions might diminish a bias against novelty.

CONCLUSION

While an increasing amount of research has shown that people, especially those in decision-making roles, can experience an implicit bias against novelty, relatively little research has examined how people can overcome this tendency. This chapter has outlined a central mechanism examining why a person might exhibit a bias against novelty, reviewed the literature on two different perspectives around studying and defining the bias against novelty, and provided suggestions about how future research might better examine how people can overcome a tendency to reject the new, when new ideas are needed.

REFERENCES

Aldag, R.J., & Fuller, S.R. 1993. Beyond fiasco: A reappraisal of the groupthink phenomenon and a new model of group decision processes. *Psychological Bulletin*, 113(3): 533–552.

Amabile, T. 1988. A model of creativity and innovation in organizations. In B.K. Staw (ed.), *Research in organization behavior* (Vol. 10): 123–167. Greenwich, CT: JAI Press.

Amabile, T.M., Conti, R., Coon, H., Lazenby, J., & Herron, M. 1996. Assessing the work environment for creativity. *Academy of Management Journal*, 39(5): 1154–1184.

Amabile, T.M., & Pratt, M.G. 2016. The dynamic componental model of creativity and innovation in organizations: Making progress, making meaning. *Research in Organizational Behavior*, 36: 157–183.

Anderson, N., Potočnik, K., & Zhou, J. 2014. Innovation and creativity in organizations a state-of-the-science review, prospective commentary, and guiding framework. *Journal of Management*, 40(5): 1297–1333.

Bantel, K.A., & Jackson, S.E. 1989. Top management and innovations in banking: Does the composition of the top team make a difference? *Strategic Management Journal*, 10(S1): 107–124.

Berg, J.M. 2016. Balancing on the creative highwire: Forecasting the success of novel ideas in organizations. *Administrative Science Quarterly*, 61(3): 433–468.

Berger, C.R. 1986. Uncertain outcome values in predicted relationships uncertainty reduction theory then and now. *Human Communication Research*, 13(1): 34–38.

Blair, C.S., & Mumford, M.D. 2007. Errors in idea evaluation: Preference for the unoriginal? *Journal of Creative Behavior*, 41(3): 197–222.

Boudreau, K.J., Guinan, E.C., Lakhani, K.R., & Riedl, C. 2016. Looking across and looking beyond the knowledge frontier: Intellectual distance, novelty, and resource allocation in science. *Management Science*, 62(10): 2765–2783.

Brownstein, A.L. 2003. Biased predecision processing. *Psychological Bulletin*, 129(4): 545–568.

Campbell, D.T. 1960. Blind variation and selective retentions in creative thought as in other knowledge processes. *Psychological Review*, 67(6): 380–400.

Chia, R. 1994. The concept of decision: A deconstructive analysis. *Journal of Management Studies*, 31(6): 781–806.

Choi, J.N., & Kim, M.U. 1999. The organizational application of groupthink and its limitations in organizations. *Journal of Applied Psychology*, 84(2): 297.

Cialdini, R.B. 1998. *The psychology of persuasion*. New York: Quill.

Cooper, R. 2006. Managing technology development projects. *Research Technology Management*, 49(6): 23–31.

Criscuolo, P., Dahlander, L., Grohsjean, T., & Salter, A. 2017. Evaluating novelty: The role of panels in the selection of R&D projects. *Academy of Management Journal*, 60: 433–460.

Csikszentmihalyi, M. 1988. Motivation and creativity: Toward a synthesis of structural and energistic approaches to cognition. *New Ideas in Psychology*, 6(2): 159–176.

Csikszentmihalyi, M. 1999. Implications of a systems perspective for the study of creativity. In R.J. Sternberg (ed.), *Handbook of creativity*: 313–335. New York: Cambridge University Press.

Day, D. 1994. Raising radicals: Different processes for championing innovative corporate ventures. *Organization Science*, 5(2): 148–172.

De Dreu, C.K.W., & West, M.A. 2001. Minority dissent and team innovation: The importance of participation in decision making. *Journal of Applied Psychology*, 86(6): 1191–1201.

Detert, J.R., & Burris, E.R. 2007. Leadership behavior and employee voice: Is the door really open? *Academy of Management Journal*, 50(4): 869–884.

Diedrich, J., Benedek, M., Jauk, E., & Neubauer, A.C. 2015. Are creative ideas novel and useful? *Psychology of Aesthetics, Creativity, and the Arts*, 9(1): 35.

Drazin, R., Glynn, M.A., & Kazanjian, R.K. 1999. Multilevel theorizing about creativity in organizations: A sensemaking perspective. *Academy of Management Review*, 24(2): 286–307.

Dutton, J.E., Ashford, S.J., O'Neill, R.M., & Lawrence, K.A. 2001. Moves that matter: Issue selling and organizational change. *Academy of Management Journal*, 44(4): 716–736.

Edmondson, A. 1999. Psychological safety and learning behavior in work teams. *Administrative Science Quarterly*, 44(2): 350–383.

Eidelman, S., & Crandall, C.S. 2012. Bias in favor of the status quo. *Social and Personality Psychology Compass*, 6(3): 270–281.

Eidelman, S., Crandall, C.S., & Pattershall, J. 2009. The existence bias. *Journal of Personality and Social Psychology*, 97(5): 765–775.

Eidelman, S., Pattershall, J., & Crandall, C.S. 2010. Longer is better. *Journal of Experimental Social Psychology*, 46(6): 993–998.

Elsbach, K.D., & Kramer, R.M. 2003. Assessing creativity in hollywood pitch meetings: Evidence for a dual-process model of creativity judgments. *Academy of Management Journal*, 46(3): 283–301.

Escoffier, N., & McKelvey, B. 2015. The wisdom of crowds in the movie industry: Towards new solutions to reduce uncertainties. *International Journal of Arts Management*, 17(2): 52–63.

Farh, J.-L., Lee, C., & Farh, C.I. 2010. Task conflict and team creativity: A question of how much and when. *Journal of Applied Psychology*, 95(6): 1173.

Ferguson, J.-P., & Carnabuci, G. 2017. Risky recombinations: Institutional gatekeeping in the innovation process. *Organization Science*, 28(1): 133–151.

Fiske, S., & Taylor, S. 1991. *Social cognition*. New York: McGraw-Hill.

Flowers, S. 2008. Harnessing the hackers: The emergence and exploitation of Outlaw Innovation. *Research Policy*, 37(2): 177–193.

Forbes, D.P., & Milliken, F.J. 1999. Cognition and corporate governance: Understanding boards of directors as strategic decision-making groups. *Academy of Management Review*, 24(3): 489–505.

Ford, C.M., & Gioia, D.A. 2000. Factors influencing creativity in the domain of managerial decision making. *Journal of Management*, 26(4): 705–732.

Ford, C.M., Sharfman, M.P., & Dean, J.W. 2008. Factors associated with creative strategic decisions. *Creativity and Innovation Management*, 17(3): 171–185.

Ford, C.M., & Sullivan, D.M. 2005. Selective retention processes that create tensions between novelty and value in business domains. In J.C. Kaufman & J. Baer (eds), *Creativity across domains: Faces of the muse*: 245–259: Mahwah, NJ: Lawrence Erlbaum Associates Publishers.

Fox, C.R., & Levav, J. 2000. Familiarity bias and belief reversal in relative likelihood judgment. *Organizational Behavior and Human Decision Processes*, 82(2): 268–292.

Frijda, N.H. 1986. *The emotions*. New York: Cambridge University Press.

George, J.M. 2007. Chapter 9: Creativity in organizations. *Academy of Management Annals*, 1(1): 439–477.

Goncalo, J.A., Polman, E., & Maslach, C. 2010. Can confidence come too soon? Collective efficacy, conflict and group performance over time. *Organizational Behavior and Human Decision Processes*, 113(1): 13–24.

Gong, Y., Zhou, J., & Chang, S. 2013. Core knowledge employee creativity and firm performance: The moderating role of riskiness orientation, firm size, and realized absorptive capacity. *Personnel Psychology*, 66(2): 443–482.

Greenwald, A.G., & Banaji, M.R. (1995). Implicit social cognition: Attitudes, self-esteem, and stereotypes. *Psychological Review*, 102(1): 4–27.

Grégoire, D.A., Barr, P.S., & Shepherd, D.A. 2010. Cognitive processes of opportunity recognition: The role of structural alignment. *Organization Science*, 21(2): 413–431.

Harrison, S.H., & Rouse, E.D. 2014. Let's dance! Elastic coordination in creative group work: A qualitative study of modern dancers. *Academy of Management Journal*, 57(5): 1256–1283.

Harrison, S.H., & Rouse, E.D. 2015. An inductive study of feedback interactions over the course of creative projects. *Academy of Management Journal*, 58(2): 375–404.

Harvey, S., & Mueller, J.S. 2021. Staying alive: Towards a diverging consensus model of overcoming a bias against novelty in groups. *Organization Science*, 32: 293–314.

Hogg, M., & Mullin, B. 1999. Joining groups to reduce uncertainty: Subjective uncertainty reduction and group identification. In D. Abrams & M.A. Hogg (eds), *Social identity and social cognition*: 249–279. Oxford: Blackwell Publishing.

Huang, L., & Pearce, J.L. 2015. Managing the unknowable: The effectiveness of early-stage investor gut feel in entrepreneurial investment decisions. *Administrative Science Quarterly*, 60(4): 634–670.

Janis, I. 1982. *Groupthink*. Boston, MA: Houghton Mifflin.

Kahneman, D., Slovic, S.P., Slovic, P., & Tversky, A. 1982. *Judgment under uncertainty: Heuristics and biases*. Cambridge: Cambridge University Press.

Kanter, R.M. 1988. When a thousand flowers bloom: Structural, collective, and social conditions for innovation in organizations. In B. Staw & L.L. Cummings (eds), *Research in organizational behavior* (Vol. 10): 169–211. Greenwich, CT: JAI Press.

Klein, K.J., & Knight, A.P. 2005. Innovation implementation: Overcoming the challenge. *Current Directions in Psychological Science*, 14(5): 243–246.

Knudsen, T., & Levinthal, D.A. 2007. Two faces of search: Alternative generation and alternative evaluation. *Organization Science*, 18(1): 39–54.

Kornish, L.J., & Ulrich, K.T. 2011. Opportunity spaces in innovation: Empirical analysis of large samples of ideas. *Management Science*, 57(1): 107–128.

Kornish, L.J., & Ulrich, K.T. 2014. The importance of the raw idea in innovation: Testing the sow's ear hypothesis. *Journal of Marketing Research*, 51(1): 14–26.

Lazarus, R.S., & Folkman, S. 1984. *Stress, coping, and adaptation*. New York: Springer.

Lee, F. 2001. Recombinant uncertainty in technological search. *Management Science*, 47(1): 117.

Lerner, J.S., & Keltner, D. 2001. Fear, anger, and risk. *Journal of Personality and Social Psychology*, 81(1): 146.

Li, Q., Maggitti, P.G., Smith, K.G., Tesluk, P.E., & Katila, R. 2013. Top management attention to innovation: The role of search selection and intensity in new product introductions. *Academy of Management Journal*, 56(3): 893–916.

Licuanan, B.F., Dailey, L.R., & Mumford, M.D. 2007. Idea evaluation: Error in evaluating highly original ideas. *Journal of Creative Behavior*, 41(1): 1–27.

Lifshitz-Assaf, H. 2017. Dismantling knowledge boundaries at NASA: The critical role of professional identity in open innovation. *Administrative Science Quarterly*. 0001839217747876.

Loewenstein, J., & Mueller, J. 2016. Implicit theories of creative ideas: How culture guides creativity assessments. *Academy of Management Discoveries*, 2(4): 320–348.

Loewenstein, J., Raghunathan, R., & Heath, C. 2011. The repetition-break plot structure makes effective television advertisements. *Journal of Marketing*, 75(5): 105–119.

Mandler, G. 1982. The structure of value: Accounting for taste. In M.S. Clark & S.T. Fiske (eds), *Affect and cognition: The 17th annual Carnegie symposium*: 3–36. Hillsdale, NJ: Erlbaum.

McCauley, C. 1998. Groupthink dynamics in Janis's theory of groupthink: Backward and forward. *Organizational Behavior and Human Decision Processes*. Special Issue: Theoretical perspectives on groupthink: A twenty-fifth anniversary appraisal, 73(2–3): 142–162.

McIntosh, T., Mulhearn, T.J., & Mumford, M.D. 2019. Taking the good with the bad: The impact of forecasting timing and valence on idea evaluation and creativity. *Psychology of Aesthetics, Creativity, and the Arts*, 15(1): 111–124.

Miron-Spektor, E., & Beenen, G. 2015. Motivating creativity: The effects of sequential and simultaneous learning and performance achievement goals on product novelty and usefulness. *Organizational Behavior and Human Decision Processes*, 127: 53–65.

Mollick, E. 2012. People and process, suits and innovators: The role of individuals in firm performance. *Strategic Management Journal*, 33(9): 1001–1015.

Moreau, C.P., Lehmann, D.R., & Markman, A.B. 2001. Entrenched knowledge structures and consumer response to new products. *Journal of Marketing Research*, 38(1): 14–29.

Moshinsky, A., & Bar-Hillel, M. 2010. Loss aversion and status quo label bias. *Social Cognition*, 28(2): 191–204.

Mueller, J. 2017. *Creative change: Why we resist it … How we can embrace it*. New York: Houghton Mifflin Harcourt.

Mueller, J.S., Melwani, S., & Goncalo, J.A. 2012. The bias against creativity: Why people desire but reject creative ideas. *Psychological Science*, 23: 13–17.

Mueller, J.S., Melwani, S., Loewenstein, J., & Deal, J. 2018. Reframing the decision-makers' dilemma: Towards social context model of creative idea recognition. *Academy of Management Journal*, 61(1): 1–17.

Mueller, J.S., Wakslak, C.J., & Krishnan, V. 2014. Construing creativity: The how and why of recognizing creative ideas. *Journal of Experimental Social Psychology*, 51: 81–87.

Mumford, M.D. 1999. Blind variation or selective variation? Evaluative elements in creative thought. *Psychological Inquiry*, 10(4): 344–348.

Murnighan, J.K., & Conlon, D.E. 1991. The dynamics of intense work groups: A study of British string quartets. *Administrative Science Quarterly*, 36(2): 165–186.

Paulus, P.B., & Yang, H.-C. 2000. Idea generation in groups: A basis for creativity in organizations. *Organizational Behavior and Human Decision Processes*, 82(1): 76–87.

Perry-Smith, J.E., & Mannucci, P.V. 2017. From creativity to innovation: The social network drivers of the four phases of the idea journey. *Academy of Management Review*, 42(1): 53–79.

Piezunka, H., & Dahlander, L. 2015. Distant search, narrow attention: How crowding alters organizations' filtering of suggestions in crowdsourcing. *Academy of Management Journal*, 58(3): 856–880.

Putman, V.L., & Paulus, P.B. 2009. Brainstorming, brainstorming rules and decision making. *Journal of Creative Behavior*, 43(1): 23–39.

Rao, R.S., Chandy, R.K., & Prabhu, J.C. 2008. The fruits of legitimacy: Why some new ventures gain more from innovation than others. *Journal of Marketing*, 72(4): 58–75.

Rao, H., Greve, H.R., & Davis, G.F. 2001. Fool's gold: Social proof in the initiation and abandonment of coverage by Wall Street analysts. *Administrative Science Quarterly*, 46(3): 502–526.

Rietzschel, E.F., Nijstad, B.A., & Stroebe, W. 2010. The selection of creative ideas after individual idea generation: Choosing between creativity and impact. *British Journal of Psychology*, 101(1): 47–68.

Ritov, I., & Baron, J. 1992. Status-quo and omission biases. *Journal of Risk and Uncertainty*, 5(1): 49–61.

Rosenkopf, L., & McGrath, P. 2011. Advancing the conceptualization and operationalization of novelty in organizational research. *Organization Science*, 22(5): 1297–1311.

Runco, M.A., & Smith, W.R. 1992. Interpersonal and intrapersonal evaluations of creative ideas. *Personality and Individual Differences*, 13(3): 295–302.

Salganik, M.J., Dodds, P.S., & Watts, D.J. 2006. Experimental study of inequality and unpredictability in an artificial cultural market. *Science*, 311(5762): 854–856.

Salganik, M.J., & Watts, D.J. 2009. Web-based experiments for the study of collective social dynamics in cultural markets. *Topics in Cognitive Science*, 1(3): 439–468.

Schilling, M.A., & Hill, C.W. 1998. Managing the new product development process: Strategic imperatives. *Academy of Management Executive*, 12(3): 67–81.

Siler, K., Lee, K., & Bero, L. 2015. Measuring the effectiveness of scientific gatekeeping. *Proceedings of the National Academy of Sciences*, 112(2): 360–365.

Siler, K., & Strang, D. 2017. Peer review and scholarly originality: Let 1,000 flowers bloom, but don't step on any. *Science, Technology, and Human Values*, 42(1): 29–61.

Silvia, P.J. 2006. *Exploring the psychology of interest*. New York: Oxford University Press.

Silvia, P.J. 2009. Looking past pleasure: anger, confusion, disgust, pride, surprise, and other unusual aesthetic emotions. *Psychology of Aesthetics, Creativity, and the Arts*, 3(1): 48.

Staw, B.M. 1995. Why no one really wants creativity. In C. Ford & D.A. Gioia (eds), *Creative action in organizations: Ivory tower visions and real world voices*. Thousand Oaks, CA: SAGE Publications.

Tahirsylaj, A.S. 2012. Stimulating creativity and innovation through Intelligent Fast Failure. *Thinking Skills and Creativity*, 7(3): 265–270.

Tversky, A., & Kahneman, D. 1991. Loss aversion in riskless choice: A reference-dependent model. *Quarterly Journal of Economics*, 106(4): 1039–1061.

Van de Ven, A.H. 1986. Central problems in the management of innovation. *Management Science*, 32: 590–607.

Van de Ven, A.H., & Delbecq, A.L. 1974. The effectiveness of nominal, delphi, and interacting group decision making processes. *Academy of Management Journal*, 17(4): 605–621.

Weary, G., Jacobson, J.A., Edwards, J.A., & Tobin, S.J. 2001. Chronic and temporarily activated causal uncertainty beliefs and stereotype usage. *Journal of Personality and Social Psychology*, 81(2): 206–219.

West, M.A., & Anderson, N.R. 1996. Innovation in top management teams. *Journal of Applied Psychology*, 81(6): 680–693.

Whitson, J., & Galinsky, A. 2008. Lacking control increases illusory pattern perception. *Science*, 322(5898): 115.

Zajonc, R.B. 2001. Mere exposure: A gateway to the subliminal. *Current Directions in Psychological Science*, 10(6): 224–228.

Zhou, J., Wang, X.M., Bavato, D., Tasselli, S., & Wu, J. 2019. Understanding the receiving side of creativity: A multidisciplinary review and implications for management research. *Journal of Management*. 0149206319827088.

Zhou, J., Wang, X. M., Song, L.J., & Wu, J. 2017. Is it new? Personal and contextual influences on perceptions of novelty and creativity. *Journal of Applied Psychology*, 102(2): 180.

14. Who is the creator? How uncertainty, threat and implicit models create paradoxical evaluations of creativity

Kerrie L. Unsworth and Aleksandra Luksyte

Creativity is usually defined as "the development of ideas about products, practices, services, or procedures that are (a) novel and (b) potentially useful to the organization" (Shalley et al., 2004: 934). In an ideal world, one would hope – and this constitutes one of the core assumptions of the literature on idea evaluation – that this assessment of novelty and usefulness is based on the idea itself, that it is a fair and unbiased evaluation made purely on the idea's attributes. Yet, research does not provide strong support for this assumption. Studies are starting to examine how highly original ideas are often rejected not only by others (e.g., Dailey & Mumford, 2006; Licuanan et al., 2007; Rietzschel et al., 2019; Zhou et al., 2019), but by creators themselves (Berg, 2016, 2019). These highly creative ideas with the most potential tend to be underestimated because the evaluation of creative ideas is a subjective process that is not devoid of biases. In this chapter, we build on and expand this growing literature about inaccuracies in idea evaluation by considering the characteristics of the creator in this process. Does it matter who the creator is? We argue that creativity evaluation is a subjective process, full of biases, and this process becomes even more subjective and biased depending on the creator's characteristics.

In particular, a growing body of research has started to examine how characteristics of the receiver, and their environment, affects the evaluation of creativity (e.g., Zhou et al., 2019; Zhou et al., 2017). We build on research about the subjective nature of perceived creativity to examine the other side of the equation. We explore how perceptions of the person generating the idea (that is, the creator) affects how creative products, ideas, processes, and procedures are assessed, evaluated, and recognized. In particular, we focus on the way in which the fit between implicit models (of male/female, younger/older, and a "creative" person) will affect assessments of the idea's novelty, and how uncertainty and the identity threat posed by the creator will affect assessments of the idea's usefulness.

We focus on the gender and age of the creators because these demographic characteristics are associated with stereotypes that are likely to influence others' perceptions of creative behaviors and outputs of creators who belong to these demographic groups. Specifically, creativity is associated with novelty, divergent thinking, challenging status quo, flexibility (Shalley et al., 2004); all these attributes are stereotypically not associated with either female creators or older creative employees (Posthuma & Campion, 2009; Proudfoot et al., 2015). We further argue that by engaging in creative work behavior women and older employees may not receive adequate recognition for their creativity in comparison to younger men, whose creativity will be expected and thus recognized and rewarded. We posit that such differential treatment and evaluation of creativity is problematic because it means discrimination. By unpacking how and why creative women and older employees (defined as those older than 40 years old; cutoff based on Equal Employment Opportunity Commission guidelines regarding age discrimination) are evaluated and treated differently, we will help organizations to minimize discrimination associated with rewarding employees based on their demographics, not their contributions (that is, creativity). This will further aid organizations in encouraging creativity among all their talented creative employees irrespective of their gender and age.

Exploring the differential evaluation of creativity for demographically diverse creators is important because of rapidly growing diversification of labor forces across the world. For example, the participation rates of women have been increasing in Australia (that is, 59 percent; Australian Bureau of Statistics, 2011). Demographic projections have shown that by 2030, nearly 30 percent of the total Australian workforce will be aged 55 or older (Australian Bureau of Statistics, 2011). There also has been a growing recognition of the importance of utilizing the talents of all employees irrespective of their demographics (Avery, 2011). Rejecting ideas because they are perceived as not novel, too novel, or not useful – based on the creator's characteristics and not the idea's characteristics – will be harmful to organizations both now and in the future. In light of these statistics, it is critical to better understand how and why creativity may be viewed differently for male and female, and younger and older creators. In doing so, in this chapter we will increase awareness and outline potential steps for managers on how to reduce biases in perceptions of creativity, minimize interpersonal mistreatment of female creators and creative older employees, and encourage creativity among talented men and women of all ages. Organizations will reduce both formal and interpersonal discrimination of their creative women and older workers and will foster an overall favorable climate in which all employees, irrespective of their gender or age, feel that they can put forward creative ideas, which will be evaluated based on their qualities, not on who generated these ideas.

In the sections that follow we discuss the consequences of creativity and the potential for different evaluations of the same idea to emerge. We then integrate small but growing research on how and why others may view and treat creativity of female and older employees differently than that produced by their male and younger counterparts. We conclude our chapter with the practical steps for organizations that strive to promote creativity among all their employees, irrespective of their demographic and cultural background. Figure 14.1 summarizes our proposed conceptual model for this chapter.

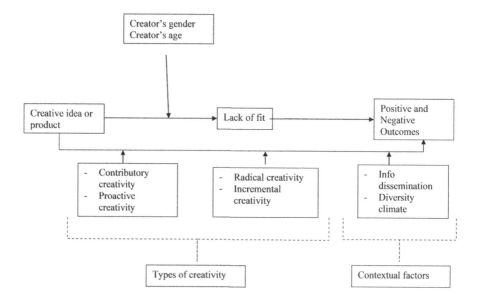

Figure 14.1   Effects of creator characteristics on evaluation of creative outcomes

CREATIVITY PARADOX: WHY IS IT POSITIVE FOR SOME, NEGATIVE FOR OTHERS?

Although being creative is integral to many jobs, often employees are reluctant to engage in creativity (Hon et al., 2014) and observers often reject creative ideas (Mueller et al., 2012) and those who put them forward (Mueller et al., 2011). We argue that one reason for such unwillingness to engage in creativity is because creativity, especially when evaluated and judged by others (Zhou et al., 2019), may bring benefits for some creators yet may accrue penalties for other creative employees. Further, others tend to reject creative ideas because there is a some level of uncertainty regarding how practical and easy it will be to use the new ideas, processes, and procedures (Mueller et al., 2012). Combining these two perspectives, we propose that individual creativity is, to some extent, a paradoxical organizational behavior, that can be evaluated both negatively and positively; and this asymmetrical assessment can be applied to some, but not other creators.

On the one hand, individual creativity is likely to be an organizationally valued behavior because it is intended to bring about improvements (Janssen et al., 2004). In fact, it has been included in wider models of performance (Griffin et al., 2007), such that good performance would incorporate creativity. Given the importance of creativity for nearly all jobs, appraisers will likely reward employee creativity to encourage these behaviors. Research indeed has supported this idea by showing that creative employees receive favorable performance evaluations and are perceived as deserving awards such as a pay raise or promotion (Luksyte et al., 2018; Proudfoot et al., 2015). Recent research has also suggested that being creative may increase employees' well-being because when they are in a creative state they may approach stressful events with more alternative options, responses, and interpretations than when they are in a less creative state (Helzer & Kim, 2019). As such, a creative idea is associated with positive outcomes, and others will likely view favourably the creators of these novel ideas.

On the other hand, the very nature of creativity is such that it involves effort as well as change and risk for those affected by the creative solutions. This is why creativity breeds uncertainty, which employees strive to minimize (Mueller et al., 2012). Creativity requires additional time and being creative at work may have a toll on family life; employees spending time at work searching for creative solutions and generating ideas may then allocate less time with their spouses at home (Harrison & Wagner, 2016). Also, others may be jealous of creative people because of the potential benefits associated with creativity (for example, recognition, praise, expert status; Proudfoot et al., 2015). And those who are creative are also likely to engage in dishonest behaviors by increasing individuals' ability to justify their unethical actions (Gino & Ariely, 2012). Thus, engaging in creative processes may be associated with negative outcomes for the creator.

From the evaluator's side, creativity is associated with uncertainty because "the more novel an idea, the more uncertainty can exist about whether the idea is practical, useful, error free, and reliably reproducible" (Mueller et al., 2012: 13). Thus, uncertainty is likely to affect perceptions of usefulness. For those affected by the idea, creativity may bring anxiety and frustration due to uncertainty and new learning requirements (Argyris & Schon, 1978). Due to this uncertainty, followers tend to rate their creative leaders as less effective than their conservative leaders (Mueller et al., 2011).

According to uncertainty reduction theory (Hogg, 2000), people are motivated to predict and control the world and events around them. When they feel uncertain about how to behave and what to expect from others, they feel a lack of control over their lives and strive to reduce that uncertainty to regain controllability and predictability. Given that people are motivated to reduce uncertainty, we argue that assessing creativity, and in particular the usefulness of an idea, may be closely intertwined with engaging in activities that are aimed to reduce this uncertainty. Further, building on the conceptualization of creativity as uncertainty-filled work behavior, we argue that for some creators this uncertainty will be amplified. The prototypical creator tends to be portrayed as a young man (Posthuma & Campion, 2009; Proudfoot et al., 2015), so uncertainty is increased when the actual creator does not fit this prototype. As such, in this chapter we integrate research on creativity as uncertainty (Mueller et al., 2012) and implicit theories of creativity (e.g., Elsbach & Kramer, 2003) to examine how and why creators of certain demographic backgrounds – for example, older women – may receive less favorable evaluations for their creativity than their younger male creative counterparts.

TRADITIONAL APPROACH

Much of the literature assumes that others assess the novelty and usefulness dimensions of creative ideas based on the idea itself. While it is clear that there is no such thing as an objective evaluation of creativity – that is, a "true" rating of creativity that sits outside subjective perceptions – the most common approach has been a normative evaluation (Amabile, 1982). Amabile's (1982) consensual assessment technique uses a group of experts to rate each creative idea, product, or process. The technique assumes that the creativity of an idea, object, or process is its defining characteristic and that the evaluation is done without knowledge of the creator. Often these assessments have been conducted in laboratory settings using set tasks such as brainstorming, Torrance tests of creative thinking (Torrance, 1972), and similar tasks (see e.g., Dollinger & Shafran, 2005). In non-laboratory situations, experts have assessed products such as children's poetry and stories (e.g., Baer et al., 2004) and children's musical compositions (e.g., Hickey, 2001) with varying degrees of reliability. Across both laboratory and non-laboratory settings, the creator is unknown and the experts are reviewing tens, if not hundreds, of separate creative products.

We do not dispute the ability of Amabile's (1982) consensual assessment technique as a methodological tool. It is a well-validated and generally reliable tool to measure the end-product of the creative process. We noted earlier that research has begun to uncover ways in which the ratings of creativity are affected by issues such as the evaluator's associated affect and creative identity (Zhou et al., 2019; Unsworth & Robinson, forthcoming) which may reduce reliability. However, by using a large number of these evaluators, the consensual assessment technique can minimize the influence of these factors on the creative measure. In essence, the consensual assessment technique can potentially smooth out any idiosyncratic biases held by each evaluator by computing an average rating. As such, the technique is useful for research where it is important to capture the inherent creativity of each product; namely, research that aims to determine the antecedents or moderators of creative products. Nonetheless, we argue that in real-world situations, particularly in the workplace, this is only part of the story.

In real-world settings, the identity of the creators of ideas or products is generally not anonymous, as it is in laboratory settings. Instead, in most situations, the creator is known to the evaluator(s). If we recognize that the evaluators and stakeholders of the creative process are "people" and are subject to human perceptual biases, then the consensual assessment technique is less likely to be appropriate and the creator's demographic and cultural characteristics are likely to play a role not only in face-to-face relationships but also in virtual interactions (Martins & Shalley, 2011). We argue that perceptions of the novelty and usefulness of an idea or product will depend not only on the idea or product itself (cf. Amabile, 1982), nor the receiver alone (cf. Unsworth & Robinson, forthcoming; Zhou et al., 2019), but also on perceptions of the creator. We suggest that novelty ratings will be affected by the creator's fit with mental models of a creative person (Proudfoot et al., 2015), and that usefulness ratings will be affected by the threat and uncertainty inherent in the creative paradox (Mueller et al., 2012), especially when associated with non-prototypical creators such as older and female creative employees.

THREAT OR UNCERTAINTY PERCEPTIONS

In our conceptualization of the paradoxical nature of creativity, creativity can be seen as threatening and uncertain, on the one hand, and invoke jealousy of the creator due to potential positive benefits, on the other. In fact, research has shown that it has many negative effects on bystanders (Mueller et al., 2012); a phenomenon known as "bias against creativity." Evaluators, particularly those who are likely to be affected by the idea, are therefore likely to want to devalue the new idea or product. Such devaluation and denigration desires could be explained by the uncertainty triggered by a creative idea (Mueller et al., 2012), and deeply ingrained motivation to reduce uncertainty (Hogg, 2000). To date, this understanding of evaluators' perceptions can be seen most prominently in Zhou and colleagues' associative evaluation theory (Zhou & Woodman, 2003; Zhou et al., 2017). This theory, and supporting empirical studies, show that when the perceiver associates the idea with a positive memory then they rate the idea as more creative. Thus, uncertainty is reduced for the perceiver and they are able to focus on the positive side of the creativity paradox. Other work has shown that influence tactics used on the evaluator (Lu et al., 2019), and the evaluator's own creative identity (Unsworth & Robinson, forthcoming), affect creativity ratings; again, we suggest that these might be indicative of uncertainty and threat reduction.

We take this argument one step further and theorize the implications based on the creator's characteristics. That is, rather than focusing just on the evaluator's own experiences, we also look at the evaluator's perception of the creator. As such, we argue that certain characteristics of the creator that induce threat are likely to increase the already high level of uncertainty inherent in creativity and thereby provoke negative ratings from evaluators. It is important to note that we are not proposing a Machiavellian evaluator figure who consciously derides their opponent; instead, we propose that this is most often a subconscious social comparison process, which is triggered by the uncertainty associated with creativity and the desire to reduce uncertainty (Hogg, 2000).

What creator characteristics are likely to invoke perceptions of threat and uncertainty? Research into threat appraisal is often linked to violence, stress, bullying, or physical or psychological harm (e.g., Barling, 1996; Johnson & Joshi, 2016; Sinclair et al., 2002). This is unlikely to be relevant in the evaluation of creativity, because it is arguable that if the new idea creates such outcomes then it truly deserves low ratings of usefulness.

On the other hand, identity threat – not being the person you want to be, or not being seen as the person you want to be (e.g., Deaux & Ethier, 1998; Pagliaro et al., 2011; Stone et al., 2012) – is much more relevant to creativity evaluation. Identity threat is related to psychosocial stress (Thoits, 1991) which will then be enhanced by the uncertainty associated with creativity. Therefore, we argue that when an evaluator's identity is threatened by the creator, they will be motivated to reduce this threat by devaluing the creative product; in essence, by removing any chance of positive consequences for the creator.

Indeed, research shows that identity threat is linked to resistance to change; for example, Eilam and Shamir (2005) suggest that threats to self-determination, self-distinctiveness, self-enhancement, and self-continuity lead to resistance to change. Along the same lines, therefore, we argue that a creator who makes an evaluator feel threatened in these ways will receive lower creativity ratings than the same idea posed by a less threatening creator. We believe it will most likely affect usefulness ratings, rather than novelty ratings, as uncertainty in creativity appears to be linked with decreased perceptions of viability (Mueller et al., 2012).

Which types of identities are most likely to be threatened when assessing creativity? Identity threat is related to status and perceived status differences (Thoits, 1991), and research often focuses on identities such as gender (Kinias & Sim, 2016), masculinity (Ashcraft, 2005), race (Pietri et al., 2018), and culture (Wright, 2015). We believe that all of these, and others, may play a role in creativity evaluation, and any form of identity threat will result in decreased assessments of the idea's usefulness. Nonetheless, we focus in this chapter on two aspects that are linked to the second part of our theoretical development – fit with implicit models – namely, gender and age.

FIT WITH IMPLICIT MODELS OF "A CREATIVE PERSON"

Integrating research on the uncertainty of creativity (Mueller et al., 2012) with implicit models of creativity (Elsbach & Kramer, 2003), we will argue that for female and older creators, being creative will mainly result in negative consequences. In contrast, for male and younger creative employees, creativity will bring positive outcomes. Implicit theories of creativity are pre-existing knowledge and mental constructions of what constitutes creativity and a prototypical creative person (Zhou et al., 2019). These implicit models influence others' evaluations of creativity as well as how much they value the novelty and usefulness dimensions of creativity. Research has examined the impact of cultural background in this domain, and shown that employees from individualistic cultures that emphasize achievement and self-actualization value novelty more so than usefulness (Loewenstein & Mueller, 2016). In contrast, those from collectivistic cultures appreciate usefulness more than novelty. Building on and integrating this research on implicit theories of creativity, we argue that these instinctive ideas about creativity and creative people will influence differential evaluations of creative males and females, as well as creative employees of various ages.

IMPLICIT THEORIES OF CREATIVITY AND CREATORS' GENDER

When we consider implicit creativity models and uncertainty for gender and age, we must consider the related issues of role congruity theory (Diekman & Eagly, 2000) and lack of fit theory (Heilman, 2012). These theories are based on differential perceptions of leadership effectiveness for male and female leaders. They propose that: (1) many of the attributes of successful leaders (that is, assertive, decisive, independent, opinionated; Epitropaki & Martin, 2004) are incongruent with communal characteristics (that is, nurturing, compassionate, empathetic, warm; Ely et al., 2011) traditionally ascribed to women (Schein, 2001); and (2) this discrepancy between leader and gender roles often results in women being perceived as ineffective leaders (Eagly & Karau, 2002).

Scholars have applied this theory to explain why the same work behavior is evaluated differently for men and women. In essence, this research has suggested that when women engage in stereotype-inconsistent work behaviors such as innovating, advocating self-interests during negotiations, or demonstrating explicit dominant behaviors, they are penalized for violating the behavioral expectations (Amanatullah & Tinsley, 2013; Heilman, 2012; Luksyte et al., 2018; Williams & Tiedens, 2016). Ironically, when women engage in work behaviors that are consistent with gender stereotypes, such as being helpful and advocating other interests during negotiations, their contributions are either ignored or not rewarded to the same extent as those of men (Heilman & Chen, 2005; Kulik & Olekalns, 2012).

Integrating with implicit models of creativity, we propose that engaging in creative activities represents a lack of fit for women and for older workers, but not for men or younger workers. With regard to gender, our theorizing is consistent with empirical evidence that has shown that creative and innovative work behaviors and creative thinking are stereotypically ascribed to men and not to women (Luksyte et al., 2018; Proudfoot et al., 2015). This is because being creative captures thinking outside the box, putting forward divergent, original ideas; actions that are likely to be associated with men, but represent lack of fit for women (Proudfoot et al., 2015). We also propose that female creativity will be associated with more uncertainty than that of men, leading to more negative outcomes for the former than the latter. Increased uncertainty results in effortful information processing (Heilman, 2012), and we argue that raters will have to put more effort into assessing female creativity than that of men because creativity is a stereotype-inconsistent behavior for the former. Such biased expectations of raters lead to biased evaluations, which negatively affect the formation of an overall impression of female workers engaging in stereotype-inconsistent behavior by generating creative ideas. Because of the increased effort to process such behaviors, these actions may be ignored, interpreted differently for men and women, or not remembered.

Supporting our theorizing, research shows that female negotiators are perceived as competent but not likeable if they adopt stereotypically masculine negotiation strategies such as self-advocating and asserting their own interests during negotiations

(Amanatullah & Tinsley, 2013). Conversely, creative men will reap the benefits associated with being creative because individual creativity is a stereotypically masculine behavior (Luksyte et al., 2018; Proudfoot et al., 2015).

In addition to accruing mainly negative consequences for engaging in creative activities, we argue that both aspects of creativity will be perceived differentially for women and men. In particular, being creative captures the generation of novel and useful ideas (Zhou et al., 2019). The novelty aspect of creativity is likely to be associated with originality, divergent and outside-the-box thinking; all masculine attributes (Proudfoot et al., 2015). Similarly, the usefulness aspect is associated with competence, proficiency, and knowledge, which again are associated negatively for women; women are perceived as less competent than men (Fiske, 2017). Given this, we argue that both aspects of creativity – usefulness and novelty – will be assessed as lower for ideas generated by women than for the same ideas generated by men.

IMPLICIT THEORIES OF CREATIVITY AND CREATORS' AGE

Lack of fit theory (Heilman, 2012) may also prove useful in explaining: (1) why older creative employees may receive negative outcomes for their creativity; and (2) how novelty and usefulness aspects of creativity may be viewed differently for older versus younger creators. Research on age stereotypes suggests that older people are perceived to be less creative, less adaptable, less flexible, and more resistant to change (Posthuma & Campion, 2009). Although meta-analytic evidence failed to support any age differences in the enactment of creative behaviors (Ng & Feldman, 2013a), stereotypes about how older workers lack creativity persist (Rietzschel et al., 2016). Based on this literature, we argue that creative older employees will receive more negative outcomes than their younger counterparts because older workers' creativity is inconsistent with negative stereotypes (for example, less creative) about older people.

In essence, being creative represents a lack of fit for older employees because creative people are usually portrayed as challenging status quo trailblazers (Proudfoot et al., 2015). Older employees do not fit this prototype because they are stereotypically viewed as lacking these characteristics (Fiske, 2017). As such, the creativity exhibited by older employees will require effortful processing and will likely be viewed with increased uncertainty. Conversely, being creative is more fitting to an image of a younger worker, who is viewed as bold, flexible, having strength and energy to challenge the status quo. Because of this, younger employees are likely receive more positive outcomes for their creativity than their older co-workers. This is because perceiving their creativity does not require additional effort associated with overcoming stereotypes and increased uncertainty.

In terms of the usefulness and novelty aspects of the creative process, we argue that older employees' creativity will be evaluated as high in usefulness, but low in novelty. We base these predictions on the content of the age stereotypes and prototypical nature of creativity. Older people are viewed as those accumulating many resources such as knowledge, power, and connections; all these resources should equip them to generate useful, easy-to-implement ideas, processes, procedures, and solutions (Ng & Feldman, 2013a). Yet, older employees are stereotypically described as lacking flexibility and creativity, and scoring lower on openness to new experiences. Given the centrality of these characteristics for the perceived novelty of creativity (Loewenstein & Mueller, 2016), we argue that older people will be viewed as low on this aspect of creativity. Unfortunately, to our knowledge there is no research that has examined the evaluation of ideas generated by older employees compared to those generated by younger employees. Given the nature of our aging populations around the world, this neglect is a significant concern and one which research must address.

DOES TYPE OF CREATIVITY MATTER?

There are different types of creativity. For example, we can differentiate between radical and incremental creativity (Madjar et al., 2011). We can also differentiate types of creativity based on the motivational driver and the initial problem to be solved, leading to proactive, contributory, expected, and responsive creativity (Unsworth, 2001; Unsworth & Luksyte, 2015). People have different motivations to engage in the creative process. Some may be driven to be creative because their job requires creative output (for example, architects), others may be creative because they are internally curious to discover something new even though their job does not require creativity. Unsworth (2001) therefore developed a theory of creativity types based on why people engage in creativity (internally driven versus externally driven) and what problem they try to solve (open versus closed problems): (1) proactive creativity is internally driven and an open problem; (2) contributory creativity is internally driven and a closed problem; (3) expected creativity is externally driven and an open problem; and (4) responsive creativity is externally driven and a closed problem. Unsworth and Luksyte (2015) show how these types have been used in creativity research. More interestingly, we believe that they will prompt different reactions to evaluations of ideas produced by those of varying gender and age.

Gender

Given that radical creativity and creativity driven by open problems (that is, proactive and expected creativity) generate the most uncertainty, we suggest that these are most likely to be situations where evaluator identity threat comes to the fore for female creative employees. Nonetheless, when taking role congruity also into account, we expect that female creative employees will experience most formal and interpersonal discrimination when they engage in a type of creativity that is driven solely by intrinsic motivation and concerns solving either open problems (that is, proactive creativity) or closed problems (that is, contributory creativity).

In this sense, contributory creativity is voluntary and research shows that there are differences in how volitional work behaviors (for example, helping; Heilman & Chen, 2005) are viewed and appraised for men and women. Consequently, women who engage in contributory creativity would likely be ignored or not appraised positively because being helpful is stereotypically a female type of behaviour (Heilman & Chen, 2005). Notably, some helping behaviors (for example, civic virtue, sportsmanship) are considered to be stereotypically masculine behaviors because they require agentic characteristics such as assertiveness (Heilman, 2012). Because of this lack of fit, helping employees to perform creatively may be viewed as stereotypically masculine behavior (Luksyte et al., 2018). In addition to being ignored for being helpful (stereotypically feminine behaviour), women who engage in contributory creativity may be appraised negatively as they violate gender stereotypes by assisting with creativity-required solutions.

Further, women who engage in proactive creativity will likely proactively violate gender stereotypes because they perform stereotypically masculine behaviors (Luksyte et al., 2013), and they are not expected to do that. In contrast to contributory creativity, women who engage in proactive creativity may have violated stereotypical norms about how they should behave (for example, being nice and warm and not challenging the status quo; Eagly & Karau, 2002). As such, they may have experienced negative consequences (Luksyte et al., 2013) and be unlikely to engage in another proactive creativity attempt. Thus, we argue that creative women who engage in either contributory or proactive creativity will experience more formal discrimination in terms of more negative performance evaluations and less promotion than creative men. Women who engage in these types of creativity will also receive more interpersonal discrimination manifested in increased incivility and jealousy.

Age

Flexibility, willingness to take risks, challenging status quo, and technological savvy is more associated with younger than older employees. Accordingly, when older employees engage in proactive creativity they behave inconsistently with stereotypes: they are intrinsically driven to make a discovery that requires much mental capacity and excellent technology skills. Thus, older workers who proactively attempt to discover better work processes (proactive creativity), may receive more negative outcomes from their co-workers (for example, greater resistance, dissatisfaction, and so on). In terms of contributory creativity and age, we propose that, similar to women engaging in this type of creativity, others will either ignore or not reward to the same degree older compared to younger creators. In comparison to younger employees, older workers are stereotyped as more reliable, loyal, dependable, and thus are expected to help others by, for example, transferring their knowledge to less experienced co-workers (Truxillo et al., 2012). Further, older workers are also expected to accumulate much procedural and declarative knowledge, which they are expected to use for solving concrete, organization-specific issues. In essence, we argue that, due to these stereotypes, older workers are expected to engage in contributory creativity, wherein they willingly assist their co-workers with specific, work-related problems.

We further propose that because of these stereotypical expectations, older workers will not receive as much credit for their contributory creativity as their younger counterparts. Recent research indirectly supports our predictions by showing that older employees who lacked interdepartmental collaboration were perceived as less creative, and thus were penalized for not conforming to age stereotypes about being helpful with lower performance and promotability ratings (Guillen & Kunze, 2019).

DOES THE IMPLEMENTATION OF TYPES OF CREATIVITY MATTER?

Gender

In addition to different types of creativity, the creativity process may vary at its implementation stage. People may be either radically creative and bring about significant breakthroughs, or their creativity may be incremental, which represent modifications to existing processes (Ettlie et al., 1984). Because radical creativity entails a complete revamping of the existing work processes and because people are inherently resistant to change (Oreg, 2003), it is logical to assume that radical creativity will result in more negative consequences than incremental creativity. We also argue that creative women will receive more negative outcomes the more radical their creative outputs and behaviors are. Because implementation of radical breakthroughs requires a willingness to take risks and career commitment (Madjar et al., 2011), it is likely to be more associated with men than women. Because of this masculine nature of radical creativity, women who aspire to generate and implement radical breakthroughs will violate stereotypical norms and expectations of a prototypical creator, who tends to be a man (Luksyte et al., 2018). Thus, they will receive more negative outcomes for their creativity, the greater radicalness of their creativity is.

Conversely, incremental improvements to the systems usually grow from organizational conformity and the presence of creative (and potentially helpful) co-workers (Madjar et al., 2011). Although, in general, being creative is associated more with men than women (Luksyte et al., 2018; Proudfoot et al., 2015), engaging in incremental creativity may be more consistent with stereotypically acceptable female behaviors such as helpfulness. As such, female innovators who implement incremental improvements will receive fewer negative outcomes than innovative women engaging in radical creativity.

Age

We further propose that others will perceive radical and incremental creativity exhibited by older and younger employees differently. In particular, older employees are attributed with such positive characteristics as loyalty to the organization, reliability, accuracy, and interpersonal skills (Ng & Feldman, 2013b; Posthuma & Campion, 2009). These characteristics are likely to play an important role in incremental creativity, where employees must have a thorough understanding of an organization and its processes to improve them. As such, we argue that when older employees engage in incremental creativity they behave consistently with positive stereotypes about them and thus will receive positive outcomes. On the other hand, negative stereotypes describe older people as lacking "hard" qualities such as physical and mental capacity, the willingness to learn, flexibility, risk-taking, and new technology skills (Posthuma & Campion, 2009). Radical creativity likely necessitates these characteristics. Accordingly, when older employees engage in radical creativity they may receive negative consequences because they violate negative stereotypes about them.

IMPLICATIONS FOR RESEARCHERS

To date, much of the advice for creativity researchers has been to use manager (or peer) ratings of employee creativity (see Anderson et al., 2014). We do not disagree that this removes error due to self-reporting biases and impression management. Furthermore, when the creator is anonymous and/or many evaluators are providing creativity ratings of the ideas, then the consensual assessment technique (Amabile, 1982) is a strong and well-validated approach. However, what do we do when evaluators are affected not only by their own views of creativity (Zhou et al., 2019), but also by the stereotypes and threat suggested by the characteristics of the creator? The former can be accounted for by ensuring that the same manager rates all employees in question; this will control for the individual difference in creativity associations. Yet, how do we account for differential ratings of female and older creative employees? It becomes difficult to trust ratings by others when assessing research outcomes. Instead, we suggest that research needs to combine both self-ratings with manager or peer ratings of creativity. This combination does not generate a perfect score without any bias; however, each may compensate for the biases associated with the other source.

   We also recognize that we have probably opened up a Pandora's box of biases that may affect the evaluation of creativity. Not only are there other characteristics likely to engender identity threat, such as status or experience, but other factors involved in the relationship between the evaluator and the creator are likely to affect the rating. For example, while leader–member exchange has been associated with increased employee creativity (e.g., Liao et al., 2010; Tierney et al., 1999), and while it has been shown in meta-analysis to have a relationship with objective performance (Martin et al., 2016), it is likely that the paradoxical nature of creativity will mean that the exchange relationship will bias creativity evaluations. In particular, an outgroup exchange member will be more likely to receive the negative reactions to their creative idea, while an ingroup member will be more likely to receive the positive reactions. These, and other interpersonal factors, are likely to affect creativity evaluations, and much more research needs to examine them.

IMPLICATIONS FOR ORGANIZATIONS

Increasing participation and creative contributions of women and older employees will lift productivity and economic growth around the world. Yet, this may not happen if, as our research suggests, these employees are not recognized and/or not rewarded to the same extent as their younger male counterparts for their creativity, representing another form of discrimination. What can organizations do to rectify this? One potential means might be to systematically address the stereotypical associations with creativity of men and younger employees as opposed to women and older workers. Stereotypes are often a function of ignorance, as many employees simply could be unaware that women and older employees were responsible for many great creative products. Specifically, female creators are responsible for such innovations as the circular saw, liquid paper, windshield wipers, and Kevlar, among others. Further, although the stereotypes about how creativity belongs to the young are prevalent, meta-analytic evidence has failed to show any age differences in actual creativity (Ng & Feldman, 2013a). This meta-analytic evidence is corroborated by statistics that more than 54 percent of innovations were created by innovators older than 40 years old (Alexander, 2015). Accordingly, educational initiatives that inform participants about the ability of both genders and both younger and older people to generate novel and useful ideas and thus be creative could prove highly beneficial. For instance, simply exposing employees to information about noteworthy female and older creative minds and, thus, eliminating their "blind spot" on this issue, may help to attenuate the younger male creator association (Pronin & Kugler, 2007).

Despite the biased nature of idea evaluation process, scholarship has unpacked several strategies that proved useful in minimizing these biases among both evaluators and creators (Licuanan et al., 2007). These biases could be eliminated if evaluators actively discuss the properties of these ideas with others (Licuanan et al., 2007). Creators could also be trained to detect their creative idea with the most potential if they focus on the abstract or "bigger picture" aspects of these ideas (Berg, 2019).

This can be done either formally through training sessions, or informally via creating a favorable diversity and inclusion climate, wherein all employees feel that their creative contributions are welcomed, supported, and rewarded irrespective of their gender or age (Richard et al., 2019). In particular, during training, managers could be educated about the biasing effects of gender and age on evaluation of employees' creativity. They could be informed about how and why these biases adversely impact promotion of fair employment practices, and managers could be trained to avoid exercising these biases in their decision-making (Lee et al., 2015). Considering recent evidence that training reduced managers' penchant to attribute stereotype-consistent behaviours of their Black employees (Stewart et al., 2010), such organizational efforts may prove useful in minimizing discrimination in the workplace. Providing managers with clear performance criteria for ratings and detailed records of past behavior (for example, examples of creative work behaviors) may help supervisors to eliminate biases when evaluating creative work behaviors and outputs of their older and female employees.

Further, organizations may eliminate formal and interpersonal discrimination of their creative employees based on their demographics by fostering a favorable diversity climate. This refers to employee shared perceptions about how well their organization adheres to fair personnel practices and integrates minority incumbents into work (McKay et al., 2008). In a favorable diversity climate, employment decisions (for example, promotion) are based on people's contributions (for example, creativity), not their demographics (McKay et al., 2008); and people have equal access to valuable organizational resources, which help them to succeed. Although a hospitable diversity climate is beneficial for all employees (Avery et al., 2013; Hicks-Clarke & Iles, 2000), it has a particularly positive impact on minority employees' work experience, which is manifested in reduced turnover (McKay et al., 2007) and increased sales performance (McKay et al., 2008). Thus, based on this research we suggest that organizations can reduce formal and interpersonal discrimination of female creative workers and creative older employees by increasing awareness of the debilitating effects of biases in the treatment and evaluation of creators of different ages and gender, as well as fostering a favorable diversity climate wherein all employees, irrespective of their gender and age, feel recognized for their creativity.

CONCLUSION

To conclude our chapter, we wish to return to our original question: Does it matter who the creator is? Unfortunately, we believe that the answer is "Yes." The perception, assessment, and evaluation of ideas, when the creator is known to the evaluator, will be biased by perceptions of threat and uncertainty, together with the fit of the creator to the implicit model of a creative person. This means that women and older employees who present ideas will be less likely to have their ideas evaluated positively, particularly when they are proactive, contributory, or radical ideas, than a man or younger employee presenting the same idea. From a research perspective, this raises concerns about peer and managerial ratings of creativity. From a practical perspective, this sets off serious alarm bells for discrimination and loss of potential innovation. We encourage all those involved in creativity to pay attention to how and why creativity is evaluated the way it is.

REFERENCES

Alexander, S. 2015. Some of the greatest minds over 50. *Telegraph*, September 25.
Amabile, T.M. 1982. Social psychology of creativity: A consensual assessment technique. *Journal of Personality and Social Psychology*, 43(5): 997.
Amanatullah, E.T., & Tinsley, C.H. 2013. Punishing female negotiators for asserting too much ... or not enough: Exploring why advocacy moderates backlash against assertive female negotiators. *Organizational Behavior and Human Decision Processes*, 120: 110–122.

Anderson, N., Potočnik, K., & Zhou, J. 2014. Innovation and creativity in organizations: A state-of-the-science review, prospective commentary, and guiding framework. *Journal of Management*, 40(5): 1297–1333.

Argyris, C., & Schon, D. 1978. *Organizational learning*. Reading, MA: Addison-Wesley.

Ashcraft, K.L. 2005. Resistance through consent? Occupational identity, organizational form, and the maintenance of masculinity among commercial airline pilots. *Management Communication Quarterly*, 19(1): 67–90.

Australian Bureau of Statistics. 2011. *Labor force, Australia*.

Avery, D.R. 2011. Why the playing field remains uneven: Impediments to promotions in organizations. In S. Zedeck (ed.), *APA handbook of industrial and organizational psychology: Maintaining, expanding, and contracting the organization* (Vol. 3): 577–613. Washington, DC: American Psychological Association.

Avery, D.R., Volpone, S.D., Stewart, R.W., Luksyte, A., Hernandez, M., et al. 2013. Examining the draw of diversity: How diversity climate perceptions affect job-pursuit intentions. *Human Resource Management*, 52: 175–193.

Baer, J., Kaufman, J.C., & Gentile, C.A. 2004. Extension of the consensual assessment technique to nonparallel creative products. *Creativity Research Journal*, 16(1): 113–117.

Barling, J. 1996. The prediction, experience, and consequences of workplace violence. In G.R. VandenBos & E.Q. Bulatao (eds), *Violence on the job: Identifying risks and developing solutions*: 29–49. American Psychological Association. https://doi.org/10.1037/10215-001.

Berg, J.M. 2016. Balancing on the creative highwire: Forecasting the success of novel ideas in organizations. *Administrative Science Quarterly*, 61(3): 433–468.

Berg, J.M. 2019. When silver is gold: Forecasting the potential creativity of initial ideas. *Organizational Behavior and Human Decision Processes*, 154: 96–117.

Dailey, L., & Mumford, M.D. 2006. Evaluative aspects of creative thought: Errors in appraising the implications of new ideas. *Creativity Research Journal*, 18(3): 367–384.

Deaux, K., & Ethier, K.A. 1998. Negotiating social identity. In J.K. Swim & C. Stangor (eds), *Prejudice*: 301–323. Cambridge, MA: Elsevier.

Diekman, A.B., & Eagly, A.H. 2000. Stereotypes as dynamic constructs: Women and men of the past, present, and future. *Personality and Social Psychology Bulletin*, 26: 1171–1188.

Dollinger, S.J., & Shafran, M. 2005. Note on consensual assessment technique in creativity research. *Perceptual and Motor Skills*, 100(3): 592–598.

Eagly, A.H., & Karau, S.J. 2002. Role congruity theory of prejudice toward female leaders. *Psychological Review*, 109: 573–598.

Eilam, G., & Shamir, B. 2005. Organizational change and self-concept threats: A theoretical perspective and a case study. *Journal of Applied Behavioral Science*, 41(4): 399–421.

Elsbach, K.D., & Kramer, R.M. 2003. Assessing creativity in Hollywood pitch meetings: Evidence for a dual-process model of creativity judgments. *Academy of Management Journal*, 46(3): 283–301.

Ely, R.J., Ibarra, H., & Kolb, D.M. 2011. Taking gender into account: Theory and design for women's leadership development programs. *Academy of Management Learning and Education*, 10: 474–493.

Epitropaki, O., & Martin, R. 2004. Implicit leadership theories in applied settings: Factor structure, generalizability, and stability over time. *Journal of Applied Psychology*, 89: 293–310.

Ettlie, J.E., Bridges, W.P., & Okeefe, R.D. 1984. Organization strategy and structural differences for radical versus incremental innovation. *Management Science*, 30: 682–695.

Fiske, S.T. 2017. Prejudices in cultural contexts: Shared stereotypes (gender, age) versus variable stereotypes (race, ethnicity, religion). *Perspectives on Psychological Science*, 12(5): 791–799.

Gino, F., & Ariely, D. 2012. The dark side of creativity: Original thinkers can be more dishonest. *Journal of Personality and Social Psychology*, 102(3): 445–459.

Griffin, M.A., Neal, A., & Parker, S.K. 2007. A new model of work role performance: Positive behavior in uncertain and interdependent contexts. *Academy of Management Journal*, 50: 327–347.

Guillen, L., & Kunze, F. 2019. When age does not harm innovative behavior and perceptions of competence: Testing interdepartmental collaboration as a social buffer. *Human Resource Management*, 58(3): 301–316.

Harrison, S.H., & Wagner, D.T. 2016. Spilling outside the box: The effects of individuals' creative behaviors at work on time spent with their spouses at home. *Academy of Management Journal*, 59(3): 841–859.

Heilman, M.E. 2012. Gender stereotypes and workplace bias. *Research in Organizational Behavior: An Annual Series of Analytical Essays and Critical Reviews*, 32: 113–135.

Heilman, M.E., & Chen, J.J. 2005. Same behavior, different consequences: Reactions to men's and women's altruistic citizenship behavior. *Journal of Applied Psychology*, 90: 431–441.

Helzer, E.G., & Kim, S.H. 2019. Creativity for workplace well-being. *Academy of Management Perspectives*, 33(2): 134–147.

Hickey, M. 2001. An application of Amabile's consensual assessment technique for rating the creativity of children's musical compositions. *Journal of Research in Music Education*, 49(3): 234–244.

Hicks-Clarke, D., & Iles, P. 2000. Climate for diversity and its effects on career and organisational attitudes and perceptions. *Personnel Review*, 29: 324–345.

Hogg, M.A. 2000. Subjective uncertainty reduction through self-categorization: A motivational theory of social identity processes. *European Review of Social Psychology*, 11: 223–255.

Hon, A.H.Y., Bloom, M., & Crant, J.M. 2014. Overcoming resistance to change and enhancing creative performance. *Journal of Management*, 40(3): 919–941.

Janssen, O., van de Vliert, E., & West, M. 2004. The bright and dark sides of individual and group innovation: A Special Issue introduction. *Journal of Organizational Behavior*, 25: 129–145.

Johnson, T.D., & Joshi, A. 2016. Dark clouds or silver linings? A stigma threat perspective on the implications of an autism diagnosis for workplace well-being. *Journal of Applied Psychology*, 101(3): 430.

Kinias, Z., & Sim, J. 2016. Facilitating women's success in business: Interrupting the process of stereotype threat through affirmation of personal values. *Journal of Applied Psychology*, 101(11): 1585.

Kulik, C.T., & Olekalns, M. 2012. Negotiating the Gender Divide: Lessons From the Negotiation and Organizational Behavior Literatures. *Journal of Management*, 38(4): 1387–1415.

Lee, S.Y., Pitesa, M., Thau, S., & Pillutla, M.M. 2015. Discrimination in selection decisions: Integrating stereotype fit and interdependence theories. *Academy of Management Journal*, 58(3): 789–812.

Liao, H., Liu, D., & Loi, R. 2010. Looking at both sides of the social exchange coin: A social cognitive perspective on the joint effects of relationship quality and differentiation on creativity. *Academy of Management Journal*, 53(5): 1090–1109.

Licuanan, B.F., Dailey, L.R., & Mumford, M.D. 2007. Idea evaluation: Error in evaluating highly original ideas. *Journal of Creative Behavior*, 41(1): 1–27.

Loewenstein, J., & Mueller, J. 2016. Implicit theories of creative ideas: How culture guides creativity assessments. *Academy of Management Discoveries*, 2(4): 320–348.

Lu, S., Bartol, K.M., Venkataramani, V., Zheng, X., & Liu, X. 2019. Pitching novel ideas to the boss: The interactive effects of employees' idea enactment and influence tactics on creativity assessment and implementation. *Academy of Management Journal*, 62(2), 579–606.

Luksyte, A., Unsworth, K.L., & Avery, D. 2013. Innovation and gender: Why are women not rewarded for innovative work behaviours. *2013 Australia and New Zealand Academy of Management Conference*. Hobart, Tasmania.

Luksyte, A., Unsworth, K.L., & Avery, D.R. 2018. Innovative work behavior and sex-based stereotypes: Examining sex differences in perceptions and evaluations of innovative work behavior. *Journal of Organizational Behavior*, 39: 292–305.

Madjar, N., Greenberg, E., & Chen, Z. 2011. Factors for radical creativity, incremental creativity, and routine, noncreative performance. *Journal of Applied Psychology*, 96: 730–743.

Martin, R., Guillaume, Y., Thomas, G., Lee, A., & Epitropaki, O. 2016. Leader–member exchange (LMX) and performance: A meta-analytic review. *Personnel Psychology*, 69(1): 67–121.

Martins, L.L., & Shalley, C.E. 2011. Creativity in virtual work: Effects of demographic differences. *Small Group Research*, 42(5): 536–561.

McKay, P.F., Avery, D.R., & Morris, M.A. 2008. Mean racial-ethnic differences in employee sales performance: The moderating role of diversity climate. *Personnel Psychology*, 61: 349–374.

McKay, P.F., Avery, D.R., Tonidandel, S., Morris, M.A., Hernandez, M., & Hebl, M.R. 2007. Racial differences in employee retention: Are diversity climate perceptions the key? *Personnel Psychology*, 60: 35–62.

Mueller, J.S., Goncalo, J.A., & Kamdar, D. 2011. Recognizing creative leadership: Can creative idea expression negatively relate to perceptions of leadership potential? *Journal of Experimental Social Psychology*, 47: 494–498.

Mueller, J.S., Melwani, S., & Goncalo, J.A. 2012. The bias against creativity: Why people desire but reject creative ideas. *Psychological Science*, 23: 13–17.

Ng, T.W.H., & Feldman, D.C. 2013a. A meta-analysis of the relationships of age and tenure with innovation-related behaviour. *Journal of Occupational and Organizational Psychology*, 86(4): 585–616.

Ng, T.W.H., & Feldman, D.C. 2013b. A meta-analysis of the relationships of age and tenure with innovation-related behaviour. *Journal of Occupational and Organizational Psychology*, 86: 585–616.

Oreg, S. 2003. Resistance to change: Developing an individual differences measure. *Journal of Applied Psychology*, 88: 680–693.

Pagliaro, S., Alparone, F.R., Pacilli, M.G., & Mucchi-Faina, A. 2011. Managing a social identity threat. *Social Psychology*, 43(1): 41–45.

Pietri, E.S., Johnson, I.R., & Ozgumus, E. 2018. One size may not fit all: Exploring how the intersection of race and gender and stigma consciousness predict effective identity-safe cues for Black women. *Journal of Experimental Social Psychology*, 74: 291–306.

Posthuma, R.A., & Campion, M.A. 2009. Age stereotypes in the workplace: Common stereotypes, moderators, and future research directions. *Journal of Management*, 35: 158–188.

Pronin, E., & Kugler, M.B. 2007. Valuing thoughts, ignoring behavior: The introspection illusion as a source of the bias blind spot. *Journal of Experimental Social Psychology*, 43: 565–578.

Proudfoot, D., Kay, A.C., & Koval, C.Z. 2015. A gender bias in the attribution of creativity archival and experimental evidence for the perceived association between masculinity and creative thinking. *Psychological Science*, 26: 1751–1761.

Richard, O.C., Avery, D.R., Luksyte, A., Boncoeur, O.D., & Spitzmueller, C. 2019. Improving organizational newcomers' creative job performance through creative process engagement: The moderating role of a synergy diversity climate. *Personnel Psychology*, 72(3): 421–444.

Rietzschel, E.F., Nijstad, B.A., & Stroebe, W. 2019. Why great ideas are often overlooked. In P.B. Paulus & B.A. Nijstad (eds), *The Oxford handbook of group creativity and innovation*: 179–200. Oxford: Oxford University Press.

Rietzschel, E.F., Zacher, H., & Stroebe, W. 2016. A Lifespan Perspective on Creativity and Innovation at Work. *Work Aging and Retirement*, 2(2): 105–129.

Schein, V.E. 2001. A global look at psychological barriers to women's progress in management. *Journal of Social Issues*, 57: 675–688.

Shalley, C.E., Zhou, J., & Oldham, G.R. 2004. The effects of personal and contextual characteristics on creativity: Where should we go from here? *Journal of Management*, 30(6): 933–958.

Sinclair, R.R., Martin, J.E., & Croll, L.W. 2002. A threat-appraisal perspective on employees' fears about antisocial workplace behavior. *Journal of Occupational Health Psychology*, 7(1): 37.

Stewart, T.L., Latu, I.M., Kawakami, K., & Myers, A. 2010. Consider the situation: Reducing automatic stereotyping through situational attribution training. *Journal of Experimental Social Psychology*, 46: 221–225.

Stone, J., Harrison, C.K., & Mottley, J. 2012. "Don't call me a student-athlete": The effect of identity priming on stereotype threat for academically engaged African American college athletes. *Basic and Applied Social Psychology*, 34(2): 99–106.

Thoits, P.A. 1991. On merging identity theory and stress research. *Social Psychology Quarterly*, 54(2): 101–112.

Tierney, P., Farmer, S.M., & Graen, G.B. 1999. An examination of leadership and employee creativity: The relevance of traits and relationships. *Personnel Psychology*, 52(3): 591–620.

Torrance, E.P. 1972. Predictive validity of the Torrance tests of creative thinking. *Journal of Creative Behavior*, 6(4): 236–252.

Truxillo, D.M., McCune, E.A., Bertolino, M., & Fraccaroli, F. 2012. Perceptions of older versus younger workers in terms of big five facets, proactive personality, cognitive ability, and job performance. *Journal of Applied Social Psychology*, 42(11): 2607–2639.

Unsworth, K.L. 2001. Unpacking creativity. *Academy of Management Review*, 26: 289–297.

Unsworth, K.L., & Luksyte, A. 2015. Is all creativity created equal? Examining different types and levels of creativity. In C.E. Shalley, M. Hitt, & J. Zhou (eds), *Oxford handbook of creativity, innovation, and entrepreneurship: Multilevel linkages*: 279–301. Oxford: Oxford University Press.

Unsworth, K.L. & Robinson, M. Forthcoming. On a scale from … Creativity survey scales. In V. Doerfler & M. Stierand (eds), *Handbook of research methods on creativity*. Cheltenham, UK and Northampton, MA, USA: Edward Elgar Publishing.

Williams, M.J., & Tiedens, L.Z. 2016. The subtle suspension of backlash: A meta-analysis of penalties for women's implicit and explicit dominance behavior. *Psychological Bulletin*, 142(2): 165–197.

Wright, J. 2015. A social identity and social power perspective on terrorism. *Contemporary Voices: St Andrews Journal of International Relations*, 6(3): 76–83.

Zhou, J., Wang, X.M., Bavato, D., Tasselli, S., & Wu, J.F. 2019. Understanding the receiving side of creativity: A multidisciplinary review and implications for management research. *Journal of Management*, 45(6): 2570–2595.

Zhou, J., Wang, X.M., Song, L.J., & Wu, J. 2017. Is it new? Personal and contextual influences on perceptions of novelty and creativity. *Journal of Applied Psychology*, 102(2): 180.

Zhou, J., & Woodman, R.W. 2003. Managers' recognition of employees' creative ideas. In L.V. Shavinina (ed.), *International handbook on innovation*: 631–640. Hillsdale, NJ: Erlbaum.

15. Using qualitative methods to generate divergence in creativity theory

Elizabeth D. Rouse and Michael G. Pratt

INTRODUCTION

After a period of steady growth of research and convergence around the definition of creativity as the production of novel and useful ideas, the very foundations of creativity are currently being questioned. As we elucidate in more detail below, this questioning extends to how we conceptualize, elicit, and measure creativity. Even the componential model, arguably the most influential model of creativity, has been recently revised, adding new and heretofore un- and underexplored linkages inherent in creativity and innovation (Amabile & Pratt, 2016). Because of the questioning of some of the foundational underpinnings underlying creativity, perhaps it is also time to rethink how we study creativity itself. In particular, this chapter explores methodologies that would be well suited to explore new and underexamined dynamics in creativity, potentially generating divergence in theory.

To date much of the research in creativity has utilized quantitative methods. Quantitative creativity research focuses primarily on the generation of novel and useful ideas. Recent reviews chronicle just how much we have learned (Anderson et al., 2014; Zhou & Hoever, 2014). For example, we know a great deal about the key individual, social, and contextual factors that enable people to generate creative ideas. However, scholars have also begun to question whether the field of creativity has perhaps been too narrow in its approach (Perry-Smith & Mannucci, 2017): is there more to creativity than just understanding how ideas are generated? Considering creative ideas as the primary dependent variable focuses our attention on some questions, while placing others out of view. For example, we know much more about creativity as an outcome than as a process. This outcome-oriented focus also raises a number of questions around the assessment of creativity. Who should assess creativity: the individual, the individual's supervisor, or a collective via the consensual assessment technique (Amabile, 1982; Park et al., 2016)? Should we measure novelty and usefulness separately? What are effective tasks for capturing creativity: asking people to draw aliens, or to come up with different uses for a brick? Taking a step back, the field has also focused narrowly on specific methodologies, particularly laboratory experiments and field surveys. As such, our knowledge of creativity to date is largely acontextual or undercontextualized. Unsworth (2001) raises the possibility that our methodologies have focused our attention on certain types of creativity and not others. Methodological narrowness likely contributes to the narrowness of the questions we ask. Indeed, specific research methodologies excel at answering certain questions and not others (McGrath, 1981). Given our field's focus on experimental and survey designs, what we lack are methods that can better incorporate the specificity and realism that are critical for understanding creativity dynamics within the contexts of organizations.

To be clear, such focus might have been necessary to bring creativity from the periphery of our field to the core; creativity research is now regularly published in the top management journals, where it once was not (see Amabile's, 2018, OB Academy of Management lifetime achievement address). However, to borrow from Isaac Newton (who borrowed it from others), professional knowledge builds by standing on the shoulders of giants, not lining up behind them. Amabile herself claimed in her recent lifetime achievement address that "it [a social psychology of creativity] is clearly a work in progress" and research will "go on for many, many decades." To continue to develop our theories of creativity, a broadening of the field seems needed. Changes and added complexities in organizations have outpaced changes in our theories. Considering technological advances specifically, Anderson and colleagues argue that "management science research has, if anything, lagged behind practice" (Anderson et al., 2014: 1323). They suggest that:

> there remains a real need for more, and more radical, theory-building contributions. Some of the most influential theories in the field have been around 20 to 30 years or even longer now (e.g., Amabile, 1983, 1988; West, 1990), and yet more recent theoretical contributions, or for that matter, counterpoint articles critical of existing theories and models, remain notable only by their absence. For a subfield whose *raison d'être* is to advance understanding of how new and innovative ideas flourish into implemented and valuable innovations, this is both paradoxical and perplexing. (ibid.: 1318)

In this chapter, we answer the call for more radical theory building by discussing a set of methods that excel at theory building and elaborating: field-based inductive qualitative methods (hereafter: "qualitative methods"). Although there have been some qualitative studies of creativity, we believe that, as a field, creativity has yet to take full advantage of these methodologies. We believe that broadening our methodological approach to creativity in this way can and will open up the opportunity to explore new questions and potentially provide pathways toward more creative creativity theory. Next, we offer an overview of qualitative research. Then, we discuss three key theoretical shifts that suggest potential paths forward for using qualitative research to expand creativity theories and the techniques and methodologies that might be particularly useful in tackling these shifts.

WHAT IS QUALITATIVE RESEARCH, AND HOW CAN IT ADDRESS SOME OF THE DEFICIENCIES IN THE CURRENT CREATIVITY LITERATURE?

Broadly defined, qualitative research is "any type of research that produces findings not arrived at by statistical procedures or other means of quantification" (Strauss &

Corbin, 1998: 10). More specifically, Locke & Golden-Biddle (2002: 100) suggest three characteristics that are central to qualitative research:

> In the first act, qualitative research takes place in natural settings ... Second, in the act of analysis, qualitative researchers work with verbal language rather than numerical language as indicators of the phenomenon of interest ... And finally, qualitative researchers communicate the results of that analysis in a textual form that verbally represents the empirical world studied.

Defined in this way, qualitative research is field research that collects and analyzes verbal data and presents the results in the form of text. "Qualitative" does not refer to a single methodology; rather, there are a variety of different methodologies in qualitative research including, but not limited to, ethnography, grounded theory, hermeneutics, narrative analysis, discourse analysis, phenomenology, and some forms of case studies. Our focus in this chapter is on inductive qualitative research, although deductive qualitative research is also possible (see Bitektine, 2008). As such, we focus on those qualitative methods that are used to build and extend theory rather than to test it.

Although different methodologies have different ontological and epistemological assumptions (and sometimes the same method, such as grounded theory, can be used from a variety of ontological perspectives; Locke, 2001), there are some commonalities among many qualitative methodologies. As noted in Table 15.1, qualitative methods tend to have different strengths and foci when compared to their quantitative brethren. Qualitative methods address specific types of research questions, collect specific types of data, and use sampling and analysis techniques that are different, by design, than other methodologies. In introducing the table, we want to begin with two important provisos. Firstly, the table outlines differences in how such methods are typically employed in management research; however, as noted with the example of deductive qualitative research, exceptions are possible. Secondly, although many of the data collection strategies we discuss in the table could be used to gather qualitative data, or could yield data that can be analyzed quantitatively (for example, number counts of observations for videos), we focus on their qualitative applications.

As noted by McGrath (1981), methods cannot be simultaneously strong in precision (for example, the ability to discern cause-and-effect relationships) like experimental methods, statistical generalizability like survey methods, and realism (for example, capturing unique contextual data) like qualitative methods. By gathering rich data in the field, qualitative methods allow a deep understanding of the phenomena being examined, allowing researchers a strong empirical scaffolding upon which to build or extend theory.

Qualitative methods also tend to ask different questions than those asked by quantitative methods, focusing more on "how?" and "why?"[1] questions rather than "how many?" and "how much?" Indeed, if you are wanting to explore how many people will change their behavior based on an intervention, such as the use of brainstorming on the production of creative ideas, qualitative research would not be a strong choice.

Table 15.1   Comparing the strengths and foci of qualitative and quantitative methods

	Qualitative	Quantitative
Overall strengths	Realism Theory building primarily (as inductive methods)	Generalizability (surveys), Precision (experimental studies) Theory testing primarily
Research question types	How and why	How many and how much
Common types of data collected	Semi-structured interviews, field observations (participant or non-participant), archival and other written documents, videos	Surveys or experimental observations
Who is studied	Informants	Subjects or respondents
Sampling	Purposive and theoretical	Random (ideally) or Convenience
Analysis	Process of moving from codes that are close to the data to ones that are more abstract, and ultimately using one's emergent theory to cast light on extant theorizing	Generating hypotheses from theory, collecting and analyzing data to test hypotheses

However, if your research questions are about how video game designers think about creativity (Rouse, 2013) or why an advertising specialist pitches some ideas and not others, then qualitative research will be better utilized. Such insights are strengthened by the types of data qualitative studies usually employ and the perspective that qualitative research takes with regard to those people studied.

With regard to the latter, qualitative research flips the traditional relationship between researcher and researched, allowing the researched to be the "experts" or "informants" who provide insights that the researcher will use to build new theory. This perspective is quite different than viewing those researched as experimental "subjects" where the researcher attempts to discover if their theoretically derived manipulations reveal the desired theoretical outcomes; or viewing others as respondents (as in a survey) to see whether their theories and resulting hypotheses are supported or not. In surveys and experiments, learning from those researched are in support of existing theory. However, if theory is lacking or is perhaps outdated – and as we have noted, our main theories of creativity are decades old – then new theories need to be built or existing theory needs to be modified or extended (Pratt & Bonaccio, 2016). In these situations, learning from the people "in the field" not only provides up-close knowledge of how organizational members think about and enact their environment, but it also allows for the formation of theories that are unique to organizational contexts (that is, "Big-O theories"; see Heath and Sitkin, 2001).

To get at these insights from informants, qualitative methods collect particular types of data. Semi-structured interviews, for example, allow you to "get into people's heads" and observations allow the researcher to see "what people do." Combined, they can provide insights into how creative workers interact with feedback providers (Harrison & Rouse, 2015) or how modern dancers coordinate in a flexible manner in the creation of new dance compositions (Harrison & Rouse, 2014). Collected over time, these methods also provide unique insights into processes, such as how and why progress facilitates the creative process (Amabile & Kramer, 2011).

Two additional and unique features of qualitative research involve sampling and analysis. Sampling occurs in both the choice of the context, and what to look at within a context. In general, sampling in qualitative studies is purposeful versus random. That is, the "cases" being examined should be ones where the dynamics the researcher is seeking to study should be visible. It is for this reason that qualitative researchers often pick "extreme cases" (Eisenhardt, 1989). Even after choosing an organization or group to study, qualitative researchers need to further identify what they are going to study, be it individuals, practices, events, processes, interactions, and so on. Patton (1990) offers several different choices for sampling strategies, including maximum variation sampling where the researcher attempts to sample broadly and on multiple dimensions (for example, tenure, organizational role, occupation) and stratified purposeful sampling that explores "characteristics of particular subgroups of interest" which "facilitates comparisons" among those subgroups (Patton, 1990: 182).[2] As more data is gathered and the researcher begins to form their own preliminary theories, sampling shifts from purposeful to "theoretical" in that the sampling changes based on emerging theoretical insights. To illustrate, in his study of Amway distributors, Pratt (2000) originally sampled people who loved or hated Amway. As he collected data, however, he also realized that there were other significant groups of Amway distributors: those who were in it but had mixed feelings about all aspects of the organization, and those who quit but did not hate the organization. Sampling these various groups was critical in developing a model of distributors that predicted strong positive identification, strong negative disidentification, neutral deidentification, and ambivalent identification.

Analysis in inductive research also varies across different qualitative methods, but also differs from quantitative methods. Methods such as grounded theory and ethnography, two of the more popular methods in management research, have a similar approach to data analysis. Whether referring to them as open (grounded theory) or first-order (ethnography) codes, one begins by coding very close to one's data. Put another way, initial codes often reflect or use *in vivo* terms used by the informants themselves. The end result is many codes, sometimes numbering in the hundreds or more. The next step is to see which codes "go together" and then label them using a more abstract code. For example, in Pratt's (2000) ethnography of Amway distributors, several practices such as cutting out a picture of something one desires and putting it on your desk for motivation, going to a car dealer and looking for the car you want most, and "getting out of your comfort zone," were abstracted as types of sensebreaking practices. The third general phase of analysis in grounded theory and ethnography is to see how these various axial codes "fit together" in the creation of new theory. In Pratt's (2000) case, success or failure in sensebreaking activities, combined with success or failure in sensegiving activities, were associated with the various identification outcomes he found (for example, identification, deidentification, disidentification, and ambivalent identification).

Taken together, as methods designed to build and extend theory rather than to test it, qualitative research differs from its quantitative, theory-testing, counterparts on a number of dimensions (see Table 15.1). As such, we suggest those wanting to adopt a qualitative methodology should do so after receiving some formalized training in that methodology (see Pratt & Bonaccio, 2016 for avenues for gaining qualitative methods training).

HOW EMBRACING QUALITATIVE RESEARCH MAY HELP TO SHIFT AND EXPAND THE QUESTIONS CREATIVITY RESEARCHERS EXPLORE: BUILDING FROM EXISTING STUDIES

To illustrate how qualitative methods may open up new areas of research, we consider three major theoretical shifts in creativity. In particular, we examine: (1) a shift from a focus on creative outcomes to a focus on creative processes; (2) a shift from thinking about inner work life as an independent variable to more of a dependent variable; and (3) a shift from creativity being "Big B" research to more "Big O" research. In this section, we zoom in by drawing upon illustrative examples of qualitative studies on creativity to show how some of these shifts are already occurring, or at least are aspirational. In the next section, we zoom out by discussing more generally what types of qualitative research techniques (for example, interviewing) or methodologies (for example, grounded theory) may be helpful in addressing these and similar creativity-related research in the future.

Shifting from a Focus on Creative Outcomes to a Focus on Creative Processes

As noted earlier, much of creativity research has been dominated by trying to understand how to increase the novelty and or usefulness of outcomes. Yet, papers have pointed to the importance of understanding the processes and activities that make up the creative process, and how people engage creative processes. For example, Drazin et al. (1999: 290) define creative engagement as "a process in which an individual behaviorally, cognitively, and emotionally attempts to produce creative outcomes" and claim that "creativity as a process is a necessary, but not sufficient, condition for creative outcomes." Considering attempts at creativity raises the possibility that creative engagement and the processes associated with it are important to understand whether or not they actually lead to an idea or product that is deemed creative. Zhang and Bartol (2010: 111–112) define creative process engagement as "employee involvement or engagement in creativity-relevant cognitive processes, including (1) problem identification, (2) information searching and encoding, and (3) idea and alternative generation." They developed an 11-item scale to measure creative process engagement that includes items such as "I spend considerable time trying to understand the nature of the problem," "I consult a wide variety of information," and "I generate a significant number of alternatives to the same problem before I choose the final solution." This type of quantitative measure provides a way to begin to capture how and when different stages of the creative process occur.

Quantitative survey measures (such as the creative process engagement scale), experiments, and archival measures (see Dean Simonton's work, as an example) are well suited to provide information about how often and when certain processes enable the generation of creative ideas and products. Qualitative methods, however, allow researchers to zoom in and zoom out of processes as they occur, to focus on more momentary experiences (zooming in) and more longitudinal dynamics (zooming out). As more qualitative researchers have taken up questions related to creativity, there has been a burgeoning area that explores creative processes in more social contexts and begins to challenge the idea that there is one creative process characterized by particular stages or activities. For example, some creative processes may involve more or fewer stages that may vary the order in which they occur. We discuss some of these studies, focusing on the methods, to provide a foundation for thinking about how future qualitative studies might both deepen and broaden our understanding of creative processes.

The study of moments of collective creativity by Hargadon and Bechky (2006) was instrumental to introducing qualitative methods into research on creative processes. They examined how six organizations (two management consulting firms, two product design consulting firms, and two internal consulting groups within management) solved problems to provide creative products to clients. The data consisted of interviews, project post-mortems, observations of work, tracking of particular projects, as well as documents and artifacts. The analysis involved an iterative process moving between data, theory, and literature that resulted in actions of categories related to collective creativity. The actions they describe – help-seeking, help-giving, reflective reframing, and reinforcing – combined insights from interviews, archives, technological artifacts, and field notes. Archival materials such as organizational handbooks provided insights about how people should solve problems, observations provided insights about how people actually solved problems, and interviews provided insights about how people perceived and interpreted how they solved problems.

As they write, Hargadon and Bechky's (2006) meso-level framework "shifts the focus from individuals to the interactions between them, and from a constant phenomenon (that is, creative individuals and organizations) to a series of momentary, transient phenomena (that is, creative moments in organizations)" (ibid.: 489); they theorize "how such collective moments of creativity happen in organizations, and explain the activities that make them possible" (ibid.: 489). This study reveals how qualitative methods, and observations in particular, can zoom in to understand actions and interactions in situ. Rather than focusing on the creativity of the outputs, this study builds new theory by focusing on the activities people engage in, in service of generating creative solutions.

Harrison and Rouse (2014) built on the foundation provided by Hargadon and Bechky (2006). They studied the group interactions of six modern dance groups over the course of ten weeks to better understand how groups coordinate their collective efforts in developing creative products. Although they completed interviews throughout the groups' processes, observations were the primary data. Recognizing the difficulty of capturing observations in field notes in the moment, particularly in a context that has a large non-verbal component (dance) and where actions are difficult to label and note, they video recorded the majority of the groups' meetings. These video recordings allowed Harrison and Rouse to return to key interactions and phases of the process once they were out of the field, as they iteratively moved through their data analysis. If something emerged as interesting in one group, they could return to the other groups' videos to see if the same dynamic was present in other groups, and compare and contrast the groups. They also conducted focus groups which allowed the groups to collectively reflect on their process once the product was complete, and allowed the researchers to support and expand their emerging theory. The interviews, in-person observations, video observations, and focus groups enabled the researchers to capture the majority of the interactions over time. In writing up their paper, Harrison and Rouse were able to incorporate detailed transcripts of interactions to "show" their data (Golden-Biddle & Locke, 2007; Pratt, 2009).

Observing creative workers' attempts to produce creative outputs enabled Harrison and Rouse to challenge, elaborate, and provide nuance to existing stage models of the creative process. As they write:

> Our model also extends our current understanding of creativity by challenging the dominant view of creativity as a linear process and, instead, suggesting the importance of cyclical group interactions that, over time, produce a creative composition. While stage models offer one view of the creative process, recent research in collective creativity has emphasized the importance of momentary interactions (Hargadon & Bechky, 2006). Yet, it is possible that, over the course of a creative project, these interactions occur in a sort of rhythm. (Harrison and Rouse, 2014: 1276)

Similarly, Harvey and Kou (2013) provide a more sophisticated understanding of how the sequences of the creative process occur over time in considering the "situated nature" of idea evaluation. Their study focused on four cross-functional United States healthcare policy groups attempting to produce policy recommendations (a form of creative output). The primary data were full verbatim transcripts for five meetings in each group over the course of five months (up until the point the first creative deliverable was due); these transcripts were publicly available. Meeting data was supplemented by other archival data such as agendas, presentations, and formal recommendations. Their analysis strategy moved from smaller units of time to larger: "we began by focusing on group interactions over a single idea, then placed these interactions in the context of meetings, and finally the group process over time" (Harvey and Kou, 2013: 353). They coded data moving from open coding to comparing codes. They then used visual maps (Langley, 1999) to examine the activities during the course of individual meetings, leading to an understanding of different modes of interactions. In the last stage of analysis, they zoomed out to consider how these modes occurred longitudinally across the meetings for each group.

Through their study, Harvey and Kou (2013) challenge how the role of idea evaluation in groups has been theorized. As they write:

Until now, research has concentrated on ways to improve idea generation in groups to answer this question. This approach assumes that the collective creative process mirrors that of individual creativity ... The problem is that this approach neglects the evaluative processes that are situated in the on-going interactions of creative groups. (ibid.: 347)

Their study suggests that evaluation is the point at which the process moves from individuals to a collective.

What becomes evident from these papers is not that creative output is unimportant, rather that understanding the activities, events, and actions that people engage in is critical to understanding how to achieve creative outputs. These studies show how observations, in particular, can enable the study of both more momentary interactions and more longitudinal processes.

Shifting from Thinking about Inner Work Life as an Independent Variable to more of a Dependent Variable

Amabile and Kramer (2007, 2011) have called attention to the importance of understanding "inner work lives" or the interplay of perceptions (sensemaking about work day events including organizations, people, work, and accomplishment), emotions (reactions to work day events), and motivations (the desire to do the work) that people experience. In regard to creativity specifically, though, scholars have studied most extensively the role of mood, affect, and motivation (cf. George, 2007). This research has been primarily directed at uncovering antecedents related to creativity. As George notes, "theorizing and research [in within-individual internal processes] was dominated by a quest to determine singular internal processes responsible for creativity" (George, 2007: 453). The primary goal of extant research on within-individual internal processes in creativity has been to uncover antecedents (such as motivation and emotions) that relate to creative outputs.

Amabile and Kramer's work provides a roadmap for how we might expand our inquiry into inner work life to better understand creativity and the experiences of creative workers. They studied 238 employees over the course of 19 weeks (on average) using daily diary-style questionnaires which included several quantitative scales and two open-ended narrative questions: one question asked the participants to describe one event from the day that stood out for them, and the other provided an open space for anything else that participants wanted to report. The data included 11,637 diary entries. For the qualitative analyses, the authors first read through the narratives. Then they conducted detailed "index" coding to catalogue various aspects of the events. From this catalogue they categorized major types of events, and created stories to capture both the experiences of individuals and the experiences of the teams of which they were a part over time. Through their study, they found that inner work life relates to people's creativity, productivity, work commitment, and collegiality.

Although this study speaks to inner work life broadly, we still lack profound insights and understandings about how people feel when they create, how people relate to what they create, and how creative workers feel about their work more generally. Moreover, the dynamic relationship between inner work life and its consequences are undertheorized. For example, we do not have a full understanding of how creative workers experience and perceive their work, or how these experiences and perceptions impact their ability to stay engaged in work over time, to work with clients, or to adapt to changing work environments. In other words, it seems important to consider what new research questions open up when we make the internal experiences of people creating central to our research, rather than an antecedent to creative outputs (Weiss & Rupp, 2011).

Recent work on identity serves as example of how qualitative methods develop and open up new research streams. Using quantitative approaches, scholars have grown interested in creative role identity (Jaussi et al., 2007; Tierney & Farmer, 2011; Wang & Cheng, 2010) – that is, the degree to which "the role of creative employee had been incorporated into self-identity" (Farmer et al., 2003: 623) – and its impact on creative outputs, both as an independent and and a moderating variable. Using qualitative approaches, however, deepens and transforms the focus of our understanding of creative identity. Elsbach and colleagues, for example, focus on identity as core to understanding creative collaboration in organizations. Elsbach (2009) studied how creative workers affirm their identities by developing signature styles. The analysis focused on interviews with ten creative workers and non-participant observation of four creative workers as they designed new toy cars. Elsbach observed brainstorming sessions, focus groups, prototype testing, and other meetings, as well as shadowed creative workers. She used finished toy cars to confirm that signature styles were identifiable in retail products. She found that designers used signature styles to confirm their identities as either independent or idealistic creators, even in corporate contexts. In a related study, Elsbach and Flynn (2013) considered how creative workers' personal identities impacted their willingness to collaborate at work. The study reveals that differences in personal identities can partially explain when and how creative workers collaborate. The data included interviews with 40 designers who were actively designing prototypes, and 100 hours of observation. For both of these studies, an iterative data analysis approach was used. To understand personal identity categorizations, Elsbach and Flynn coded the interview transcripts. To understand the collaborative behaviors, both the interviews and observations were coded.

Taken together, these studies highlight the importance of better understanding how creative workers think about themselves and their work in order to understand how effective creativity occurs in organizations. As Elsbach (2009: 1043) articulated:

> [M]ost of this research begins with the assumption that creative workers will be satisfied with producing products that fit the needs of consumers and will be willing to adhere to the practical constraints imposed by budget, safety, and marketing needs ... These perspectives appear to discount the importance of individual, creative vision for creative workers and the associated professional identities that these workers hold.

These studies recognize that creative workers are not just idea-generating machines that produce ideas on demand; instead, creative workers have varying inner work lives that shape when and how they want to create in organizations. This approach enriches our understanding of creativity, without needing to quantitatively measure creativity.

Qualitative research has proved important to understanding people's identities and sense of work meaningfulness, or work that is perceived to be "at minimum, purposeful and significant" (Pratt & Ashforth, 2003: 311). In efforts to understand creativity more fully, researchers are beginning to take up these topics. In addition to the work on personal identities described above, Amabile and Pratt (2016), in revising the componential model of creativity, theorize the importance of meaningfulness in the creative process. They write:

> With regard to meaningful work, given that most of the linkages we have suggested to meaningful work have been either unexplored or under-explored, we believe that empirical research in this area is critical. Most basically, we wonder if there is indeed a connection between meaningful work and positive affect, and if so, under what conditions this relationship might be strengthened or weakened. (Amabile and Pratt, 2016: 180)

Although there has been research on traditional job characteristics (for example, autonomy) and employee creativity, little research has been done on the impact of the social and contextual dimensions of work (see Oldham & Fried, 2016). We would go further, moving beyond characteristics of jobs to how work is perceived in the minds of the workers. Qualitative methods can be fruitful in pushing these streams of research forward, since they are well suited to understanding questions related to people's interpretations and experiences. As Amabile and Kramer (2011: 18) observe, "Inner work life is the mostly invisible part of each individual's experience"; qualitative methods help to surface these invisible experiences, making them more visible. It would also be possible to consider these inner work life experiences in concert with quantifiable indicators of creativity.

Shifting from Creativity being "Big-B" Research to more "Big-O" Research

In reviewing existing research on organizational behavior, Heath and Sitkin (2001) offer a typology that weights differently the "O" and "B" in organizational behavior. They suggest that Big-B research focuses on interesting behavior that might be relevant to organizations (for example, decision-making, escalation of commitment, brainstorming); contextualized-B research focuses on behavior that, by definition, occurs in an organizational context (for example, job satisfaction or organizational commitment); and Big-O research focuses on behavior that is central to the task of organizing, that is, how people organize and carry out their goals (for example, organizational communication, coordination, or transactive memory). Heath and Sitkin argue that Big-O research is more likely to be cross-level, might lead to additional theory development, and might have greater impact on organizations.

Given creativity's roots in psychology, it is not surprising that much of our understanding of creativity focuses on behaviors that are somewhat decontextualized and can be readily measured in a lab. Many of the individual factors that have been studied in relation to creativity – traits, goal orientations, values, affect, for example – add to our understanding of creativity despite being acontextual. When scholars consider contextual factors that impact creativity – job complexity, leadership, for example – the study of creativity moves more into the domain of contextualized-B research. Although Big-O research might not be of interest to all creativity scholars, given its focus on contributing to organizing more broadly, additional opportunities for theorizing might open up if researchers designed studies that pushed in this direction, or at the very least linked creativity with other processes central to the organizing process.

Heath and Sitkin (2001) use Sutton and Hargadon (1996) as a prime example of Big-O research. The study could have just been about brainstorming (Big-B research), but it also speaks to the way the organization (IDEO) and employees organize themselves, offering insights about communication and learning (Big-O research). Their study began with a general research question, "How does IDEO innovate routinely?" Sutton and Hargadon motivate their paper by recognizing that historically most research on brainstorming has been conducted via experiments with participants who have little training and experience in brainstorming and have no prior relationships with one another. These conditions do not often hold in organizations that regularly use brainstorming. Data included 24 observed brainstorming sessions (in person and/or video), 60 interviews, many informal discussions, archival materials about IDEO (the organization) and a brainstorming survey. The authors also tracked design teams as they developed new products. Sutton and Hargadon (1996: 710–711) revealed that:

> [B]rainstorms may not be the most efficient means for generating ideas or for doing any other single task, but they are efficient for accomplishing a variety of important tasks at once. In addition to generating possible design solutions, brainstorms support the organization's memory of technical solutions, provide skill variety, support an attitude of wisdom in and outside the session, create a status auction that maintains a focus on designing products, and they impress clients and generate income.

Thus, while the study advances our understanding about the role of brainstorming in innovation, it also speaks to broader questions around organizing.

Similarly, Lingo and O'Mahony's (2010) study theoretically advances our understanding of creativity, as well as a second theoretical domain related to organizing: brokerage. Lingo conducted a three-year field study of the Nashville country music industry; the data included 85 interviews, 100 hours of observations of meetings, recording sessions, and breaks. She also co-produced a song herself, engaging in participant observation. In their analysis, Lingo and O'Mahony: (1) wrote vignettes focusing on the producers' experiences in order to map the music production process; (2) used the vignettes, interviews, and field notes to identify and compare the producer's work practices; and (3) created a matrix to document the frequency and timing of practices over the course of projects. The paper builds creativity theory by identifying different types of ambiguity that are encountered in different phases of the creative process, as well as the actions that are taken to manage this ambiguity. It also challenges theories of brokerage by showing how, through nexus work, producers intertwined *tertius gaudens* and *tertius iungens* approaches, which had been previously conceptualized as contradictory.

These papers illustrate that Big-O research can require a study that involves deep immersion in the context, often combining multiple sources of data to gain different views of the phenomenon (Rouse & Harrison, 2016). Elsbach and Kramer's (2003) study of Hollywood pitch meetings provides an example of a study that might not qualify as Big-O research, but nonetheless touches on central organizing processes, such as the identification and selection of talent. Their study starts with a challenge for managers of creative work: How do you identify employees with high-creative potential? They motivated their study by reviewing how studies of creativity assessment had focused almost entirely on personality. Like Sutton and Hargadon (1996), they argue that within organizations, people making these types of judgments have experience and expertise, so studying non-experts' judgments via experiments provide only limited insights; also, survey measures fail to capture the dynamism of social judgments and assessments. Their data collection included 36 interviews with screenwriters, agents, and producers, and observations of 28 pitches (live, video, and re-enacted). Elsbach also attended three screenwriting classes. Through their iterative analysis process, they developed a dual process model of creativity assessments in which both writer prototypes and pitcher–catcher relationships prototypes play a key role in the assessment of creative potential. In attempting to understand the contextualized process of assessment, they highlight how creative assessments are both dynamic and relational.

HOW EMBRACING QUALITATIVE RESEARCH MAY HELP TO SHIFT AND EXPAND THE QUESTIONS CREATIVITY RESEARCHERS EXPLORE: BUILDING AN AGENDA FOR THE FUTURE

The aforementioned questions and illustrative examples home in on issues of process, inner life (how people think and feel), and contextualization. In this section, we take these three broad areas and discuss some qualitative methods and techniques that may be the most relevant for researchers looking to expand the field of creativity in these areas.

At a very general level, any given inductive methodology can get at some or each of these general areas of research. However, some qualitative methods are particularly attuned to questions of process, or a person's inner life, or contextualization. For example, Ann Langley has done considerable work in developing qualitative methods for capturing process (e.g., Langley, 1999). As she writes, process data focuses on events and matters of "who did what when" (Langley, 1999: 692); as such, observational data is particularly well suited to capture these actions over time. Narrative methods (e.g., Boje, 2001; Riessman, 2008), by contrast, capture thinking and feeling of an individual as they tell their stories about themselves and their life.[3] Narratives may be combined with process-oriented methods to see how individuals' or groups' thoughts and feelings change over time (e.g., Sonenshein, 2010). Ethnographic methods, broadly defined as studies of culture and illustrated by the work of Spradley (1980), are not only tailored to understanding how people think and feel, but also provide the researcher with considerable insights into the context they are examining. Given that ethnographies can occur over long periods of time, they can be used or adapted to get at process. That said, when considering methods for creativity or other qualitative research, researchers can borrow from different methodologies once sufficiently trained, and researchers can gather data using one methodology but analyze it with a different one, typically using methods that share similar ontologies and epistemologies (Pratt et al., forthcoming).

Drilling down from general methodologies to techniques utilized within and across methodologies, there are a variety of ways to gather data on process, inner life, and context. We summarize our arguments in Table 15.2. As with Table 15.1, although many of the data collections strategies we discuss in the table could be used to gather qualitative data or could yield data that can be analyzed quantitatively, we once again focus on their qualitative applications.

Capturing Process

One of the best ways to capture how people are being creative is to observe them actually being creative. Observations can be viewed via the human eye directly (on-site) or mediated via recording technology. Direct and video observations enable the understanding of interactions and processes both in the moment and over time. An observational approach allows researchers to capture more ephemeral interactions and ongoing experiences. When designing observations, it is important to consider who, what, when, and how long to observe. For example, based on the research question, is it more important to observe creative workers collaborating as they work with ideas or to observe how creative workers interact with clients? In considering how to conduct observations, it is often helpful to develop an observational protocol (see Whyte, 1984) as well as an observational strategy (Wolcott, 1994). This advice is most often focused on direct observations when there is an individual or team of researchers observing creativity and other dynamics on-site.

Video methods (Heath et al., 2010) which capture observations using video recording technology are now more frequently used in top-tier journals (for a review, see Christianson, 2018). Video technology can be used by the researcher on-site, placed by researchers who are not on-site, utilized by the people you are studying, and/or gathered by someone else and examined as a type of archival data. In addition to providing an enduring record (a feature which Harrison and Rouse leveraged), video also allows for the capturing of more precise timing information about when and how often behaviors and interactions occur, as well as providing a record of

Table 15.2   *Qualitative techniques for exploring process, inner life, and contextualizing in creativity research*

Area of focus	Techniques for data gathering	Illustrative citations	Sample research questions
Process	Direct field observations Field video methods	Whyte (1984), Wolcott (1994), Christianson (2018), Heath et al. (2010), LeBaron et al. (2018)	• In what ways, if any, do craftspeople use both traditional and new work practices in their creative work? • How do changes in team membership shift creative processes over the course of a project? • How do groups comprised of people with different work orientations interact during the creative process? • In what ways, if any, does working virtually influence how people collaborate on creative projects over time? • When, how, and from whom do individuals seek help as they develop creative ideas for work? • How do groups manage transitions between creativity and implementation in long-term projects?
Inner life	Interviews (including semi-structured and narrative interviews) Open-ended diaries	Atkinson (1998), Riessman (2008), Rubin and Rubin (2005), Seidman (1998), Bolger et al. (2003), Iida et al. (2012)	• How do professional artists think about their creative work when hired to work within a corporate context? • How do creative workers cognitively shift between creative and non-creative tasks? • How do creative workers think about the trajectories of their careers in terms of their creative outputs? • In what ways, and during what parts of the creative process, do creative workers derive meaning from their work? • How does a creative worker's developmental network shape their approach to creative work over time? • In what ways, if any, do experienced creative workers think about their legacy?
Contextualizing	All of the above (potentially) Participant observation	Spradley (1980), Spradley (2016)	• How do creative workers learn, challenge, and adapt externally imposed project management strategies when they create (e.g., agile)? • How, if at all, do different levels and types of attachment with the organization or product shape collective creative processes? • How do creative workers and their managers negotiate which ideas to pitch to clients?

nonverbal communications which might be important for understanding emotions (Christianson, 2018). For the study of creativity, being able to capture interactions not only with other people, but also with objects and the environment, seems particularly valuable. LeBaron et al. (2018) in their Table 1 provide a list of decisions and issues to keep in mind if using video methods.

Capturing Inner Life

Interviews, including semi-structured and narrative interviews, and open-ended diaries, are especially potent tools for getting an understanding of how people think and feel. Perhaps the most common interview type is semi-structured, which allows the researcher the opportunity to map out particular areas of inquiry while also allowing informants the opportunity to take conversations in unexpected directions. One of the key strengths of interviews is that they allow targeted investigation around particular themes and allow the opportunity for people to discuss their own perceptions of their work. Unlike diary entries, where the questions asked do not change, as we discuss below, interviews are more malleable. With interviews, the types of questions may change during the interview itself as the interviewee brings up new information and sparks new questions. When done with iterative inductive approaches, such as grounded theory, semi-structured interview questions shift and change as more is learned about the topic and/or phenomenon (Charmaz, 2006; Corbin & Strauss, 2008; Locke, 2001).

When exploring the interface of identity and creativity, researchers may want to gather a more specific type of interview: life story or narrative interviews. Scholars suggest that narratives are a key way for understanding identity (Ashforth et al., 2008; Larkey & Morrill, 1995; Scott et al., 1998). Mishler (1999: 19) claims that: "We express, display, make claims for who we are – and who we would like to be – in the stories we tell and how we tell them." Narratives are also useful in understanding other aspects of inner work life. Mishler, for example, used a narrative approach in interviewing craft artists to understand "how they came to their work, what it meant to them, and how it functioned in their lives" (ibid.: 21). Generating narratives requires that the participant has extended time to talk and to tell stories, therefore interview protocols need to be designed to elicit stories (Atkinson, 1998; Riessman, 2008). For example, a researcher could ask a creative worker to tell the story of how an idea came to be or the story of a creative project.

Finally, the work of Amabile and Kramer (2011) reveals the power of open-ended diaries for capturing people's internal worlds over time. Although they used daily diaries, Rouse (2013) used weekly diaries to understand how people related to their ideas over time. Rouse tailored Amabile's and Kramer's question to focus the respondent's attention on events related to their ideas: "Briefly describe one event from the past week that stands out in your mind as relevant to the lifecycle of your ideas (that is generation, development, and/or closure around your ideas) and your reactions to that event." Like Amabile and colleagues (Amabile et al., 2004), she also included an open-ended question: "add anything else you would like to report about this past week," in order to capture any other information that was particularly salient. Diary methods focus on ongoing experiences and offer a way to reduce the time lag between the experience and the retelling of the experience (Bolger et al., 2003). In both of the studies described, the researchers chose to keep the question consistent over time. Although this limits the ability to engage in an iterative approach where the protocol shifts with new insights, it does allow for the comparability of entries over time. Diary methods are particularly appropriate, then, for considering within-person changes over time and individual differences in these changes over time (Bolger et al., 2003).

Contextualizing

Any of the aforementioned techniques could be helpful in contextualizing one's study and one's theorizing, depending on where and what you are observing and what questions you ask in your interviews or diary entries. Indeed, given that the strength of qualitative methods is their ability to provide rich and realistic insights (McGrath, 1981) and given that these methods are field-based (Pratt & Bonaccio, 2016), these methods are designed to build and extend theories in ways that pay particular attention to context. That said, participant observation, where you engage in the work that your informants are doing, is likely to be especially helpful in conducting creativity studies that bring in the "O." Participant observations are at the heart of many ethnographic methods, though there are relatively few methodology books dedicated to the subject (see Spradley, 1980 as an exception). In organizational research, Van Maanen's classic work on police (e.g., Van Maanen, 1978), Bechky's (2006) work on film sets, and Pratt's (2000) foray as an Amway distributor, each illustrate how participant observations can ground a researcher's theorizing in the specific context they are examining.

To our knowledge, there are no studies of creative work that employ participant observation as its primary approach. That said, Bechky, although not looking at creativity per se, did discuss how film crews respond to surprising situations to showcase how they come up with creative solutions via organizational bricolage (Bechky & Okhuysen, 2011). Moreover, it is important to note that Rouse was a professional dancer for five years prior to her work with Harrison on the creativity of dance groups (Harrison & Rouse, 2015, 2014). Thus, she was able to bring her own experience into that work when generating new theoretical insights. Given the paucity of work using this methodological technique, new research using it may be particularly impactful.

When considering using participant observation, one must consider how long one has to gather data, given that studies employing this technique often involve a significant investment of time. Moreover, one must engage in work that one can do at least somewhat competently (although too much competence stemming from significant past experience in work may unduly influence one's ability to learn from the informants you are currently studying). Finally, a participant observer has to be careful that their own contribution to the group they are studying is not significant enough that failure to perform well, or their exit from the group, will not cause undue harm to those they are studying.

CONCLUSION

To close, as research in creativity is beginning to question some of its core assumptions, and continues to grow in new and different areas, qualitative methods may be an effective way to build and extend new theory in this area. Our chapter provides an overview of qualitative methods, offers some areas where new research in creativity is currently being explored, and suggests some methods and techniques for future work. In particular, we discuss how qualitative research may generate theories of creativity that are more process-oriented, that explore the inner life of creative workers, and that are more contextualized and organization-specific.

ACKNOWLEDGEMENTS

We thank Greg Fetzer and Greg Oldham for their feedback on earlier versions of this chapter.

NOTES

1. As noted in Pratt and Bonaccio (2016: 697) quantitative methods may attempt to answer "why" questions via mediation models, but do so in a more constrained or limited way.
2. Not all of the sampling strategies noted by Patton (1990) are equally valuable in all methodologies. For example, convenience sampling is ill-fitting with grounded theory; in addition, snowball sampling should be done when there are either no other alternatives, or when your research study wants to take advantage of ego networks.
3. Phenomenological studies are also well attuned to getting at a person's inner life, but are not as well used in management research. Interested parties might start with Sanders (1982) and Tomkins and Eatough (2013).

REFERENCES

Amabile, T.M. 1982. Social psychology of creativity: A consensual assessment technique. *Journal of Personality and Social Psychology*, 43: 997.

Amabile, T.M. 1983. The social psychology of creativity: A componential conceptualization. *Journal of Personality and Social Psychology*, 45: 357–376.

Amabile, T.M. 1988. A model of creativity and innovation in organizations. In B.M. Staw & L.L. Cummings (eds), *Research in organizational behavior*, Vol. 10: 123–167. Greenwich, CT: JAI Press.

Amabile, T. 2018. *Lifetime achievement award address*. Academy of Management, OB Division.

Amabile, T.M., & Kramer, S.J. 2007. Inner work life: Understanding the subtext of business performance. *Harvard Business Review*, 85: 72–83.

Amabile, T.M., & Kramer, S.J. 2011. *The progress principle: Using small wins to ignite joy, engagement, and creativity at work*. Cambridge, MA: Harvard University Press.

Amabile, T.M., & Pratt, M.G. 2016. The dynamic componential model of creativity and innovation in organizations: Making progress, making meaning. *Research in Organizational Behavior*, 36: 157–183.

Amabile, T.M., Schatzel, E.A., Moneta, G.B., & Kramer, S.J. 2004. Leader behaviors and the work environment for creativity: Perceived leader support. *Leadership Quarterly*, 15: 5–32.

Anderson, N., Potočnik, K., & Zhou, J. 2014. Innovation and creativity in organizations: A state-of-the-science review, prospective commentary, and guiding framework. *Journal of Management*, 40: 1297–1333.

Ashforth, B.E., Harrison, S.H., & Corley, K.G. 2008. Identification in organizations: An examination of four fundamental questions. *Journal of Management*, 34: 325–374.

Atkinson, R. 1998. *The life story interview*. Thousand Oaks, CA: SAGE.

Bechky, B.A. 2006. Gaffers, gofers, and grips: Role-based coordination in temporary organizations. *Organization Science*, 17: 3–21.

Bechky, B.A., & Okhuysen, G.A. 2011. Expecting the unexpected? How SWAT officers and film crews handle surprises. *Academy of Management Journal*, 54: 239–261.

Bitektine, A. 2008. Prospective case study design: qualitative method for deductive theory testing. *Organizational Research Methods*, 11: 160–180.

Boje, D.M. 2001. *Narrative methods for organizational and communication research*. London: SAGE.

Bolger, N., Davis, A., & Rafaeli, E. 2003. Diary methods: Capturing life as it is lived. *Annual Review of Psychology*, 54: 579–616.

Charmaz, K. 2006. *Constructing grounded theory: A practical guide to qualitative analysis*. Thousand Oaks, CA: SAGE.

Christianson, M.K. 2018. Mapping the terrain: The use of video-based research in top-tier organizational journals. *Organizational Research Methods*, 21: 261–287.

Corbin, J., & Strauss, A.L. 2008. *Basics of qualitative research*. Thousand Oaks, CA: SAGE.

Drazin, R., Glynn, M.A., & Kazanjian, R.K. 1999. Multilevel theorizing about creativity in organizations: A sensemaking perspective. *Academy of Management Review*, 24: 286–307.

Eisenhardt, K.M. 1989. Building theory from case study research. *Academy of Management Review*, 14: 532–550.

Elsbach, K.D. 2009. Identity affirmation through signature style: A study of toy car designers. *Human Relations*, 62: 1041–1072.

Elsbach, K.D., & Flynn, F.J. 2013. Creative collaboration and the self-concept: A study of toy designers. *Journal of Management Studies*, 50: 515–544.

Elsbach, K.D., & Kramer, R.M. 2003. Assessing creativity in Hollywood pitch meetings: Evidence for a dual-process model of creativity judgments. *Academy of Management Journal*, 46: 283–301.

Farmer, S.M., Tierney, P., & Kung-Mcintyre, K. 2003. Employee creativity in Taiwan: An application of role identity theory. *Academy of Management Journal*, 46: 618–630.

George, J.M. 2007. Creativity in organizations. *Academy of Management Annals*, 1: 439–477.

Golden-Biddle, K. & Locke, K. 2007. *Composing qualitative research, 2nd edition*. Thousand Oaks, CA: SAGE.

Hargadon, A., & Bechky, B. 2006. When collections of creatives become creative collectives: A field study of problem solving at work. *Organization Science*, 17: 484–500.

Harrison, S.H., & Rouse, E.D. 2014. Let's dance! Elastic coordination in creative group work: A qualitative study of modern dancers. *Academy of Management Journal*, 57: 1256–1283.

Harrison, S., & Rouse, E. 2015. An inductive study of feedback interactions over the course of creative projects. *Academy of Management Journal*, 58: 375–404.

Harvey, S., & Kou, C.Y. 2013. Collective engagement in creative tasks: The role of evaluation in the creative process in groups. *Administrative Science Quarterly*, 58: 346–386.

Heath, C., Hindmarsh, J., & Luff, P. 2010. *Video in qualitative research: Analysing social interaction in everyday life*. Thousand Oaks, CA: SAGE.

Heath, C., & Sitkin, S.B. 2001. Big-B versus Big-O: What is organizational about organizational behavior? *Journal of Organizational Behavior*, 22: 43–58.

Iida, M., Shrout, P.E., Laurenceau, J.-P., & Bolger, N. 2012. Using diary methods in psychological research. In H. Cooper, P. Camic, D. Long, A. Panter, D. Rindskopf, & K. Sher (eds), *APA handbooks in psychology®. APA handbook of research methods in psychology, Vol. 1. Foundations, planning, measures, and psychometrics*: 277–305. Washington, DC: American Psychological Association.

Jaussi, K.S., Randel, A.E., & Dionne, S.D. 2007. I am, I think I can, and I do: The role of personal identity, self-efficacy, and cross-application of experiences in creativity at work. *Creativity Research Journal*, 19: 247–258.

Langley, A. 1999. Strategies for theorizing from process data. *Academy of Management Review*, 24: 691–710.

Larkey, L., & Morrill, C. 1995. Organizational commitment as symbolic process. *Western Journal of Communication*, 59: 193–213.

LeBaron, C., Jarzabkowski, P., Pratt, M.G., & Fetzer, G. 2018. *An introduction to video methods in organizational research*. Los Angeles, CA: SAGE Publications.

Lingo, E.L., & O'Mahony, S. 2010. Nexus work: Brokerage on creative projects. *Administrative Science Quarterly*, 55: 47–81.

Locke, K. 2001. *Grounded theory in management research*. Thousand Oaks, CA: SAGE.

Locke, K., & Golden-Biddle, K. 2002. An introduction to qualitative research: Its potential for industrial and organizational psychology. In S. Rogelberg (ed.), *Handbook of research methods in industrial and organizational psychology*: 99–118. Malden, MA: Blackwell.

McGrath, J.E. 1981. Dilemmatics: The study of research choices and dilemmas. *American Behavioral Scientist*, 25: 179–210.

Mishler, E.G. 1999. *Storylines: Craftartists' narratives of identity*. Cambridge, MA: Harvard University Press.

Oldham, G. & Fried, Y. 2016. Job design research and theory: Past, present, and future. *Organizational Behavior and Human Decision Processes*, 136: 20–35.

Park, N.K., Chun, M.Y., & Lee, J. 2016. Revisiting individual creativity assessment: Triangulation in subjective and objective assessment methods. *Creativity Research Journal*, 28: 1–10.

Patton, M.Q. 1990. *Qualitative evaluation and research methods*, 2nd edn. Newbury Park, CA: SAGE.

Perry-Smith, J., & Mannucci, P.V. 2017. From creativity to innovation: The social network drivers of the four phases of the idea journey. *Academy of Management Review*, 42: 53–79.

Pratt, M.G. 2000. The good, the bad, and the ambivalent: Managing identification among Amway distributors. *Administrative Science Quarterly*, 45: 456–493.

Pratt, M.G. 2009. From the Editors: For the lack of a boilerplate: Tips on writing up (and reviewing) qualitative research. *Academy of Management Journal*, 52(5): 856–862.

Pratt, M.G. & Ashforth, B. 2003. Fostering meaningfulness in and at work. In K. Cameron, J. Dutton, and R. Quinn (eds), *Positive organizational scholarship*: 309–327. San Francisco, CA: Berrett-Koehler Publishers.

Pratt, M.G., & Bonaccio, S. 2016. Qualitative research in IO psychology: Maps, myths, and moving forward. *Industrial and Organizational Psychology*, 9: 693–715.

Pratt, M.G., Sonenshein, S., & Feldman, M.S. Forthcoming. Moving beyond templates: A bricolage approach to conducting trustworthy qualitative research, *Organizational Research Methods*.

Riessman, C.K. 2008. *Narrative methods for the human sciences*. Newbury Park, CA: SAGE Publications.

Rouse, E. 2013. *Kill your darlings? Experiencing, maintaining, and changing psychological ownership in creative work*. Dissertation, Boston College.

Rouse, E.D., & Harrison, S.H. 2016. Triangulate and expand. In K.D. Elsbach & R.M. Kramer (eds), *Handbook of Qualitative Organizational Research: Innovative Pathways and Methods*: 286–297. New York: Routledge.

Rubin, H., & Rubin, I. 2005. *Qualitative interviewing: The art of hearing data*. Thousand Oaks, CA: SAGE.

Sanders, P. 1982. Phenomenology: A new way of viewing organizational research. *Academy of Management Review*, 7: 353–360.

Scott, C.R., Corman, S.R., & Cheney, G. 1998. Development of a structurational model of identification in the organization. *Communication Theory*, 8: 298–336.

Seidman, I. 1998. *Interviewing as qualitative research*. New York: Teachers College Press.

Sonenshein, S. 2010. We're changing – Or are we? Untangling the role of progressive, regressive, and stability narratives during strategic change implementation. *Academy of Management Journal*, 53: 477–512.

Spradley, J. 1980. *Participant observation*. New York: Holt Rinehart & Winston.

Spradley, J.P. 2016. *The ethnographic interview*. Long Grove, IL: Waveland Press.

Strauss, A., & Corbin, J. 1998. *Basics of qualitative research techniques*. Thousand Oaks, CA: SAGE.

Sutton, R.I., & Hargadon, A. 1996. Brainstorming groups in context: Effectiveness in a product design firm. *Administrative Science Quarterly*, 41: 685–718.

Tierney, P., & Farmer, S.M. 2011. Creative self-efficacy development and creative performance over time. *Journal of Applied Psychology*, 96: 277–293.

Tomkins, L., & Eatough, V. 2013. The feel of experience: Phenomenological ideas for organizational research. *Qualitative Research in Organizations and Management: An International Journal*, 8: 258–275.

Unsworth, K. 2001. Unpacking creativity. *Academy of Management Review*, 26: 289–297.

Van Maanen, J. 1978. The asshole. In P. Manning & J. Van Maanen (eds), *Policing: A view from the street*: 221–238. Santa Monica, CA: Goodyear Publishing.

Wang, A.C., & Cheng, B.S. 2010. When does benevolent leadership lead to creativity? The moderating role of creative role identity and job autonomy. *Journal of Organizational Behavior*, 31: 106–121.

Weiss, H.M., & Rupp, D.E. 2011. Experiencing work: An essay on a person-centric work psychology. *Industrial and Organizational Psychology*, 4: 83–97.

West, M.A. 1990. The social psychology of innovation in groups. In M.A. West & J.L. Farr (eds), *Innovation and creativity at work: Psychological and organizational strategies*: 309–333. Chichester: Wiley.

Whyte, W. 1984. *Learning from the field*. Beverly Hills, CA: SAGE.

Wolcott, H. 1994. *Tranforming qualitative data*. Thousand Oaks, CA: SAGE.

Zhang, X., & Bartol, K.M. 2010. Linking empowering leadership and employee creativity: The influence of psychological empowerment, intrinsic motivation, and creative process engagement. *Academy of Management Journal*, 53: 107–128.

Zhou, J., & Hoever, I.J. 2014. Research on workplace creativity: A review and redirection. *Annual Review of Organizational Psychology and Organizational Behavior*, 1: 333–359.

Index

Printed and bound by CPI Group (UK) Ltd, Croydon, CR0 4YY

16/04/2025

14658377-0004